Revealed Preference Theory

Pioneered by American economist Paul Samuelson, revealed preference theory is based on the idea that the preferences of consumers are revealed in their purchasing behavior. Researchers in this field have developed complex and sophisticated mathematical models to capture the preferences that are "revealed" through consumer choice behavior. This study of consumer demand and behavior is closely tied up with econometrics (especially nonparametric econometrics), where testing the validity of different theoretical models is an important aspect of research. The theory of revealed preference has a very long and distinguished tradition in economics, but until now there has been no systematic presentation of the theory. This book deals with basic questions in economic theory, such as the relation between theory and data, and studies the situations in which empirical observations are consistent or inconsistent with some of the best-known theories in economics.

Christopher P. Chambers is an associate professor of economics at the Department of Economics, University of California, San Diego. He has published articles in the *American Economic Review*, *Econometrica*, *Games and Economic Behavior*, *Journal of Economic Theory*, and *Theoretical Economics*. He is an associate editor of the *Journal of Economic Theory*, *Journal of Mathematical Economics*, and *Social Choice and Welfare*. He is also co-editor of *Mathematical Social Sciences*.

Federico Echenique is a professor of economics at the Division of the Humanities and Social Science, California Institute of Technology. He has published articles in the *American Economic Review*, *Econometrica*, *Journal of Political Economy*, *Games and Economic Behavior*, *Journal of Economic Theory*, and *Theoretical Economics*. He is an associate editor of the *Journal of Economic Theory*, *Economic Journal*, *Economic Theory*, and *ACM Transactions on Economics and Computation*

Econometric Society Monographs

Editors:

Jeffrey Ely, Northwestern University
Donald W. K. Andrews, Yale University

The Econometric Society is an international society for the advancement of economic theory in relation to statistics and mathematics. The Econometric Society Monograph series is designed to promote the publication of original research contributions of high quality in mathematical economics and theoretical and applied econometrics.

Other titles in the series:

G. S. Maddala, *Limited dependent and qualitative variables in econometrics*, 9780521241434, 9780521338257
Gerard Debreu, *Mathematical economics: Twenty papers of Gerard Debreu*, 9780521237369, 9780521335614
Jean-Michel Grandmont, *Money and value: A reconsideration of classical and neoclassical monetary economics*, 9780521251419, 9780521313643
Franklin M. Fisher, *Disequilibrium foundations of equilibrium economics*, 9780521378567
Andreu Mas-Colell, *The theory of general equilibrium: A differentiable approach*, 9780521265140, 9780521388702
Truman F. Bewley, Editor, *Advances in econometrics – Fifth World Congress (Volume I)*, 9780521467261
Truman F. Bewley, Editor, *Advances in econometrics – Fifth World Congress (Volume II)*, 9780521467254
Hervé Moulin, *Axioms of cooperative decision making*, 9780521360555, 9780521424585
L. G. Godfrey, *Misspecification tests in econometrics: The Lagrange multiplier principle and other approaches*, 9780521424592
Tony Lancaster, *The econometric analysis of transition data*, 9780521437899
Alvin E. Roth and Marilda A. Oliviera Sotomayor, Editors, *Two-sided matching: A study in game-theoretic modeling and analysis*, 9780521437882
Wolfgang Hardle, *Applied nonparametric regression*, 9780521429504
Jean-Jacques Laffont, Editor, *Advances in economic theory – Sixth World Congress (Volume I)*, 9780521484596
Jean-Jacques Laffont, Editor, *Advances in economic theory – Sixth World Congress (Volume II)*, 9780521484602
Halbert White, *Estimation, inference and specification*, 9780521252805, 9780521574464
Christopher Sims, Editor, *Advances in econometrics – Sixth World Congress (Volume I)*, 9780521444590, 9780521566100
Christopher Sims, Editor, *Advances in econometrics – Sixth World Congress (Volume II)*, 9780521444606, 9780521566094
Roger Guesnerie, *A contribution to the pure theory of taxation*, 9780521629560
David M. Kreps and Kenneth F. Wallis, Editors, *Advances in economics and econometrics – Seventh World Congress (Volume I)*, 9780521589833
David M. Kreps and Kenneth F. Wallis, Editors, *Advances in economics and econometrics – Seventh World Congress (Volume II)*, 9780521589826
David M. Kreps and Kenneth F. Wallis, Editors, *Advances in economics and econometrics – Seventh World Congress (Volume III)*, 9780521580137, 9780521589819
Donald P. Jacobs, Ehud Kalai, and Morton I. Kamien, Editors, *Frontiers of research in economic theory: The Nancy L. Schwartz Memorial Lectures*, 1983–1997, 9780521632225, 9780521635387

(continued after Index)

Revealed Preference Theory

Christopher P. Chambers
Department of Economics,
University of California San Diego

Federico Echenique
Division of the Humanities and Social Science,
California Institute of Technology

CAMBRIDGE
UNIVERSITY PRESS

University Printing House, Cambridge CB2 8BS, United Kingdom

One Liberty Plaza, 20th Floor, New York, NY 10006, USA

477 Williamstown Road, Port Melbourne, VIC 3207, Australia

4843/24, 2nd Floor, Ansari Road, Daryaganj, Delhi - 110002, India

79 Anson Road, #06-04/06, Singapore 079906

Cambridge University Press is part of the University of Cambridge.

It furthers the University's mission by disseminating knowledge in the pursuit of education, learning and research at the highest international levels of excellence.

www.cambridge.org
Information on this title: www.cambridge.org/9781107087804

First published 2016

A catalogue record for this publication is available from the British Library

Library of Congress Cataloging in Publication data
Names: Chambers, Christopher P., 1975– author. | Echenique, Federico, author.
Title: Revealed preference theory / Christopher P. Chambers, Federico Echenique.
Description: New York : Cambridge University Press, [2016] |
Series: Econometric society monographs | Includes bibliographical references and index.
Identifiers: LCCN 2015040826| ISBN 9781107087804 (hardback) |
ISBN 9781107458116 (pbk.)
Subjects: LCSH: Revealed preference theory. | Consumption (Economics) |
Consumers' preferences–Econometric models.
Classification: LCC HB801.C3945 2016 | DDC 339.4/7–dc23
LC record available at http://lccn.loc.gov/2015040826

ISBN 978-1-107-08780-4 Hardback
ISBN 978-1-107-45811-6 Paperback

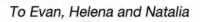

To Evan, Helena and Natalia

Contents

Preface

0.1 WHAT IS REVEALED PREFERENCE THEORY?

"Revealed preference" is a term with several interpretations in economic theory, all closely related but possessing subtle philosophical differences. The central theme common to all interpretations is that of understanding what economic models say about the observable world. Most practitioners of revealed preference theory recognize that an economic model is useful for organizing data and making predictions, but they would not go so far as to admit that the model is, or represents, "reality." Economic models usually consist of multiple interacting parts. Some parts are theoretical in nature, and are not meant to be observed. These unobservable parts are then tied to objects which could potentially be observed and measured.

Let us begin with the canonical example of revealed preference theory. Economists often view individuals as making decisions consistent with some objective function, usually interpreted as "utility." So, the theory posits that an individual chooses that option which gives her the highest utility among all feasible options. This has proved to be a useful and tractable model in many branches of economics; in fact, the concept is ubiquitous. But it has been recognized at least since Pareto (1906) that, even if an individual optimizes a utility, the cardinal structure of said utility function (that is, the numerical values assigned to potential choices by the utility) cannot be inferred from choice behavior. Utility is a "theoretical" concept. The only empirically meaningful statements that can be gleaned from data relate to whether one option exhibits a higher utility than another. Once this is recognized, it is natural to ask: what are the predictions of the utility maximization model for observable choice behavior? Obviously, the predictions will have to be made *across* different choice situations. A theory that claims an individual chooses the best available option from those in front of her will have little to say without imposing constraints on the notion of "best." So, the next step was to understand what these predictions are. These questions form the first few chapters of this book.

The revealed preference approach seeks to understand what a given model says about data. Observable economic data are either consistent with a given model or not. If the data are consistent with the model, this does not provide evidence that the model is right, but instead tells us that – at least in terms of economically observable phenomena – we may without loss of generality treat the economic system under consideration as if the model is right.

As an illustration of this phenomenon, the words "as if" are frequently applied in revealed preference analysis: a decision maker behaves "as if" she possesses a utility function, a firm behaves "as if" it is profit-maximizing, a group of agents behave "as if" they make agreements according to a Nash bargaining solution. Importantly, common to all uses of the "as if" qualification is the idea that there is some procedural aspect to behavior which is unobserved, and which cannot be observed using economic data.

It is true, however, that this "as if" approach often generates parameters which are intended to be applied outside of the model. For example, the theory of subjective expected utility can be used to elicit a probability measure over states of the world. Whether or not this probability measure actually represents a probability measure the agent in question possesses, it is often treated as such. Researchers often assume that the agent possesses a probability measure, and that the behaviorally elicited probability measure is a good enough proxy. Assumptions like these obviously cannot be tested using economic data, and thus fall in the realm of philosophy.

What does the standard revealed preference exercise look like? A model is specified by hypothesizing the existence of some objects, which are not observable as data, even in principle. Thus, a revealed preference theory is existential in nature. We can refer to these unobservable objects as theoretical objects. These objects are hypothesized to interact with observable objects in a certain way. Generally speaking, theoretical objects live in a large space (though this need not always be the case). The standard example of the exercise we have in mind is the utility function over commodity space: the set of utility functions is obviously quite large. We can never see a utility function, but what we might be able to see are demand observations at a finite list of prices. Thus the question arises: does there exist a utility function which could generate these demand observations by a process of maximization? In general, such questions are by no means trivial to answer. For the utility example, because there are an infinite number of potential utility functions, searching through every possible utility function to verify whether or not one of them could lead to observed data is an impossible task. A different approach is needed, some way of simplifying the problem. This approach is revealed preference theory.

We wish to emphasize that the role of revealed preference theory is not to make any claim on the notion of what constitutes an economic theory, or to discuss the "realism" or meaning of theoretical concepts in an economic theory.[1] In fact, revealed preference theory has nothing to say about the

[1] Some essays by Paul Samuelson (1963, 1964, 1965) have sometimes been interpreted as suggesting that a theory is equivalent to its theoretical predictions.

interpretation of these theoretical concepts. Rather, the driving force of revealed preference theory is understanding the implications of our theories and models for the real world.[2] Similarly, while the theory has been formulated for choice data, there is nothing inherent in revealed preference theory that precludes using other sources of datasets.[3]

0.2 DIFFERENT APPROACHES IN REVEALED PREFERENCE

In broad terms, revealed preference theory can be divided into two main subfields. The first assumes that all relevant and potentially observable economic data are in fact observed. For example, the integrability question of demand theory asks when a fully specified demand function can be rationalized by an (unobserved) preference relation which the consumer maximizes. Another example is standard in decision theory, where one observes a complete preference relation, meaning that one observes the outcome of all pairwise comparisons between objects of choice. We study a few such questions in this book, but not many. On the other hand, the second subfield assumes that economic data are only partially observable. We observe consumer demand a finite number of times. We observe production a finite number of times. Or we see how agents interact a finite number of times.

Within this second subfield, there are again two underlying themes, which are two sides of the same coin. One theme deals with refutability, or falsifiability. This approach studies the revealed preference implications of a model by studying what the model rules out. Given data, we want to check whether or not these data falsify the model in question. A canonical example is the equivalence of the generalized axiom of revealed preference (GARP) and rationalizability. GARP is a statement that rules out "revealed preference cycles," any demonstration of which falsifies the model. So, the idea is to characterize those potential observations which would directly falsify the model. GARP characterizes these observations as those which exhibit "preference cycles." The absence of a preference cycle, on the other hand, says nothing about the truth of the model. It only establishes that the model has not been falsified.

An alternative approach attempts to verify that given data are consistent with the model. The driving force in this framework is that of "reducing" the search for unobservables to a smaller space. The canonical example of this approach is the equivalence of the Afriat inequalities and the hypothesis of maximizing a utility function. The Afriat inequalities are a finite list of linear inequalities that are derived directly from observed data. If the inequalities have a common

[2] In a final chapter, we will describe a "theory" as a kind of class of potential relations that might hold in the real-world. This turns out to be a useful construction for understanding the empirical content that a theory has, but it may not conform to the notion of a theory as philosophers of science define it.

[3] Indeed, the most common empirical application of revealed preference theory uses data from non-incentivized consumption surveys. These surveys are not, strictly speaking, choice data.

solution, then one can claim that the observed data could have been generated by utility maximization; in other words, the model has not been falsified. On the other hand, if there is no such solution, then we have falsified the model. Directly verifying that data are consistent with utility maximization involves searching an infinite-dimensional space (the space of utility functions). Finding a solution to the Afriat inequalities involves searching a finite dimensional space. Indeed, there are well-known linear programming algorithms which can be used to determine whether the Afriat inequalities have a solution. However, with either approach, the hypothesis refers to "unobservable" or "theoretical" concepts (the utility function in the first place, the solution to the inequalities in the other).

In this book, we focus on the first approach. Our interest in this book is in understanding the data which falsify a given model. It is natural that our interest will therefore be in directly characterizing such datasets. However, it is important to understand that, quite generally, the two approaches are mathematically equivalent, and neither is "better" than the other. At times, one approach, and at other times the other, will be more useful. To illustrate, consider Afriat's Theorem: this beautiful theorem establishes that GARP, satisfaction of the Afriat inequalities, and consistency with the maximization of a utility function are all equivalent. Thus, Afriat's Theorem not only provides a direct method of falsifying the model (GARP), but a simple method of verifying when the model is not refuted (the Afriat inequalities). It is now know that this duality holds relatively generally; this was first described in economics by Brown and Matzkin (1996). In practice, however, the more difficult problem is often in exhibiting classes of data which refute the given model, eliminating all unobservable and theoretical concepts.

0.3 SCOPE OF THE BOOK

This book arose from courses taught by the authors at Caltech and UCSD, and by no means claims to be exhaustive, complete, or definitive: the selection of material covered inevitably reflects our own interests and expertise. There are many areas of revealed preference theory, both old and modern, which we discuss very little. In particular, we include no discussion whatsoever of the theory of household consumption, which is an area of revealed preference theory that has been especially active. In addition, there are already several fine existing surveys of revealed preference theory; Richter (1971), Mas-Colell (1982), Carvajal, Ray, and Snyder (2004), Varian (2006), Cherchye, Crawford, De Rock, and Vermeulen (2009), and Crawford and De Rock (2014) are excellent and highly recommended references which have helped us to shape our own ideas.

Our presentation of the material emphasizes some concepts that we have found particularly important in our own understanding and teaching of revealed preference theory.

In the classical choice or demand theoretic setting, while there are several objects that might rightfully be called a revealed preference relation, the literature often refers to revealed preference as if it is a single concept. This can lead to substantial confusion on the part of students. While everyone readily understands the notion that x is revealed preferred to y if x is chosen when y is available, somewhat more subtle is the notion of revealed strict preference: that x is chosen when y is available and y is not chosen. The subtlety lies in the fact that the revealed strict preference need not be the strict part of the revealed preference. Indeed, the role of the most famous of revealed preference axioms, the weak axiom of revealed preference, is simply to ensure that revealed strict preference does not contradict revealed preference: it is impossible for x to be revealed preferred to y while y is revealed strictly preferred to x. We chose, therefore, to introduce a technology in this book which makes these concepts clear. Instead of referring to a revealed preference, we refer throughout to a revealed preference *pair*: the pair consisting of the revealed preference and the revealed strict preference.

Much of this book focuses on the idea of "eliminating" existentially quantified theoretical concepts, as described in our discussion of utility maximization above. The elimination of quantifiers can often be facilitated by some simple mathematical results which prove to be extremely powerful. One of the important mathematical results that we use over and over is called the Theorem of the Alternative. Geometrically, it is very simple. At the same time, it is very powerful, and often lets us convert existential quantification in one set of variables to universal quantification in another. It relates pairs of linear inequalities. The theorem tells us that one of the systems (the primal) has a solution if and only if the other (the dual) does not. The key aspect is that these two systems are systems of inequalities in different variables. The variables of the primal correspond to the constraints of the dual, and conversely. Often, we are lucky enough to be able to reduce the search for a theoretical object to a list of linear inequalities. For example, it may not be obvious, but the existence of a utility function representing a preference on a finite set is equivalent to the existence of a solution to a collection of linear inequalities, where the utility function is viewed as a vector living in a finite-dimensional space. By the Theorem of the Alternative, there is no solution to this collection of linear inequalities if and only if the dual set of linear inequalities has a solution. Thus, falsifying the hypothesis of the existence of a utility is simplified: instead of demonstrating that all potential solutions cannot be solutions, we simply have to demonstrate one solution to the dual set of linear inequalities. And the dual set of linear inequalities has a variable for each constraint of the primal set. It turns out that in this context, one can show that a solution to the dual set of linear inequalities corresponds to a revealed preference cycle, so that a utility function exists if and only if there is no revealed preference cycle. Importantly, what the Theorem of the Alternative has allowed us to do is to remove any existential mention of the theoretical object.

This technique proves useful because tests for many economic models can be reduced to collections of linear inequalities. But this is not always the case. Tests for some economic models turn out to be best studied by systems of polynomial inequalities. And in fact, for polynomial inequalities, there are similar notions to the Theorem of the Alternative. One, which has not yet found widespread application in economics, is called the Positivstellensatz. The Positivstellensatz claims that a system of polynomial inequalities has a solution if and only if some dual set has no solution. Though in general it may be difficult to test whether this dual set of polynomial inequalities has a solution, there are algorithms that seem to work well in practice. Another related idea is the Tarski–Seidenberg result. Tarski–Seidenberg asks whether a given collection of polynomial inequalities has a solution. It turns out that there is an algorithm for checking whether or not this is so (this algorithm, unfortunately, is generally computationally very costly).

The Tarski–Seidenberg algorithm is a beautiful application of a model-theoretic construct called quantifier elimination. Quantifier elimination is a rare property that certain theories can have; and it just so happens that the theory of real closed fields (of which the real numbers are an example) has this property. Quantifier elimination is said to hold if existentially quantified first-order sentences can always be shown to be equivalent to sentences with no existential quantification. As most revealed preference exercises are existential in nature (that is, one wants to search for the existence of a utility function, or preference, or choice correspondence), quantifier elimination proves to be an extremely powerful tool in revealed preference theory.

The book is laid out into chapters whose titles are, for the most part, self-explanatory. Chapter 1 begins with some mathematical preliminaries which will be useful throughout the text. Chapters 2–6 investigate the revealed preference question in classical environments, ranging from abstract choice, to demand, to production. Chapter 7 is an investigation into the stochastic choice model, which generalizes the abstract choice-theoretic model to allow choice over options to be random. Chapter 8 describes some of the basic economic models of uncertainty, and how they can be investigated with revealed preference techniques. Chapters 9–11 are devoted to studying revealed preference-style questions in models of group choice; general equilibrium theory, game theory, and political science topics are addressed here.

The final two chapters are more methodological and abstract. Chapter 12 formalizes an underlying theme of the book: that finding rationalizations in many revealed preference models turns out to be equivalent to finding a satisfaction to a collection of polynomial inequalities. This observation is not new, of course, but we describe some tools deriving from the mathematical discipline of real algebraic geometry which we believe could be useful for practitioners. Chapter 13 is devoted to studying notions of revealed preference, empirical content, and falsifiability from an abstract perspective. This chapter is mostly based on the authors' joint work with Eran Shmaya.

Finally, we are very grateful to Kim C. Border, Jun Chen, SangMok Lee, Ce Liu, Efe Ok, Juan Sebastián Pereyra, John N. Rehbeck, Eran Shmaya, and Gerelt Tserenjigmid for corrections, references, and very useful comments on early drafts of the book. Kevin Li, in particular, proofread most of the material and helped us improve the writing and the exposition in the book significantly. We also received very useful feedback from five anonymous reviewers from Cambridge University Press. Special thanks are due to our coauthors Yaron Azrieli, Takashi Hayashi, PJ Healy, SangMok Lee, Kota Saito, Matt Shum, Eran Shmaya, and Bumin Yenmez for work that has shaped our understanding of revealed preference theory, and for letting us use our joint research for some of the material included in the book.

CHAPTER 1

Mathematical Preliminaries

We begin by reviewing basic mathematical facts and notation that we shall use repeatedly in the book. The basic results we need relate to binary relations and their extensions and representations, and to solutions to systems of inequalities.

1.1 BASIC DEFINITIONS AND NOTATIONAL CONVENTIONS

1.1.1 Relations

Let X be a set. An *n-ary relation on* X is a subset of X^n. A *binary relation on* X is a subset of $X \times X$. When R is a binary relation on X, we write $(x,y) \in R$ as $x\,R\,y$. When R is an n-ary relation, we also write $R(x_1,\ldots,x_n)$ instead of $(x_1,\ldots,x_n) \in R$.

Given a binary relation R, define its *strict part*, or *asymmetric part*, P_R by $(x,y) \in P_R$ iff $(x,y) \in R$ and $(y,x) \notin R$. Define its *symmetric part*, or *indifference relation*, I_R by $(x,y) \in I_R$ iff $(x,y) \in R$ and $(y,x) \in R$.

Two elements $x,y \in X$ are *unordered* by R if $(x,y) \notin R$ and $(y,x) \notin R$. Two elements are *ordered* by R when they are not unordered by R. We say that a binary relation B is an *extension* of R if $R \subseteq B$ and $P_R \subseteq P_B$. A binary relation B is a *strict extension* of R if it is an extension, and in addition there is a pair that is unordered by R but ordered by B. Finally, a binary relation is *complete* if it leaves no pair of elements unordered. That is, R is complete if for all x and y, $x\,R\,y$ or $y\,R\,x$ (or both).

The following are standard properties of binary relations. A binary relation R is:

- *transitive* if, for all x, y, and z, $x\,R\,y$ and $y\,R\,z$ imply that $x\,R\,z$;
- *quasitransitive* if, for all x, y, and z, $x\,P_R\,y$ and $y\,P_R\,z$ imply that $x\,P_R\,z$;
- *reflexive* if $x\,R\,x$ for all x;
- *irreflexive* if $(x,x) \notin R$ for all x;
- *symmetric* if, for all x and y, $(x,y) \in R$ implies that $(y,x) \in R$;
- *antisymmetric* if, for all x and y with $x \neq y$, $(x,y) \in R$ implies that $(y,x) \notin R$.

Observe that if a binary relation is complete, then it is reflexive.

The following are types of binary relations: A binary relation is a(n)

- *weak order* if it is complete and transitive;
- *linear order* if it is complete, transitive, and antisymmetric;
- *equivalence relation* if it is reflexive, symmetric, and transitive;
- *partial order* if it is reflexive, transitive, and antisymmetric.

1.1.2 Partially ordered sets

If $\geq$ is a partial order on X, an *upper bound* on $A \subseteq X$ (with respect to $\geq$) is an element $x \in X$ such that $x \geq y$ for all $y \in A$; a *lower bound* on $A \subseteq X$ is an element $x \in X$ such that $y \geq x$ for all $y \in A$. A *least upper bound* on A is an upper bound x on A such that if y is an upper bound on A then $y \geq x$. A *greatest lower bound* on A is a lower bound x on A such that if y is a lower bound on A then $x \geq y$. We write $x \vee y$, called the *join* of x and y, for the least upper bound on the set $\{x,y\}$; and $x \wedge y$, called the *meet* of x and y, for the greatest lower bound on the set $\{x,y\}$. A set X, with a partial order $\geq$ on X, is a *lattice* if, for all x and y in X, $x \vee y$ and $x \wedge y$ are defined in X with respect to $\geq$.

Let X, with the partial order $\geq$, be a lattice. A function $u : X \to \mathbf{R}$ is *supermodular* if for all $x, y \in X$,

$$u(x) + u(y) \leq u(x \vee y) + u(x \wedge y),$$

and *submodular* if $-u$ is supermodular.

If $\geq$ is a partial order on X, a *chain* is a subset $Y \subseteq X$ such that for all $x, y \in Y$, either $x \geq y$ or $y \geq x$. The following result, known as *Zorn's Lemma*, is one of the many equivalents of the axiom of choice in set theory. It allows one to extend many induction-style proofs to sets of arbitrary cardinality. We shall use it several times.

Zorn's Lemma *Let $\geq$ be a partial order on a set X, and suppose that for every chain $Y \subseteq X$ there is an upper bound of Y in X (with respect to $\geq$). Then there exists $x^* \in X$ such that, for all $x \in X$, $x \geq x^*$ implies $x = x^*$.*

An element like x^* in the statement of Zorn's Lemma, with the property that $x \geq x^*$ implies $x = x^*$, is a *maximal element* for $\geq$ in X.

1.1.3 Euclidean spaces

We use $\mathbf{R}$ to denote the real numbers, $\mathbf{Q}$ to denote the rational numbers, and $\mathbf{Z}$ to denote the integers. When $X = \mathbf{R}$, we have the following familiar binary relation: $> \subseteq \mathbf{R}^2$ defined as $x > y$ if there is some $z \neq 0$ such that $x = y + z^2$. The relation $\geq$ is defined by $x \geq y$ if either $x = y$ or $x > y$. We often write $x > y$ as $y < x$, and $x \geq y$ as $y \leq x$. For any $x, y \in \mathbf{R}$ with $x < y$, the open interval $\{z \in \mathbf{R} : x < z < y\}$ is denoted by (x,y).

Let $X = \mathbf{R}^n$; $x_i \in \mathbf{R}$ is the ith *component* of the *vector* x, for $i = 1, \ldots, n$. The *inner product* of two vectors x and y is $x \cdot y = \sum_{i=1}^{n} x_i y_i$. Define the binary relation $\geq$ by $x \geq y$ if $x_i \geq y_i$ for $i = 1,\ldots,n$. Define $>$ and $\gg$ by $x > y$ if $x \geq y$ and $x \neq y$; and $x \gg y$ if $x_i > y_i$ for $i = 1,\ldots,n$. Denote by $\mathbf{R}^n_+$ the set of $x \in \mathbf{R}^n$ with $x \geq 0$; and by $\mathbf{R}^n_{++}$ the set of $x \in \mathbf{R}^n$ with $x \gg 0$.

Note that $\geq$ on $\mathbf{R}^n$ is a partial order, while $\geq$ on $\mathbf{R}$ is a linear order. The set $\mathbf{R}^n$ with the order $\geq$ is a lattice, and for any $x = (x_i)_{i=1}^n$ and $y = (y_i)_{i=1}^n$ we have $x \vee y = (\max\{x_i, y_i\})_{i=1}^n$ and $x \wedge y = (\min\{x_i, y_i\})_{i=1}^n$.

The usual (Euclidean) norm on $\mathbf{R}^n$ is $\|x\| = \sqrt{\sum_{i=1}^n x_i^2}$. The *interior* of a set $A \subseteq \mathbf{R}^n$ is the set of $x \in A$ for which there is $\varepsilon > 0$ such that if $\|x - y\| < \varepsilon$ then $y \in A$. The interior of A is denoted by $\operatorname{int} A$. We say that x is interior to A if $x \in \operatorname{int} A$.

We use standard notational conventions for functions and correspondences. Let X and Y be sets. We denote by $u : X \to Y$ a function with domain X and range a subset of Y. A *correspondence* is a function $\varphi : X \to 2^Y$, which we denote by $\varphi : X \rightrightarrows Y$. When $X \subseteq \mathbf{R}^n$, $Y = \mathbf{R}$, $x \in X$, and $u : X \to Y$ is differentiable (the definition of which is omitted), then $\nabla u(x)$ denotes the *gradient* of u at x.

We use $\mathbf{1}$ to denote an *indicator function*: for $E \subseteq X$, $\mathbf{1}_E : X \to \mathbf{R}$ is the function $\mathbf{1}_E(x) = 1$ if $x \in E$ and $\mathbf{1}_E(x) = 0$ if $x \notin E$; $\mathbf{1}_x$ denotes $\mathbf{1}_{\{x\}}$.

The notation for indicator functions is also used as an *indicator vector*. When $E \subseteq \{1,\ldots,n\}$, $\mathbf{1}_E$ is the vector in $\mathbf{R}^n$ that has a 1 in the ith component if $i \in E$, and has a 0 in the ith component if $i \notin E$. The vector $\mathbf{1}_i$ is called the ith *unit vector*. Finally, we write $\mathbf{1}$ for $\mathbf{1}_{\{1,\ldots,n\}}$, the vector all of whose components are 1.

1.2 PREFERENCE AND UTILITY

A *(rational) preference relation* on X is a binary relation $\succeq \subseteq X \times X$ that is a weak order. A preference relation that is a linear order is called a *strict preference* or a *strict preference relation*.

When we use the $\succeq$ notation for a binary relation, we write $\succ$ for $P_\succeq$, its strict part, and $\sim$ for its symmetric part $I_\succeq$. Note that when $\succeq$ is a preference relation then $\succ$ is asymmetric and transitive, while $\sim$ is an equivalence relation.

1.2.1 Properties of preferences

For a preference relation $\succeq$ on $X \subseteq \mathbf{R}^n$, we can define the following standard properties. We say that $\succeq$ is:

- *locally nonsatiated* if for all x and $\varepsilon > 0$, there is some $y \in X$ such that $\|x - y\| < \varepsilon$ and $y \succ x$;
- *monotonic* if $x \gg y$ implies $x \succ y$;
- *strictly monotonic* if $x > y$ implies $x \succ y$;
- *continuous* if the sets $\{z \in X : z \succeq x\}$ and $\{z \in X : x \succeq z\}$ are relatively closed in X for every x.

The set $\{z \in X : z \succeq x\}$ is the *upper contour set* of $\succeq$ at x: the set of elements that are at least as good as x. The *strict upper contour set* of $\succeq$ at x is $\{z \in X : z \succ x\}$. And the set $\{z \in X : x \succeq z\}$ is the *lower contour set* of $\succeq$ at x.

In the case when $X \subseteq \mathbf{R}^n$ is a convex set, it is often useful to understand the relation between a preference and convex combinations of elements in X. Say that a binary relation $\succeq$ is

- *convex* if $\lambda \in (0,1)$, $y \succeq x$, and $z \succeq x$ implies that $\lambda y + (1-\lambda)z \succeq x$;
- *strictly convex* if $\lambda \in (0,1)$, $y \succeq x$, $z \succeq x$, and $y \neq z$ implies that $\lambda y + (1-\lambda)z \succ x$.

So a preference relation $\succeq$ is convex if the upper contour set of $\succeq$ at x is a convex set, for all $x \in X$.

1.2.2 Utility

Preference relations are often described through a *utility function* $u : X \to \mathbf{R}$ by $x \succeq y$ iff $u(x) \geq u(y)$. We say that u *represents* $\succeq$. In that case we say that u is locally nonsatiated, monotonic, or strictly monotonic if the preference relation it represents has those properties. A utility function is *quasiconcave* if the preference relation it represents is convex; and *strictly quasiconcave* if the preference relation it represents is strictly convex. Additionally, we say that u is continuous or concave if it satisfies those properties according to its ordinary definitions. A *smooth* utility is one for which all partial derivatives of all orders exist.

We have the following general theorem.

Theorem 1.1 *A preference relation has a utility function that represents it iff there exists an (at most) countable set $Z \subseteq X$ with the following property: for all $x, y \in X$ for which $x \succ y$, there exists $z \in Z$ for which $x \succeq z \succeq y$.*

Proof. First, we show that if there exists such a utility representation, then there exists a countable set $Z \subseteq X$ satisfying the property in the statement of the theorem.

We shall exhibit a two-part construction. Let $A = u(X) \subseteq \mathbf{R}$, a nonempty set of real numbers. Consider two countable sets of open intervals. The first, denoted by $\mathcal{I}$, is the set of all open intervals with rational endpoints. The second, denoted by $\mathcal{I}'$, is the set of open intervals (x,y) with $x, y \in A$ and $(x,y) \cap A = \varnothing$. We show that $\mathcal{I}'$ is countable by the following argument: For $(x,y) \in \mathcal{I}'$, choose $q_{(x,y)} \in \mathbf{Q}$ such that $x < q_{(x,y)} < y$.[1] Note that, since any two intervals in $\mathcal{I}'$ are disjoint, the mapping $(x,y) \mapsto q_{(x,y)}$ is one-to-one. Since $\mathbf{Q}$ is countable, $\mathcal{I}'$ is countable.

Now, for each $I \in \mathcal{I}$, if $I \cap A \neq \varnothing$, pick $a \in I \cap A$ and denote this by a_I. Denote the set $\mathcal{A} = \{a_I : I \in \mathcal{I}, I \cap A \neq \varnothing\}$, and note that this set is at most countable

[1] This does not require the axiom of choice. Enumerate $\mathbf{Q} = \{q_1, q_2, \ldots\}$, and choose $q_{(x,y)}$ to be the element of $\mathbf{Q}$ for which $x < q_{(x,y)} < y$ associated with the lowest index in the enumeration.

because $\mathcal{I}$ is countable. Define $\mathcal{A}'$ to be the set of all x for which $(x,y) \in \mathcal{I}'$, for some y. Note that $\mathcal{A}'$ is at most countable because $\mathcal{I}'$ is.

Using the axiom of choice, for each $a \in \mathcal{A} \cup \mathcal{A}'$, choose one element $x(a) \in X$ such that $u(x(a)) = a$. Let $Z = \{x(a) : a \in \mathcal{A} \cup \mathcal{A}'\}$. It is clear that Z is at most countable and satisfies the requisite property.

Conversely, suppose that there exists an at most countable set Z satisfying the property in the hypothesis. Suppose that Z is countable, and label it as $\{z_k\}_{k=1}^{\infty}$. Define the number $u_k = 1/2^k$. Clearly, $\sum_{k=1}^{\infty} u_k < \infty$. For all $x \in X$, define $u(x) = \sum_{\{k:x \succ z_k\}} u_k - \sum_{\{k:z_k \succ x\}} u_k$. To verify that it is indeed a utility representation, first suppose that $x \succeq y$. Then $\{k : y \succ z_k\} \subseteq \{k : x \succ z_k\}$, so that $\sum_{\{k:y \succ z_k\}} u_k \leq \sum_{\{k:x \succ z_k\}} u_k$, and $\{k : z_k \succ x\} \subseteq \{k : z_k \succ y\}$, so that $\sum_{\{k:z_k \succ x\}} u_k \leq \sum_{\{k:z_k \succ y\}} u_k$. We conclude that $\sum_{\{k:y \succ z_k\}} u_k - \sum_{\{k:z_k \succ y\}} u_k \leq \sum_{\{k:x \succ z_k\}} u_k - \sum_{\{k:z_k \succ x\}} u_k$, or $u(y) \leq u(x)$.

For the strict preference, suppose that $x \succ y$. By the property of Z, there exists some z_k such that $x \succeq z_k \succeq y$. Then by completeness and transitivity, either $x \succ z_k$ or $z_k \succ y$. If the former, then $\{j : y \succ z_j\} \subsetneq \{j : x \succ z_j\}$, so that $\sum_{\{j:y \succ z_j\}} u_j < \sum_{\{j:x \succ z_j\}} u_j$. If the latter, then $\{j : z_j \succ x\} \subsetneq \{j : x \succ z_j\}$, so that $\sum_{\{j:z_j \succ x\}} u_j < \sum_{\{j:z_j \succ y\}} u_j$. In either case, we conclude that $\sum_{\{j:y \succ z_j\}} u_j - \sum_{\{j:z_j \succ y\}} u_j < \sum_{\{j:x \succ z_j\}} u_j - \sum_{\{j:z_j \succ x\}} u_j$, or $u(x) > u(y)$.

The proof is similar in the case where Z is finite.

1.3 ORDER PAIRS, ACYCLICITY, AND EXTENSION THEOREMS

An *order pair* on X is a pair of binary relations $\langle R, P\rangle$ such that $P \subseteq R$. If R is a binary relation, then $\langle R, P_R\rangle$ is an order pair, but we shall encounter order pairs $\langle R, P\rangle$ in which P may not be the strict part of R. An order pair $\langle R', P'\rangle$ is an *order pair extension* of $\langle R, P\rangle$ if $R \subseteq R'$ and $P \subseteq P'$. (Our previous definition of when a binary relation B is an extension of R corresponds to $\langle R, P_R\rangle$ being an order pair extension of $\langle B, P_B\rangle$.)

An order pair $\langle R, P\rangle$ is *acyclic* if there is no sequence $x_1, x_2, \ldots, x_L$ such that

$$x_1 \, R \, x_2 \, R \ldots R \, x_L,$$

and $x_L \, P \, x_1$. A sequence in the situation above is called a *cycle* of $\langle R, P\rangle$, and L is the *length of the cycle*. A single binary relation R is acyclic if the order pair $\langle R, R\rangle$ is acyclic.

Observation 1.2 *If $\langle R, P\rangle$ is acyclic, then $\langle R \cup (x,x), P\rangle$ is acyclic for any $x \in X$. Hence, any acyclic $\langle R, P\rangle$ has an acyclic extension $\langle R', P'\rangle$ in which R' is reflexive.*

The *transitive closure* of a binary relation R is the binary relation R^T defined by $x \, R^T \, y$ if there is a sequence $x_1, x_2, \ldots, x_L$ such that

$$x = x_1 \, R \, x_2 \, R \ldots R \, x_L = y.$$

Equivalently, R^T is the smallest transitive relation containing R, or

$$R^T = \bigcap \{R' : R' \text{ is transitive and } R \subseteq R'\}.$$

Thus, $\langle R,P\rangle$ is acyclic iff there is no x and y with $x\, R^T\, y$ and $y\, P\, x$. Note also that $\langle R,P\rangle$ is acyclic iff $\langle R^T,P\rangle$ is acyclic.

Acyclicity captures a basic property of rational preference. If a binary relation $\succeq$ is complete and $\succ$ is the strict part of $\succeq$, then $\succeq$ is transitive (and hence a rational preference relation) iff $\langle \succeq, \succ\rangle$ is acyclic. As we shall see, acyclicity is essentially what is left of rationality when $\succeq$ is only partially observed, in the sense that we observe some $R \subsetneq \succeq$.

Many problems in revealed preference theory are extension exercises, in the sense that we are given an order pair $\langle R,P\rangle$ and we need to find some well-behaved order pair extension of $\langle R,P\rangle$. The problem then amounts to comparing elements that are left uncompared in R; the following lemma is a basic result on adding comparisons.

Lemma 1.3 (Extension Lemma). *Let $\langle R,P\rangle$ be an acyclic order pair, and $x,y \in X$ be two distinct elements, unordered by R. Then one of the following statements holds true:*

I) $\langle R\cup\{(x,y)\}, P\cup\{(x,y)\}\rangle$ *is acyclic.*
II) $\langle R\cup\{(y,x)\}, P\cup\{(y,x)\}\rangle$ *is acyclic.*
III) $\langle R\cup\{(x,y),(y,x)\}, P\rangle$ *is acyclic.*

Proof. Define a binary relation S by letting $w\, S\, z$ if there is a sequence $x_1, x_2, \ldots, x_L$ such that

$$w = x_1\, R\, x_2\, R \ldots R\, x_L = z,$$

and for which $x_l\, P\, x_{l+1}$ for some $l = 1,\ldots,L-1$. Note that if $x\, S\, y$, then none of the pairs (x_l, x_{l+1}) can equal (x,y) or (y,x) because x and y are unordered by R.

Suppose that (III) is not true: we show that one of the other statements must hold. Because $\langle R,P\rangle$ is acyclic, if $\langle R\cup\{(x,y),(y,x)\},P\rangle$ has a cycle, either $\langle R\cup\{(x,y)\},P\rangle$ has a cycle, or $\langle R\cup\{(y,x)\},P\rangle$ has a cycle. Note that if $\langle R\cup\{(x,y)\},P\rangle$ has a cycle, then $y\, S\, x$; and if $\langle R\cup\{(y,x)\},P\rangle$ has a cycle, then $x\, S\, y$. This implies that if (III) is not true then $x\, S\, y$ or $y\, S\, x$.

Suppose that $x\, S\, y$. We show that (I) follows. Since $\langle R,P\rangle$ is acyclic, any cycle of $\langle R\cup\{(x,y)\}, P\cup\{(x,y)\}\rangle$ must involve (x,y). But $x\, S\, y$ implies that a cycle with the same initial and terminal points could be constructed in $\langle R,P\rangle$. So there can be no cycles in $\langle R\cup\{(x,y)\}, P\cup\{(x,y)\}\rangle$.

Similarly, $y\, S\, x$ implies (II).

We present two fundamental results on extending a binary relation. The first is called Szpilrajn's Theorem, and deals with extending a partial order to a linear order. The second is a basic and useful result on extensions of acyclic order pairs to preference relation.

Theorem 1.4 (Szpilrajn). *Suppose that $\succeq$ is a partial order. Then there is a linear order $\succeq'$ which extends $\succeq$.*

Proof. We present a proof for the case when X is finite. The general result relies on Zorn's Lemma: see the proof of Theorem 1.5. We shall use the notation from the proof of Lemma 1.3.

Since $\succeq$ is a partial order, it is antisymmetric. Consider any antisymmetric order R and its strict part P. Suppose x and y are unordered according to R. If we apply Lemma 1.3 to $\langle R,P\rangle$, then in fact (I) or (II) must hold. The reason is that if x and y are distinct elements, and there is a sequence $x_1,x_2,\ldots,x_L$ such that

$$x = x_1\ R\ x_2\ R \ldots R\ x_L = y,$$

then antisymmetry implies that some R may be replaced by P, and hence $x\ S\ y$. As a consequence, if (II) does not hold, there must exist a sequence $x_1,x_2,\ldots,x_L$ as above, which means that $x\ S\ y$. In turn, $x\ S\ y$ implies (I), by the argument in the proof of Lemma 1.3.

The proof is completed by induction. We can define a sequence $(\succeq_n)_{n=0}^N$ of binary relations as follows. Let $\succeq_0 = \succeq$. Now suppose we have given $\succeq_{n-1}$ such that $\langle \succeq_{n-1}, \succ_{n-1}\rangle$ is acyclic and $\succeq_{n-1}$ is antisymmetric. Suppose there is a pair x,y unordered according to $\succeq_{n-1}$. Applying Lemma 1.3, either (I) or (II) must hold. Without loss, suppose $\langle \succeq_{n-1} \cup \{(x,y)\}, \succ_{n-1} \cup \{(x,y)\}\rangle$ is acyclic. Define $\succeq_n = \succeq_{n-1} \cup \{(x,y)\}$ and note that $\succ_{n-1} \cup \{(x,y)\}$ is its strict part. Further, $\succeq_n$ retains antisymmetry. Since X is finite, there is N such that $\succeq_N$ is complete, and by construction transitive since $\langle \succeq_N, \succ_N\rangle$ is acyclic.

The following result is perhaps the first "revealed preference theorem" in the book. Its significance will become clear in the next few chapters.

Theorem 1.5 *Let $\langle R,P\rangle$ be an order pair. There is a preference relation $\succeq$ such that $\langle \succeq, \succ\rangle$ is an order pair extension of $\langle R,P\rangle$ iff $\langle R,P\rangle$ is acyclic.*

Proof. It is obvious that if $\succeq$ exists, then $\langle R,P\rangle$ is acyclic. We proceed to prove the converse. Suppose that $\langle R,P\rangle$ is acyclic. By Observation 1.2, we can assume without loss of generality that R is reflexive.

The proof proceeds by first showing that there is a transitive, though not necessarily complete, relation $\hat{R}$ for which $\langle \hat{R}, P_{\hat{R}}\rangle$ is an order pair extension of $\langle R,P\rangle$. Then we use Lemma 1.3 in an induction argument to show that the relation $\hat{R}$ can be completed.

In the first step, define $\hat{R} = (R)^T$, the transitive closure of R. It is obvious that $R \subseteq \hat{R}$. Further, suppose that $x\ P\ y$. Then, by acyclicity of $\langle R,P\rangle$, it follows that $y\ (R)^T\ x$ is impossible, so that $x\ P_{\hat{R}}\ y$.

Now, let $\mathcal{W}$ be the collection of all acyclic order pairs $\langle R^*,P^*\rangle$ that satisfy (a) that $\langle R^*,P^*\rangle$ is an order pair extension of $\langle R,P\rangle$, and (b) that P^* is the strict part of R^*, $P^* = P_{R^*}$. By the first step of the proof, $\mathcal{W} \neq \varnothing$. Order $\mathcal{W}$ by pointwise set inclusion; so that $\langle R^1,P^1\rangle \leq \langle R^2,P^2\rangle$ if $R^1 \subseteq R^2$ and $P^1 \subseteq P^2$. That is, $\langle R^1,P^1\rangle \leq \langle R^2,P^2\rangle$ if $\langle R^2,P^2\rangle$ is an order pair extension of $\langle R^1,P^1\rangle$.

We shall use Zorn's Lemma. Let $\langle R_\lambda, P_\lambda \rangle_{\lambda\in\Lambda}$ be a chain in $\mathcal{W}$. We claim that $\langle \bigcup_{\lambda\in\Lambda} R_\lambda, \bigcup_{\lambda\in\Lambda} P_\lambda \rangle \in \mathcal{W}$. Clearly it is an extension of $\langle R,P\rangle$. It is also clearly acyclic; for, suppose that there is a cycle $x_1 \left(\bigcup_{\lambda\in\Lambda} R_\lambda\right) x_2 \ldots x_n \left(\bigcup_{\lambda\in\Lambda} R_\lambda\right) x_1$, with at least one instance of $\bigcup_{\lambda\in\Lambda} P_\lambda$. Then by definition, there is $\lambda \in \Lambda$ for which $x_1 R_\lambda x_2 \ldots x_n R_\lambda x_1$, with at least one instance of P_λ. Finally, it is clear that $\bigcup_{\lambda\in\Lambda} P_\lambda$ is the strict part of $\bigcup_{\lambda\in\Lambda} R_\lambda$, for if $(x,y) \in \bigcup_{\lambda\in\Lambda} P_\lambda$ and $(y,x) \in \bigcup_{\lambda\in\Lambda} R_\lambda$, there is $\lambda \in \Lambda$ for which $x\, P_\lambda\, y$ and $y\, R_\lambda\, x$, contradicting our hypothesis. And if $(x,y) \in \bigcup_{\lambda\in\Lambda} R_\lambda$ but $(y,x) \notin \bigcup_{\lambda\in\Lambda} R_\lambda$, then there is $\lambda \in \Lambda$ for which $x\, R_\lambda\, y$ but not $y\, R_\lambda\, x$, so that $x\, P_\lambda\, y$.

By Zorn's Lemma, there exists a maximal acyclic order pair $\langle \tilde{R}, \tilde{P}\rangle$ for which $\tilde{P}$ is the strict part of $\tilde{R}$ and which extends $\langle R,P\rangle$. Since R is reflexive, so is $\tilde{R}$. We claim that $\tilde{R}$ is complete. If not, then there are $x,y \in X$ with $x \neq y$ which are unranked. By Lemma 1.3, there is an acyclic order pair extension of $\langle \tilde{R}, \tilde{P}\rangle$ and satisfying the relevant property, which also clearly extends $\langle R,P\rangle$, contradicting maximality of $\langle \tilde{R}, \tilde{P}\rangle$. The desired relation is then $\tilde{R}$.

Theorem 1.5 has a direct application to a family $(\langle R_\lambda, P_\lambda\rangle)_{\lambda\in\Lambda}$ of order pairs.

Corollary 1.6 *There is a preference relation* $\succeq$ *such that for all* $\lambda \in \Lambda$, $\langle \succeq, \succ \rangle$ *is an order pair extension of* $\langle R_\lambda, P_\lambda\rangle$ *iff* $\langle \bigcup_{\lambda\in\Lambda} R_\lambda, \bigcup_{\lambda\in\Lambda} P_\lambda\rangle$ *is an acyclic order pair.*

We will say that an order pair $\langle R,P\rangle$ is *quasi-acyclic* if there is no sequence $x_1, x_2, \ldots, x_L$ such that

$$x_1\, P\, x_2\, P \ldots P\, x_L,$$

and $x_L\, R\, x_1$.

The following provides a result related to Theorem 1.5, but guaranteeing quasitransitive preference instead of transitive preference.

Lemma 1.7 *There is a complete, quasitransitive relation* $\succeq$ *such that* $\langle \succeq, \succ \rangle$ *is an order pair extension of* $\langle R,P\rangle$ *iff* $\langle R,P\rangle$ *is quasi-acyclic.*

Proof. As in the proof of Theorem 1.5, one direction is obvious. Suppose instead that $\langle R,P\rangle$ is quasi-acyclic. Define $x \succeq y$ iff it is not the case that $y\, P^T\, x$. We claim that $\succeq$ is the appropriate relation.

We first show that $x \succ y$ iff $x\, P^T\, y$. If $x \succ y$, then since $y \succeq x$ is false, it follows that $x\, P^T\, y$ is true. If, instead, $x\, P^T\, y$ is true, then by acyclicity, $y\, P^T\, x$ is false (this uses the property that $P \subseteq R$). As a consequence, we obtain $x \succeq y$. And since $x\, P^T\, y$, we know that $y \succeq x$ is false, so that $x \succ y$.

Now, note that if $x\, R\, y$, it follows that $y\, P^T\, x$ is false (by quasi-acyclicity), so that $x \succeq y$. Further, if $x\, P\, y$, then by the preceding paragraph, we know that $x \succ y$. This proves that $\langle \succeq, \succ \rangle$ is an extension of $\langle R,P\rangle$.

Further, $\succeq$ is complete. Suppose by means of contradiction that it is not: then there is a pair x,y which are unordered according to $\succeq$. By definition, it must be that $x\, P^T\, y$ and $y\, P^T\, x$. But then we have $x\, P^T\, x$, contradicting quasi-acyclicity (this uses the hypothesis that $P \subseteq R$). And $\succ$ is transitive as $\succ = P^T$, which is by definition transitive.

Finally, we establish one more result. It should be clear by now that, in an order pair $\langle R,P\rangle$, P might not equal P_R, the strict part of R. Starting from Theorem 1.5, however, we have established extensions to pairs in which the second order indeed equals the strict part of the first order. This motivates the question of when such extensions are possible.

Say that an order pair $\langle R,P\rangle$ is *asymmetric* if there are no x,y for which $x\,P\,y$ and $y\,R\,x$. An asymmetric order pair may have cycles, *but it has no cycles of length 2.*

Lemma 1.8 *There is a complete relation $\succeq$ such that $\langle\succeq,\succ\rangle$ is an order pair extension of $\langle R,P\rangle$ iff $\langle R,P\rangle$ is asymmetric.*

Proof. One direction is obvious. For the other direction, define $x \succeq y$ iff it is not the case that $y\,P\,x$. Then it is clear that this relation is complete, as $P \subseteq R$ and $\langle R,P\rangle$ is asymmetric (so that it is impossible that $x\,P\,y$ and $y\,P\,x$). To see that $\langle\succeq,\succ\rangle$ is an extension of $\langle R,P\rangle$: whenever $x\,R\,y$, we have $y\,P\,x$ is false, and consequently that $x \succeq y$. And whenever $x\,P\,y$, then $x\,R\,y$, so that $x \succeq y$. And since $x\,P\,y$, by definition, $(y,x) \notin \succeq$. Thus $x \succ y$.

1.4 CYCLIC MONOTONICITY

Let $X \subseteq \mathbf{R}^n$ be nonempty, and $\rho : X \rightrightarrows \mathbf{R}^n$ be a correspondence. Say that ρ is *cyclically monotone* (or that it satisfies cyclic monotonicity) if, for every finite sequence $x_1,\ldots,x_L$, with $L > 1$ and $x_L = x_1$, and every choice of $z_i \in \rho(x_i)$ for $i = 1,\ldots,L-1$, it holds that

$$\sum_{i=1}^{L-1} z_i \cdot (x_{i+1} - x_i) \geq 0.$$

The property of cyclic monotonicity is important in revealed preference theory. It is a multidimensional generalization of *monotonicity*: suppose that $n = 1$. Then a function $\rho : X \to \mathbf{R}$ is monotone decreasing if $(y - x)$ and $(\rho(y) - \rho(x))$ are of opposite signs; put differently, if

$$0 \leq (y-x)(\rho(x) - \rho(y)) = \rho(x)(y-x) + \rho(y)(x-y).$$

By analogy with the case when $n = 1$, we can say that a correspondence $\rho : X \rightrightarrows \mathbf{R}^n$ is monotone when for all $x,y \in X$ and all $z_x \in \rho(x)$, $z_y \in \rho(y)$,

$$0 \leq z_x \cdot (y-x) + z_y \cdot (x-y).$$

The notion of cyclic monotonicity generalizes the idea of monotonicity to account for all finite cycles in X, not only cycles of length two.

Theorem 1.9 *Suppose that one of the following two hypotheses is satisfied:*

- *For all $x \in X$, $\rho(x) \neq \varnothing$.*
- $|\{x \in X : \rho(x) \neq \varnothing\}| < +\infty$ *and* $0 < \left|\bigcup_{x\in X} \rho(x)\right| < +\infty$.

Then the following statements are equivalent:

I) ρ *is cyclically monotone.*
II) *There is a function* $u : X \to \mathbf{R}$ *such that for all* $x, y \in X$ *and all* $z_x \in \rho(x)$,

$$u(y) - u(x) \leq z_x \cdot (y - x).$$

III) *There is a function* $u : X \to \mathbf{R}$ *such that for all* $y \in X$,

$$u(y) = \inf\{u(x) + z_x \cdot (y - x) : x \in X, z_x \in \rho(x)\}.$$

Proof. It is obvious that (III) implies (II). To show that (II) implies (I), note that for any sequence $x_1, \ldots, x_L$, with $x_L = x_1$, it holds that $0 = \sum_{l=1}^{L-1}(u(x_{l+1}) - u(x_l))$.

To prove the theorem, we shall prove that (I) implies the existence of a function u that satisfies the properties stated in (II) and in (III). Let $\rho : X \rightrightarrows \mathbf{R}^n$ be cyclically monotone. Fix an arbitrary $x^* \in X$ for which $\rho(x^*) \neq \varnothing$ (this exists under either of the two hypotheses). Fix $z^* \in \rho(x^*)$.

Let $x \in X$. Here is how we define $u(x)$. Denote by Σ_x the set of all finite sequences $((x_1, z_1), (x_2, z_2), \ldots, (x_{M-1}, z_{M-1}), (x_M))$, with $M \geq 1$, $x_1 = x^*$, $x_M = x$, $z_i \in \rho(x_i)$ and $z_1 = z^*$. Think of sequences $((x_1, z_1), (x_2, z_2), \ldots, (x_{M-1}, z_{M-1}), (x_M))$ as *paths* connecting x^* and $x = x_M$ for which there is $z_i \in \rho(x_i)$ for all x_i, except for x_M. Define $u(x)$ as follows:

$$u(x) = \inf\{\sum_{m=1}^{M-1} z_m \cdot (x_{m+1} - x_m) : ((x_1, z_1), \ldots, (x_M)) \in \Sigma_x\}.$$

The function $u : X \to \mathbf{R}$ is then well defined under either of the two hypotheses. Under the first hypothesis, for any sequence ending in x_M, we may fix $z_M \in \rho(x_M)$ and note that for $((x_1, z_1), \ldots, (x_M))_{m=1}^{M} \in \Sigma_x$,

$$\sum_{m=1}^{M-1} z_m \cdot (x_{m+1} - x_m) + z_M \cdot (x^* - x_M) \geq 0,$$

as ρ is cyclically monotone. Therefore, $z_M \cdot (x - x^*)$ is a lower bound on $\sum_{m=1}^{M-1} z_m \cdot (x_{m+1} - x_m)$ for $((x_1, z_1), \ldots, (x_M))_{m=1}^{M} \in \Sigma_x$, and thus the infimum in the definition of $u(x)$ is defined in $\mathbf{R}$. Under the second hypothesis, it is enough to observe that by cyclic monotonicity we may without loss of generality restrict to the subset of Σ_x which has no repetitions of elements, which by assumption is finite. Hence, the infimum becomes a minimum. Note that, under either case, $u(x^*) = 0$.

We finish the proof by showing that the function u satisfies the properties in (II) and (III). Fix $x, y \in X$ and $z_x \in \rho(x)$. For any $((x_1, z_1), \ldots, (x_M)) \in \Sigma_x$, by definition of $u(y)$,

$$u(y) \leq z_x \cdot (y - x) + \sum_{m=1}^{M-1} z_m \cdot (x_{m+1} - x_m);$$

and hence $u(y) - z_x \cdot (y - x)$ is a lower bound on the set in the right hand side of the definition of $u(x)$. Thus $u(y) - z_x \cdot (y - x) \leq u(x)$. This establishes (II).

To prove (III), note that (II) implies that $u(y)$ is a lower bound on $\{u(x) + z \cdot (y - x) : x \in X, z \in \rho(x)\}$. Fix $\varepsilon > 0$. By definition of $u(y)$ there is some $((x_1, z_1), \ldots, (x_M)) \in \Sigma_y$ such that $u(y) + \varepsilon > \sum_{m=1}^{M-1} z_m \cdot (x_{m+1} - x_m)$. Let $\hat{x} = x_{M-1}$ and $\hat{z} = z_{M-1}$. Then

$$u(y) + \varepsilon > \hat{z} \cdot (y - \hat{x}) + \sum_{m=1}^{M-2} z_m \cdot (x_{m+1} - x_m) \geq \hat{z} \cdot (y - \hat{x}) + u(\hat{x});$$

which finishes the proof.

When X is convex, the theorem has the important implication that the function u is concave. We record this fact as follows:

Corollary 1.10 *Let $X \subseteq \mathbf{R}^n$ be a convex set. Under either of the hypotheses of Theorem 1.9, the following statements are equivalent:*

I) *ρ is cyclically monotone.*

II) *There is a concave function $u : X \to \mathbf{R}$ such that for all $x, y \in X$ and $z_x \in \rho(x)$*

$$u(y) - u(x) \leq z_x \cdot (y - x).$$

III) *There is a concave function $u : X \to \mathbf{R}$ such that for all $y \in X$,*

$$u(y) = \inf\{u(x) + z \cdot (y - x) : x \in X, z \in \rho(x)\}.$$

Proof. The definition $u(y) = \inf\{u(x) + z \cdot (y - x) : x \in X, z \in \rho(x)\}$ in statement (III) implies that u is concave, as it is the lower envelope of affine functions. The result follows because the function constructed in the proof of statements (II) and (III) of Theorem 1.9 is the same.

Versions of these results exist even without either of the hypotheses of Theorem 1.9. However, one must allow for the possibility that u is no longer real-valued.

The importance of (II) in Corollary 1.10 should be clear from the following result.

Proposition 1.11 *Let $X \subseteq \mathbf{R}^n$ be convex, and $u : X \to \mathbf{R}$ be a concave function. Then, for all $x \in int\ (X)$ there is $p \in \mathbf{R}^n$ such that*

$$u(y) \leq u(x) + p \cdot (y - x),$$

for all $y \in X$.

The proof of Proposition 1.11 is an application of the separating hyperplane theorem, and is omitted.

For any function $u : X \to \mathbf{R}$ and $x \in X$, if $p \in \mathbf{R}^n$ has the property that $u(y) \leq u(x) + p \cdot (y - x)$, for all $y \in X$, then p is a *supergradient* of u at x. Proposition 1.11 says that if u is concave then it has a supergradient at any interior point of its domain. The set of all supergradients of u at x is called the *superdifferential* of u at x.

When u is concave and differentiable at x the only supergradient at x is the gradient of u at x. So the superdifferential of u at x is $\rho(x) = \{\nabla u(x)\}$.

1.5 THEOREM OF THE ALTERNATIVE

Many results in revealed preference theory can be formulated using some version of the Theorem of the Alternative, or Farkas' Lemma. We state a version (Lemma 1.12) that may involve either real or rational coefficients and solutions. The usefulness of such a result is that it allows one to state a problem involving real solutions to a system of linear inequalities, and find a revealed preference axiom from the rational solution to the alternative linear system.

For a matrix B, we denote by B_i its ith row.

Lemma 1.12 *Let* $\mathbf{F}$ *be either the set of real numbers* $\mathbf{R}$, *or the set of rational numbers* $\mathbf{Q}$. *Let* B *be a* $(M_1 + M_2) \times K$ *matrix with entries in* $\mathbf{F}$. *Consider the systems of inequalities S1 and S2:*

$$S1 : \begin{cases} B_i \cdot \theta \geq 0, i = 1, \ldots, M_1 \\ B_i \cdot \theta > 0, i = M_1 + 1, \ldots, M_1 + M_2 \end{cases}$$

$$S2 : \begin{cases} \eta \cdot B = 0 \\ \eta \geq 0, \end{cases}$$

where θ *is the* K*-dimensional unknown in S1 and* η, *of dimension* $(M_1 + M_2)$, *is the unknown in S2. Then S1 has a solution* $\theta \in \mathbf{F}^K$ *iff S2 has no solution* $\eta \in \mathbf{F}^{M_1+M_2}$ *with* $\eta_i > 0$ *for some* $i \in \{M_1 + 1, \ldots, M_1 + M_2\}$.

Lemma 1.13 *(Integer–Real Farkas) Let* $\{A_i\}_{i=1}^M$ *be a finite collection of vectors in* $\mathbf{Q}^K$. *Then one and only one of the following statements is true:*

I) *There exists* $y \in \mathbf{R}^K$ *such that for all* $i = 1, ..., L$, $A_i \cdot y \geq 0$ *and for all* $i = L+1, ..., M$, $A_i \cdot y > 0$.

II) *There exists* $z \in \mathbf{Z}_+^M$ *such that* $\sum_{i=1}^M z_i A_i = 0$, *where* $\sum_{i=L+1}^M z_i > 0$.

Proof. Both (I) and (II) cannot simultaneously hold. To see why, suppose that there exist y and z as stated in (I) and (II). Then $A_i \cdot y \geq 0$ for all $i = 1, \ldots, L$ and $A_i \cdot y > 0$ for all $i = L+1, \ldots, M$. Consider $\sum_{i=1}^M z_i A_i \cdot y$. Since $\sum_{i=1}^M z_i A_i = 0$, we know that $\sum_{i=1}^M z_i A_i \cdot y = 0$. Furthermore, since there is some $j \in \{L+1, \ldots, M\}$ for which $z_j A_j \cdot y > 0$, and for all i, $z_i A_i \cdot y \geq 0$, we conclude that $\sum_{i=1}^M z_i A_i \cdot y > 0$, a contradiction.

We now establish that if (II) does not hold, (I) holds. Note that (II) holds iff there is $z \in \mathbf{Q}_+^M$ satisfying the statement in (II). (The reason being that M is finite and that z satisfies the statement in (II) iff Nz satisfies it, for any positive integer N.) By Lemma 1.12 if (II) does not hold, there exists $y \in \mathbf{Q}^K$ such that for all $i = 1,...,L, A_i \cdot y \geq 0$ and for all $i = L+1,...,M, A_i \cdot q > 0$. Since $\mathbf{Q}^K \subseteq \mathbf{R}^K$, $y \in \mathbf{R}^K$.

Finally, the following nonhomogeneous version, which is easily proved using Lemma 1.12, often comes in useful.

Lemma 1.14 *Let B be an $M \times K$ matrix with real entries and let γ be an M-vector with real entries. Consider the systems of inequalities S1 and S2:*

$$S1 : B_i \cdot \theta \geq \gamma_i, i = 1, \ldots, M$$

$$S2 : \begin{cases} \eta \cdot B = 0 \\ \eta \geq 0 \\ \eta \cdot \gamma > 0 \end{cases}$$

where θ is the K-dimensional unknown in S1 and η, of dimension M, is the unknown in S2. Then S1 has a solution $\theta \in \mathbf{R}^K$ iff S2 has no solution $\eta \in \mathbf{R}^M$.

1.6 CHAPTER REFERENCES

Szpilrajn's Theorem (Theorem 1.4) is due to Szpilrajn (1930). Theorem 1.5 generalizes Szpilrajn's Theorem, and is due to Richter (1966) and Hansson (1968). It appears in the form stated here in Suzumura (1976b). Sen (1969) popularized the notion of quasitransitivity. The original proofs of Theorem 1.1 were based on a construction due to Cantor (1895), which shows that any two countable dense linearly ordered sets without endpoints are order-isomorphic, and first appears in economics in Debreu (1954).

Theorem 1.9 and Corollary 1.10 are standard results in convex analysis: see Rockafellar (1997). The idea of cyclic monotonicity and the fact that it characterizes subsets of superdifferentials first appears in Rockafellar (1966). Rockafellar also observes that monotonicity is equivalent to cyclic monotonicity for $X = \mathbf{R}$. The condition of cyclic monotonicity appears frequently in the mechanism design literature as well. Rochet (1987) is a direct generalization of Rockafellar's result. Since monotonicity is necessary and sufficient for cyclic monotonicity in one dimension, one might conjecture that eliminating cycles of length n is necessary and sufficient for cyclic monotonicity in $n-1$ dimensions. This turns out to be false. An example appears in Asplund (1970) (a mapping which rotates every $x \in \mathbf{R}^2$ by $\frac{\pi}{n}$ is cyclically monotonic of order n but not $n+1$). See also Bartz, Bauschke, Borwein, Reich, and Wang (2007). However, there are characterizations of monotonic correspondences which naturally generalize the Rockafellar result; see Krauss (1985) or Fitzpatrick (1988).

Theorems of the Alternative, such as Lemma 1.12, make an early appearance in Farkas (1902); classic references in economics are Kuhn and Tucker (1956) and Gale (1960b). The version here for the real numbers appears first in

Motzkin (1936), and can be derived from the more general formulation due to Slater (1951). The rational version is essentially Theorem 3.2 of Fishburn (1973b). A general result along these lines is Theorem 1.6.1 in Stoer and Witzgall (1970). A more recent general reference is Schrijver (1998). Lemma 1.14 can be found, for example, in Gale (1960b), and Lemma 1.13 in Chambers and Echenique (2014b).

CHAPTER 2

Classical Abstract Choice Theory

We start our development of revealed preference theory by discussing the abstract model of choice. All revealed preference problems have two components: *data*, and *theory*. Given a family of possible data, and a particular theory, a revealed preference exercise seeks to describe the particular instances of data that are compatible with the theory. We shall illustrate the role of each component for the case of abstract choice. The data consist of observed choices made by an economic agent. A theory describes a criterion, or a mechanism, for making choices.

Given is a set X of objects that can possibly be chosen. In principle, X can be anything; we do not place any structure on X. A collection of subsets $\Sigma \subseteq 2^X \setminus \{\varnothing\}$ is given, called the *budget* sets. Budget sets are potential sets of elements from which an economic agent might choose. A *choice function* is a mapping $c : \Sigma \to 2^X \setminus \{\varnothing\}$ such that for all $B \in \Sigma$, $c(B) \subseteq B$. Importantly, choice from each budget is nonempty.

For the present chapter, choice functions are going to be our notion of data. The interpretation of a choice function c is that we have access to the choices made by an individual agent when facing different sets of feasible alternatives. A particular choice function, then, embodies multiple observations.

The main theory is that of the maximization of some binary relation on X. The theory postulates that the agent makes choices that are "better" than other feasible choices, where the notion of better is captured by a binary relation. The theory will be refined by imposing assumptions on the binary relation: for example that the relation is a preference relation (i.e. a weak order).

Given notions of data and theory, the problem is to understand when the former are consistent with the latter. We are mainly going to explore two ways of formulating this notion of consistency.

We say that a binary relation $\succeq$ on X *strongly rationalizes* c if for all $B \in \Sigma$,

$$c(B) = \{x \in B : \forall y \in B, x \succeq y\}.$$

When there is such a binary relation, we say that c is *strongly rationalizable.*

The idea behind strong rationalizability is that $c(B)$ should comprise *all* of the best elements of B according to $\succeq$.

In contrast, we may only want to require that $c(B)$ be among the best elements in B: Say that a binary relation $\succeq$ on X *weakly rationalizes* choice function c if for all $B \in \Sigma$,

$$c(B) \subseteq \{x \in B : \forall y \in B, x \succeq y\}.$$

A utility function u weakly rationalizes the choice function c if the binary relation $\succeq$ defined by $x \succeq y \Leftrightarrow u(x) \geq u(y)$ weakly rationalizes c.

Weak rationalizability allows for the existence of feasible alternatives that are equally as good as the chosen ones, but that were not observed to be chosen.

It should be clear from the definitions that all choice functions are weakly rationalizable by the binary relation $X \times X$ – meaning the binary relation defined by $x \succeq y$ for all x and y (or, in other words, that $x \sim y$ for all $x, y \in X$). For the exercise to be interesting, one must impose constraints on the rationalizing $\succeq$: such constraints can be thought of as a *discipline* on the revealed preference exercise. The need to impose various kinds of discipline shall emerge more than once in this book.

In contrast with weak rationalizability, strong rationalizability does rule out some choice functions: There are choice functions that are not strongly rationalizable. We say that strong rationalizability is *testable*, or that it has *observable implications*. Our first results, in Section 2.1 to follow, seek to describe precisely those choice functions that are strongly rationalizable, and to discuss rationalization by binary relations with particular properties.

2.1 STRONG RATIONALIZATION

Given a choice function c, we can define its *revealed preference pair* $\langle \succeq^c, \succ^c \rangle$ by $x \succeq^c y$ iff there exists $B \in \Sigma$ such that $\{x, y\} \subseteq B$ and $x \in c(B)$, and $x \succ^c y$ iff there exists $B \in \Sigma$ such that $\{x, y\} \subseteq B$, $x \in c(B)$, and $y \notin c(B)$. The binary relations in $\langle \succeq^c, \succ^c \rangle$ give rise to the name "revealed preference theory." The idea, of course, is that if an agent's choices are guided by a preference relation, then $x \in c(B)$ and $y \in B$ when x is at least as good as y according to the agent's preferences. Thus $x \succeq^c y$ captures those binary comparisons which are revealed by c to be part of the agent's preferences.

It is important to recognize that, in general, $\succ^c$ need not be asymmetric, and it need not be the strict part of $\succeq^c$. In general, though, $\succ^c \subseteq \succeq^c$. Thus, it is an order pair according to our definition. In fact, the notion of an order pair is meant to capture precisely the pairs of orders arising in revealed preference theory.

The theory developed here is based on the revealed preference pair. It is, however, important to caution that there may be relevant information in a choice function that is not contained in the revealed preference pair. The following example presents two choice functions that give rise to the same revealed preference pair. The first is strongly rationalizable (by a quasitransitive relation), while the other is not.

Example 2.1 *Let $X = \{x, y, z, w\}$. Consider $\Sigma = \{\{x, y, z, w\}, \{y, z, w\}\}$. Define a choice function $c(\{x, y, z, w\}) = \{x, y\}$ and $c(\{y, z, w\}) = \{y, z\}$. This choice function is rationalizable by the reflexive binary relation which ranks $x \sim y$, $x \succ z$, $y \sim z$ and each of x, y, and z above w. This relation is quasitransitive.*

Now, let $\Sigma' = \{\{x, y\}, \{y, z\}, \{x, z\}, \{x, w\}, \{y, z, w\}\}$ where $c'(\{x, y\}) = \{x, y\}$, $c'(\{y, z\}) = \{y\}$, $c'(\{x, z\}) = \{x\}$, $c'(\{x, w\}) = \{x\}$, and $c'(\{y, z, w\}) = \{y, z\}$. Note this generates exactly the same revealed preference pair as the preceding, but c' is not rationalizable by any relation: The reason is that a rationalizing relation would have to have $y \succ z$ (from $c'(\{y, z\}) = \{y\}$) and $y \sim z$ (from $c'(\{y, z, w\}) = \{y, z\}$).

We begin with a description of strongly rationalizable choice functions. The following observation, a direct consequence of the definition, almost gives us our first answer.

Proposition 2.2 *A choice function c is strongly rationalizable iff it is strongly rationalizable by $\succeq^c$.*

Proof. Suppose c is strongly rationalizable. Then there exists $\succeq$ which strongly rationalizes c. Let $B \in \Sigma$, and let $x \in c(B)$. By definition, for all $y \in B$, $x \succeq^c y$. On the other hand, suppose that $x \succeq^c y$ for all $y \in B$. For any $y \in B$, since $x \succeq^c y$, there is $B_y \in \Sigma$ for which $y \in B_y$ and $x \in c(B_y)$. Since $\succeq$ strongly rationalizes c, we conclude that $x \succeq y$ and thus that for all $y \in B$, $x \succeq y$. Then $x \in c(B)$ as $\succeq$ strongly rationalizes c.

Given Proposition 2.2, it is easy to formulate a condition that says that $\succeq^c$ rationalizes c. The condition is called the V-*axiom*: A choice function c satisfies the V-axiom if for all $B \in \Sigma$ and all $x \in B$, if $x \succeq^c y$ for all $y \in B$, then $x \in c(B)$.

Theorem 2.3 *A choice function is strongly rationalizable iff it satisfies the V-axiom.*

Proof. By Proposition 2.2, we need to show that the V-axiom is equivalent to strong rationalizability by $\succeq^c$. But that $x \in c(B)$ and $y \in B$ implies $x \succeq^c y$ is just the definition of $\succeq^c$, so strong rationalizability by $\succeq^c$ is the statement that $x \in c(B)$ iff for all $y \in B$, $x \succeq^c y$, which is just the V-axiom.

Many revealed preference exercises boil down to an extension exercise; in which, given a revealed preference pair, we seek an order pair extension with particular properties. Recall that when we write the order pair $\langle \succeq, \succ \rangle$, then $\succ$ is the strict part of $\succeq$. This may not be the case for $\langle \succeq^c, \succ^c \rangle$.

Theorem 2.4 *A binary relation $\succeq$ strongly rationalizes c if $\langle \succeq, \succ \rangle$ is an order pair extension of $\langle \succeq^c, \succ^c \rangle$.*

Proof. Suppose that $\langle \succeq, \succ \rangle$ is an order pair extension of $\langle \succeq^c, \succ^c \rangle$. We need to show that for all $B \in \Sigma$, $x \in c(B)$ if and only if $x \succeq y$ for all $y \in B$. So suppose that $x \in c(B)$ and $y \in B$. Then by definition, $x \succeq^c y$. Consequently, $x \succeq y$. Now suppose that $x \succeq y$ for all $y \in B$. Since $c(B) \neq \varnothing$, if $x \notin c(B)$ then there is $y \in B$ for which $y \succ^c x$. Then $y \succ x$, as $\langle \succeq, \succ \rangle$ is an order pair extension of $\langle \succeq^c, \succ^c \rangle$, which would contradict that $x \succeq y$ for all $y \in B$. So $x \in c(B)$.

A converse to Theorem 2.4 is available when $\succeq$ is a preference relation:

Theorem 2.5 *A preference relation $\succeq$ strongly rationalizes c iff $\langle \succeq, \succ \rangle$ is an order pair extension of $\langle \succeq^c, \succ^c \rangle$.*

Proof. Given Theorem 2.4, we shall only prove the necessity of order pair extension.

Suppose that c is strongly rationalizable by some preference relation $\succeq$. The definition of strong rationalization implies that if $x \succeq^c y$, then $x \succeq y$. Suppose that $x \succ^c y$. Then there is B for which $\{x, y\} \subseteq B$, $x \in c(B)$ and $y \notin c(B)$. Since $y \notin c(B)$, completeness of $\succeq$ implies that there is $z \in B$ with $z \succ y$. Since $x \in c(B)$, we know $x \succeq z$. By transitivity of $\succeq$, $x \succ y$.

We now turn to strong rationalization by a preference relation (a weak order). The condition should be familiar from our discussion in Chapter 1. Say that a choice function c is *congruent* if $\langle \succeq^c, \succ^c \rangle$ is acyclic. Our next result is the fundamental characterization of rationalization by a preference relation; it follows quite directly from the results we have established in Chapter 1.

Theorem 2.6 *A choice function is strongly rationalizable by a preference relation iff it is congruent.*

Proof. By Theorem 2.5, there is a preference relation $\succeq$ rationalizing c iff there is a preference relation $\succeq$ for which $\langle \succeq, \succ \rangle$ is an order pair extension of $\langle \succeq^c, \succ^c \rangle$. By Theorem 1.5, this is true iff $\langle \succeq^c, \succ^c \rangle$ is acyclic.

It is frequently convenient to work with single-valued choice functions, choice functions such that for every $B \in \Sigma$, $c(B)$ is a singleton. The following result says that many natural assumptions one could want to place on such choice functions are equivalent: one could say *observationally equivalent*, in the sense that they strongly rationalize the same choice functions.

Proposition 2.7 *Suppose for all $B \in \Sigma$, B is finite, and $|c(B)| = 1$. Then the following statements are equivalent:*

I) *c is strongly rationalizable by a complete, quasitransitive relation.*
II) *c is strongly rationalizable by a preference relation.*
III) *c is strongly rationalizable by a strict preference relation.*
IV) *$\succ^c$ is acyclic.*

Proof. That (III) implies (II) and (II) implies (I) are obvious, the latter because a transitive relation is always quasitransitive. We show that (I) implies (III). First, note that $\succeq^c = (\succ^c \cup =)$, because c is single-valued. We know that there is a complete and quasitransitive $\succeq$ which rationalizes c. We will show that $\succ^c$

$\subseteq \succ$. So suppose that $x \succ^c y$. This means that there is $B \in \Sigma$ for which $\{x,y\} \subseteq B$, $x \in c(B)$ and $y \notin c(B)$. Because $y \notin c(B)$ and $\succeq$ is complete, there exists $y_2 \in B$ for which $y_2 \succ y_1 = y$. If $y_2 \notin c(B)$, there is $y_3 \in B$ for which $y_3 \succ y_2$. We can inductively continue this construction, and because $\succeq$ is quasitransitive, $\succ$ is acyclic, and B is finite, there is y_k such that $y_k \succ y_{k-1} \succ \ldots y_1 = y$, where $y_k \in c(B)$. By quasitransitivity, $y_k \succ y$. But since $c(B)$ is single-valued, $y_k = x$, so that $x \succ y$, which is what we wanted to show.

Now, we let $\succeq^*$ be a strict preference relation for which $x \succ y$ implies $x \succ^* y$, which exists by Theorem 1.4 (note that $(\succ \cup =)$ is a partial order by quasitransitivity of $\succeq$). We claim that $\succeq^*$ rationalizes c. So let $x \in c(B)$, which means that for all $y \in B$ where $y \neq x$, $x \succ^c y$, so that $x \succ y$ and finally $x \succ^* y$. Conversely, suppose that $x \succeq^* y$ for all $y \in B$. Then it must be that $x \succeq y$ for all $y \in B$, as otherwise, there would exist $y \in B$ for which $y \succ x$, which would imply $y \succ^* x$. Consequently, as $\succeq$ rationalizes c, we have $x \in c(B)$.

Finally, (I) is equivalent to (IV). It is easy to see that if c is single-valued and quasitransitive rationalizable, then $\succ^c$ is acyclic. Conversely, suppose that $\succ^c$ is acyclic. Since c is single-valued, $\succeq^c = (\succ^c \cup =)$. By Lemma 1.7, there is a quasitransitive $\succeq$ for which $\succeq^c \subseteq \succeq$ and $\succ^c \subseteq \succ$. The result now follows by Theorem 2.4.

2.1.1 Weak axiom of revealed preference

Congruence in Theorem 2.6 requires one to rule out cycles of any length (using the terminology of Chapter 1). A weaker condition only rules out cycles of length two. We say that a choice function satisfies the *weak axiom of revealed preference* if whenever $x \succeq^c y$, it is not the case that $y \succ^c x$.[1]

While the weak axiom of revealed preference has less bite than congruence, its weakness can be compensated for by a condition on Σ, the domain of the choice function. Note that the larger is the collection Σ, the more restrictive is the weak axiom. So one can make up for the weakness of the weak axiom by demanding a large collection Σ. In particular, if Σ includes all sets of cardinality at most three, the weak axiom of revealed preference is equivalent to rationalizability by a preference relation.

The following pair of results gives the implications of the weak axiom for choice on arbitrary domains. We then present a result which gives the implications of the weak axiom when Σ is rich, in a sense to be made precise.

Theorem 2.8 *A choice function c satisfies the weak axiom of revealed preference iff there exists a complete binary relation $\succeq$ which strongly rationalizes c such that $\succ$ extends $\succ^c$* (i.e. $\succ^c \subseteq \succ$).

[1] The weak axiom of revealed preference is an instance of the condition we termed asymmetry of an order pair in Chapter 1. Indeed, by Lemma 1.8, the weak axiom of revealed preference is the weakest hypothesis that establishes the existence of a complete relation $\succeq$ such that $\langle \succeq, \succ \rangle$ is a order pair extension of $\langle \succeq^c, \succ^c \rangle$.

Proof. First, let $\succeq$ be a complete rationalizing relation such that $\succ$ extends $\succ^c$. Since $\succeq$ strongly rationalizes c, $\succeq^c \subseteq \succeq$. Therefore, if $x \succeq^c y$ and $y \succ^c x$, we would have $x \succeq y$ and $y \succ x$, a contradiction with the definition of $\succ$.

On the other hand, suppose c satisfies the weak axiom of revealed preference. By Lemma 1.8, there is a complete $\succeq$ for which $\succeq^c \subseteq \succeq$ and $\succ^c \subseteq \succ$. By Theorem 2.4, $\succeq$ rationalizes c.

Theorem 2.9 *Suppose that Σ contains all sets of cardinality at most three. Then c is strongly rationalizable by a preference relation iff it satisfies the weak axiom of revealed preference.*

Proof. That a choice function rationalizable by a preference relation satisfies the weak axiom of revealed preference is obvious, as the weak axiom is implied by congruence. Conversely, suppose that c satisfies the weak axiom of revealed preference. By assumption, for all $x, y \in X$, $\{x, y\} \in \Sigma$. Since $c(\{x, y\}) \neq \varnothing$, this implies that $\succeq^c$ is complete. Next, we claim that it is transitive. For suppose that $x \succeq^c y$ and $y \succeq^c z$. If either $x = y$, $y = z$, or $x = z$, then it is obvious that $x \succeq^c z$. So suppose they are all distinct. To prove $x \succeq^c z$, we will show that $x \in c(\{x, y, z\})$, for if not, either $y \in c(\{x, y, z\})$, in which case $y \succ^c x$ (contradicting the weak axiom); or $y \notin c(\{x, y, z\})$ and $z \in c(\{x, y, z\})$, in which case $z \succ^c y$, again contradicting the weak axiom. Thus $x \in c(\{x, y, z\})$, so that $x \succeq^c z$, and $\succeq^c$ is transitive. This shows that $\succeq^c$ is a preference relation.

Finally, $\succ^c$ is the strict part of $\succeq^c$. Clearly, $x \succ^c y$ implies $x \succeq^c y$, and, by the weak axiom, also implies that $y \succeq^c x$ is false. Conversely, if $x \succeq^c y$ and $y \succeq^c x$ is false, we know that $x = c(\{x, y\})$, so that $x \succ^c y$. By Theorem 2.4, c is strongly rationalizable by $\succeq^c$.

Note that, under the hypotheses of Theorem 2.9, the revealed preference relation $\succeq^c$ strongly rationalizes c (Proposition 2.2). By observing choice from all sets of cardinality two, one can identify uniquely the rationalizing preference. For all x and y, $\{x, y\} \in \Sigma$, so $c(\{x, y\})$ is defined and nonempty. So x and y must be ordered by $\succeq^c$.

There are two conditions that are well known to "decompose" the weak axiom of revealed preference. We give them the names first used by Sen (1969), and we show that they are equivalent to the weak axiom.

Say that c satisfies *condition α* if, for any $B, B' \in \Sigma$ where $B \subseteq B'$, $c(B') \cap B \subseteq c(B)$. Say that c satisfies *condition β* if for all $B, B' \in \Sigma$ where $B \subseteq B'$, if $\{x, y\} \subseteq c(B)$, then $x \in c(B')$ if and only if $y \in c(B')$.

The weak axiom refers implicitly to choice from two sets: the set at which x is chosen over y when we say that $x \succeq^c y$, and the set at which y is chosen over x when we say that $y \succ^c x$. Conditions α and β talk explicitly about these sets; α constrains choice from a smaller set, given what was chosen at a larger set, while condition β goes in the opposite direction. The following result explains that α and β can be said to decompose the weak axiom.

Theorem 2.10 *If a choice function satisfies the weak axiom, then it satisfies conditions α and β. Conversely, suppose that either of the two following properties is satisfied:*

I) *Σ has the property that whenever $B, B' \in \Sigma$ have nonempty intersection, then $B \cap B' \in \Sigma$*
II) *For all x, y, $\{x, y\} \in \Sigma$.*

Then if a choice function satisfies conditions α and β, it satisfies the weak axiom.

Proof. Let c be a choice function with domain Σ. Suppose that c satisfies the weak axiom. We shall prove that it satisfies α and β. Let $B, B' \in \Sigma$ with $B \subseteq B'$.

Consider first condition α. Suppose that $x \in c(B') \cap B$. Then $x \succeq^c y$ for all $y \in B'$. In particular, $x \succeq^c y$ for any $y \in c(B)$, as $B \subseteq B'$. If $x \notin c(B)$, then there is $z \in c(B)$ (which is assumed nonempty), so that $z \succ^c x$, violating the weak axiom. Hence $x \in c(B)$.

Second, consider condition β. Let $\{x, y\} \subseteq c(B)$ and $B \subseteq B'$. Then $x \succeq^c y$ and $y \succeq^c x$. Suppose $x \in c(B')$. If $y \notin c(B')$, we have $y \succ^c x$, contradicting the weak axiom. Hence $y \in c(B')$. A symmetric argument establishes that if $y \in c(B')$, then $x \in c(B')$.

Conversely, suppose c satisfies conditions α and β. Suppose, toward a contradiction, that there are x and y with $x \succeq^c y$ and $y \succ^c x$. There are then $A, A' \in \Sigma$ with $\{x, y\} \subseteq A \cap A'$, $x \in c(A)$, $y \in c(A')$ and $x \notin c(A')$. Let $B = A \cap A'$ if condition (I) is satisfied, and let $B = \{x, y\}$ if condition (II) is satisfied. Then by condition α, $x \in c(A)$ and $y \in c(A')$ imply that $x, y \in c(B)$. Now condition β implies that we cannot have $y \in c(A')$ and $x \notin c(A')$. Hence c satisfies the weak axiom.

Corollary 2.11 *Suppose that Σ contains all sets of cardinality at most three. Then c is strongly rationalizable by a preference relation iff it satisfies conditions α and β.*

Proof. Follows from Theorem 2.9 and Theorem 2.10.

When choice $c(B)$ is a singleton for all B, then condition β has no bite. Our next result considers choice functions with singleton values. It explains why some authors reserve the phrase "weak axiom of revealed preference" for what we have called condition α.

Theorem 2.12 *Suppose that Σ has the property that whenever $B, B' \in \Sigma$ have nonempty intersection, then $B \cap B' \in \Sigma$. Suppose further that for all $B \in \Sigma$, $|c(B)| = 1$. Then c satisfies the weak axiom of revealed preference iff it satisfies condition α.*

Proof. Note that condition β is vacuous under the single-valuedness hypothesis. The result therefore follows directly from Theorem 2.10.

2.1.2 Maximal rationalizability

Strong rationalizability requires that $c(B)$ consist of the "best" alternatives in B for a binary relation. Instead, one can require that $c(B)$ contain all the elements of B that cannot be "improved" upon. If the binary relation in question is complete, the two approaches will be equivalent. In general, however, they differ.

Say that a binary relation $\succeq$ *maximally rationalizes* c if

$$c(B) = \{x \in B : \nexists y \in B, y \succ x\}.$$

That is, $c(B)$ corresponds to a set of undominated elements.

If there exists a binary relation $\succeq$ that maximally rationalizes c, then there exists a binary relation $\succeq'$ which strongly rationalizes c. Namely, $x \succeq' y$ if $y \succ x$ is false.[2] When $\succeq$ is complete, it is easy to see that $\succeq' = \succeq$.

The following example shows that there are choice functions that are strongly rationalizable but not maximal rationalizable.

Example 2.13 *Let $\Sigma = \{\{x,y\},\{x,z\},\{x,y,z\}\}$, and $c(\{x,y\}) = \{x,y\}$, $c(\{x,z\}) = \{x,z\}$, and $c(\{x,y,z\}) = \{x\}$. Then this choice function is strongly rationalizable, but is not maximal rationalizable. The relation $\succeq$ that strongly rationalizes c is given by $x \succeq y$, $y \succeq x$, $x \succeq z$, $z \succeq x$, $x \succeq x$, $y \succeq y$, and $z \succeq z$. Note that $\succeq$ is not complete.*

To see that c is not maximal rationalizable, suppose that $\succeq$ maximally rationalizes c. Then because $c(\{x,y,z\}) = \{x\}$, it must be that either $x \succ y$ or $z \succ y$. But $x \succ y$ is impossible, as $c(\{x,y\}) = \{x,y\}$. On the other hand, suppose that $z \succ y$. Then it follows that $x \succ z$, or else $z \in c(\{x,y,z\})$. But this contradicts $z \in c(\{x,z\})$.

2.1.3 Quasitransitivity

The previous analysis makes use of the property of transitivity of a preference relation. In contrast, a quasitransitive relation presents a challenge. In particular, a version of Theorem 2.6 for strong rationalization by a quasitransitive relation is not available (see also Theorem 11.2). But one can easily prove a similar result in one direction:

Proposition 2.14 *If $\langle \succeq^c, \succ^c \rangle$ is quasi-acyclic, then there is a complete and quasitransitive relation strongly rationalizing c.*

Proof. Suppose $\langle \succeq^c, \succ^c \rangle$ is quasi-acyclic. By Lemma 1.7, there is a complete and quasitransitive relation $\succeq$ for which $\succeq^c \subseteq \succeq$ and $\succ^c \subseteq \succ$. By Theorem 2.4, $\succeq$ strongly rationalizes c.

But quasi-acyclicity of $\langle \succeq^c, \succ^c \rangle$ is not necessary for strong rationalization by a quasitransitive relation, as shown by our next example.

[2] $\succeq'$ is then termed the *canonical conjugate* of $\succ$ (Kim and Richter, 1986). This object appears often in revealed preference theory.

Example 2.15 *Suppose* $X = \{x,y,z\}$, *and let* $\Sigma = \{\{x,y\},\{y,z\},\{x,z\},\{x,y,z\}\}$. *Define* $c(\{x,y\}) = \{x,y\}$, $c(\{y,z\}) = \{y,z\}$, $c(\{x,z\}) = \{x\}$, *and* $c(\{x,y,z\}) = \{x,y\}$. *Then c is strongly rationalizable by the relation* $\succeq$ *given by*

$$\succeq = \{(x,y),(y,x),(y,z),(z,y),(x,z),(x,x),(y,y),(z,z)\};$$

that is, all pairs are indifferent except for x and z. The relation $\succeq$ *is quasitransitive. However,* $z \succeq^c y$ *and* $y \succ^c z$ *so that* $\langle \succeq^c, \succ^c \rangle$ *is not quasi-acyclic.*

Proposition 2.7 presents a characterization of quasitransitive strong rationalization in the case when c is singleton-valued. In general, however, it is difficult to find a simple characterization of quasitransitive rationalizability. The reasoning is simple. When we have a preference relation $\succeq$ strongly rationalizing c, we know that if $x \in c(B)$ and $y \in B$, but $y \notin c(B)$, then $x \succ y$. The same cannot be said to hold for quasitransitive relations. In fact, suppose that $\succeq$ is a complete relation on a finite set X for which $\succ$ is acyclic. A relatively easy proposition states that this $\succeq$ is a preference relation iff for all finite B, if $y \in B$ but $y \notin c(B)$, then *for all* $x \in c(B)$, $x \succ y$. On the other hand, it can be shown that $\succeq$ is quasitransitive iff for all finite sets B, if $y \in B$ and $y \notin c(B)$, then *there exists* $x \in c(B)$, $x \succ y$.

2.2 SATISFICING

The notion of strong rationalization can be adapted to the study of a theory of "bounded rationality," the theory of satisficing behavior. The theory, which was first proposed by Herbert Simon, claims that an individual always makes choices which are "good enough," though not necessarily optimal. In our context, the assumption is that if an individual chooses an alternative, then she also chooses anything which is at least as good.

We will say that a choice function c is *satisficing rationalizable* by $\succeq$ if for all $B \in \Sigma$ and all $x,y \in B$, $x \in c(B)$ and $y \succeq x$ imply $y \in c(B)$.

The following two results characterize various notions of satisficing rationalizability. They are essentially extension results, whereby instead of searching for $\succeq$ for which $\succeq^c \subseteq \succeq$ and $\succ^c \subseteq \succ$, we simply require $\succ^c \subseteq \succ$.

Theorem 2.16 *The following statements are equivalent:*

I) *c is satisficing rationalizable by a strict preference relation.*
II) *c satisficing rationalizable by a preference relation.*
III) $\succ^c$ *is acyclic.*

Proof. First, note that if c is satisficing rationalizable by a strict preference relation, then it is obviously satisficing rationalizable by a preference relation.

Second, we prove that (II) implies (III). So suppose that c is satisficing rationalizable by a preference relation $\succeq$, but suppose that there is a cycle $x_1 \succ^c x_2 \ldots \succ^c x_K \succ^c x_1$. We claim that $x_i \succ^c x_{i+1}$ implies that $x_i \succ x_{i+1}$. Note that as $x_i \succ^c x_{i+1}$, there exists $B \in \Sigma$ for which $\{x_i,x_{i+1}\} \subseteq B$, $x_i \in c(B)$, and

$x_{i+1} \notin c(B)$. Because $\succeq$ satisficing rationalizes c, it follows that $x_i \succ x_{i+1}$; as otherwise, we must have $x_{i+1} \in c(B)$. This demonstrates that there is a $\succ$ cycle, contradicting the fact that $\succeq$ is a preference relation. This shows that (II) implies (III).

Finally, we show that (III) implies (I). So suppose that $\succ^c$ admits no cycles. We can consider the transitive closure of the relation $\{(x,y) : x \succ^c y$ or $x = y\}$; denote it by $\succeq'$. By acyclicity of $\succ^c$, $\succeq'$ is a partial order. By Szpilrajn's Theorem (Theorem 1.4), it admits an extension to a strict preference relation $\succeq$. We claim that $\succeq$ satisficing rationalizes c. To see this, suppose that $B \in \Sigma$, $x \in c(B)$, and $y \succeq x$. Then it must be the case that $y \in c(B)$, as otherwise, we would have $x \succ^c y$, which would imply $x \succ y$, a contradiction.

We say a choice function satisfies the *weakened weak axiom of revealed preference* if $\succ^c$ is asymmetric. The following theorem states that the weakened weak axiom is necessary and sufficient for the existence of a complete binary relation $\succeq$ for which $\succ^c \subseteq \succ$.

Theorem 2.17 *A choice function is satisficing rationalizable by a complete binary relation iff it satisfies the weakened weak axiom of revealed preference.*

Proof. First, suppose that c is satisificing rationalizable by a complete binary relation $\succeq$, and suppose by way of contradiction that there exist x and y for which $x \succ^c y$ and $y \succ^c x$. Then there exist $B, B' \in \Sigma$ for which $\{x,y\} \subseteq B \cap B'$, $x \in c(B)$, $y \notin c(B)$, $y \in c(B')$, $x \notin c(B')$. As $\succeq$ satisficing rationalizes c, we therefore conclude that $x \succ y$ and $y \succ x$, a contradiction.

On the other hand, suppose that c satisfies the weakened weak axiom of revealed preference. We define $x \succeq y$ when $y \succ^c x$ is false. Note that by the weakened weak axiom of revealed preference, $\succeq$ is complete. Further, $\succeq$ satisficing rationalizes c. To see this, suppose that $\{x,y\} \in B$ for some $B \in \Sigma$, and that $x \in c(B)$ and $y \succeq x$. Then if $y \notin c(B)$, we know that $x \succ^c y$. This implies that $y \succ^c x$ is false (by the weakened weak axiom), so that $x \succeq y$. And since $x \succ^c y$, we know that $y \succeq x$ is false (by definition of $\succeq$). We conclude that $x \succ y$, a contradiction.

Note that there is an obvious parallel between Theorem 2.6 and Theorem 2.16 on the one hand, and between Theorem 2.8 and Theorem 2.17 on the other. However, there is no counterpart of Theorem 2.9 here. For example, a choice function c defined on all finite subsets of $\{x,y,z\}$ by $c(\{x,y\}) = \{x\}$, $c(\{y,z\}) = \{y\}$, $c(\{x,z\}) = \{z\}$, $c(\{x,y,z\}) = \{x,y,z\}$ satisfies the weakened weak axiom of revealed preference, but there is no transitive relation $\succeq$ that satisficing rationalizes c.

2.3 WEAK RATIONALIZATION

The notion of strong rationalization is based on the assumption that $c(B)$ could capture all the choices that an agent might potentially make from a set B. In general, though, in an empirical environment, we have no reason to expect that we will be able to observe such an object. What we usually observe is a choice that an agent makes; but this does not preclude the possibility of other choices being reasonable for that agent. The notion of weak rationalization is intended to capture this idea.

The following theorem is an analogue to Theorem 2.5. However, it does not require the hypothesis that $\succeq$ be a preference relation. Thus, in general, the property of being weakly rationalizable by a relation $\succeq$ is completely characterized by the revealed preference pair.

Theorem 2.18 *A binary relation $\succeq$ weakly rationalizes c iff the revealed preference pair $\langle \succeq^c, \succ^c \rangle$ satisfies $\succeq^c \subseteq \succeq$.*

Proof. Suppose c is weakly rationalizable by some $\succeq$. Note that if $x \succeq^c y$, then by definition, $x \succeq y$. So $\succeq^c \subseteq \succeq$.

On the other hand, suppose that the revealed preference pair $\langle \succeq^c, \succ^c \rangle$ satisfies $\succeq^c \subseteq \succeq$. Then we claim that $\succeq$ weakly rationalizes c. We need to show that for all $B \in \Sigma, x \in c(B)$ implies $x \succeq y$ for all $y \in B$. So suppose that $x \in c(B)$. Then by definition, $x \succeq^c y$. Consequently, $x \succeq y$.

Weak rationalization is trivial if we place no restrictions on the order which can weakly rationalize a choice function. This is because complete indifference weakly rationalizes anything. To this end, we will study rationalization by preference relations which have *monotonicity* properties. Monotonicity will be a discipline imposed on the revealed preference exercise.

Let $\langle \geq, > \rangle$ be an acyclic order pair. Say that a binary relation $\succeq$ is *monotonic* with respect to $\langle \geq, > \rangle$ if $\langle \succeq, \succ \rangle$ is an order pair extension of $\langle \geq, > \rangle$. The meaning of $\langle \geq, > \rangle$ is that $\geq$ and $>$ reflect some observable characteristics of the alternatives under consideration, and that we can require the unobservable rationalizing relations to somehow conform to $\geq$ and $>$.

The order pair $\langle \geq, > \rangle$ suggests a structure on budget sets. Say that $B \subseteq X$ is *comprehensive* with respect to order pair $\langle \geq, > \rangle$ if whenever $x \in B$ and $x \geq y$, $y \in B$. The notion of a comprehensive budget is natural when budgets are defined to be a set of objects that are "affordable." Suppose that B is defined by some notion of what the agent can purchase, like a budget defined from prices and income (see Chapter 3). Then, if $x \in B$ because the cost of purchasing x is below the agent's income, and $x \geq y$ implies that the cost of purchasing y cannot exceed that of purchasing x, then of course we have that $y \in B$.

For a fixed $\langle \geq, > \rangle$, define the order pair $\langle \succeq^R, \succ^R \rangle$ by $x \succeq^R y$ if $x \succeq^c y$ and define $x \succ^R y$ if there exists $B \in \Sigma$ and $z \in B$ where $\{x, y, z\} \subseteq B$, $x \in c(B)$ and $z > y$.

The following theorem shows that the order pair $\langle \succeq^R, \succ^R \rangle$ is the proper tool for studying rationalization by a preference relation which is monotonic with respect to $\langle \geq, > \rangle$. We say that a choice function satisfies the *generalized axiom of revealed preference* if the order pair $\langle \succeq^R, \succ^R \rangle$ is acyclic. Theorem 2.19 is relevant to the issues we shall study in Chapter 3.

Theorem 2.19 *Suppose that the acyclic order pair $\langle \geq, > \rangle$ satisfies $x > y \geq z$ implies $x > z$, and that all $B \in \Sigma$ are comprehensive. Then there exists a preference relation which is monotonic with respect to order pair $\langle \geq, > \rangle$ and which weakly rationalizes c iff $\langle \succeq^R, \succ^R \rangle$ satisfies the generalized axiom of revealed preference. In addition, if there is a countable set $Y = \{y_1, y_2, \ldots\}$ such that for all x, z satisfying $x > z$, there is k such that $x > y_k > z$, then the preference relation can be chosen to have a utility representation.*

Proof. Suppose preference relation $\succeq$ is monotonic with respect to $\langle \geq, > \rangle$ and weakly rationalizes c. Suppose by way of contradiction that $\langle \succeq^R, \succ^R \rangle$ is not an acyclic order pair. If it is not acyclic, there is $x_1, \ldots, x_L$ for which $x_1 \succeq^R x_2 \ldots \succeq^R x_L$ and $x_L \succ^R x_1$. Since $x_L \succ^R x_1$, there is z for which $x_L \succeq^R z$ and $z > x_1$. Since $\succeq$ weakly rationalizes c, we have $x_1 \succeq ... \succeq x_L \succeq z$, and by monotonicity, we have $z \succ x_1$, a contradiction to the fact that $\succeq$ is a preference relation.

Conversely, suppose that $\langle \succeq^R, \succ^R \rangle$ is an acyclic order pair. We shall demonstrate that $\langle \succeq^R \cup \geq, > \rangle$ is also an acyclic order pair.[3] It will therefore follow by Theorem 1.5 that there is a preference relation $\succeq$ for which $\succeq^R \subseteq \succeq$, $\geq \subseteq \succeq$, and $> \subseteq \succ$. As a consequence, $\succeq$ will be monotonic with respect to $\langle \geq, > \rangle$, and by Theorem 2.18, $\succeq$ will weakly rationalize c (since $\succeq^R = \succeq^c$). So, suppose for a contradiction that $\langle \succeq^R \cup \geq, > \rangle$ is not an acyclic order pair. The key observations here are that for all $x, y, z \in X$:

- $x \succeq^R y \geq z$ implies $x \succeq^R z$
- $x \succeq^R y > z$ implies $x \succ^R z$
- $x \succ^R y \geq z$ implies $x \succ^R z$

Indeed, the first implication follows because if $x \succeq^R y$, there exists $B \in \Sigma$ for which $\{x, y\} \subseteq B$ and $x \in c(B)$. But if $y \in B$, by comprehensivity, $z \in B$ as well, so that $x \succeq^R z$. The second implication follows by definition. The third implication follows since, if $x \succ^R y$, then there exist $B \in \Sigma$ and $w \in B$ for which $x \in c(B)$ and $w > y$. As B is comprehensive and $y \geq z$, $z \in B$. Further, as $w > y \geq z$, we have by assumption that $w > z$. Consequently $x \succ^R z$.

Since $\langle \succeq^R \cup \geq, > \rangle$ is not acyclic, there is a $\langle \succeq^R \cup \geq, > \rangle$-cycle. For simplicity, let $Q = (\succeq^R \cup \geq)$. Let $x_1 \, Q \ldots Q \, x_L > x_1$ be a $\langle \succeq^R \cup \geq, > \rangle$-cycle, where $L \geq 2$. By the preceding observations, we can, without loss of generality, assume that this cycle takes the form

$$x_1 \geq x_2 \geq \ldots \geq x_K \succeq^R \ldots \succeq^R x_L > x_1 \tag{2.1}$$

by converting all relations of the form $x_i \succeq^R x_{i+1} \geq x_{i+2}$ to $x_i \succeq^R x_{i+2}$.

If $K \neq L$, then we have $x_{L-1} \succeq^R x_L > x_1$. Here, the second observation implies that $x_{L-1} \succ^R x_1$. But $x_1 \geq \ldots \geq x_K$, so by repeatedly applying the third observation, we would have $x_{L-1} \succ^R x_K$. But then $x_K \succeq^R \ldots \succeq^R x_{L-1} \succ^R x_K$, contradicting acyclicity of $\langle \succeq^R, \succ^R \rangle$.

[3] For future reference, note that this also implies that $\langle \succeq^R \cup \geq, \succ^R \cup > \rangle$ is an acyclic order pair.

On the other hand, if $K = L$, then the cycle in equation (2.1) is a $\langle \geq, > \rangle$ cycle, contradicting the acyclicity of $\langle \geq, > \rangle$. We have therefore established that $\langle \succeq^R \cup \geq, > \rangle$ is acyclic.

To see the statement about the utility representation, let $S = (\succeq^R \cup \geq)$, and let $T = (\succ^R \cup >)$. Define the relation U by $x\ U\ y$ if there are $x_1, \ldots, x_k$ with $x = x_1\ V \ldots V\ x_k = y$, where each $V \in \{S, T\}$, and at least one instance coincides with T. Note that U is transitive. Define $u(x) = \sum_{\{k: xUy_k\}} 2^{-k}$.

First, we claim that u represents $\succeq$ which weakly rationalizes c. Thus, suppose that $x \in c(B)$, and that $y \in B$. Now, if $y\ U\ y_k$, then we have $x \succeq^R y\ U\ y_k$, whereby $x\ U\ y_k$, so that $u(x) \geq u(y)$. Second, we claim that $\succeq$ is also monotonic with respect to $\langle \geq, > \rangle$. Thus, suppose $x \geq y$. Again, if $y\ U\ y_k$, then by definition $x \geq y\ U\ y_k$, so that $x\ U\ y_k$. Hence $u(x) \geq u(y)$. Now, suppose that $x > y$. Then there is y_k for which $x > y_k > y$. We claim that $y\ U\ y_k$ is false (obviously $x\ U\ y_k$). So, suppose by way of contradiction that $y\ U\ y_k$ holds, so that $y\ U\ y_k > y$. This implies the existence of a $\langle \succeq^R \cup \geq, > \rangle$ cycle, which we previously demonstrated to be impossible.

If one is willing to sacrifice the transitivity of indifference, nearly any choice function becomes weakly rationalizable by a monotonic binary relation. As we shall see, the relevant property of c is that for all x, $x \succ^R x$ is false. In fact, any choice function satisfying this property can be rationalized by the relation defined as $x \succeq y$ if $y > x$ is false. Let us denote this relation as $>^{-1}$.

Proposition 2.20 *Suppose $\langle \geq, > \rangle$ is an acyclic order pair for which $x > y \geq z$ implies $x > z$. Then $>^{-1}$ is complete, quasitransitive, and monotonic with respect to $\langle \geq, > \rangle$.*

Proof. To show that $>^{-1}$ is complete, suppose that it is not. Then there are x, y for which $x > y$ and $y > x$. But this contradicts the acyclicity of order pair $\langle \geq, > \rangle$ (as $> \subseteq \geq$). Further, $>^{-1}$ is quasitransitive. Suppose $x >^{-1} y$ and $y >^{-1} z$, but that $y >^{-1} x$ and $z >^{-1} y$ are false. It follows that $x > y$ and $y > z$ must be true. As a consequence of our assumption that $x > y \geq z$ implies $x > z$, this implies that $x > z$, which implies by acyclicity that $x >^{-1} z$, and of course $z >^{-1} x$ is false. It is clear by acyclicity that $>^{-1}$ is monotonic with respect to $\langle \geq, > \rangle$.

Theorem 2.21 *Suppose that the acyclic order pair $\langle \geq, > \rangle$ satisfies $x > y \geq z$ implies $x > z$, and that all $B \in \Sigma$ are comprehensive. Then the following statements are equivalent:*

I) *There exists a complete binary relation which is monotonic with respect to order pair $\langle \geq, > \rangle$ and which weakly rationalizes c.*
II) *For all x, $x \succ^R x$ is false.*
III) *$>^{-1}$ weakly rationalizes c.*

Proof. First, we show that (I) implies (II). So suppose that there is a complete order monotonic with respect to order pair $\langle \geq, > \rangle$ and weakly rationalizing c.

We claim that for all x, $x \succ^R x$ is false. Suppose by way of contradiction that there exists x for which $x \succ^R x$. Then by definition there exists $B \in \Sigma$ and $y \in B$ for which $x \in c(B)$ and $y > x$. But since $y > x$ and $\succeq$ is monotonic with respect to order pair $\langle \geq, > \rangle$, it follows that $y \succ x$. This implies that $x \notin c(B)$, as $\succeq$ weakly rationalizes c, a contradiction.

To see that (II) implies (III), we need to show that $>^{-1}$ weakly rationalizes c; suppose that $x \in c(B)$. Suppose by way of contradiction that there is $y \in B$ such that $y >^{-1} x$ and $x >^{-1} y$ is false. Then it follows that $y > x$. But since $x \in c(B)$, $y \in B$, and $y > x$, it follows that $x \succ^R x$, a contradiction.

Finally, that (III) implies (I) is obvious.

The theorem demonstrates that the only empirical content of quasitransitive choice is that for all B, if $x \in c(B)$, then x lies on the "boundary" of B. The equivalence of (I) and (III) establishes that, amongst binary relations monotonic with respect to $\langle \geq, > \rangle$, the assumption of quasitransitivity adds no additional empirical content to the hypothesis of weak rationalization by a complete binary relation. This stands in strong contrast to weak rationalization by a preference relation.

2.4 SUBRATIONALIZABILITY

A dual notion to the notion of weak rationalizability is what we will call subrationalizability. We will say that a choice function c is *subrationalizable* by $\succeq$ if for all $B \in \Sigma$,

$$\varnothing \neq \{x \in B : x \succeq y \text{ for all } y \in B\} \subseteq c(B).$$

Thus, a subrationalizable choice function admits all dominant elements of $\succeq$, but may admit other alternatives. We might be interested in such a condition in an environment where an individual potentially makes mistakes.

Fishburn introduces the following notions. For a finite collection $\Sigma' \subseteq \Sigma$, we define

$$\mathcal{C}(\Sigma') = \left\{ x \in \bigcup_{B \in \Sigma'} B : \text{For all } B \in \Sigma', x \in B \Rightarrow x \in c(B) \right\}.$$

That is, $\mathcal{C}(\Sigma')$ is the set of all alternatives that are always chosen from Σ' when they are available. We will say that choice function c satisfies *partial congruence* if for all $\Sigma' \subseteq \Sigma$ where $0 < |\Sigma'| < +\infty$, $\mathcal{C}(\Sigma') \neq \varnothing$.

As its name suggests, partial congruence is weaker than congruence.

Proposition 2.22 *If c satisfies congruence, then it satisfies partial congruence.*

Proof. Suppose c violates partial congruence, and let $\Sigma' \subseteq \Sigma$ for which $0 < |\Sigma'| < +\infty$ and $\mathcal{C}(\Sigma') = \varnothing$. Now, for each $x \in \bigcup_{B \in \Sigma'} c(B)$, there is $y \in \bigcup_{B \in \Sigma'} c(B)$ for which $y \succ^c x$. Pick an arbitrary $x \in \bigcup_{B \in \Sigma'} c(B)$, and label this x_1. For each x_i, find $x_{i+1} \in \bigcup_{B\in\Sigma'} c(B)$ for which $x_{i+1} \succ^c x_i$. Since $|\Sigma'| < \infty$, eventually there will be $i > j$ for which there is $B \in \Sigma'$ so that $\{x_i, x_j\} \subseteq c(B)$. Observe that $x_i \succ^c \ldots \succ^c x_j$, and $x_j \succeq^c x_i$, contradicting congruence.

The following result characterizes subrationalizability by preference relations.

Theorem 2.23 *Suppose a choice function has the property that $|c(B)| < +\infty$ for all $B \in \Sigma$. Then the following are equivalent:*

I) *c is subrationalizable by a preference relation.*
II) *c is subrationalizable by a strict preference relation.*
III) *c satisfies partial congruence.*

The requirement that $|c(B)| < +\infty$ for all $B \in \Sigma$ is necessary to complete a critical induction step in the proof. The general characterization of subrationalizable choice functions remains open. The condition of partial congruence may be problematic from a falsifiability perspective. The reason is that if $\bigcup_{E\in\Sigma'} E$ is an infinite set, the statement that there exists $x \in \mathcal{C}(\Sigma')$ is existential. This means that it postulates the existence of a certain object. If our process of scientific observation consists of observing chosen elements of choice sets one by one, and if we suppose that we can only observe finite data, we can never falsify the hypothesis that such an element exists.

Proof. To see that (I) implies (II), suppose that c is subrationalizable by a preference relation. One simply needs to "break ties." To see this, suppose that $\succeq$ is a preference relation subrationalizing c. Let $\geq$ be a well-ordering of X.[4] We define $\succeq'$ by $x \succeq' y$ if $x \succ y$ or $x \sim y$ and $y \geq x$. First, for every $B \in \Sigma$, there exists a $\succeq'$-maximal element. To see this, consider the collection of $\succeq$-maximal elements, and pick the $\geq$-minimal element (this necessarily exists because $\geq$ is a well-ordering). Then this element is clearly $\succeq'$-maximal. And further, every $\succeq'$-maximal element of B is also $\succeq$-maximal. So $\succeq'$ subrationalizes c, and is a strict preference relation.

To see that (II) implies (III), suppose c is subrationalizable by a strict preference relation $\succeq$. We need to show that it satisfies partial congruence. To this end, let $\Sigma' \subseteq \Sigma$ be a finite subcollection of budgets. Then for each $B \in \Sigma'$, there exists a unique maximal element $x(B) \in B$ according to $\succeq$. By letting x^* be the maximal element of $\{x(B) : B \in \Sigma'\}$ (this exists as Σ' is a finite collection), we see that $x^* \in \mathcal{C}(\Sigma')$.

To see that (III) implies (I), suppose that c satisfies partial congruence. We add to Σ all singleton and binary sets which are not originally present, and extend c to these sets by $c(\{x,y\}) = \{x,y\}$. This new choice function is also clearly partially congruent, and we will show that it is subrationalizable (this

4 A *well-ordering* of a set X is a strict preference relation for which every nonempty subset of X has a minimal element. Existence of well-orderings is guaranteed by the axiom of choice.

will establish that c is subrationalizable). So, without loss, we can assume that Σ includes all binary sets.

Now, let $\mathcal{E}$ be the collection of finite subsets of Σ. For a partial order $\succeq$ and $\Sigma' \in \mathcal{E}$, we define $\mathcal{C}(\Sigma',\succeq) = \{x \in \bigcup_{E\in\Sigma'} E : \nexists y \in \bigcup_{E\in\Sigma'} E, y \succ x\}$. That is, $\mathcal{C}(\Sigma',\succeq)$ are the $\succeq$-maximal elements of $\bigcup_{E\in\Sigma'} E$.

We consider the collection $\mathcal{R}$ of all partial orders $\succeq$ on X such that for all $\Sigma' \in \mathcal{E}$, $\mathcal{C}(\Sigma',\succeq) \cap \mathcal{C}(\Sigma') \neq \varnothing$. We know that $\mathcal{R}$ is nonempty, as the relation $\Delta = \{(x,x) : x \in X\}$ satisfies $\Delta \in \mathcal{R}$. We will show that $\mathcal{R}$ contains at least one strict preference relation $\succeq$; this will be enough to complete the proof. To see why, note that if $\Sigma' \in \mathcal{E}$ is $\Sigma' = \{B\}$, $\mathcal{C}(\Sigma',\succeq)$ is just the $\succeq$-maximal element of B. And $\mathcal{C}(\Sigma') = c(B)$, so that we conclude that the $\succeq$-maximal element of B is an element of $c(B)$.

So, we order $\mathcal{R}$ by set inclusion. For any chain $\{\succeq_\lambda\}_{\lambda\in\Lambda} \subseteq \mathcal{R}$, we claim that $\succeq' = \left(\bigcup_{\lambda\in\Lambda} \succeq_\lambda\right) \in \mathcal{R}$. We will thus be able to use Zorn's Lemma to establish the existence of a maximal element. First, it is easy to verify that $\succeq'$ is a partial order; we will skip the details. We need to show that $\succeq'$ satisfies $\mathcal{C}(\Sigma',\succeq') \cap \mathcal{C}(\Sigma') \neq \varnothing$ for all $\Sigma' \in \mathcal{E}$. For a contradiction, suppose that there exists some $\Sigma' \in \mathcal{E}$ for which $\mathcal{C}(\Sigma',\succeq') \cap \mathcal{C}(\Sigma') = \varnothing$. In particular, this implies that for every $x \in \mathcal{C}(\Sigma')$, there exists $y \in \bigcup_{B\in\Sigma'} B$ for which $y \succ' x$. Now, note that as $c(E)$ is finite for each $E \in \Sigma$, this necessarily implies that $\mathcal{C}(\Sigma')$ is also finite (since Σ' is finite). This in particular implies that there exists $\succeq_\lambda$ such that for each $x \in \mathcal{C}(\Sigma')$, there exists $y \in \bigcup_{B\in\Sigma'} B$ for which $y \succ_\lambda x$. But this contradicts the fact that $\succeq_\lambda \in \mathcal{R}$. We conclude by Zorn's Lemma that there exists a maximal $\succeq^* \in \mathcal{R}$. Our only task now is to show that $\succeq^*$ is complete.

Now, suppose conversely that $\succeq^*$ is not complete. Then there exist $x', y' \in X$ for which x' and y' remain unranked according to $\succeq^*$. Recall from Chapter 1 that ^{T} denotes transitive closure. We consider two possible extensions of $\succeq^*$: $\succeq^1 = \left(\succeq^* \cup \{(x',y')\}\right)^T$, and $\succeq^2 = \left(\succeq^* \cup \{(y',x')\}\right)^T$. The two differ in how they rank x' and y'. It is easy to verify that $x \succeq^1 y$ if $x \succeq^* y$ or $x \succeq^* x'$ and $y' \succeq^* y$, and that $x \succeq^2 y$ if $x \succeq^* y$ or $x \succeq^* y'$ and $x' \succeq^* y$.

Because $\succeq^*$ is maximal and each of $\succeq^1$ and $\succeq^2$ are partial orders (antisymmetry can be proved by supposing it to be false and establishing a contradiction that x' and y' were ranked according to $\succeq^*$), we conclude that there exist $\Sigma^1, \Sigma^2 \in \mathcal{E}$ for which $\mathcal{C}(\Sigma^1) \cap \mathcal{C}(\Sigma^1,\succeq^1) = \varnothing$ and $\mathcal{C}(\Sigma^2) \cap \mathcal{C}(\Sigma^2, \succeq^2) = \varnothing$.

This implies that

$$w \in \mathcal{C}(\Sigma^1) \cap \mathcal{C}(\Sigma^1,\succeq^*) \Rightarrow \exists x \in \bigcup_{E\in\Sigma^1} E \text{ such that } x \succeq^* x' \text{ and } y' \succeq^* w, \tag{2.2}$$

and that

$$z \in \mathcal{C}(\Sigma^2) \cap \mathcal{C}(\Sigma^2,\succeq^*) \Rightarrow \exists x \in \bigcup_{E\in\Sigma^2} E \text{ such that } x \succeq^* y' \text{ and } x' \succeq^* z. \tag{2.3}$$

Finally, let $\Sigma^* = \Sigma^1 \cup \Sigma^2 \cup \{\{x',y'\}\}$. Since Σ includes all singleton and binary sets, $\Sigma^* \in \mathcal{E}$, so that $\mathcal{C}(\Sigma^*) \cap \mathcal{C}(\Sigma^*,\succeq^*) \neq \varnothing$. So pick $b \in \mathcal{C}(\Sigma^*) \cap$

$\mathcal{C}(\Sigma^*,\succeq^*)$. We claim that $b \in \{x',y'\}$. Observe that

$$\mathcal{C}(\Sigma^*)\cap\mathcal{C}(\Sigma^*,\succeq^*)\subseteq\left[\mathcal{C}(\Sigma^1)\cap\mathcal{C}(\Sigma^1,\succeq^*)\right]\cup\left[\mathcal{C}(\Sigma^2)\cap\mathcal{C}(\Sigma^2,\succeq^*)\right]\cup\{x',y'\}.$$

So, suppose that $b \in \mathcal{C}(\Sigma^1)\cap\mathcal{C}(\Sigma^1,\succeq^*)$. By (2.2), we conclude that $b = y'$—otherwise, (2.2) tells us that $y' \succ^* b$ (recall $\succeq^*$ is a partial order), so that $b \notin \mathcal{C}(\Sigma^*)\cap\mathcal{C}(\Sigma^*,\succeq^*)$. Analogously, by (2.3), if $b \in \mathcal{C}(\Sigma^2)\cap\mathcal{C}(\Sigma^2,\succeq^*)$, we conclude that $b = x'$.

This establishes that $b \in \{x',y'\}$. So, suppose without loss of generality that $b = x'$. Since $\mathcal{C}(\Sigma^1)\cap\mathcal{C}(\Sigma^1,\succeq^*)\neq\varnothing$, we can conclude by (2.2) that there exists $z \in \bigcup_{E\in\Sigma^1} E$ such that $z \succeq^* x'$. But unless we have $z = x'$, it would follow that $x' \notin \mathcal{C}(\Sigma^*,\succeq^*)$, which we know to be false. So we must conclude that $x' = z \in \bigcup_{E\in\Sigma^1} E$. But by definition of $\mathcal{C}$, this implies that $x' \in \mathcal{C}(\Sigma^1)$, as $x' \in \mathcal{C}(\Sigma^*)$. Finally, $x' \in \mathcal{C}(\Sigma^*,\succeq^*)$ implies $x' \in \mathcal{C}(\Sigma^1,\succeq^1)$, as $z \succ^1 x'$ implies $z \succ^* x'$.

So we have shown that $\mathcal{C}(\Sigma^1)\cap\mathcal{C}(\Sigma^1,\succeq^1)\neq\varnothing$, a contradiction. Similarly, if we assume that $b = y'$, we arrive at the conclusion that $\mathcal{C}(\Sigma^1)\cap\mathcal{C}(\Sigma^2,\succeq^2)\neq\varnothing$. As either possibility arrives at a contradiction, we have established that $\succeq^*$ is complete, and hence a strict preference relation.

2.5 EXPERIMENTAL ELICITATION OF CHOICE

Until now, we have abstained from assigning any concrete interpretation to the notion of a choice function. However, for choice to be an empirical concept, it must be observable. There are conceptual and practical issues that arise when we operationalize the idea that choice should be observable.

Imagine a choice-theoretic experiment, the goal of which is to study a particular subject's choice function. In the experiment, the subject may be presented with multiple budgets. If the goal of the experiment is to understand what the individual would choose from each of the budgets, we run into a basic problem. Imagine an individual presented with choices from the two budgets: {hat, left shoe}, {jacket, right shoe}. Suppose that, when presented with the budget {hat, left shoe}, the choice would be the hat, and when presented with the choice {jacket, right shoe}, the choice would be the jacket. If presented with both choices simultaneously, it is possible that the subject might choose the pair of shoes. The two shoes are complements. The presence of complementarities distorts choice.

There is a classical solution to this problem. The idea is to ask the subject to announce which choice she would make from each budget, and then to randomly select a budget, paying the subject the announced choice from that budget. Suppose Σ is finite. Consider a finite set of states of the world Ω, to be realized in the future, and associate each $B \in \Sigma$ with some state $\omega_B \in \Omega$. If the subject is asked to report a single-valued choice function, and announces c, the subject is paid the random variable paying off the single element of $c(B)$ in state ω_B, which we can also call c with a slight abuse of notation. This mechanism is referred to as the *random decision selection* mechanism.

Note that under the random decision selection mechanism, the subject's ultimate payoff is an element of X^Ω, rather than of X. Thus, what matters for her choices is her preference over X^Ω, rather than her preference over X. We would expect there to be some relation between preferences on X and preferences on X^Ω. We can say a preference $\succeq^*$ over X^Ω is *monotonic* with respect to a preference $\succeq$ over X if whenever $f, g \in X^\Omega$ satisfy $f(\omega) \succeq g(\omega)$ for all $\omega \in \Omega$, then $f \succeq^* g$, with a strict preference if in addition there is $\omega \in \Omega$ for which $f(\omega) \succ g(\omega)$.[5] Monotonicity is usually understood as the claim that, if the subject is made better off *ex-post*, regardless of which state obtains, then the subject is made better off *ex-ante*.[6]

The punchline is that if $\succeq$ is a complete and transitive relation over X, and $\succeq^*$ over X^Ω is monotonic with respect to $\succeq$, then a single-valued choice function c $\succeq^*$ dominates all elements of X^Ω iff for all $B \in \Sigma$, if $c(B) = \{y\}$, then $y \succeq x$ for all $x \in B$. Thus, if we are willing to assume monotonicity, then the random decision selection mechanism is a good way of eliciting choice. Importantly, monotonicity requires no form of separability (such as Savage's P2 "sure thing" principle), or an expected utility hypothesis.

2.6 CHAPTER REFERENCES

Probably one of the first works to mention abstract choice theory is Arrow (1951). The theory is mostly a generalization of the classical demand context, described in the next section. Uzawa (1956) is one of the first papers to study the revealed preference approach in an abstract environment, followed shortly thereafter by Arrow (1959), to whom Theorem 2.9 is due. Corollary 2.11 and Theorem 2.12 are due to Sen (1971), while condition α first appears in Chernoff (1954). Theorem 2.6 is first established in full generality in the independent works of Richter (1966) and Hansson (1968). The main contribution in those papers was to describe restrictions on budget sets; prior to this, most works in abstract choice assumed that every finite set could be a potential budget set.

The term "congruence" is due to Richter. Theorem 2.3 on rationalizability is due to Richter (1971). A related result, characterizing maximal rationalizability, is provided by Bossert, Sprumont, and Suzumura (2005). Theorem 2.8 on the class of choice functions satisfying the weak axiom of revealed preference is from Wilson (1970), see also Mariotti (2008). Wilson notes the connection between choice functions satisfying the weak axiom and those induced as von Neumann–Morgenstern stable sets. See also Plott (1974). The characterizations of satisficing rationalizability by preference relation

[5] This assumes no state is null, so that we believe each state might possibly occur; see Chapter 8.

[6] This statement is compelling so long as the *ex-post* notion of "better off" coincides with the *ex-ante* notion. That is, in evaluating *ex-post* outcomes, the *ex-ante* preference $\succeq$ over certain prospects is applied. There are classical examples (Diamond, 1967 or Machina, 1989) where we would not expect this relationship to hold.

and strict preference relations appear in Aleskerov, Bouyssou, and Monjardet (2007) and Tyson (2008). The notion of the weakened weak axiom of revealed preference is due to Ehlers and Sprumont (2008), Theorem 2.17 appears there, and the concept in that characterization appears in Wilson (1970) as the notion of a "Q cut." Theorem 2.23 is due to Fishburn (1976).

Theorem 2.19 is related to Afriat's Theorem, discussed formally in the next chapter. A result along the lines of Theorem 2.19 appears in Quah, Nishimura, and Ok (2013).

The theory of satisficing behavior in Section 2.2 was proposed by Simon (1955). The observations on the distinction between rationalizability and dominant rationalizability are due to Suzumura (1976a). Kim (1987) studies generalized transitivity concepts which we have not discussed, all of which turn out to be empirically equivalent to the standard concept. Bossert and Suzumura (2010) is a detailed work devoted to studying the empirical content of many generalized choice models, some of which we describe here.

A recent literature has used choice as a primitive to study various "behavioral" theories. Manzini and Mariotti (2007) consider choice by the successive application of different binary relations. Masatlioglu, Nakajima, and Ozbay (2012) study attention, and formalize the notion that a decision maker may only consider a subset of the available alternatives. Ok, Ortoleva, and Riella (2014) develop a model of reference-dependent choice. Green and Hojman (2007), de Clippel and Eliaz (2012), Cherepanov, Feddersen, and Sandroni (2013), and Ambrus and Rozen (2014) describe models of agents with multiple motivations. Finally, we should mention the paper by de Clippel and Rozen (2012), which studies some of these behavioral developments under the assumption of limited observability that is very relevant to the notion of empirical content.

In a similar spirit, Green and Hojman (2007), Bernheim and Rangel (2007), Chambers and Hayashi (2012), and Bernheim and Rangel (2009) use choice theory to propose welfare criteria that remain valid when standard revealed preference axioms fail.

The random decision selection mechanism is originally due to Allais (1953), and discussed also by Savage (1954) and his "hot man" example. The idea is also used in the famous elicitation mechanism of Becker, DeGroot, and Marschak (1964). The framework described here is taken from Azrieli, Chambers, and Healy (2012).

CHAPTER 3

Rational Demand

Revealed preference theory started out as an exploration into the testable implications of neoclassical demand theory, and while it has expanded in many different directions, the analysis of rational demand is the most actively researched area in revealed preference theory. In this chapter, we present an exposition of the basic results in the revealed preference theory of rational demand.

We suppose here that we have observations on the purchasing decisions of a single consumer. The consumer makes a sequence of independent choices at different price vectors. The data consists of the consumer's choices, and we seek to understand the implications of rational consumption behavior for such data.

The material on rational demand is divided into three chapters. In Chapter 3 we discuss the basic results on weak and strong rationalization, including Afriat's Theorem, the main result in the revealed preference theory of rational demand. In Chapter 4 we turn to specific properties of demand functions; and in Chapter 5 to some of the practical issues that arise when applying the results of revealed preference theory to empirical research.

3.1 WEAK RATIONALIZATION

Consider an agent choosing a bundle of n goods to purchase. Consumption space is $X \subseteq \mathbf{R}^n_+$, meaning that the consumer chooses $x \in X$. We assume that for any $x \in X$ and $\varepsilon > 0$, there is ε' with $0 < \varepsilon' < \varepsilon$ and $x + \varepsilon' \mathbf{1} \in X$; this means that it is possible to add more of every good to any bundle in X and still remain in X.[1]

Given a preference relation $\succeq$ on X, let $d : \mathbf{R}^n_{++} \times \mathbf{R}_+ \to 2^X$ be the *demand correspondence* associated to $\succeq$; it is defined as

$$d(p,m) = \{x \in X : p \cdot x \leq m \text{ and } (\forall y \in X)(y \succ x \Longrightarrow p \cdot y > m)\}.$$

[1] This assumption is used to guarantee the existence of locally nonsatiated rationalizations.

We refer to d as a *demand function* if $d(p,m)$ is always a singleton.

A *consumption dataset* D is a collection (x^k,p^k), $k = 1,\dots K$, with $K \geq 1$ an integer, $x^k \in X$ and $p^k \in \mathbf{R}^n_{++}$. For each k, x^k is the consumption bundle purchased by the consumer at prices p^k. We shall assume that the consumer exhausts all his income, so that the expenditure $p^k \cdot x^k$ is also the total income devoted to consumption at the time at which the purchases were made. This assumption is in principle unavoidable, because if we were to allow for unspent (and unobservable) income, then any dataset is rationalizable. Section 3.2.3 discusses some related issues. As we shall see, the assumption that income equals expenditure amounts to an implicit assumption of local nonsatiation.

We seek to understand when the consumer's behavior is compatible with the basic theory of rational choice. Formally, a preference relation $\succeq$ *weakly rationalizes* a consumption dataset D if, for all k and $y \in X$, $p^k \cdot x^k \geq p^k \cdot y$ implies that $x^k \succeq y$. In other words, if d is the demand correspondence associated to $\succeq$, then $\succeq$ weakly rationalizes D if $x^k \in d(p^k, p^k \cdot x^k)$ for all k. Say that D is *weakly rationalizable* if there is a preference relation that weakly rationalizes D. There is a stronger version of rationalizability, which we shall discuss in Section 3.2.

We often specify a preference relation through a utility function. Say that a utility $u : X \to \mathbf{R}$ weakly rationalizes the data if for all k and $y \in X$, $p^k \cdot x^k \geq p^k \cdot y$ implies that $u(x^k) \geq u(y)$.

If we place no restrictions on $\succeq$, then any dataset is weakly rationalizable. We can just let $\succeq$ indicate indifference among all the elements of X. The resulting theory is not very interesting or useful: it explains everything because it predicts nothing. For this reason, we are going to impose some basic discipline on our exercise by requiring that the rationalizing $\succeq$ be monotonic.

Consider the situation in Figure 3.1. The figure illustrates a dataset $D_0 = \{(x^1,p^1),(x^2,p^2)\}$. The bundle x^2 is affordable at a budget in which x^1 was demanded. If the consumer were rational we could infer that she likes x^1 at least as much as x^2: we say that x^1 is *revealed preferred* to x^2. At the same time, x^2 is revealed preferred to x^1. We would conclude that a rational consumer who made these choices would regard x^1 and x^2 as equally good. Any rationalizing preference must impose indifference between x^1 and x^2.

Now we see that if the rationalizing preference is required to be monotone, then indifference is impossible. When the consumer in Figure 3.1 purchased x^1, she could have chosen x^2 by spending strictly less than she did at x^1. We should then conclude that she cannot regard the two choices as exactly equivalent: the consumer could have afforded a bundle $x^* \gg x^2$ at prices p^1 and expenditure $p^1 \cdot x^1$. By monotonicity of the rationalizing preference, the bundle x^* must be strictly preferred to x^2. At the same time, x^1 must be at least as good as x^*. So x^* must be strictly preferred to x^2; the consumer cannot be indifferent between the two. We infer that the observations in Figure 3.1 constitute a refutation of the hypothesis that the consumer is rational and his preferences are monotonic.

Generally, we say that a consumption dataset D satisfies the *weak axiom of revealed preference (WARP)* if there is no pair of observations (x^k,p^k) and (x^l,p^l) such that $p^k \cdot x^k \geq p^k \cdot x^l$ while $p^l \cdot x^l > p^l \cdot x^k$. In words, there is no pair

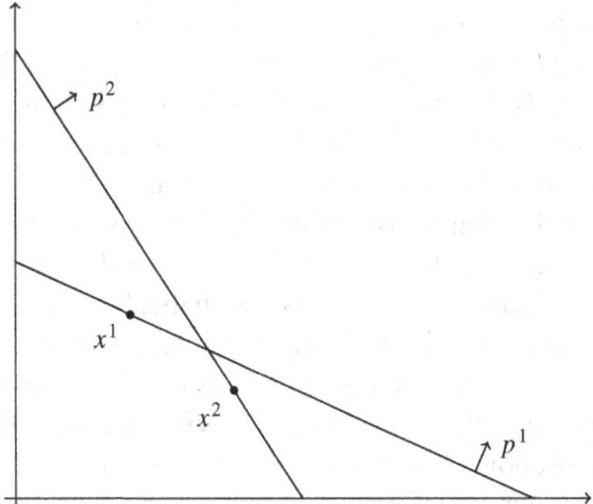

Fig. 3.1 A violation of WARP.

of observations such that the first is revealed preferred to the second, while the second is *strictly* revealed preferred to the first. The dataset in Figure 3.1 exhibits a violation of WARP (recall the discussion of WARP in 2.1.1).

To go beyond the example in Figure 3.1 it is useful to introduce some general definitions.

Given a consumption dataset $D = \{(x^k, p^k)\}_{k=1}^K$, we can define an order pair $\langle \succeq^R, \succ^R \rangle$ on X by $x \succeq^R y$ iff there is k such that $x = x^k$ and $p^k \cdot x^k \geq p^k \cdot y$; and $x \succ^R y$ iff there is k such that $x = x^k$ and $p^k \cdot x^k > p^k \cdot y$. Note that $\succ^R \subseteq \succeq^R$, but that $\succ^R$ will typically not be the strict binary relation associated to $\succeq^R$.[2] The pair $\langle \succeq^R, \succ^R \rangle$ is *D*'s *revealed preference pair*. A dataset satisfies WARP iff there is no $x, y \in X$ with $x \succeq^R y$ and $y \succ^R x$.

Revealed preference pairs, as we have just defined them, are special cases of the notions introduced in Section 2.3 of Chapter 2. The primitives in Chapter 2 are: a set X, a collection of subsets $\Sigma \subseteq 2^X \backslash \{\varnothing\}$, and a choice function $c : \Sigma \to 2^X \backslash \{\varnothing\}$ such that for all $B \in \Sigma$, $c(B) \subseteq B$. Here, $X \subseteq \mathbf{R}^n_+$ is our given consumption space; the collection Σ of budget sets is defined as $\Sigma = \{B_k\}$, where $B_k = \{y \in X : p^k \cdot x^k \geq p^k \cdot y\}$; and $c(B) = \bigcup \{x^k : B_k = B\}$. Then the notion of revealed preference order pair coincides with the definition in Chapter 2, and the definition of WARP we have just given is equivalent to that of Chapter 2.

Observe that the relations $\succeq^R$ and $\succ^R$ are typically very incomplete, in the sense that many alternatives in X are not comparable according to these relations; the problem of rationalizability can be viewed as the problem of completing (or extending) these relations in a way that preserves transitivity.

We saw in the discussion of Figure 3.1 that WARP is necessary for weak rationalization by a monotonic preference. It will be shown below that WARP is not sufficient. The (stronger) property that is both necessary and sufficient for weak rationalization by a monotonic preference is defined as follows:

[2] This property of $\langle \succeq^R, \succ^R \rangle$ is in fact why we introduced the notion of order pairs.

A dataset satisfies the *generalized axiom of revealed preference* (GARP) if its revealed preference pair is an acyclic order pair. Note that the requirement that $\langle \succeq^R, \succ^R \rangle$ is an order pair implies that $\succ^R$ must be asymmetric. We also say that the revealed preference order pair satisfies GARP. Again, the concept of GARP corresponds to the definition in 2.3.

Define the *indirect revealed preference* relation to be the binary relation $(\succeq^R)^T$, the transitive closure of $\succeq^R$. In that sense, we can think of $\succeq^R$ as a *direct revealed preference* relation, and of $\succ^R$ as a *direct strict revealed preference* relation. Thus, one equivalent way to phrase GARP is to say that if x is indirectly revealed preferred to y, then y cannot be revealed strictly preferred to x.

GARP is also equivalent to the following property. For any sequence of data points $((x^{k_1}, p^{k_1}), \ldots, (x^{k_L}, p^{k_L}))$, if the following inequalities hold:

$$p^{k_1} \cdot x^{k_1} \geq p^{k_1} \cdot x^{k_2}$$

$$p^{k_2} \cdot x^{k_2} \geq p^{k_2} \cdot x^{k_3}$$

$$\vdots$$

$$p^{k_{L-1}} \cdot x^{k_{L-1}} \geq p^{k_{L-1}} \cdot x^{k_L}$$

$$p^{k_L} \cdot x^{k_L} \geq p^{k_L} \cdot x^{k_1},$$

then they must hold with equality.

Theorem 3.1 *A dataset is weakly rationalizable by a monotonic preference relation iff its revealed preference pair satisfies GARP.*

With the identification made above between the primitives of this chapter and those of Chapter 2, Theorem 3.1 is easily seen to be a special case of Theorem 2.19. Simply verify that the conditions of Theorem 2.19 are satisfied; namely, 1) that each B_k is comprehensive with respect to the natural ordering $\langle \geq, > \rangle$; and 2) that $x \succ^R y$ iff $x \succeq^R y$ and there exists k with $x, y, z \in B_k$ $x \in c(B_k)$ and $z > y$. In fact, because all prices are strictly positive, the same properties hold with respect to the order pair $\langle \geq, \gg \rangle$.

Remark 3.2 The proof of Theorem 3.1 reveals a bit more than stated: GARP implies the existence of a strictly monotone rationalizing preference. Thus monotonicity and strict monotonicity are observationally equivalent. Further, we can impose local nonsatiation on our rationalizing preference. In that case, the existence of a locally nonsatiated weak rationalization implies GARP. So local nonsatiation and strict monotonicity are observationally equivalent.

Remark 3.3 When the consumption space is discrete, say it is $\mathbf{Z}^n_+$, then Theorem 3.1 must be modified. In this environment it is possible that $p^k \cdot x^l < p^k \cdot x^k$ but there is no $x \in \mathbf{Z}^N_+$ for which $x^l < x$ and $p^k \cdot x \leq p^k \cdot x^k$. For example, if $n = 2$, this occurs with the two-observation consumption dataset specified by $(x^1, p^1) = ((1,2),(4,3))$ and $(x^2, p^2) = ((2,0),(5,2))$. This consumption dataset

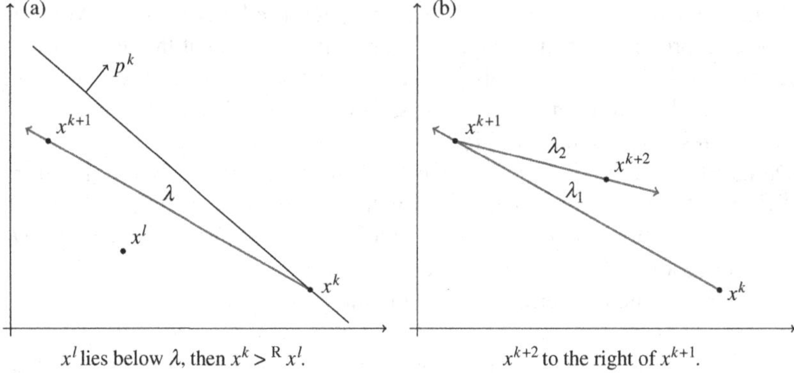

Fig. 3.2 An illustration of the proof of Theorem 3.4.

is weakly rationalizable by a strictly monotonic preference, yet $p^1 \cdot x^2 < p^1 \cdot x^1$ and $p^2 \cdot x^1 < p^2 \cdot x^2$. The issue is that the notion $x^k \succ^R x^l$ as defined in Chapter 2 does not coincide with $p^k \cdot x^l < p^k \cdot x^k$ in this case.

The importance of the difference between WARP and GARP is brought out by our next results, Theorem 3.4 and Remark 3.5.

Theorem 3.4 *Suppose that there are exactly two goods ($n = 2$). Then a dataset satisfies GARP if and only if it satisfies WARP.*

Proof. We show that if a consumption dataset D fails GARP, then there must exist a cycle of length two. To this end, we will argue by contradiction and consider a cycle of minimal length, supposing that it has length at least three. The proof is geometric.

Suppose then that $(x^1, p^1), \ldots, (x^L, p^L)$ is a sequence of observations in D that imply a violation of GARP. So they form a cycle C:

$$x^1 \succeq^R x^2 \succeq^R \cdots \succeq^R x^L \succ^R x^1,$$

with $L \geq 3$. Suppose, toward a contradiction, that there are no shorter cycles.

We first show that no observed bundle is larger than another. Suppose to the contrary that $x^k \geq x^l$ for $k \neq l$. Working with indices modulo L, $x^{k-1} \succeq^R x^k$ would then imply $x^{k-1} \succeq^R x^l$, for $p^{k-1} \cdot x^{k-1} \geq p^{k-1} \cdot x^k \geq p^{k-1} \cdot x^l$. Then we may remove $x^k, \ldots, x^{l-1}$ from the cycle to form one of shorter length, retaining the strict inequality if it lies in this part of the cycle – a contradiction, as C was minimal.

So suppose that no observed bundle is larger than another. Since $n = 2$, the observed bundles can be ordered by the quantity of good 1 consumed in each bundle.

The basic observation is the following. Let x^k be a bundle in C. Consider the half-line in $\mathbf{R}^2_+$ starting from x^k and passing through x^{k+1}. See Figure 3.2(a). The half-line, named λ in the figure, will lie wholly within the budget at which

x^k was purchased. So if x^l is on or below the half-line, then $x^k \succeq^R x^l$. And $x^k \succ^R x^l$ when $x^k \succ^R x^{k+1}$, or when x^l is strictly below λ.

Now suppose that x^k has more of good 1 than x^{k+1}, so x^{k+1} lies to the left of x^k. Consider x^{k+2}, a bundle distinct from x^k and x^{k+1}. Let λ_1 be the half-line starting from x^k and passing through x^{k+1}, and λ_2 be the half-line starting from x^{k+1} and passing through x^{k+2}. Note that x^{k+2} cannot lie strictly below λ_1, or we would obtain $x^k \succ^R x^{k+2}$ and a shorter cycle than C.

We shall prove that x^{k+2} must be to the left of x^{k+1}. Suppose, toward a contradiction, that x^{k+2} has more of good 1 than x^{k+1}; so it lies to the right, as in Figure 3.2(b). If x^k were strictly below λ_2, we would have the cycle of length two $x^k \succeq^R x^{k+1} \succ^R x^k$. So the only possibility is that x^k lies on λ_2. Thus x^k, x^{k+1}, and x^{k+2} are all on the same line. But this configuration always leads to a shorter cycle than C, because it implies that $x^k \succeq^R x^{k+1} \succeq^R x^k$ and that $x^k \succeq^R x^{k+2}$. Thus, if $x^k \succ^R x^{k+1}$, or if $x^{k+1} \succ^R x^{k+2}$ (which implies $x^{k+1} \succ^R x^k$), then there is a shorter cycle – in fact a cycle of length two. And if $\neg(x^k \succ^R x^{k+1})$ and $\neg(x^{k+1} \succ^R x^{k+2})$ then the strict comparison in C lies elsewhere, so $x^k \succeq^R x^{k+2}$ leads to a shorter cycle. Thus x^{k+2} must be to the left of x^{k+1}.

The argument we have just made says that whenever x^{k+1} lies to the left of x^k, x^{k+2} must lie to the left of x^{k+1}. Now, C is a cycle, so (1) there is some k such that x^{k+1} is to the left of x^k; and (2) it cannot be true that x^{k+1} is to the left of x^k for all k. We are left with a contradiction.

Remark 3.5 Theorem 3.4 fails dramatically when $n \geq 3$. For each k there is an example of a dataset that is not weakly rationalizable, but that has no cycles of length less than k. Hence, when $n \geq 3$ there is no hope of simplifying GARP to some axiom that would only require ruling out cycles of certain lengths.

Consider the set $\{x \in \mathbf{R}^3_+ : \sum_i x_i = 1\}$. Draw on the face of this set a regular, convex polygon with k vertices (a regular k-gon). The vertices of the polygon will be the demand observations (these are vectors in $\mathbf{R}^3_+$). One needs to construct prices which result in a cycle of length k, but no shorter cycle. Consider going clockwise around the polygon. Any vertex, say observation x^j, has an adjacent vertex x^{j+1} (connected by an edge) in the clockwise direction. It is clear that one can separate the convex hull $\{x^j, x^{j+1}\}$ from the convex hull of $\{x^i\}_{i=1}^k \backslash \{x^j, x^{j+1}\}$. In fact, by a simple continuity argument, we can pick a hyperplane with normal vector q^j such that x^j lies on the hyperplane, $q^j \cdot x^{j+1} < q^j \cdot x^j$, and for all $i \notin \{j, j+1\}$, $q^j \cdot x^i > q^j \cdot x^j$. Then for α small enough, $p^j = \alpha q^j + (1, \ldots, 1)$ will be a vector of strictly positive prices for which $p^j \cdot x^{j+1} < p^j \cdot x^j$, and for all $i \notin \{j, j+1\}$, $p^j \cdot x^i > p^j \cdot x^j$ (recall that $\sum_{l=1,2,3} x^i_l = 1$ for all i). This gives a cycle of length k, but of no shorter length.

Theorem 3.1 answers the question of which datasets are weakly rationalizable. As we observed in Remark 3.2, consumption datasets cannot distinguish between a locally nonsatiated and a strictly monotonic preference relation. It turns out that much more can be said about the possible rationalizing preference relation: the following remarkable result says that the hypotheses of rationalization via a concave, strictly increasing, and continuous utility function are empirically indistinguishable from the hypothesis of rationalization via a locally non-satiated preference.

Afriat's Theorem *Let X be a convex consumption space, and $D = \{(x^k, p^k)\}_{k=1}^K$ be a consumption dataset. The following statements are equivalent:*

I) *D has a locally non-satiated weak rationalization;*
II) *D satisfies GARP;*
III) *There are strictly positive real numbers U^k and λ^k, for each k, such that*

$$U^k \leq U^l + \lambda^l p^l \cdot (x^k - x^l)$$

for each pair of observations (x^k, p^k) and (x^l, p^l) in D;
IV) *D has a continuous, concave, and strictly monotonic rationalization $u : X \to \mathbf{R}$.*

The inequalities in Statement III of Afriat's Theorem are called *Afriat inequalities*.

Remark 3.6 We can replace the system of inequalities in (III) by a smaller system, which only requires the inequalities to hold for k and l for which $p^l \cdot (x^k - x^l) \leq 0$. This fact is evident from the proof of the theorem in 3.1.1.

Before we give the proof, it is useful to interpret (III), the Afriat inequalities. The inequalities come from the first-order conditions for the maximization of a utility function subject to a budget set: Suppose for simplicity that the data is rationalizable by a utility function u that is differentiable. The first order condition would demand that

$$\nabla u(x)|_{x=x^k} = \lambda^k p^k,$$

where λ^k is a Lagrange multiplier. If, in addition, the utility function is concave we know that $u(y) - u(x) \leq \nabla u(x) \cdot (y - x)$ (see Proposition 1.11). By letting $U^k = u(x^k)$, one obtains the Afriat inequality

$$U^k - U^l = u(x^k) - u(x^l) \leq \nabla u(x^l) \cdot (x^k - x^l) = \lambda^l p^l \cdot (x^k - x^l).$$

It should then be clear that Afriat inequalities have two sources. One is satisfaction of the first-order condition for the consumer's problem. The other is the concavity of the utility function. The numbers U^k in (III) are meant to be the utility levels achieved when consuming x^k, and λ^k is meant to be the Lagrange multiplier.

What is remarkable about Afriat's Theorem is that GARP is sufficient to ensure a solution to this system of inequalities. The idea that GARP captures rationalizability (Theorems 2.19 and 3.1) is relatively easy to see. The result that concavity comes for free is deeper.

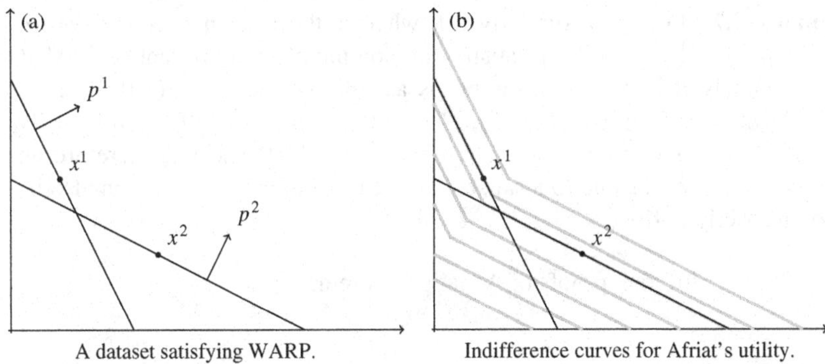

A dataset satisfying WARP. Indifference curves for Afriat's utility.

Fig. 3.3 An illustration of the utility function in Afriat's Theorem.

Given a solution to the system of inequalities (III), one can write down a rationalizing utility function that satisfies the conditions in (IV):

$$u(x) = \min\{U^k + \lambda^k p^k \cdot (x - x^k) : k = 1, \ldots, K\}.$$

This utility function is illustrated in Figure 3.3. On the left, in Figure 3.3(a) is a dataset satisfying WARP. On the right are indifference curves corresponding to the utility function defined, as above, from solutions to the Afriat inequalities for that dataset.

One last comment is in order. The utility we have just exhibited is not smooth (for a result on smooth utility, see Section 3.2.1); but we made use of smoothness when we introduced the first-order conditions. Smoothness is not crucial to the argument. The important concept is that $\lambda^k p^k$ must be a *supergradient* of the utility function. It is instructive to see why this is the case.

Assume given a solution to the Afriat inequalities. We can then string together Afriat inequalities as follows: $U^k - U^l \leq \lambda^l p^l \cdot (x^k - x^l)$ and $U^m - U^k \leq \lambda^k p^k \cdot (x^m - x^k)$ imply that

$$U^m - U^l \leq \lambda^l p^l \cdot (x^k - x^l) + \lambda^k p^k \cdot (x^m - x^k).$$

In fact, if we consider a sequence $k_1, k_2, \ldots k_L$, and $k_L = k_1$, then

$$0 = \sum_{i=1}^{L-1} (U^{k_{i+1}} - U^{k_i}) \leq \sum_{i=1}^{L-1} \lambda^{k_i} p^{k_i} \cdot (x^{k_{i+1}} - x^{k_i}).$$

The property we have just derived from a solution to the Afriat inequalities is, in the terminology of 1.4, that the correspondence $\rho(x) = \bigcup_{k:x=x^k} \{\lambda^k p^k\}$ is *cyclically monotone* (on its domain). Then, reasoning as in Theorem 1.9 (and Corollary 1.10), one obtains a rationalizing utility.

In other words, one way of understanding Afriat's Theorem is as providing numbers λ^k for which the correspondence $\rho(x) = \bigcup_{k:x=x^k} \{\lambda^k p^k\}$ is cyclically monotone. In that sense, GARP can be viewed as an ordinal version of cyclic monotonicity.

Remark 3.7 One may similarly ask whether the existence of $\lambda^k > 0$ for which $\rho(x) = \bigcup_{k:x=x^k}\{\lambda^k p^k\}$ satisfies monotonicity is equivalent to WARP. Unfortunately it is not. An example is as follows. Let $p^1 = (1,0,0)$, $x^1 = (3,3,3)$, $p^2 = (0,1,0)$, $x^2 = (2,2,5)$, $p^3 = (0,0,1)$, and $x^3 = (4,0,4)$. It is easily verified that this consumption dataset satisfies WARP, and that there are no corresponding λ^k leading to a satisfaction of monotonicity. Prices can also be chosen strictly positive.

We offer two different proofs of Afriat's Theorem.

3.1.1 Proof of Afriat's Theorem

We prove that (I) $\Longrightarrow$ (II) $\Longrightarrow$ (III) $\Longrightarrow$ (IV) $\Longrightarrow$ (I). That (I) $\Longrightarrow$ (II) follows from Theorem 3.1. That (IV) $\Longrightarrow$ (I) is obvious. We shall prove the other implications, starting from (II) $\Longrightarrow$ (III), which is the substance of this proof. The proof uses the Theorem of the Alternative, in the form of Lemma 1.12.

We shall prove that if there is no solution to the system of linear inequalities in (III), then GARP is violated. Using Lemma 1.12 it is easy to formulate the consequences of the inequalities not having a solution. We ignore the requirement that each $U^i > 0$, as any solution to the remaining inequalities can be made to satisfy this simply by adding a large enough constant to each U^i. We need to specify the matrix B that corresponds to these linear inequalities in a helpful way.

Consider all pairs $(i,j) \in \{1,...,K\}^2$ with $i \neq j$, and call this set of pairs A. We now construct a real-valued matrix of dimension $(|A|+K) \times 2K$. The first $|A|$ rows are indexed by elements of A, and the last K by $\{1,...,K\}$. The first K columns are labeled $1,...,K$, while the second K are labeled $1',...,K'$. The construction of the matrix is illustrated below.

$$
\begin{array}{c}
 \\ (1,2) \\ \vdots \\ (i,j) \\ \vdots \\ \vdots \\ i \\ \vdots
\end{array}
\begin{array}{c}
\begin{array}{ccccccc|ccccc}
1 & \cdots & i & \cdots & j & \cdots & K & 1' & \cdots & i' & \cdots & K'
\end{array} \\
\left[\begin{array}{ccccccc|ccccc}
1 & \cdots & 0 & \cdots & 0 & \cdots & 0 & p^1\cdot(x^2-x^1) & \cdots & 0 & \cdots & 0 \\
\vdots & & \vdots & & \vdots & & \vdots & \vdots & & \vdots & & \vdots \\
0 & \cdots & 1 & \cdots & -1 & \cdots & 0 & 0 & \cdots & p^i\cdot(x^j-x^i) & \cdots & 0 \\
\vdots & & \vdots & & \vdots & & \vdots & \vdots & & \vdots & & \vdots \\
\hline
\vdots & & \vdots & & \vdots & & \vdots & \vdots & & \vdots & & \vdots \\
0 & \cdots & 0 & \cdots & 0 & \cdots & 0 & 0 & \cdots & 1 & \cdots & 0 \\
\vdots & & \vdots & & \vdots & & \vdots & \vdots & & \vdots & & \vdots
\end{array}\right]
\end{array}
$$

Define the matrix B as follows: For the first $|A|$ rows, in the row corresponding to (i,j), we put zeroes in all entries except for 1 in column i, -1 in column j, and $p^i\cdot(x^j - x^i)$ in column i'. We can write this succinctly by denoting a vector of all zeroes with a single 1 in its ith entry by $\mathbf{1}_i$. Then row (i,j) is the vector $\mathbf{1}_i - \mathbf{1}_j + p^i\cdot(x^j - x^i)\mathbf{1}_{i'}$. For the last K rows, in the row corresponding to i, we put the vector $\mathbf{1}_{i'}$. Clearly, a vector

$$(U,\lambda) = (U_1,\ldots,U_K,\lambda_1,\ldots,\lambda_K)$$

satisfies the system of inequalities in (III) iff $B_{(i,j)} \cdot (U,\lambda) \geq 0$, for all $(i,j) \in A$, and $B_i \cdot (U,\lambda) > 0$ for all i.

By Lemma 1.12, the nonexistence of a solution to Afriat's inequalities means that there is for each (i,j) a $\eta_{(i,j)} \geq 0$ and for each $h \in \{1,\ldots,K\}$ a $\eta_h \geq 0$ such that

$$\sum_{(i,j)\in A} \eta_{(i,j)} B_{(i,j)} + \sum_{h=1}^{K} \eta_h B_h = 0, \tag{3.1}$$

and

$$\eta_h > 0 \qquad \text{for at least one } 1 \leq h \leq K. \tag{3.2}$$

Out of all $\eta = (\eta_{(i,j)}, \eta_h)$ satisfying (3.1) and (3.2), choose η to have a minimum number of entries that equal zero. Think of the numbers $\eta_{(i,j)}$ and η_h as weights. So Lemma 1.12 gives a weighted sum of rows that is identically zero, and where the weight is strictly positive for at least one of the last K rows of the matrix.

Let i be such that $\eta_i > 0$ as in (3.2). The weighted sum of entries in column i' is zero, so there must exist a pair (i,j) for which $p^i \cdot (x^j - x^i) < 0$ and $\eta_{(i,j)} > 0$. Then we have a positive weight on -1 in the column for j. So there must exist some k with $\eta_{(j,k)} > 0$. Then, writing the sum of entries in column j',

$$0 = \eta_j + \sum_{(j,k)} \eta_{(j,k)} p^j \cdot (x^k - x^j) = \eta_j + \sum_{\substack{(j,k)\\ \eta_{(j,k)}>0}} \eta_{(j,k)} p^j \cdot (x^k - x^j).$$

Since $\eta_j \geq 0$, it follows that there be some index k such that $p^j \cdot (x^k - x^j) \leq 0$ in addition to $\eta_{(j,k)} > 0$.

We therefore see that $x^i \succ^R x^j \succeq^R x^k$. In fact, what we proved above is the implication

$$\eta_{(i,j)} > 0 \Longrightarrow \text{there exists } k \text{ such that } \left\{\eta_{(j,k)} > 0 \text{ and } x^j \succeq^R x^k\right\}; \tag{3.3}$$

therefore, continuing in this fashion we obtain a cycle

$$x^{i_1} \succeq^R \cdots \succeq^R x^{i_L} \succeq^R x^{i_{L+1}} = x^{i_1}$$

as the set $\{x^k\}_1^K$ is finite.

There are two possibilities. Either $x^{i_a} \succ^R x^{i_{a+1}}$ for at least one a, or $p^{i_a} \cdot (x^{i_{a+1}} - x^{i_a}) = 0$ for all a. In the former case $\langle \succeq^R, \succ^R \rangle$ is not acyclic, so the data violate GARP and we are done.

In the latter case, we show that we can transform the weights η to obtain new weights η' such that $\eta'_{(i_a,i_{a+1})} = 0$ for at least one (i_a, i_{a+1}) with $p^{i_a} \cdot (x^{i_{a+1}} - x^{i_a}) = 0$. Note that, because $x^{i_1}, x^{i_2}, \ldots, x^{i_L}, x^{i_1}$ is a cycle, and

$p^{i_a} \cdot (x^{i_{a+1}} - x^{i_a}) = 0$, we have that

$$\sum_{a=1}^{L} \left[(\mathbf{1}_{i_a} - \mathbf{1}_{i_{a+1}}) + p^{i_a} \cdot (x^{i_{a+1}} - x^{i_a}) \mathbf{1}_{i'_a} \right] = 0.$$

By construction (3.3) above, $\eta_{(i_a, i_{a+1})} > 0$ for each $1 \leq a \leq L$, so set

$$\kappa = \min_{a=1,\ldots,L} \eta_{(i_a, i_{a+1})}$$

and consider

$$\eta'_{(i,j)} = \begin{cases} \eta_{(i,j)} - \kappa & \text{if } \exists a : (i_a, i_{a+1}) = (i,j) \\ \eta_{(i,j)} & \text{otherwise,} \end{cases}$$

and $\eta'_i = \eta_i$ for all i. Then,

$$\begin{aligned} \sum_{(i,j)\in A} \eta'_{(i,j)} B_{(i,j)} + \sum_{i=1}^{K} \eta'_i B_i &= \sum_{(i,j)\in A} \eta_{(i,j)} B_{(i,j)} + \sum_{i=1}^{K} \eta_i B_i \\ &\quad - \kappa \left[\sum_{a=1}^{L} (\mathbf{1}_{i_a} - \mathbf{1}_{i_{a+1}}) + p^{i_a} \cdot (x^{i_{a+1}} - x^{i_a}) \mathbf{1}_{i'_a} \right] \\ &= 0. \end{aligned}$$

Note that η' equals zero for at least one (i_{a+1}, i_a) such that $p^{i_a} \cdot (x^{i_{a+1}} - x^{i_a}) = 0$ (the ones with minimum weight in η).

Therefore, $\eta' \geq 0$ is also a vector that satisfies Equations (3.1) and (3.2), $\eta' \leq \eta$, and η' has at least one entry $= 0$ that η does not have. This is not possible, as η was chosen to contain the minimal number of zeros. Thus, it must be the case $x^{i_a} \succ^R x^{i_{a+1}}$ for some $1 \leq a \leq L$, which proves (II) $\Longrightarrow$ (III).

To prove that (III) implies (IV), define a utility function $u : X \to \mathbf{R}$ by

$$u(x) = \min\{U^k + \lambda^k p^k \cdot (x - x^k) : k = 1, \ldots, K\}.$$

Observe that u is the minimum of continuous, monotone increasing, and concave (linear) functions, and hence is itself continuous, monotone increasing, and concave.

It is easy to see that u is a weak rationalization. First, $u(x^k) = U^k$ for all k, as (III) implies that $U^k = U^k + \lambda^k p^k \cdot (x^k - x^k) \leq U^l + \lambda^l p^l \cdot (x^k - x^l)$. Second, fix an observation k and let y be such that $p^k \cdot x^k \geq p^k \cdot y$. We have that $u(x^k) \geq u(y)$ because

$$u(x^k) = U^k \geq U^k + \lambda^k p^k \cdot (y - x^k) \geq u(y).$$

Thus the preference represented by u is a weak rationalization of the data. □

3.1.2 Constructive proof of Afriat's Theorem

The substantive step in the proof of Afriat's Theorem is the implication (II) $\Longrightarrow$ (III). The proof we have given in 3.1.1 relies on Lemma 1.12, and has the advantage of illustrating a method that we use repeatedly in this book (see for instance Chapter 12; or Theorems 3.8 and 3.12 in the present chapter). We now turn to a proof that shows how one constructs numbers U^k and λ^k that solve the inequalities in (III). This proof has the advantage of giving a way of constructing a rationalizing utility by constructively finding a solution to the Afriat inequalities.[3]

Let $X_0 \subseteq X$ be the set of observed consumption bundles; that is, $X_0 = \{x^k : k = 1,\ldots,K\}$. Consider the revealed preference pair $\langle \succeq^R, \succ^R \rangle$ restricted to X_0.

By Theorem 1.5, GARP implies that there is a preference relation $\succeq$ on X_0 such that $x \succeq y$ when $x \succeq^R y$ and $x \succ y$ when $x \succ^R y$. Partition X_0 according to the equivalence classes of $\succeq$. That is, let $I_1,\ldots,I_J$ be a partition of X_0 such that $x \sim y$ for $x,y \in I_j$ and $x \succ y$ if $x \in I_j$, $y \in I_h$, and $j > h$.[4]

There are two important aspects of the partition $I_1,\ldots,I_J$. First, if $x^k, x^l \in I_j$ then $p^l \cdot (x^k - x^l) \geq 0$ and $p^k \cdot (x^l - x^k) \geq 0$; as $p^k \cdot (x^l - x^k) < 0$, for example, would imply that $x^k \succ^R x^l$ and thus $x^k \succ x^l$. Second, if $x^k \in I_j$, $x^l \in I_h$ and $h < j$, then $p^l \cdot (x^k - x^l) > 0$; as $p^l \cdot (x^k - x^l) \leq 0$ would imply that $x^l \succeq^R x^k$ and thus $x^l \succeq x^k$.

We now define $(U^k, \lambda^k)_{k=1}^K$ recursively. Set $U^k = \lambda^k = 1$ if $x^k \in I_J$.

Suppose that we have defined (U^k, λ^k) for all $x^k \in \bigcup_{h=j+1}^J I_h$. We can choose V_j such that, for all $x^l \in I_j$ and $x^k \in \bigcup_{h=j+1}^J I_h$,

$$V_j < U^k \quad \text{and} \quad V_j < U^k + \lambda^k p^k \cdot (x^l - x^k). \tag{3.4}$$

Set $U^l = V_j$ for all l with $x^l \in I_j$.

Note that the choice of U^l ensures that if $x^k \in \bigcup_{h=j+1}^J I_h$ then $U^l < U^k$. Since $p^l \cdot (x^k - x^l) > 0$ for each $x^l \in I_j$, we can choose λ^l to be

$$\lambda^l = \max_k \frac{U^k - U^l}{p^l \cdot (x^k - x^l)} \geq 0 \tag{3.5}$$

where the max is taken over k such that $x^k \in \bigcup_{h=j+1}^J I_h$.

The chosen $(U^k, \lambda^k)_{k=1}^K$ satisfy the inequalities in (III). Indeed, let k and l be such that $x^k \in I_j$, $x^l \in I_h$ and $j > h$. Then (3.4) ensures that

$$U^l \leq U^k + \lambda^k p^k \cdot (x^l - x^k),$$

and (3.5) that

$$U^k \leq U^l + \lambda^l p^l \cdot (x^k - x^l). \tag{3.6}$$

If k and l are such that $x^k, x^l \in I_j$, then $U^k = U^l$ so (3.6) follows because $\lambda^k > 0$ and $p^l \cdot (x^k - x^l) \geq 0$.

[3] It should also be mentioned that linear programming methods, applied to the linear system in the proof in 3.1.1, can also be used to construct a solution to the Afriat inequalities.

[4] Strictly speaking, the existence of $\succeq$ is not constructive, as Theorem 1.5 relies on Zorn's Lemma. In the present case, however, X_0 is finite and $\succeq$ is easily constructed.

3.1.3 General budget sets

We turn to a version of Afriat's Theorem for general budget sets, budget sets that may not be defined by a vector of prices. We can generalize the statement $p^k \cdot (x - x^k) \leq 0$, specifying when x is affordable at prices p^k, by introducing a monotonic, continuous function $g^k : X \to \mathbf{R}$ for which $g^k(x^k) = 0$. We say that x is affordable when $g^k(x) \leq 0$.

A dataset is now a collection $(x^k, B^k), k = 1, \ldots, K$; where for each k there is a monotonic and continuous function $g^k : X \to \mathbf{R}$ such that $B^k = \{z \in X : g^k(z) \leq 0\}$. We suppose that $g^k(x^k) = 0$. Note that our previous notion of a dataset is a special case, where for each k, $g^k(x) = p^k \cdot (x - x^k)$.

Adapting the definitions of revealed preference, we can define $x \succeq^R y$ when there is k such that $x = x^k$ and $g^k(y) \leq 0$; and $x \succ^R y$ when there is k such that $x = x^k$ and $g^k(y) < 0$. A dataset satisfies GARP if $\langle \succeq^R, \succ^R \rangle$ is an acyclic order pair. A dataset satisfies WARP if $x \succeq^R y$ implies that $y \succ^R x$ does not hold.

In this more general environment, WARP and GARP are no longer equivalent when $n = 2$. Consider the three points $(0,3), (2,2), (3,0)$. For any pair of these, the convex and comprehensive hull of that pair does not include the third. We can choose our g^k functions so that there are three budget sets, the convex and comprehensive hulls of the pairs. It is then easy to construct a violation of GARP for which there is no corresponding violation of WARP.

The following generalization of Afriat's Theorem is due to Forges and Minelli.

Theorem 3.8 *Let X be convex. The following are equivalent:*

I) *The data $\{(x^k, B^k)\}_{k=1}^K$ have a locally nonsatiated weak rationalization;*
II) *$\langle \succeq^R, \succ^R \rangle$ is acyclic;*
III) *There are strictly positive real numbers U^k and λ^k, for each k, such that*

$$U^l \leq U^k + \lambda^k g^k(x^l)$$

for each pair of observations k and l.

IV) *The data $\{(B^k, x^k)\}_{k=1}^K$ have a monotonic and continuous rationalization;*

Further, in the case when all the functions g^k are concave, the statements above are equivalent to the existence of a monotonic, continuous, and concave rationalization.

Proof. First, that (IV) $\Longrightarrow$ (I) $\Longrightarrow$ (II) is immediate. The substance of the proof is (II) $\Longrightarrow$ (III), just as in the proof of Afriat's Theorem. The proof follows along the same lines as our proof of Afriat's Theorem.

To prove that (II) $\Longrightarrow$ (III), construct a matrix B as follows. Let A be the set of pairs (k,l) with $k \neq l$. For the first $|A|$ rows, in the row corresponding to (k,l), we put $\mathbf{1}_k - \mathbf{1}_l + g^k(x^l)\mathbf{1}_{k'}$. For the last K rows, in the row corresponding to k, we put the vector $\mathbf{1}_{k'}$. A vector

$$(U,\lambda) = (U^1,\ldots,U^K,\lambda^1,\ldots,\lambda^K)$$

satisfies the system of inequalities in (III) iff $B_{(k,l)} \cdot (U,\lambda) \geq 0$, for all $(k,l) \in A$, and $B_k \cdot (U,\lambda) > 0$ for all k.

Suppose that there is no solution to the system in (III). By Lemma 1.12 there is $\eta \geq 0$ such that

$$\sum_{(k,l)\in A} \eta_{(k,l)} B_{(k,l)} + \sum_k \eta_k B_k = 0,$$

and $\eta_k > 0$ for at least one k. Choose η to have the least number of zero entries.

Reasoning just as in the proof of Afriat's Theorem, we know that there is l for which $\eta_{(k,l)} > 0$ and $g^k(x^l) < 0$. The negative entry in the column for l in row (k,l) must cancel out with some row (w,l) with strictly positive weight in η; in fact w can be chosen such that $g^l(x^w) \leq 0$. Thus $x^k \succ^R x^l \succeq^R x^w$. The rest of the proof is analogous to the proof of Afriat's Theorem: we obtain a cycle of $\langle \succeq^R, \succ^R \rangle$.

To prove that (III) $\Longrightarrow$ (IV) we use a similar construction to the one in Afriat's Theorem; we let

$$u(x) = \min\{U^k + \lambda^k g^k(x) : k = 1,\ldots,K\}.$$

Note that u is monotone increasing and continuous. In addition, if $g^k(y) \leq 0$ then $u(y) \leq U^k = u(x^k)$; so it is a weak rationalization.

Finally, the construction above is concave when each g^k is concave.

3.2 STRONG RATIONALIZATION

A preference relation $\succeq$ *strongly rationalizes* a consumption dataset D if, for all k and $y \in X$,

$$(p^k \cdot y \leq p^k \cdot x^k \text{ and } y \neq x^k) \Longrightarrow x^k \succ y$$

Say that D is *strongly rationalizable* if there is a preference relation that strongly rationalizes D. Note that this definition implies choice must be single-valued, which is not the case for the notion of strong rationalization presented in 2.1. Otherwise, the definition of strong rationalization here is consistent with that in 2.1 under the assumption of single-valued choice.

Recall that one can understand weak rationalization as the extension of the observed demand behavior to a demand correspondence, namely the demand correspondence generated by the rationalizing preference. In contrast, strong rationalization is about extending the observed demand behavior to a (single-valued) demand function. In particular, the dataset $\{(x^1,p^1),(x^2,p^2)\}$, with $p^1 = p^2$, $x^1 \neq x^2$, and $p^1 \cdot x^1 = p^2 \cdot x^2$, is weakly rationalizable by a preference that is indifferent among x^1 and x^2, but it is not strongly rationalizable as it is incompatible with a single-valued demand function.

Given a consumption dataset D, we can define an order pair $\langle \succeq^S, \succ^S \rangle$ by $x \succeq^S y$ iff there is k such that $x = x^k$ and $p^k \cdot x^k \geq p^k \cdot y$; and $x \succ^S y$ iff $x \succeq^S y$ and $x \neq y$. The pair $\langle \succeq^S, \succ^S \rangle$ is D's *strong revealed preference* pair.

A dataset satisfies the *strong axiom of revealed preference* (SARP) if its strong revealed preference pair is acyclic.

Theorem 3.9 *A dataset is strongly rationalizable iff it satisfies SARP.*

Remark 3.10 The rationalization can, in fact, be assumed to be strictly monotonic, as in Theorem 3.1. Since we are considering strong rationalization, there is no need to impose monotonicity or local nonsatiation to rule out a trivial rationalization.

Proof. Let D be a dataset that satisfies SARP. We can define $\langle R^M, P^M \rangle$ from $\langle \succeq^S, \succ^S \rangle$ as $R^M = \succeq^S \cup \geq$ and $P^M = \succ^S \cup >$. Then the proof of the following lemma is similar to the proof of Theorem 2.19, and therefore omitted.

Lemma 3.11 *If $\langle \succeq^S, \succ^S \rangle$ satisfies SARP then $\langle R^M, P^M \rangle$ is acyclic.*

Now the proof follows from Theorem 1.5.

The next result is in the spirit of Afriat's Theorem. It shows that if we insist on a strong rationalization, then strict concavity is observationally equivalent to local nonsatiation. Note that strict concavity is trivially testable in the context of weak rationalization, as strict concavity (indeed strict quasiconcavity) of the utility function implies that demand is single valued. It turns out that strict concavity adds no additional empirical content to the hypothesis of single-valued demand.

Theorem 3.12 *Let X be a convex consumption space, and $D = (x^k, p^k)_{k=1}^K$ be a consumption dataset. Then the following are equivalent:*

I) *D has a locally nonsatiated strong rationalization.*
II) *D satisfies SARP.*
III) *There are strictly positive real numbers U^k and λ^k, for each k, such that for all k and l,*

$$U^k \leq U^l + \lambda^l p^l \cdot (x^k - x^l);$$

and further, if $x^k \neq x^l$,

$$U^k < U^l + \lambda^l p^l \cdot (x^k - x^l).$$

IV) *D has a continuous, strictly concave, and strictly monotonic strong rationalization $u : X \to \mathbf{R}$.*

Proof. The proof that (II) $\implies$ (III) goes along familiar lines. Construct the matrix B as in Afriat's Theorem, but only include in A the pairs (i,j) with $p^i \cdot (x^j - x^i) \leq 0$ (as we remarked above, this can also be done in the proof of Afriat's Theorem). Now, partition the set A into A_1 containing the pairs

(k,l) with $x^k = x^l$, and A_2 containing the pairs (k,l) with $x^k \neq x^l$. Now, a vector $(U,\lambda) = (U^1,\dots,U^K,\lambda^1,\dots,\lambda^K)$ satisfies the inequalities in (III) iff $B_{(i,j)} \cdot (U,\lambda) \geq 0$, for all $(i,j) \in A_1$, $B_{(i,j)} \cdot (U,\lambda) > 0$, for all $(i,j) \in A_2$, and $B_i \cdot (U,\lambda) > 0$ for all i.

The nonexistence of a solution to this system of inequalities implies the existence of a vector of weights η such that

$$\sum_{(i,j)\in A_1} \eta_{(i,j)} B_{(i,j)} + \sum_{(i,j)\in A_2} \eta_{(i,j)} B_{(i,j)} + \sum_{i=1}^{K} \eta_i B_i = 0$$

with strictly positive weights $\eta_i > 0$ for some i, or $\eta_{i,j} > 0$ for some $(i,j) \in A_2$. If $\eta_i > 0$ then there is j such that $p^i \cdot (x^j - x^i) < 0$, and the proof proceeds to establish a cycle exactly as in the proof of Afriat's Theorem. If, instead, $\eta_{i,j} > 0$ for some $(i,j) \in A_2$ then $p^i \cdot (x^j - x^i) \leq 0$ and $x^i \neq x^j$ implies that $x^i \succ^R x^j$ by definition of $\langle \succeq^S, \succ^S \rangle$. Thus we start a cycle with a strict revealed preference comparison, just as in the case when $\eta_i > 0$.

The proof of (III) $\Longrightarrow$ (IV) requires more work than in the corresponding step of the proof of Afriat's Theorem. Let us fix a solution (U,λ) of the system (III).

Let $h : \mathbf{R}^n \to \mathbf{R}$ be a strictly convex and differentiable function such that $h(x) = 0$ only at 0, and is otherwise positive with globally bounded derivative (above and below) in all directions.[5] Let $\varepsilon > 0$ be small enough such that two criteria are satisfied: in the first place, such that

$$U^j < U^i + \lambda^i p^i \cdot (x^j - x^i) - \varepsilon h(x^j - x^i)$$

for all $x^i \neq x^j$; and in the second place, such that for all x and commodities i,

$$\varepsilon \nabla h(x) < \lambda^i p^i,$$

where $\leq$ is vector inequality and ∇ refers to the gradient (this is possible as h has bounded derivative in each direction and $\lambda^i p^i \in \mathbf{R}^n_{++}$).

We now define, for each i, $\varphi_i : X \to \mathbf{R}$ by

$$\varphi_i(x) = U^i + \lambda^i p^i \cdot (x - x^i) - \varepsilon h(x - x^i).$$

Finally, we define $u : X \to \mathbf{R}$ by

$$u(x) = \min_i \varphi_i(x).$$

It is obvious that u is strictly concave. We claim that it also rationalizes the data.

As a first step, we need to ensure that it is monotonic. This follows from the second property of ε above, which ensures that $\nabla \varphi_i \gg 0$.

Now, we must show that u rationalizes the data. First, note that $u(x^i) = \varphi_i(x^i) = U^i$ (this follows by the generalized Afriat inequalities in (III) and by

[5] For example, $h(x) = \sum_{i=1}^{n} (|x_i| - \ln(|x_i| + 1))$.

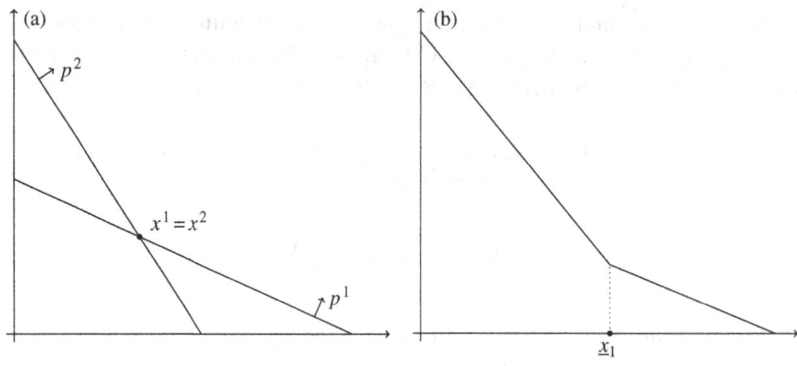

No smooth rationalization. Non-linear prices: a bulk discount.

Fig. 3.4 Smooth utility and general budget sets.

the choice of ε). Now, suppose that $p^i \cdot (x - x^i) \leq 0$ and $x \neq x^i$. Then

$$u(x) \leq \varphi_i(x) = U^i + \lambda^i p^i \cdot (x - x^i) - \varepsilon h(x - x^i) < U^i = u(x^i).$$

So u strongly rationalizes the data.

3.2.1 Smooth utility

Many economic models endow consumers with a differentiable utility, and it is natural to use consumption data to test for differentiability. Consider data $(x^1, p^1), (x^2, p^2)$ as in Figure 3.4(a); it is clear that a rationalizing utility would need to have a "kink" at x^1. The data in Figure 3.4(a) suggest a necessary condition for rationalization by a smooth function: that $x^k \neq x^l$ when $p^k \neq p^l$. This condition turns out to be the only added empirical content of smoothness, as formalized by the following result due to Chiappori and Rochet.

Theorem 3.13 *A dataset $D = (x^k, p^k)_{k=1}^K$ is strongly rationalizable by a smooth, strictly monotonic, and strictly concave utility $u : X \to \mathbf{R}$ iff D satisfies (1) SARP and (2) $x^k = x^l$ iff $p^k = p^l$.*

3.2.2 General budget sets

Finally, we discuss data with general budget sets. Let X be a convex set. A dataset is now a collection $(x^k, B^k), k = 1, \ldots, K$, where B^k is a closed set such that

I) the complement of B^k in X is a convex set;
II) if $z \notin B^k$ and $y > z$, then $y \notin z$;
III) if $y > x^k$, then $y \notin B^k$.

A consumer facing nonlinear prices is a classical example of how such data could be generated. For example, in the budget in Figure 3.4(b) there is a quantity discount: good 1 costs p_1 for quantities below $\underline{x}_1$ and $p_1' < p_1$ for quantities above.

Here (I) captures precisely the "quantity discount" idea, while (II) is a generalization of the monotonicity in standard budgets with linear prices. Requirement (III) corresponds to the standard assumption that choices exhaust all the consumer's income. A special case of this model is obtained when there are continuous, monotone increasing, and convex functions g^k such that $g^k(x^k) = 0$ and $B^k = \{y \in X : g^k(y) \leq 0\}$. It is interesting to contrast the model with the one in Section 3.1.3.

Adapting the definitions of revealed preference, we can define $x \succeq^S y$ when there is k such that $x = x^k$ and $y \in B^k$; and $x \succ^S y$ when $x \succeq^S y$ and $x \neq y$. By analogy with our previous theory, we say that the data satisfy SARP if $\langle \succeq^S, \succ^S \rangle$ is acyclic.

The following result is due to Rosa Matzkin.

Theorem 3.14 *Let X be convex and bounded. A dataset is strongly rationalizable by a strictly monotonic, and strictly concave utility iff it satisfies SARP.*

3.2.3 Partially observed prices and consumption

The analysis until now has assumed data on all relevant prices and consumptions. This assumption may not always be reasonable. For example the return on household labor, which can be seen as the price of leisure, may not be observable. Similarly, consumption surveys normally ask for information on consumption defined narrowly: supermarket purchases, purchases of non-durables, etc. The demand for all commodities may not be observable. We show in this section that such lack of observability leads to a serious lack of predictive power.

Let us begin with the case of partially observed prices. Say that we have $n+m$ commodities. We observe the consumption of all $n+m$ commodities, with K data points. However, we only observe the prices corresponding to the first n commodities.

Formally, we say that a *consumption dataset with partially observed prices* D is a collection (x^k, p^k), $k = 1, \ldots K$, with $x^k \in \mathbf{R}^{n+m}_{+}$ and $p^k \in \mathbf{R}^n_{++}$. We say that D, a consumption dataset with partially observed prices, is weakly rationalizable if for each $k = 1, \ldots, K$, there exists $q^k \in \mathbf{R}^m_{++}$ such that $(x^k, (p^k, q^k))$ is a consumption dataset which is weakly rationalizable.

Let x_n denote the projection of $x \in \mathbf{R}^{n+m}_{+}$ onto its first n coordinates; similarly define x_m to be the projection on the last m coordinates. Further, for a consumption dataset with partially observed prices, and $x \in \mathbf{R}^m_{++}$, we let $K_x = \{k \in \{1, \ldots, K\} : x^k_m = x\}$.

Theorem 3.15 *A consumption dataset with partially observed prices is weakly rationalizable by a locally nonsatiated preference iff for all $x \in \mathbf{R}^m_{++}$, the set $(x^k_n, p^k)_{k \in K_x}$ is weakly rationalizable by a locally nonsatiated preference.*

Proof. If the consumption dataset with partially observed prices is weakly rationalizable by a locally nonsatiated preference, there exist U^k, λ^k, and q^k such that for all $k,l \in K_x$, $U^k \leq U^l + \lambda^l(p^l,q^l)\cdot(x^k - x^l)$. But since $x_m^k = x = x_m^l$, these inequalities become $U^k \leq U^l + \lambda^l p^l \cdot (x_n^k - x_n^l)$, so that the Afriat inequalities are satisfied for $(x_n^k,p^k)_{k\in K_x}$.

Conversely, suppose that each $(x_n^k,p^k)_{k\in K_x}$ is weakly rationalizable by a locally nonsatiated preference. Let $q \in \mathbf{R}_{++}^m$ be such that $x_m^k \neq x_m^l$ implies $q\cdot x_m^k \neq q\cdot x_m^l$; simply choose q to be not perpendicular to any of the vectors $\{x_m^k - x_m^l\}_{k\neq l}$.

Now, for each k, let $\mu^k > 0$ be large enough so that

$$\mu^k > \max_{\{l:x_m^l\neq x_m^k\}} \left\{ \frac{p^k\cdot(x_n^l - x_n^k)}{q\cdot(x_m^k - x_m^l)}, 1 \right\}.$$

Let $q^k = \mu^k q$. Let us define our pair $\langle \succeq^R, \succ^R\rangle$ as usual, for the consumption dataset $(x^k,(p^k,q^k))$. There can be no cycles within K_x for any x, by hypothesis. We now claim that for k,l for which $x_m^k \neq x_m^l$, $q\cdot x_m^k > q\cdot x_m^l$ implies that $x^l \succeq^R x^k$ is false. To see this, $q^l\cdot(x_m^l - x_m^k) < p^l\cdot(x_n^k - x_n^l)$, so that $(p^l,q^l)\cdot x^l < (p^l,q^l)\cdot x^k$.

Now, we claim that there are no $\langle \succeq^R, \succ^R\rangle$ cycles. Suppose for a contradiction that there is a cycle, $x^1 \succeq^R x^2 \succeq^R \ldots \succeq^R x^K \succ^R x^1$. Then we claim that for all k, $q\cdot x_m^k \geq q\cdot x_m^{k+1}$, where addition is modulo K as usual. If not then there is a k for which the inequality is reversed. In this case, we must have $x_m^k \neq x_m^{k+1}$ and $q\cdot x_m^{k+1} > q\cdot x_m^k$, from which we obtain from the previous paragraph that $x^k \succeq^R x^{k+1}$ is false, which is a contradiction. Consequently, we have that for all k, $q\cdot x_m^k = q\cdot x_m^{k+1}$, from which we obtain by the assumption on q that $x_m^k = x_m^{k+1}$. This implies that all elements of the cycle must lie in a single K_x, which was assumed false. Hence there is no $\langle \succeq^R, \succ^R\rangle$ cycle.

Importantly, Theorem 3.15 demonstrates that if demand for commodities whose prices are unobserved is always distinct across observations, preference maximization implies no additional conditions.

We can also ask what happens when there is unobserved consumption. It turns out that as soon as there is some commodity whose consumption we cannot observe, there is no empirical content to preference maximization. A *consumption dataset with partially observed consumption D* is a collection (x^k,p^k) for $k = 1,\ldots,K$, where each $x^k \in \mathbf{R}_+^n$, and each $p^k \in \mathbf{R}_{++}^{n+m}$.

Theorem 3.16 *Suppose that $m \geq 1$. Then for any consumption dataset with partially observed consumption, there exists $y^k \in \mathbf{R}_+^m$ for which $((x^k,y^k),p^k)$, $k = 1,\ldots,K$, is a consumption dataset which is weakly rationalizable by a locally nonsatiated preference.*

Proof. The indices naturally order observations. We assume zero consumption for all commodities with index at least as high as $n+2$. Consumption of commodity $n+1$ is defined first for $k = 1$ as 0. Inductively it is defined to be large enough so that $\{x : p^k\cdot x \leq p^k\cdot(x_n^k,x_{n+1}^k,0,\ldots,0)\}$ is nested in the relative interior of $\{x : p^{k+1} \cdot x \leq p^{k+1} \cdot (x_n^{k+1}, x_{n+1}^{k+1}, 0, \ldots, 0)\}$. To do so, note that the set $\{x : p^k \cdot x \leq p^k \cdot (x_n^k, x_{n+1}^k, 0, \ldots, 0)\}$ is compact, so we can maximize $p^{k+1} \cdot x$ on it, and let the maximum value of this be w. Choose x_{n+1}^{k+1} so that $p^{k+1} \cdot (x_n^{k+1}, x_{n+1}^{k+1}, 0, \ldots, 0)$ is greater than w, and set $y^k = (x_{n+1}^{k+1}, 0, \ldots, 0)$. By this construction, we have that for $k > l$, $p^k \cdot (x^k, y^k) > p^k \cdot (x^l, y^l)$. Conversely, suppose that $p^k \cdot (x^k, y^k) > p^k \cdot (x^l, y^l)$. Clearly $l \neq k$. If $l > k$, then by construction, $p^k \cdot (x^l, y^l) > p^k \cdot (x^k, y^k)$; since y^l was chosen so that (x^l, y^l) is not in the set $\{x : p^k \cdot x \leq p^k \cdot (x^k, y^k)\}$. So $k > l$ iff $p^k \cdot (x^k, y^k) > p^k \cdot (x^l, y^l)$. Consequently, the data $((x^k, y^k), p^k)$ can be rationalized by a locally nonsatiated preference.

Theorems 3.15 and 3.16 allow flexibility in choosing the observed wealth, which is something which, in the setup of this chapter, has been taken to be equal to expenditure (hence determined, or observed). If wealth is observable, these results break down. It remains an open question to characterize the empirical content of preference maximization with only partially observed prices and/or consumption, especially when wealth can be observed. Results exist for the one-dimensional case where bounds are put on consumption in Theorem 3.16.

Finally, we note that empirical studies of consumption avoid the conclusion of Theorem 3.16 by assuming that preferences are separable. If one studies, for example, supermarket purchases, then one assumes that goods which are not purchased in a supermarket are separable from the ones that are. This means that if an agent conforms to the theory, she will have a budget for the supermarket. One can then treat the problem of choosing optimal consumption in the supermarket separately from the rest of the agent's consumption decisions. Separability is treated in 4.2.2.

3.3 REVEALED PREFERENCE GRAPHS

Finally, we investigate here a question which is related specifically to the structure of linear budget sets. Return to the notion of data introduced in 3.1: a collection (x^k, p^k), $k = 1, \ldots K$, with $K \geq 1$ an integer, $x^k \in X$ and $p^k \in \mathbf{R}^n_{++}$. The integer K is the cardinality of the dataset.

For a consumption dataset D of cardinality K, we can define the *revealed preference graph* $\langle \trianglerighteq, \triangleright \rangle$ on $\{1, \ldots, K\}$ by $i \trianglerighteq j$ if $p^i \cdot x^i \geq p^i \cdot x^j$ and $i \triangleright j$ if $p^i \cdot x^i > p^i \cdot x^j$. We say that $\langle \trianglerighteq, \triangleright \rangle$ is the revealed preference graph defined by D.

The following simple result states that there are no *a priori* restrictions on which order pairs can be revealed preference graphs.

Theorem 3.17 *Let $\langle \trianglerighteq, \triangleright \rangle$ be an order pair in which $\trianglerighteq$ is a reflexive binary relation and $\triangleright$ is an irreflexive binary relation on $\{1, \ldots, K\}$. Then there exists X and a consumption dataset D on X of cardinality K for which $\langle \trianglerighteq, \triangleright \rangle$ is the corresponding revealed preference graph.*

Proof. Suppose $\trianglerighteq$ is reflexive. Let $X = \mathbf{R}^K_+$ and let $x^i = \mathbf{1}_i$; the unit vector in dimension i. For each i and j, set

$$p^i_j = \begin{cases} 1/2 & \text{if } i \triangleright j \\ 1 & \text{if } i \trianglerighteq j \text{ and not } i \triangleright j \\ 2 & \text{if not } i \trianglerighteq j \end{cases}$$

It is easy to verify that D so defined has $\langle \trianglerighteq, \triangleright \rangle$ as its revealed preference order pair.

Theorem 3.17 allows flexibility in choosing consumption space. If consumption space is fixed, then the question of which order pairs can be revealed preference graphs remains open. We will encounter phenomena of this type several times; see for example Theorem 9.1 and Theorem 11.2.

Theorem 3.18 *For any $X \subseteq \mathbf{R}^n_+$ in which $n \geq 2$, for any $K \geq 1$, the following order pairs are revealed preference graphs on $\{1, \dots, K\}$:*

I) $\langle = \cup \neq, \neq \rangle$
II) $\langle =, \varnothing \rangle$

In the first graph of Theorem 3.18, every observation is strictly revealed preferred to every other observation.

Proof. To see that the first is a revealed preference graph, let $\mathcal{S}$ be the unit sphere in $\mathbf{R}^n$. Fix arbitrary $p^1, \dots, p^K \in \mathbf{R}^n_{++}$ such that p^i and p^j are not collinear whenever $i \neq j$, define $x^i = \arg\max_{\mathcal{S}} p^i \cdot x$. It is easy to verify that this data has $\langle = \cup \neq, \neq \rangle$ as its revealed preference graph. (Note that any smooth convex set with nonempty interior intersecting the strictly positive orthant will work in place of $\mathcal{S}$, so long as we can choose p^i so to have unique and distinct maximizers in the positive orthant.)

Showing that $\langle =, \varnothing \rangle$ is a revealed preference graph follows a similar construction, instead letting $\mathcal{P} = \{x \in \mathbf{R}^n_+ : \prod x_i \geq 1\}$. Choose arbitrary p^i (as long as p^i and p^j are not collinear when $i \neq j$) and let $x^i = \arg\min_{\mathcal{P}} p^i \cdot x$. Similarly, there is nothing particularly special about the set $\mathcal{P}$.

3.4 CHAPTER REFERENCES

Samuelson (1938) introduced the idea of revealed preferences, and formulated the weak axiom of revealed preference. Little (1949) and Samuelson (1948) showed how to construct indifference curves from revealed preference in the two-commodity case. Houthakker (1950) proved a version of Theorem 3.1, the first characterization of the empirical content of rational consumption. Houthakker's condition was stated for single-valued demand, and was equivalent to the condition we here call SARP. Related are the papers by

Newman (1960) and Stigum (1973).[6] Samuelson (1950) coined the phrase "strong axiom of revealed preference;" however, the concept he attributes to Houthakker is slightly different from Houthakker's actual contribution. Specifically, Samuelson required that the strong revealed preference pair be quasi-acyclic. There seems to be no general consensus on the meaning of SARP in the literature; for more on this, see Suzumura (1977). We should also mention the contribution of Mas-Colell (1978), which can be viewed as an identification result for demand functions satisfying certain revealed preference axioms.

Marcel Richter, in two important survey articles (Richter, 1971 and Richter, 1979) presents a unified view of revealed preference, discussing the commonalities and differences between the material in Chapters 2 and 3. In particular, Richter (1979) accounts for how the duality between choices and budgets translates into revealed preference theory. Richter also covers the relation to the question of integrability of demand, which is out of the scope of our book.

The observation in Remark 3.3 is due to Polisson and Quah (2013).

Theorem 3.4 is due to Rose (1958), though the result was conjectured earlier by Hicks (1956, pp. 52–54).[7] An example of a well-defined, continuous, almost everywhere differentiable demand function satisfying WARP and not GARP is given in Gale (1960a) (see also Hicks, 1956, pp. 110–111). Kihlstrom, Mas-Colell, and Sonnenschein (1976) provide a theory of such demand functions. WARP is the absence of cycles of length two: a natural conjecture is that absence of cycles of length n would suffice for rationalizability in n-dimensional space. Kamiya (1963) gives an example of finite data for three consumption goods which exhibits no cycles of length two or three, but which is not rationalizable. Shafer (1977) establishes that this non-equivalence is robust. Shafer works with demand functions (not finite data) and shows that for three commodities, one must require absence of cycles of all possible lengths, by exhibiting, for any n, single-valued demand functions which exhibit no cycles of length n, but which are not rationalizable. Peters and Wakker (1994, 1996) discuss this result for environments with more than three commodities; see also John (1997). Finally, a recent investigation into these ideas is Heufer (2007).

Afriat's Theorem appeared first in Afriat (1967), but was popularized by Hal Varian in a collection of papers ((1982; 1983a; 1985)). Recently, Fostel, Scarf, and Todd (2004) and Chung-Piaw and Vohra (2003) provided new proofs of Afriat's Theorem. Our proof in 3.1.1 is different from these, and follows basically the argument by Matzkin and Richter (1991). The first

[6] Uzawa (1960a, 1971) investigates demand functions satisfying WARP and a regularity condition. See also Bossert (1993). A series of papers investigates a related "continuous" version of an acyclicity condition; see Ville (1946); Ville and Newman (1951–1952); Hurwicz and Richter (1979).

[7] See also Newman (1955); Houthakker (1957); Newman (1960), Blackorby, Bossert, and Donaldson (1995), and Banerjee and Murphy (2006).

linear-programming-style proofs of Afriat's Theorem are due to Diewert (1973). The argument using linear combinations of rows in the proof is a form of the Poincaré–Veblen–Alexander Theorem (see Berge, 2001; the theorem is attributed to early contributors to the mathematical discipline of topology, i.e. Poincaré, 1895; Veblen and Alexander, 1912–1913). The constructive proof of Afriat's Theorem in 3.1.2 is taken from Varian (1982).

The recent paper by Reny (2014) considers infinite datasets, and shows that GARP is necessary and sufficient for the existence of a quasiconcave rationalization. Reny's result unifies the approaches based on finite datasets and demand functions. It is noteworthy that an infinite dataset satisfying GARP may not be rationalizable by a concave utility, only a quasiconcave one. The theorem of Reny also gives a particularly simple proof of a weak version of Afriat's Theorem (one ensuring a quasiconcave rationalization) for finite data. Sondermann (1982) provides a sufficient condition ensuring representation by an upper semicontinuous (closed upper contour sets) utility.

Necessary and sufficient conditions for the existence of λ^k such that $x^k \mapsto \lambda^k p^k$ is monotone are presented in John (2001), where it is also shown that the model is equivalent to rationalization by a nontransitive preference with a certain type of "utility" rationalization which has a certain convexity property.

Probably the first paper to study a version of Afriat's Theorem for nonlinear budget sets is Yatchew (1985), who investigates necessary and sufficient conditions for convex utility maximization on finite unions of polyhedra in the form of inequalities. Theorem 3.8 is from Forges and Minelli (2009). Forges and Minelli also present a stronger result, where if the functions g^k are quasiconvex and differentiable then there is a concave rationalization, if there is a rationalization. Cherchye, Demuynck, and De Rock (2014) build on this result, establishing a characterization of datasets which are weakly rationalizable by quasiconcave, locally nonsatiated, and continuous preferences on arbitrary budget sets which are closed and satisfy free disposability.

Theorem 3.12 is due to Matzkin and Richter (1991). Matzkin and Richter clarify the notions of weak and strong rationalizability, and put the previous work on revealed preference in this context. Theorem 3.13 is due to Chiappori and Rochet (1987). Matzkin and Richter (1991) also present a result on smooth rationalization, in the spirit of Theorem 3.13. The result on general budget sets in Theorem 3.14 is due to Matzkin (1991).

Theorems 3.15 and 3.16 are due to Varian (1988a); the case of $m = 1$ is established there.

Theorem 3.17 can be found in Deb and Pai (2014), as well as the first part of Theorem 3.18, though these results are implicit in other works.

Finally, we have not discussed stochastic choice in demand theory: See the papers by Bandyopadhyay, Dasgupta, and Pattanaik (1999) and Bandyopadhyay, Dasgupta, and Pattanaik (2004).

CHAPTER 4

Topics in Rational Demand

Chapter 3 established the testable implications of the hypothesis that consumers are rational. We are often interested in situations where the rationalizing preference, or demand function, satisfies additional properties. We want to know what additional structure is imposed on a dataset from demanding that the rationalization has to use a utility function with some given property. In particular, we focus on the properties of supermodularity, submodularity, homotheticity, separability, complements, and substitutes.

4.1 DISCRETE GOODS: SUPERMODULAR AND SUBMODULAR RATIONALIZATIONS

In Chapter 3 we discussed a collection of results in the spirit of Afriat's Theorem. In these results, one obtains a concave rationalization from the rationalizability of the data. Arguably, though, most consumption goods come in discrete units. Some goods seem particularly "lumpy," such as cars and houses. For such goods, the notion of concavity is not well defined. One can instead investigate super- and submodularity. Supermodularity corresponds to the notion that goods are complements: specifically, that increases in the consumption of one good become more valuable when one consumes more of the other goods. Submodularity corresponds to the property of substitute goods.

The meaning of super- and submodularity can be understood from Figure 4.1. In the figure, there are two goods. For any two bundles x and y, $x \wedge y$ is the component-wise minimum of the bundles x and y, and $x \vee y$ is the component-wise maximum (see the definitions in Chapter 1). The function $u : X \to \mathbf{R}$ is *supermodular* if for all $x, y \in X$,

$$u(x) + u(y) \leq u(x \vee y) + u(x \wedge y),$$

and *submodular* if $-u$ is supermodular.

If u is supermodular then the change in utility $u(x) - u(x \wedge y)$ cannot exceed the change $u(x \vee y) - u(y)$. Note that in Figure 4.1, the increase in good 2 when we go from $x \wedge y$ to x is the same as when we go from y to $x \vee y$. This means that

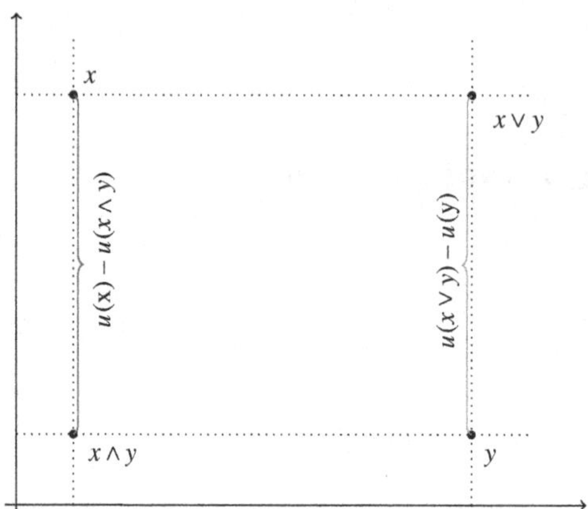

Fig. 4.1 Supermodularity.

the change in utility resulting from adding the amount of good 2 in the change from $x \wedge y$ to x, can only be larger when the quantity of good 1 is larger. This is a notion of complementary goods: the increases in utility due to increases in consumption of good 2 are larger as we consume more of good 1.

Submodularity has the opposite interpretation. If u is submodular in the figure, then the increase in utility due to the increase in consumption of good 2 is diminished by a higher consumption of good 1. Thus the two goods are substitutes.

It turns out that, when goods are discrete, supermodularity and submodularity of utility are empirically indistinguishable from rationalizability of the data. This result is in the spirit of Afriat's, but it comes from a rather different set of ideas.

Let $X \subseteq \mathbf{Z}^n_+$. A *(discrete) dataset* is a finite list of observations (x^k, B^k), $k = 1, \ldots, K$, where for each k, $x^k \in B^k \subseteq X$. The interpretation is that x^k is the chosen element from the budget B^k. Assume:

- x^k is maximal in B^k, in the sense that if $y > x^k$ then $y \notin B^k$.
- B^k satisfies the property that $z \in B^k$ whenever there is $y \in B^k$ and $z \leq y$.
- $|B^k| < +\infty$.

Given a dataset D, we can define the *strong revealed preference* pair $\langle \succeq^S, \succ^S \rangle$ as in Chapter 3 by $x \succeq^S y$ iff there is k such that $x = x^k$ and $y \in B^k$, and $x \succ^S y$ iff $x \succeq^S y$ and $x \neq y$. Then the *strong axiom of revealed preference* (SARP) is the requirement that $\langle \succeq^S, \succ^S \rangle$ is acyclic.

Note that Theorem 3.9 is valid for the model discussed here. The notion of data is different, but the assumptions we have made on the data guarantee that the proof of the theorem applies as written.

Theorem 4.1 *Let $X \subseteq \mathbf{Z}^n_+$ be a lattice. The following statements are equivalent:*

I) *D is strongly rationalizable.*
II) *D satisfies SARP.*
III) *D has a strictly monotonic and supermodular strong rationalization* $u : X \to \mathbf{R}$.
IV) *D has a strictly monotonic and submodular strong rationalization* $v : X \to \mathbf{R}$.

Proof. The equivalence of (I) and (II) is clear from previous results (Theorem 3.9). We need to prove that (II) implies (III) and (IV).

Because K is finite, and each B^k is finite, there is M such that for all $x \in \bigcup_k B^k$ and all i, $x_i < M$. Let $X_M = \{x \in \mathbf{Z}^n_+ : x_i < M \text{ for all } i\}$.

Let D satisfy SARP. Imagine first that consumption space is X_M. By Theorem 3.9, D has a strictly monotonic rationalization $\succeq$ on X_M. Since X_M is finite, there is an integer-valued utility function $v : X_M \to \mathbf{Z}_+$ defined by $v(x) = |\{y \in X_M : x \succeq y\}|$. Let $V = \sup_{x \in X_M} v(x)$. Define $g : X \to \mathbf{R}$ as follows. For $x \in X_M$, $g(x) = v(x)$. Otherwise, $g(x) = V + \sum_i x_i$. Note that g is a strictly monotonic, integer-valued function which strongly rationalizes the data.

Let $u(x) = 2^{g(x)}$; we claim that u is a supermodular strong rationalization of D. It is clearly a strong rationalization because it is a monotonic transformation of g. To see that it is supermodular, let x and y in X and suppose without loss of generality that $g(x) \geq g(y)$. If $x = x \vee y$ then $y = x \wedge y$ so there is nothing to prove. Suppose then that $x \neq x \vee y$, which implies that $x \vee y \succ x$, as $\succeq$ is strictly monotonic. Thus $g(x \vee y) \geq g(x) + 1$. Then,

$$\begin{aligned} u(x) + u(y) &= 2^{g(x)} + 2^{g(y)} \leq 2^{g(x)} + 2^{g(x)} \leq 2^{g(x)+1} \\ &\leq 2^{g(x \vee y)} = u(x \vee y) \leq u(x \vee y) + u(x \wedge y); \end{aligned}$$

so u is supermodular.

To exhibit a submodular strong rationalization, define $v : X \to \mathbf{R}$ by $v(x) = \sum_{i=0}^{g(x)} 2^{-i}$. The function v is a strong rationalization of D because v is a monotonic transformation of g. To see that v is submodular, suppose that $x \neq x \vee y$ and $x \neq x \wedge y$ (otherwise we have nothing to prove). Then,

$$v(x) - v(x \wedge y) = \sum_{j=g(x \wedge y)+1}^{g(x)} 2^{-j} \geq \left(\frac{1}{2}\right)^{g(x \wedge y)+1}.$$

On the other hand,

$$\begin{aligned} v(x \vee y) - v(y) &= \sum_{j=g(y)+1}^{g(x \vee y)} 2^{-j} \leq \sum_{j=g(y)+1}^{\infty} 2^{-j} \\ &= \left(\frac{1}{2}\right)^{g(y)} \leq \left(\frac{1}{2}\right)^{g(x \wedge y)+1} \end{aligned}$$

where the last inequality follows because $x \neq x \vee y$ implies that $y \neq x \wedge y$, so $y \succ x \wedge y$ by the strict monotonicity of $\succeq$. Thus $v(x \vee y) - v(y) \leq v(x) - v(x \wedge y)$, which shows that v is submodular.

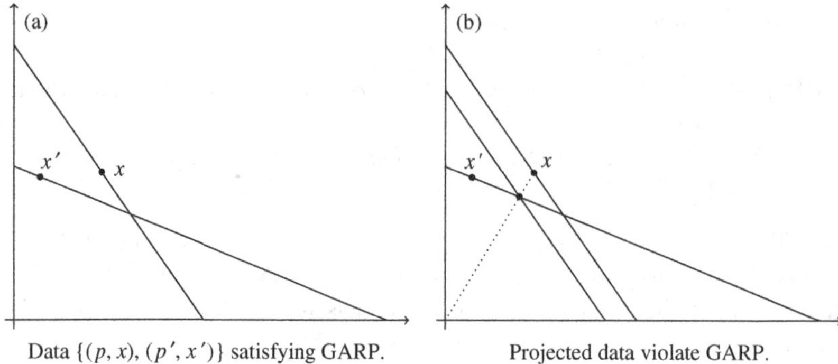

Data $\{(p, x), (p', x')\}$ satisfying GARP.

Projected data violate GARP.

Fig. 4.2 Testable implications of homothetic preferences.

4.2 DIVISIBLE GOODS

Super- and submodularity are properties of particular interest when studying discrete goods. Other properties are commonly studied in environments with divisible goods. We now turn to homotheticity, separability, complements, and substitutes.

Assume throughout that consumption space $X \subseteq \mathbf{R}^n_+$ is a convex set. The notion of dataset is the same as in 3.1: A *consumption dataset* D is a collection (x^k, p^k), $k = 1, \dots K$, with $K \geq 1$ an integer, $x^k \in X$ and $p^k \in \mathbf{R}^n_{++}$.

4.2.1 Homotheticity

Here we assume X is a *cone*, so that whenever $x \in X$ and $\alpha \geq 0$, we have $\alpha x \in X$. A preference $\succeq$ is *homothetic* if, for all $\alpha > 0$ and all x, y, $x \succeq y$ implies that $\alpha x \succeq \alpha y$. A function $u : X \to \mathbf{R}$ is *homothetic* if the preference that it represents is homothetic.

We can begin to understand the testable implications of homotheticity from Figure 4.2. Suppose that we are interested in whether the data $\{(p,x), (p',x')\}$ have a homothetic rationalization. Clearly, the data satisfy GARP so they have a rationalization. It is easy to see, however, that no homothetic rationalization exists. The reason can be gleaned from Figure 4.2(b): a homothetic rationalization would imply that demand would have to lie on the ray joining x and 0, for any budget line that is parallel to the budget line for (p,x). So if we "deflate" the budget line for (p,x) until it crosses the point where the ray crosses the budget line for (p',x') the demand would have to lie at that intersection. We would then have a violation of WARP.

Somewhat more formally, Figure 4.2 presents the following situation. If there were a homothetic rationalization, then any supporting hyperplane of the upper contour set $\{y \in X : y \succeq x\}$ would also support $\{y \in X : y \succeq \theta x\}$, for $\theta > 0$. Choose θ such that θx lies on the budget line for (p',x'), i.e. $p' \cdot (\theta x) = p' \cdot x'$; thus x' is revealed preferred to θx. By homotheticity, p supports the upper contour set of $\succeq$ at θx, so θx should be chosen at prices p and income $p\cdot\theta x$. Then WARP would require that $p\cdot(\theta x)\leq p\cdot x'$.

The reasoning above leads to the following necessary condition for rationalization by a homothetic preference:

$$\theta=\frac{p'\cdot x'}{p'\cdot x}\Longrightarrow \theta p\cdot x\leq p\cdot x';$$

or,

$$1\leq\frac{p\cdot x'}{p\cdot x}\frac{p'\cdot x}{p'\cdot x'}.$$

A strengthening of this condition turns out to be necessary and sufficient for rationalization by a homothetic preference. To simplify the notation, we shall normalize the prices in the data so that $p^k\cdot x^k=1$ for all k. If we have prices so that $p^k\cdot x^k\neq 1$, it is simple to redefine prices $q^k=\frac{p^k}{p^k\cdot x^k}$ provided each $x^k\neq 0$. Theorem 4.2 will then apply to these normalized prices.

A dataset D satisfies the *homothetic axiom of revealed preference (HARP)* if, for any sequence $k_1,\ldots,k_L$ of numbers in $\{1,\ldots,K\}$, we have

$$p^{k_L}\cdot x^{k_1}\prod_{i=1}^{L-1}p^{k_i}\cdot x^{k_{i+1}}\geq 1.$$

Observe that HARP is stronger than GARP: Fix a sequence $k_1,\ldots,k_L$ such that GARP is violated; that is $p^{k_i}\cdot x^{k_{i+1}}\leq p^{k_i}\cdot x^{k_i}$, $i=1,\ldots L-1$, and $p^{k_L}\cdot x^{k_1}<p^{k_L}\cdot x^{k_L}$. Then $p^{k_i}\cdot x^{k_i}=1$ implies that the product of the left-hand side of these inequalities is strictly less than one. Thus HARP is violated.

Finally, let us define the *homothetic revealed preference order pair* $\langle\succeq^H,\succ^H\rangle$ as $x\succeq^H y$ when there are k and $\alpha>0$ for which $\alpha x=x^k$ and $p^k\cdot x^k\geq p^k\cdot(\alpha y)$ and $x\succ^H y$ when there are k and $\alpha>0$ for which $\alpha x=x^k$ and $p^k\cdot x^k>p^k\cdot(\alpha y)$. The meaning of $\succeq^H$ should be intuitive: $x\succeq^H y$ when the data, together with the hypothesis of homothetic preferences, imply that x must be preferred to y. Specifically, if x and x^k are on the same ray, then homotheticity requires that x be demanded at the same prices as x^k. This is like adding the observation (x,p^k) to the data. Then $p^k\cdot x>p^k\cdot y$ implies that x is "revealed preferred" to y, which is precisely the meaning of $x\succeq^H y$.

The following result is due to Hal Varian.

Theorem 4.2 *Let X be a convex cone such that for all $x\in X$ and all $\varepsilon>0$, there is $\varepsilon'\in(0,\varepsilon)$ with $x+\varepsilon'\mathbf{1}\in X$. Let $D=\{(x^k,p^k)\}_{k=1}^K$ be a consumption dataset, where for all k, $p^k\cdot x^k=1$. The following statements are equivalent:*

I) *D has a locally nonsatiated and homothetic weak rationalization.*
II) *D satisfies the homothetic axiom of revealed preference.*
III) *There is a strictly positive real number U^k for each k, such that*

$$U^k\leq U^l p^l\cdot x^k$$

for each pair of observations (x^k,p^k) and (x^l,p^l) in D.

IV) *D has a concave, homothetic, continuous, and monotonic rationalization $u : X \to \mathbf{R}$.*
V) *$\langle \succeq^H, \succ^H \rangle$ is acyclic.*

Proof. We first prove that I implies II. Let $\succeq$ be a locally nonsatiated, homothetic rationalization. Fix any sequence $k_1, \ldots, k_L$ in $\{1, \ldots, K\}$.

Let the sequence $s^1, \ldots, s^{L-1}$ be defined by

$$s^1 = p^{k_1} \cdot x^{k_2}$$
$$s^2 = (p^{k_1} \cdot x^{k_2}) p^{k_2} \cdot x^{k_3} = s^1 p^{k_2} \cdot x^{k_3}$$
$$\vdots$$
$$s^{L-1} = s^{L-2} p^{k_{L-1}} \cdot x^{k_L}.$$

We first argue that $x^{k_1} \succeq x^{k_2}/s^1$. Notice that the bundle x^{k_2}/s^1 is affordable in the budget at which x^{k_1} was purchased: $p^{k_1} \cdot (x^{k_2}/s^1) = 1$. Then $x^{k_1} \succeq (x^{k_2}/s^1)$. Next, we argue that homotheticity implies $(x^{k_2}/s^1) \succeq (x^{k_3}/s^2)$. The reason is that

$$p^{k_2} \cdot x^{k_2} = p^{k_2} \cdot \left(\frac{s^1}{s^2} x^{k_3} \right) = 1,$$

so that $x^{k_2} \succeq (s^1/s^2) x^{k_3}$, and hence by homotheticity, $(x^{k_2}/s^1) \succeq (x^{k_3}/s^2)$.

By repeating this argument we obtain that

$$x^{k_1} \succeq (x^{k_2}/s^1) \succeq (x^{k_3}/s^2) \succeq \cdots \succeq (x^{k_L}/s^{L-1}).$$

By assumption, x^{k_L} is $\succeq$ maximal in the set $\{x : p^{k_L} \cdot x \leq p^{k_L} \cdot x^{k_L}\}$, so x^{k_L}/s^{L-1} is $\succeq$ maximal in the set $\{x : s^{L-1} p^{k_L} \cdot x \leq s^{L-1} p^{k_L} \cdot x^{k_L}/s^{L-1}\}$ by the homotheticity of $\succeq$. Then $x^{k_1} \succeq (x^{k_L}/s^{L-1})$ and local nonsatiation of $\succeq$ implies $s^{L-1} p^{k_L} \cdot x^{k_1} \geq s^{L-1} p^{k_L} \cdot (x^{k_L}/s^{L-1})$. Since $s^{L-1} p^{k_L} \cdot (x^{k_L}/s^{L-1}) = 1$ we have established that HARP is satisfied.

Second, we prove that II implies III. Let the number U^l be defined as the infimum of

$$\prod_{i=1}^{L-1} p^{k_i} \cdot x^{k_{i+1}}$$

over all sequences $k_1, \ldots, k_L$ in $\{1, \ldots, K\}$ with $k_L = l$. The infimum is achieved for some sequence because HARP guarantees that removing a cycle only makes the product $\prod_{i=1}^{L-1} p^{k_i} \cdot x^{k_{i+1}}$ smaller, so we can without loss of generality consider the infimum over sequences with no cycles, and there are finitely many such sequences. Let $U^l = \prod_{i=1}^{L-1} p^{k_i} \cdot x^{k_{i+1}}$ and $U^m = \prod_{i=1}^{L'-1} p^{k'_i} \cdot x^{k'_{i+1}}$; then

$$U^l = \prod_{i=1}^{L-1} p^{k_i} \cdot x^{k_{i+1}} \leq \left(\prod_{i=1}^{L'-1} p^{k'_i} \cdot x^{k'_{i+1}}\right)(p^m \cdot x^l) = U^m (p^m \cdot x^l).$$

Note that, following this construction, $U^k > 0$ for all k.

Third, we prove that III implies IV. Since we assumed that $p^l \cdot x^l = 1$ for all l, we have $U^l p^l \cdot x^k = U^l + U^l p^l \cdot (x^k - x^l)$ for all k, l, so that we have a solution to Afriat's inequalities. Define a utility function $u : X \to \mathbf{R}$ by

$$u(x) = \min\{U^k + U^k p^k \cdot (x - x^k) : k = 1, \dots, K\},$$

a construction analogous to the one in the proof of Afriat's Theorem. Then $p^k \cdot x^k \geq p^k \cdot y$ implies that $u(x^k) \geq u(y)$, so u rationalizes the data.

Clearly, u is continuous, monotonic, and homothetic. The proof that it is concave is the same as in Afriat's Theorem.

Finally, we demonstrate that (II) and (V) are equivalent. Suppose by means of contradiction that there is a cycle $z^1 \succeq^H \dots \succeq^H z^L \succ^H z^1$. For each $i = 1, \dots, L$, suppose $\alpha^i z^i = x^{k_i}$. Now, $z^i \succeq^H z^{i+1}$ means that $p^{k_i} \cdot x^{k_i} \geq p^{k_i} \cdot \left(\alpha^i z^{i+1}\right) = p^{k_i} \cdot \left(\frac{\alpha^{k_i} x^{k_{i+1}}}{\alpha^{k_{i+1}}}\right)$. Then for all $i = 1, \dots, L-1$, $1 = p^{k_i} \cdot x^{k_i} \geq p^{k_i} \cdot \left(\frac{\alpha^{k_i} x^{k_{i+1}}}{\alpha^{k_{i+1}}}\right)$, and $1 = p^{k_L} \cdot x^{k_L} > p^{k_L} \cdot \left(\frac{\alpha^{k_L} x^{k_1}}{\alpha^{k_1}}\right)$. Multiplying the inequalities and canceling the α terms obtains $p^{k_L} \cdot x^{k_1} \prod_{i=1}^{L-1} p^{k_i} \cdot x^{k_{i+1}} < 1$, violating HARP.

On the other hand, suppose (II) is violated, and let $k_1, \dots, k_L$ be a sequence for which $p^{k_L} \cdot x^{k_1} \prod_{i=1}^{L-1} p^{k_i} \cdot x^{k_{i+1}} < 1$. Define $z^1 = x^{k_1}$, $\alpha^1 = 1$, and for each $i = 2, \dots, L$, define $\alpha^i = p^{k_{i-1}} \cdot x^{k_i}$, and $z^i = \frac{x^{k_i}}{\prod_{j=1}^{i} \alpha^j}$. Observe that for all $i = 1, \dots, L-1$, $z^i \succeq^H z^{i+1}$, since $p^{k_i} \cdot (\alpha^i z^i) = p^{k_i} \cdot (\alpha^i z^{i+1})$. Observe also that $\left(\prod_{i=1}^{L} \alpha^L\right) p^{k_L} \cdot z^L = p^{k_L} \cdot x^{k_L} = 1$, and that $\left(\prod_{i=1}^{L} \alpha^L\right) p^{k_L} \cdot z^1 = p^{k_L} \cdot x^{k_1} \prod_{i=1}^{L-1} p^{k_i} \cdot x^{k_{i+1}} < 1$ by assumption, so that $z^L \succ^H z^1$, constituting a $\langle \succeq^H, \succ^H \rangle$ cycle.

Remark 4.3 The preceding does not allow observations of $x^k = 0$. If we did, the "non-normalized" version of HARP and condition (III) are necessary and sufficient here. The non-normalized version of HARP would read that for all sequences $\{k_1, \dots, k_n\}$, we have $p^{k_n} \cdot x^{k_1} \prod_{i=1}^{n-1} p^{k_1} \cdot x^{k_{i+1}} \geq \prod_{i=1}^{n} p^{k_i} \cdot x^{k_i}$. The non-normalized version of condition (III) is that $U^k p^l \cdot x^l \leq U^l p^l \cdot x^k$ for all k and l.

4.2.2 Separability

In practical analysis of consumer demand, separability is a very important property. In principle, a consumer chooses among many different goods, solving inter- as well as intratemporal optimization problems. Practical researchers abstract away from this complexity by considering some subset of goods in isolation. For example, classical studies of applied demand, such as Deaton (1974), work with only 9 goods. Modern applied papers often consider more goods, but still greatly simplify the universe of possible goods.

The simplification of focusing on a small subset of goods and assuming separability avoids the issues raised in Section 3.2.3. In fact, assuming separability of some kind seems unavoidable for any tractable empirical study of consumption.

Let $X \subseteq X_1 \times X_2$, with $X_i \subseteq \mathbf{R}^{n_i}_+$; and write vectors in X as (x_1, x_2), where $x_i \in X_i$. A preference relation $\succeq$ is *separable* in X_1 if for all $x_1, x_1' \in X_1$ and all $x_2, \hat{x}_2 \in X_2$ $(x_1, x_2) \succeq (x_1', x_2)$ if and only if $(x_1, \hat{x}_2) \succeq (x_1', \hat{x}_2)$. A utility function $u : X \to \mathbf{R}$ is *separable* in X_1 if there are functions $f : X_1 \to \mathbf{R}$ and $g : f(X_1) \times X_2 \to \mathbf{R}$, where for all x_2, $y \mapsto g(y, x_2)$ is strictly monotonic, such that $u(x_1, x_2) = g(f(x_1), x_2)$.

When preferences are separable, the consumer's maximization problem reduces into a "subproblem" for the goods in X_1. Given a budget to spend on goods x_1, the consumer can solve the problem of choosing x_1 independently of the specific bundle x_2 chosen: only the budget left over to spend on x_1 matters, not the actual quantities of the goods in x_2. Thus separability allows the separate analysis of demand for x_1. Of course, here we are concerned with testing for separability, so we cannot ignore the relation between choosing x_1 and x_2.

Theorem 4.4 *The following statements are equivalent:*

I) *There are strictly positive real numbers U^k, V^k, λ^k, μ^k, $k = 1, \ldots, K$ such that*

$$U^k \leq U^l + \lambda^l p_1^l \cdot (x_1^k - x_1^l) + \frac{\lambda^l}{\mu^l}(V^k - V^l), \tag{4.1}$$

$$V^k \leq V^l + \mu^l p_2^l \cdot (x_2^k - x_2^l). \tag{4.2}$$

II) *The dataset $\{(p_2^k, x_2^k)\}$ satisfies GARP; and there is a solution (V^k, μ^k) to 4.2 above such that the dataset $\{((p_1^k, 1/\mu^k), (x_1^k, V^k))\}$ satisfies GARP.*

III) *D has a concave, continuous, and monotonic rationalization $u : X \to \mathbf{R}$ that is separable in X_1.*

We present Theorem 4.4 without proof. It is important to note that Theorem 4.4 focuses on concave rationalizations (note the contrast with Afriat's Theorem, where concavity comes for free). The Afriat inequalities for this problem are described by Equations (4.1) and (4.2). These inequalities are not linear, in contrast with the original Afriat inequalities.

A special kind of separability is *additive separability*. A test for additive separability is particularly interesting for time-series data (see Section 5.3.3), in which there is a single observation (a dataset of size 1).

Let $X \subseteq X_1 \times X_2 \times \cdots \times X_T$, with $X_t = \mathbf{R}^n_+$, $t = 1, \ldots, T$. Write vectors in X as $(x_1, \ldots, x_T)$, where $x_t \in \mathbf{R}^n_+$. A preference relation $\succeq$ is *additively separable* if there is a function $u : \mathbf{R}^n_+ \to \mathbf{R}$ such that $(x_1, \ldots, x_T) \succeq (x_1', \ldots, x_T')$ iff $\sum_{t=0}^T u(x_t) \geq \sum_{t=0}^T u(x_t')$.

Say that a dataset $\{(x^k, p^k)\}_{k=1}^K$ is *additively separably rationalizable* by the function $u : \mathbf{R}^n_+ \to \mathbf{R}$ if the additively separable preferences defined from u weakly rationalize the data $\{(x^k, p^k)\}_{k=1}^K$. We provide a test for the case when $K = 1$, so the dataset is (x, p). Note that $p = (p_1, \ldots, p_T)$, with $p_t \in \mathbf{R}^n_{++}$.

Proposition 4.5 *Data (x,p) (a dataset with $K=1$) with $x \gg 0$ is additively separably rationalizable by a concave and strictly increasing function iff the correspondence $\rho(x) = \bigcup_{t:x=x_t}\{p_t\}$ satisfies cyclic monotonicity.*

Proposition 4.5 follows from using the first-order conditions for maximization of $\sum_t u(x_t)$, and Corollary 1.10.

Note that general utility maximization is not testable with a single observation, but the theory of additive separability has testable implications even when $K=1$.

4.2.3 Quasilinear utility

Many economic models assume that utility takes a quasilinear form: $u(x)+y$, for $x \in \mathbf{R}^n_+$ and $y \in \mathbf{R}$. There are $n+1$ goods, and the $(n+1)$-st is a *numeraire*. Wealth is measured in the same units as the numeraire good, which therefore always has a price of one. We shall allow consumption of the numeraire to be negative, which is a common assumption in applications of quasilinear utility. Given the assumption that y can be negative, the maximization of $u(x)+y$ subject to a budget constraint with prices p (the problem $\max_{(x,y)} u(x)+y$ subject to the constraint $p \cdot x + y \leq I$) is, when u is locally nonsatiated, equivalent to the maximization of $u(x) - p \cdot x$.

As in Proposition 4.5, the property of cyclic monotonicity described in 1.4 can be used to characterize datasets that could be rationalized by a quasilinear utility.

We take as primitive a dataset D: a collection (x^k,p^k), $k=1,\dots K$, with $K \geq 1$ an integer, $x^k \in X$ and $p^k \in \mathbf{R}^n_{++}$. There are now, however, $n+1$ goods and we seek a rationalization by a quasilinear utility function. A dataset D is *quasilinear rationalizable* if there exists a locally nonsatiated utility function $u : X \to \mathbf{R}$ such that for all k and $x \in X$,

$$u(x) - p^k \cdot x \leq u(x^k) - p^k \cdot x^k.$$

Theorem 4.6 *Let X be a convex consumption space such that for all $x \in X$ and all $\varepsilon > 0$, there is $\varepsilon' \in (0,\varepsilon)$ with $x + \varepsilon' \mathbf{1} \in X$. The following statements are equivalent:*

I) *D is quasilinear rationalizable.*
II) *For each k, there is U^k such that for all k,l,*

$$U^k \leq U^l + p^l \cdot (x^k - x^l).$$

III) *The correspondence $\rho(x) = \bigcup_{k:x=x^k}\{p^k\}$ satisfies cyclic monotonicity.*
IV) *The data are quasilinear rationalizable by a continuous, strictly increasing, concave utility function.*

Proof. That (I) implies (II) is as follows. Let u rationalize the data, and let $U^k = u(x^k)$. In particular, we have $U^l - p^k \cdot x^l \leq U^k - p^k \cdot x^k$, which establishes II.

That (II) implies (III) follows from adding up Afriat inequalities corresponding to cycles, as we discussed after stating Afriat's Theorem (and by the same argument as in the proof of Theorem 1.9). The proof that (III) implies (IV) is exactly as in Theorem (1.9): let

$$u(x) = \inf\{p^{k_1} \cdot (x - x^{k_1}) + p^{k_2} \cdot (x^{k_1} - x^{k_2}) + \ldots + p^{k_{M-1}} \cdot (x^{k_M} - x^{k_{M-1}})\},$$

where the infimum is taken over all sequences $k_1, \ldots, k_M$ with x^{k_1} fixed at some arbitrary $x_0 \in X$. (See Corollary 1.10).

That (IV) implies (I) is trivial.

Remark 4.7 If one assumes that income and quasilinear good consumption must be positive, then the equivalence of (II)–(IV) in the preceding still hold. That (IV) implies (II) holds from the first-order conditions of concave optimization. Condition (IV) could be proved by choosing I large enough so that $I - p^i \cdot x^i \geq 0$ for all i, and defining $y^i = I - p^i \cdot x^i$.

The idea behind Theorem 4.6 is similar to the argument in Theorem 1.9, and it is instructive to see why. If we reason as in the discussion of Afriat's Theorem, and assume that there is a differentiable rationalization u, then the relevant first-order condition for maximizing $u(x) - p \cdot x$ is

$$\nabla u(x) = p.$$

As was the case for Afriat's Theorem, we seek to infer marginal utilities from data, but the difference is that now the Lagrange multiplier (λ^k in Afriat's Theorem) is known and equal to one. The dataset therefore already tells us what the marginal utilities must be, if the data are to be rationalized by a quasilinear utility. Theorem 4.6 therefore asks for prices that could be marginal utilities for a concave utility function – namely cyclic monotonicity. Most of the work in proving Afriat's Theorem went into establishing the existence of multipliers λ^k such that $\rho(x) = \bigcup_{k:x=x^k}\{\lambda^k p^k\}$ is cyclically monotone. In the case of quasilinear utility, this is already taken care of by the quasilinearity assumption.

4.2.4 Gross complements and substitutes

We now turn to two basic properties of demand: the complementarity or substitutability between a pair of goods. Roughly speaking, two goods are "gross" complements if a price change that favors the consumption of one good also induces higher consumption of the second good. Common examples of complementary goods include coffee and sugar, or gin and tonic. Instead of being properties of preference, gross complements and gross substitutes are properties of demand functions.

Formally, we say that a demand function on $\mathbf{R}^2_+$ satisfies *gross complements* if for all m, $d(p,m)$ is a weakly decreasing function of p. We say that the demand function is *rational* if there exists a locally nonsatiated preference relation $\succeq$ for which there is a unique $\succeq$-maximal element of $\{x \in \mathbf{R}^n_+ : p \cdot x \leq m\}$, and $d(p,m)$ is equal to this element. A demand function satisfying gross complements is one for which both goods respond in the same direction to changes in price. On the other hand, we will say a demand function on $\mathbf{R}^2_+$ satisfies *gross substitutes* if $d_1(p,m)$ increases in p_2, and $d_2(p,m)$ increases in p_1. Note that for these definitions to be at all meaningful, demand must be single-valued. We say a demand function is a *rational demand function* if there is a monotonic preference which generates d as its demand correspondence.

It is convenient here to suppose that m is normalized; this is without loss of generality as any rational demand function is homogeneous. For the remainder of this subsection, we always assume $m = 1$, and drop the dependence of d on m.

Data come in the form of observed price/demand pairs, $D = \{(p^k, x^k)\}_{k=1}^K$. We turn to the question of when data are consistent with a rational demand function exhibiting the property of gross complements. In line with the normalization of income, assume that data has been normalized such that, for all k, $p^k \cdot x^k = 1$. Consider Figure 4.3(a), which depicts a hypothetical observation of demand $x = (x_1, x_2)$ at prices $p = (p_1, p_2)$. In principle, the two budgets in Figure 4.3(a) are not comparable, and the observations might be consistent with gross complements. However, the dotted budget line in the figure can be obtained by either starting from (x,p) and making one good cheaper, or by starting from (x',p') and making the other good cheaper. Either way, demand at the dotted budget line should be larger than both x and x'. As Figure 4.3(b) illustrates, this is not possible. In this fashion we obtain a condition on the data that is necessary for consistency with gross complements: the pointwise maximum of demands, $x \vee x'$, must be affordable for any budget larger than the p and p' budgets.

There is a second necessary condition. Consider the observed demands in Figure 4.3(c). This a situation where, when we go from p to p', demand for the good that gets cheaper decreases while demand for the good that gets more expensive increases. This is not in itself a violation of complementarity. However, consider Figure 4.3(d): were we to increase the budget from p to the dotted prices, complementarity would imply a demand at the dotted prices that is larger than x. But no point in the dotted budget line is both larger than x and satisfies the weak axiom of revealed preference (WARP) with respect to the choice of x'.

So a simultaneous increase in one price and decrease in another cannot yield opposite changes in demand. This property is a strengthening of WARP: Fix p, p' and x as in Figure 4.3(c). Then WARP requires that x' not lie below the point where the p and p' budget lines cross. Our property requires that x' not lie below the point on the p'-budget line with the same quantity of good 2 as x.

The following result states that the two necessary conditions illustrated in Figure 4.3 are in fact both necessary and sufficient. These constitute a nonparametric test of gross complements in the demand for a pair of goods.

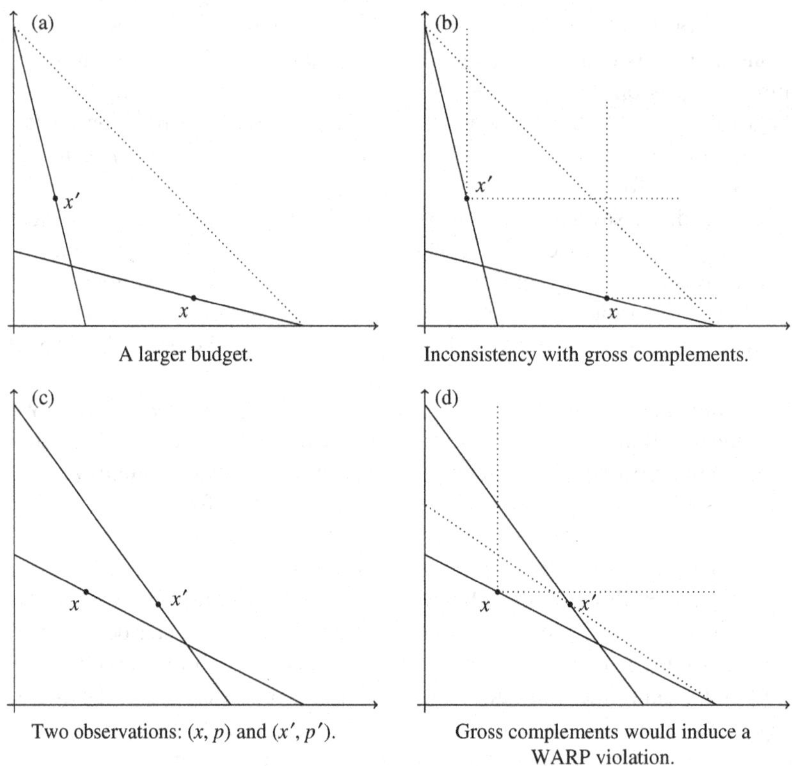

Fig. 4.3 Implications of gross complements.

Theorem 4.8 *Let $\{(p^k, x^k)\}_{k=1}^K$ be a dataset with $n = 2$ and, for all k, $p^k \cdot x^k = 1$ (a normalization). There exists a rational demand d, satisfying gross complements, such that for all k, $d(p^k) = x^k$ iff for all k,l, the following are satisfied:*

- $(p^k \wedge p^l) \cdot (x^k \vee x^l) \leq 1$
- *For all $i \neq j$, if $p^k \cdot x^l \leq 1$ and $p_i^k > p_i^l$, then $x_j^k \geq x_j^l$.*

We now turn to gross substitutes. To illustrate the implications of gross substitutes for observed demand, consider the example in Figure 4.4. We have two observations: x is the bundle purchased at prices p, and x' is purchased at prices p'. These purchases do not appear to directly violate gross substitutes. The observed choices are also consistent with the weak axiom of revealed preference, so there is an extension of these purchases to a rational demand function that is defined for all prices. There is, however, no demand function compatible with these observations which satisfies gross substitutes: Consider the prices p'' given by the dotted budget line. Gross substitutes and the choice of x at p require a decrease in the consumption of the good whose price is the same in p and in p'', so demand at p'' should lie in the northwest segment of the

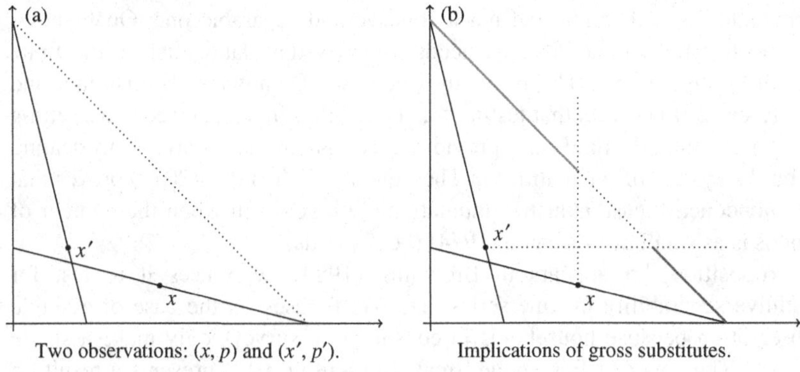

Two observations: (x, p) and (x', p'). Implications of gross substitutes.

Fig. 4.4 Implications of gross substitutes.

budget line. On the other hand, gross substitutes and the choice of x' require that demand at p'' lies in the southeast segment of the budget line. Since these two segments are disjoint, there is no demand function that extends the data and satisfies gross substitutes.

Figure 4.4 then suggests a necessary condition for observations to be consistent with a rational demand exhibiting gross substitutes. The next theorem states that the condition is both necessary and sufficient. Smoothness of demand comes for free in this case.

Theorem 4.9 *Let $\{(p^k, x^k)\}_{k=1}^K$ be a dataset with $n = 2$ and, for all k, $p^k \cdot x^k = 1$ (a normalization). There exists a smooth and rational demand function d satisfying gross substitutes such that for all k, $d(p^k) = x^k$ iff for all k, l such that $p_1^k \leq p_1^l$ and $p_2^l \leq p_2^k$, we have $p_1^l x_1^l \leq p_1^k x_1^k$.*

4.3 CHAPTER REFERENCES

A version of Theorem 4.1 appeared first in Chambers and Echenique (2009b), and was extended by Shirai (2010). Our proof of the supermodular result follows suggestions by Eran Shmaya and John Quah. The submodular utility used in the proof is a construction due to Rader (1963) (Shirai noted that this construction yields a submodular utility).

The results in Sections 4.2.1 and 4.2.2 are from Varian (1983a). The equivalence between conditions (III) and (I) in Section 4.2.1 was shown by Afriat (1972) and Diewert (1973); HARP is due to Varian, though Diewert mentions an equivalent test in a footnote. Knoblauch (1993) describes a method for predicting responses to price changes for data consistent with homotheticity.

Theorem 4.4 is due to Hal Varian. The recent paper of Quah (2013) is the first paper to treat the case of a general, possibly nonconcave, separable rationalization. In fact Quah presents an example of a dataset that has a separable rationalization, but not a concave and separable one. Quah shows that to test for separability one needs to verify that data satisfy some finite set of configurations. The paper by Cherchye, Demuynck, Hjertstrand, and De Rock (2014) shows that testing for separability in Varian's concave setting is computationally hard, and provides a computational approach to dealing with the system of inequalities in Theorem 4.4. Echenique (2013) proves that the nonconcave case is also computationally hard, even when the number of goods is as small as in Deaton (1974) (i.e. 9 goods).

Proposition 4.5 appears in Browning (1989), who uses it to test for additive separability in time series data. He focuses on the case of a single observation because households in consumption surveys only make a single choice. The paper of Echenique, Imai, and Saito (2013) presents a result on time separability for multiple observations (as well as for other models of intertemporal choice).

The result on quasilinear utility is from Brown and Calsamiglia (2007).

Theorem 4.8 is due to Chambers, Echenique, and Shmaya (2010), while Theorem 4.9 appears in Chambers, Echenique, and Shmaya (2011). Related are the papers of Kehoe and Mas-Colell (1984) and Kehoe (1992), which show that gross substitutability of demand implies a version of the weak axiom.

CHAPTER 5

Practical Issues in Revealed Preference Analysis

The tests in Chapters 3 and 4 are meant to be applicable to actual datasets, and many researchers have investigated these applications using experiments, consumption surveys, and other sources of data. Naturally, there are complications that arise when one tries to carry out the tests we have described. We shall focus on the basic application of GARP (or SARP) to data on consumption expenditures. The difficulties in applying GARP can be summarized as follows:

First, GARP is an "all or nothing" notion. A dataset either falsifies the theory of a rational consumer or it does not. One may, however, want to distinguish a grayscale of degrees of violation of the theory. It is possible that some violations can be attributed to simple mistakes on the part of a fully rational consumer. We develop concepts along these lines in 5.1.

Second, the nature of budget sets introduces problems with the power of testing for GARP. When two observed budget sets are nested, then there are no choices that can indicate a violation of GARP (actually of WARP in that case). More generally, any dataset in which budget sets have substantial overlap is biased towards the satisfaction of GARP. The problem of budget overlap is very real because often data contain more individual-level variation in expenditure levels than variation in relative prices. As we explain below (Section 5.2), these features cause budget sets to have substantial overlap.

Third, many studies do not track the identities of individual consumers. With such *cross-sectional* datasets, two observations (x^1, p^1) and (x^2, p^2) actually correspond to different individuals (or households), but they are identified as having the same preferences based on their observable characteristics. The procedure of identifying individuals based on their observable characteristics is called "matching" in statistics and econometrics. The basic problem is how to carry out this identification, or matching: when can we treat two individuals as the same for the purposes of revealed preference tests.

Moreover, certain cross-sectional datasets exacerbate the problem of power. The observations (x^1, p^1) and (x^2, p^2) in the data are of two different individuals (treated as the same agent) at similar points in time. Prices p^1 and p^2 are then

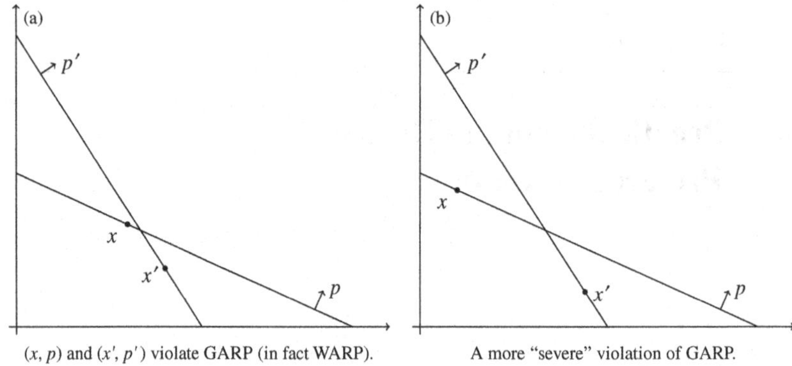

(x, p) and (x', p') violate GARP (in fact WARP).

A more "severe" violation of GARP.

Fig. 5.1 Two observations: (x, p) and (x', p').

bound to be similar, because even prices in different locations are similar at the same point in time. The main source of variation in the data must then be in expenditure levels $p^k \cdot x^k$. As a consequence budget sets tend to be nested; the power of testing for GARP is thus diminished.

5.1 MEASURES OF THE SEVERITY OF A VIOLATION OF GARP

The revealed preference tests we have seen are dichotomous: either the data satisfy the test or they do not. But we are probably also interested in the *degree* to which a test is violated. Specifically, suppose that a dataset violates GARP, but that we somehow judge the violation to be mild. We may not be willing to conclude that the agents involved behaved irrationally.

5.1.1 Afriat's efficiency index

Afriat observes that if expenditures at each observation are "deflated" by some number $e \in [0,1]$, then the violation of GARP will disappear. Afriat proposes to measure the severity of a violation by how much expenditure needs to be deflated for the data to satisfy GARP.

Formally, define a modified revealed preference relation R_e by $x^k \; R_e \; y$ iff $ep^k \cdot x^k \geq p^k \cdot y$; define P_e similarly. For $e \in [0,1]$ small enough, the pair $\langle R_e, P_e \rangle$ will be acyclic. *Afriat's efficiency index (AEI)* is defined as the supremum over all the numbers e such that $\langle R_e, P_e \rangle$ is acyclic:

$$AEI = \sup\{e \in [0,1] : \langle R_e, P_e \rangle \text{ is acyclic.}\}$$

AEI is an intuitive measure of a violation of GARP. Consider, for example, the violation in Figure 5.1. The violation represented in Figure 5.1(b) is more severe than the one in 5.1(a). The difference is reflected in the AEI because a large deflation of expenditure (a smaller e) is needed to account for the violation.

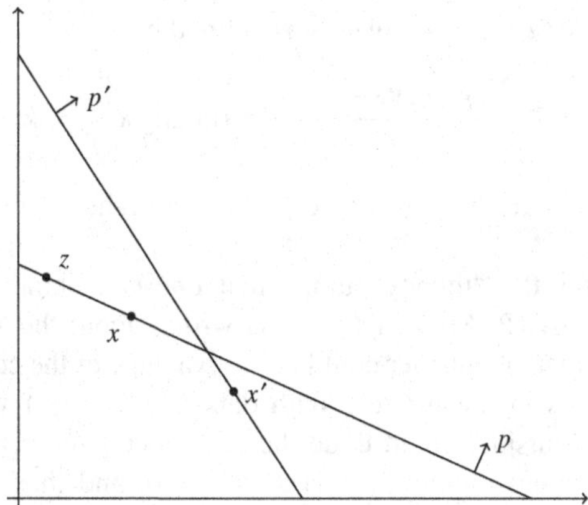

Fig. 5.2 Two violations of WARP: (x, p), (x', p') and (z, p), (x', p').

Afriat's index is also called the *critical cost efficiency index*, or CCEI in the literature.

5.1.2 Varian's version of AEI

Varian modifies Afriat's index by allowing e to vary across the different price vectors. Consider a vector $\theta = (e^k)_{k=1}^K$ of numbers in $[0,1]$, one for each observation. Define the binary relation R_θ as $x^k \, R_\theta \, x^l$ if $e^k p^k \cdot x^k \geq p^k \cdot x^l$. Define the strict relation P_θ analogously. There is a set Θ of vectors θ such that the corresponding $\langle R_\theta, P_\theta \rangle$ satisfies GARP. *Varian's efficiency index (VEI)* is the closest distance of a vector θ to the unit vector ($e^k = 1$ for all k), among those θ for which $\langle R_\theta, P_\theta \rangle$ is acyclic. Formally,

$$VEI = \inf\{\|\mathbf{1} - \theta\| : \langle R_\theta, P_\theta \rangle \text{ is acyclic.}\}$$

5.1.3 The Money Pump Index

Both Afriat's and Varian's indices have a problem. Consider the example in Figure 5.2. The AEI is the same for the two violations in the figure: the data $\{(x,p),(x',p')\}$ and the data $\{(z,p),(x',p')\}$ have the same AEI. This is counterintuitive. Arguably $\{(z,p),(x',p')\}$ presents a worse violation than $\{(x,p),(x',p')\}$. The source of the problem is that every violation of GARP involves at least one cycle, and AEI (or VEI) try to break the cycle at its "weakest link." In the example in Figure 5.2, this requires deflating expenditure to the point that x' is on the budget set for x.

If one instead treats each "link" equally, then the problem goes away. Let the sequence $x^{k_1}, x^{k_2}, \ldots, x^{k_n}$ define a violation of GARP, a cycle of $\langle \succeq^R, \succ^R \rangle$.

The *money pump index (MPI)* of this violation is defined by

$$MPI_{\{(x^{k_1},p^{k_1}),\ldots,(x^{k_n},p^{k_n})\}} = \frac{\sum_{l=1}^{n} p^{k_l} \cdot (x^{k_l} - x^{k_{l+1}})}{\sum_{l=1}^{n} p^{k_l} \cdot x^{k_l}} \quad \text{(taking } k_{n+1} = k_1\text{)}. \quad (5.1)$$

It is easy to see that, in Figure 5.2, $\{(z,p),(x',p')\}$ has a higher level of MPI than $\{(x,p),(x',p')\}$.

The MPI is named for the "money pump" that one can obtain from a consumer who violates GARP. Arguably, what is wrong about the situation in Figures 5.1 and 5.2 is that an outsider could take advantage of the consumer that exhibits the behaviors in the figures. With data (x,p), (x',p') violating WARP, for example, the outsider could trade the consumer x for x' at prices p, thereby getting an amount of money $p \cdot (x - x') > 0$, and then trade x' back for x at prices p', thereby getting an amount of money $p' \cdot (x' - x) > 0$. The total amount obtained by manipulating the consumer in such a way is $p \cdot (x - x') + p' \cdot (x' - x)$. The MPI simply expresses this magnitude as a fraction of total expenditure.

Under certain assumptions, the MPI is the basis for a statistical test of rational consumer behavior. If one assumes a source of statistical errors, one can construct a critical region, so that rational consumer behavior is rejected (beyond what can be explained as an error) if the MPI lies in this critical region.

5.2 POWER OF TESTING GARP

Failure to reject GARP can sometimes be caused by how budgets vary in the data. In fact, certain datasets are problematic in the sense that it is intrinsically hard to observe violations of GARP in them. Consider the example in Figure 5.3(a). No matter what the consumer chooses at these budgets, there will be no violation of GARP.

The figure is a stark example of a common phenomenon: when incomes vary more than prices, it is harder to detect a violation of GARP. In cross-sectional consumption data one has many observations of consumption chosen by different households (individuals) at similar prices. The econometrician tries to identify choices by different individuals as coming from the same (or similar) preference relations, but since prices vary little, and individual incomes can vary widely, GARP is easily satisfied. The situation is similar for aggregate time-series data, meaning time-series data for a whole economy. Such data often exhibit large year-on-year changes in aggregate expenditure (which equals aggregate incomes), and comparatively small changes in relative prices.

One might argue that the issue of power does not apply to the realm of revealed preference analysis. The theory only claims that agents' behavior is *as if* they were maximizing a utility function. So what if the budgets are not set up in a way that might detect a violation of GARP? There is no sense in which utility maximization could be a true model other than when behavior satisfies GARP: this is in contrast to statistical models in which one affirms

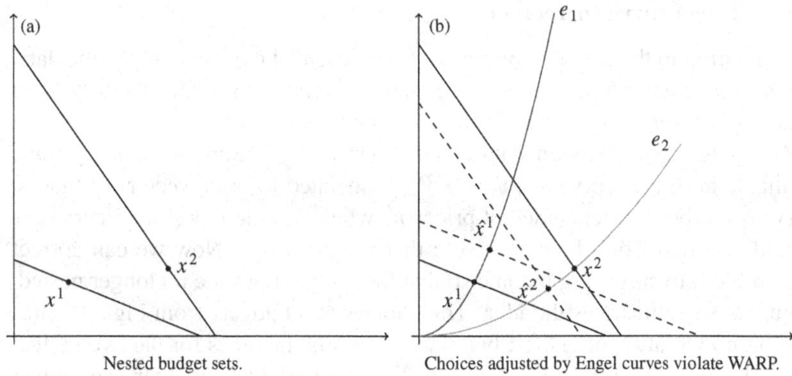

Nested budget sets.

Choices adjusted by Engel curves violate WARP.

Fig. 5.3 Power of GARP.

the existence of an unknown true parameter. Having mentioned this point of view, we shall nevertheless proceed with an exploration of the role of power in revealed preference tests.

5.2.1 Bronars' index

Recognizing the problems with the power of GARP, Stephen Bronars proposes an index that tries to measure the power of using any particular collection of budgets for testing GARP. His idea is: Given a collection of budget sets $B^1,\ldots,B^K$, simulate an "irrational" consumer choosing from these sets and see how frequently the consumer violates GARP. Bronars assumes a consumer who chooses a consumption bundle fully at random from the budget set.

The *Bronars' index* of a collection of budget sets is the probability that randomly chosen consumption bundles $x^1,\ldots,x^K$ violate GARP, where x^k is chosen uniformly at random on the boundary (budget line) of the budget B^k.

The index is implemented using Monte Carlo simulation. If there are L goods, one method draws $s_1^k,\ldots,s_L^k$ at random and chooses $x^k \in B^k$ such that the budget share of good l is s_l^k. This is done in such a way that the distribution over the budget line is uniform. A second method targets the actual budget shares in the data: If θ_l^k is the actual observed budget share of good l in observation k, let $s_l^k = \theta_l^k z_l^k / \sum_h \theta_h^k z_h^k$, where the variables $z_1^k,\ldots,z_L^k$ are drawn uniformly and independently from $[0,1]$.

Bronars' index is now routinely used in experimental studies of GARP. When designing an experiment, researchers choose budgets so as to exhibit a high Bronars' index. An alternative measure of power, introduced by Andreoni, Gillen and Miller, is based on having data from many agents choosing from the same budget sets. One draws one choice at random, among the observed choices, from each budget set. Then one tests if the resulting "bootstrapped" choices pass GARP.

5.2.2 Engel curve correction

One solution to the problem of power is to use Engel curves to adjust the data. Let d be a demand function. For given p, the *Engel curve* associated to p is the function $m \mapsto d(p,m)$.

Given is a consumption dataset $D = \{(x^k, p^k)\}_{k=1}^K$. Suppose that we have available an Engel curve $e_k : \mathbf{R}_+ \to \mathbf{R}^l_+$ associated to price vector p^k; that is, $e_k(y)$ is the bundle demanded at prices p^k when income is y (Engel curves e_k would be fitted from the data). Note that $y = p^k \cdot e_k(y)$. Now we can correct the problem by adjusting income so that the budget lines are no longer nested. Figure 5.3(b) illustrates the idea. The choices and budgets from Figure 5.3(a) exhibit no violation of GARP, but if we adjust the incomes for the two budget lines (keeping the prices the same) to the two dashed lines, then the budget sets are no longer nested and there is scope for a violation of GARP. Indeed, at these hypothetical budgets, we can find the choices consistent with Engel curves e_1 and e_2. The choices induced by the Engel curves present a violation of WARP.

The idea of using Engel curves was developed by Blundell, Browning, and Crawford. They propose to consider a fixed sequence of choices and prices

$$x^{k_1}, \ldots, x^{k_l}, \ldots x^{k_L},$$

with a distinguished choice x^{k_l}. Transform the sequence as follows. For each k, we let $e_k : \mathbf{R}_+ \to \mathbf{R}^n_+$ be an Engel curve for prices p^k. That is, e_k satisfies the following properties:

- For all k, $e_k(p^k \cdot x^k) = x^k$.
- For all k and all $y \leq y'$, $e_k(y) \leq e_k(y')$.
- For all k and all y, $p^k \cdot e_k(y) = y$.

So, these Engel curves need not come from preference maximization, but importantly, the second criterion requires that the Engel curves are associated with normal demand.

We proceed to describe the construction. For $x^{k_{l-1}}$, the term preceding x^{k_l} in the sequence, we use the Engel curve for prices $p^{k_{l-1}}$ to find a hypothetical choice $\hat{x}^{k_{l-1}}$ on a budget line such that $\hat{x}^{k_{l-1}}$ is revealed preferred to x^{k_l}. Specifically, let $\hat{m}^{k_{l-1}} = p^{k_{l-1}} \cdot x^{k_l}$ and $\hat{x}^{k_{l-1}} = e_{k_{l-1}}(\hat{m}^{k_{l-1}})$. Given $\hat{x}^{k_{l-1}}$, we can use the same idea to construct $\hat{x}^{k_{l-2}}$ from $\hat{x}^{k_{l-1}}$. That is, let $\hat{m}^{k_{l-2}} = p^{k_{l-2}} \cdot \hat{x}^{k_{l-1}}$ and $\hat{x}^{k_{l-2}} = e_{k_{l-2}}(\hat{m}^{k_{l-2}})$. Continuing in this fashion, we construct $\hat{x}^{k_1}, \ldots, \hat{x}^{k_{l-1}}$ with the property that

$$\hat{x}^{k_1} \succeq^R \hat{x}^{k_2} \succeq^R \cdots \succeq^R \hat{x}^{k_{l-1}} \succeq^R x^{k_l}.$$

The construction of $\hat{x}^{k_{l+1}}, \ldots, \hat{x}^{k_L}$ is similar. Let $\hat{m}^{k_{l+1}}$ be the solution to the equation

$$p^{k_l} \cdot x^{k_l} = p^{k_l} \cdot e_{k_{l+1}}(\hat{m}^{k_{l+1}})$$

(such a solution exists and is unique under our assumptions on Engel curves; namely, continuity is implied by normality). Let $\hat{x}^{k_{l+1}} = e_{k_{l+1}}(\hat{m}^{k_{l+1}})$ and note that $x^{k_l} \succeq^R \hat{x}^{k_{l+1}}$ by construction. Given, $\hat{x}^{k_{l+1}}$ and $\hat{m}^{k_{l+1}}$, let $\hat{m}^{k_{l+2}}$ be the solution to the equation $\hat{m}^{k_{l+1}} = p^{k_{l+1}} \cdot e_{k_{l+2}}(\hat{m}^{k_{l+2}})$; and set $\hat{x}^{k_{l+2}} = e_{k_{l+2}}(\hat{m}^{k_{l+2}})$. Continuing in this fashion we obtain a sequence $x^{k+l} \succeq^R \hat{x}^{k_{l+1}} \succeq^R \cdots \succeq^R \hat{x}^{k_L}$.

The usefulness of the construction follows from the following proposition. The construction never eliminates a violation of GARP. Thus every sequence exhibiting a violation of GARP remains a violation after being adjusted by Engel curves. In other words, transforming a sequence in this way can only increase the chances of observing a violation of GARP.

Proposition 5.1 *If $x^{k_1},\ldots,x^{k_L}$ is a sequence with $x^{k_1} \succeq^R \cdots \succeq^R x^{k_L} \succ^R x^{k_1}$ and $\hat{x}^{k_1},\ldots,\hat{x}^{k_L}$ is the Engel-curve adjusted sequence when x^{k_L} is the distinguished element, then $\hat{x}^{k_1} \succeq^R \cdots \succeq^R \hat{x}^{k_L} \succ^R \hat{x}^{k_1}$.*

Proof. Let $m^{k_l} = p^{k_l} \cdot x^{k_l}$. It is easy to see by induction that $m^{k_l} \geq \hat{m}^{k_l}$ for $l = 1,\ldots,L$. By construction,

$$\hat{m}^{k_{L-1}} = p^{k_{L-1}} \cdot x^{k_L} \leq p^{k_{L-1}} \cdot x^{k_{L-1}} = m^{k_{L-1}},$$

where the inequality follows from $x^{k_{L-1}} \succeq^R x^{k_L}$. Then, the normality of demand implies that

$$x^{k_{L-1}} = e_{k_{L-1}}(m^{k_{L-1}}) \geq e_{k_{L-1}}(\hat{m}^{k_{L-1}}) = \hat{x}^{k_{L-1}},$$

so we obtain that

$$m^{k_{L-2}} = p^{k_{L-2}} \cdot x^{k_{L-2}} \geq p^{k_{L-2}} \cdot x^{k_{L-1}} \geq p^{k_{L-2}} \cdot \hat{x}^{k_{L-1}} = \hat{m}^{k_{L-2}}.$$

By continuing in this fashion, we show that $m^{k_l} \geq \hat{m}^{k_l}$ for $l = 1,\ldots,L$. Then, $x^{k_L} \succ^R x^{k_1}$ implies that

$$p^{k_L} \cdot x^{k_L} > p^{k_L} \cdot x^{k_1} \geq p^{k_L} \cdot \hat{x}^{k_1},$$

as $x^{k_1} = e_{k_1}(m^{k_1}) \geq e_{k_1}(\hat{m}^{k_1}) = \hat{x}^{k_1}$. Hence, $x^{k_L} \succ^R \hat{x}^{k_1}$; so the fact that $\hat{x}^{k_1} \succeq^R \cdots \succeq^R x^{k_L}$ establishes the result, using the fact that $\hat{x}^{k_L} = x^{k_L}$.

5.3 AN OVERVIEW OF EMPIRICAL STUDIES

We briefly describe some of the best-known empirical studies of GARP, classified by the kind of datasets that they use.

5.3.1 Panel data

Koo (1963) may be the first empirical study of revealed preference in consumption. He uses a panel dataset of consumption choices, and finds that relatively few households (panelists) in his sample satisfy GARP fully. It is interesting that such an early study uses panel data, a kind of data that corresponds closely to the theory, and presents fewer complications than some of the later uses of cross-sectional and time-series data. Koo introduces a measure of the degree of satisfaction of GARP, based on the idea that some subset of the observed choices could be consistent with GARP. His measure is flawed, however, as pointed out by Dobell (1965).

5.3.2 Cross-sectional data

Famulari (1995) tests for violations of GARP using a cross-sectional dataset obtained from a consumer expenditure survey. She focuses on budget sets that involve similar levels of expenditure, as a way of addressing the standard problems of the power of GARP. She assumes that bundles with similar costs, and where goods have similar expenditure shares, may be difficult to compare for consumers. Hence she focuses on comparing observations where the consumption bundles have similar costs, but dissimilar expenditure shares. Famulari also uses Afriat's efficiency index to account for possible measurement errors that could lead her to find spurious violations of GARP.

Based on their economic and demographic characteristics, Famulari groups her sample of some four thousand "consumer units" into 43 different types of households (this methodology is called "matching" in statistics and econometrics). She defines a rate of violation of GARP as follows: a pair of observations x^k and x^l constitute a violation if x^k stands in the transitive closure of the revealed preference relation to x^l (x^k is indirectly revealed preferred to x^l), while x^l is strictly revealed preferred to x^k. Famulari's *rate of violation of GARP* is the number of pairs that induce a violation divided by the total number of pairs in the data. Her results are that violation rates are quite small, and they are attributable to measurement errors (using Afriat's efficiency index).

Dowrick and Quiggin (1994) use a revealed preference approach to cross-country welfare comparisons. As a first step, they test for GARP using cross-country aggregate consumption data. Specifically, they obtain one observation (p^k, x^k) for each country in a sample of 60 countries (using data from 1980). For country k, x^k is a per-capita aggregate consumption bundle, and p^k is a country-specific price index. They treat the cross-country dataset as a consumption dataset, the idea being that a common representative consumer could exist across these countries. They use revealed preference comparisons as a comparison in the standard of living. They find almost no violations of GARP (and that GARP is very close to WARP). The results are consistent with the existence of seven categories of countries, such that the bundle consumed by a high-category country is always revealed preferred to a lower-category country; and such that most countries in the same category are not comparable according to revealed preference.

The study of Blundell, Browning, and Crawford (2003) is also worth mentioning here. They use cross-sectional data and introduce the technique described in Section 5.2.2.

5.3.3 Time-series data

Varian (1982) studies yearly aggregate data on consumption in the period 1947–1978. A test for GARP in this case can be interpreted as a test for the existence of an aggregate representative consumer. Varian finds no violation of GARP. The test, however, has very low power for yearly aggregate data. In the post-war period, the US aggregate income was increasing markedly year after year, while relative prices were relatively stable. This fact is emphasized by Varian in his paper: an observation that prompted later researchers to be concerned with the power of testing for GARP. Landsburg (1981) conducts a similar study on UK consumption data, and also notes that increasing income is problematic, attributing the observation to Gary Becker. See also Chalfant and Alston (1988). Swofford and Whitney (1986, 1987) are early related studies on the demand for financial assets.

Browning (1989) is another well-known study using time-series data. Instead of testing for GARP, Browning is interested in the maximization of a utility function of a particular form: an additively time-separable utility function, with no discounting and a per-period utility index that is constant over time. The test for rationalizability by this kind of utility turns out to be cyclic monotonicity: see Proposition 4.5.

Using aggregate time-series data from the UK and the US, Browning finds that GARP can never be rejected, which is in line with Varian's findings and the comments on the power of GARP we made above. Cyclic monotonicity is rejected, but there are fairly long periods of time for which cyclic monotonicity holds. Given that the data satisfy GARP, we know that there are multipliers for the prices for which the data with "adjusted prices" pass cyclic monotonicity (see the discussion after Afriat's axiom on Page 41). Browning proceeds to calculate such multipliers, and uses them to inquire about the reasons behind the falsification of the additively separable model.

5.3.4 Experimental data

Battalio, Kagel, Winkler, Fischer, Basmann, and Krasner (1973) ran a field experiment in the female ward of a psychiatric hospital. Patients (who were diagnosed psychotic) could exchange tokens for different consumption goods. By varying the value of the tokens, the authors induce a variety of different budget sets, and record the patients' purchases. Battalio *et al.* found that many patients satisfied GARP. In particular, if one allows for small measurement errors in quantities, then almost all the psychiatric patients' behavior is consistent with GARP. The authors also look at the dynamic behavior of the few patients who violate GARP, and argue that the patients reacted to price changes in the correct direction, but that they failed to fully adjust to the new prices. It is possible that if patients had had sufficient time to get used to the price change, then no violations would have been observed.

Sippel (1997) presented individuals with a menu of choices, determined by standard budget sets. Subjects were according to the random decision selection mechanism. Individuals were paid in consumption goods, and were required to consume the goods at the experiment. Overall, subjects were found to be inconsistent with classical demand theory. By setting an AEI of 95%, most subjects were found to be consistent with the predictions of preference maximization, but the power of the test also decreased substantially. The study then chose perturbed demand close to actual demand, finding that the number of violations changes little after perturbation, suggesting that inconsistency cannot be due to error alone.

Andreoni and Miller (2002) are motivated by the standard experimental finding that agents are too generous when asked to split a given amount of money. In "dictator game" experiments, subjects are asked to split x dollars between themselves and another subject, who is completely anonymous. Andreoni and Miller run such dictator-game experiments, and test if the observed altruistic behavior is utility-maximizing, by a utility that depends on the monetary rewards received by both agents. They find that 98% of subjects make choices that are consistent with utility maximization. Andreoni and Miller go further than most revealed-preference exercises in estimating a parametric function of a utility function accounting for subject's choices (about half the subjects can be classified as using a linear, CES (constant elasticity of substitution), or Leontief utility).

Harbaugh, Krause, and Berry (2001) perform an experiment using seven- and eleven-year-old children, as well as college students. They test each of these populations for compliance with GARP, after making them choose from several budget sets. They find a relatively small number of violations of GARP. Seven-year-olds violate GARP much more than older children (but still exhibit a relatively small number of violations). Eleven-year-old children behave close to rationally, and there are few differences between college-age adults and eleven-year-old children. It is interesting that the authors find that violations of GARP are largely uncorrelated with the results of a test that measures mathematical ability in children.

Choi, Kariv, Müller, and Silverman (2014) run an experiment on choices from budgets, and correlate the degree of consistency with GARP (as measured by the Afriat efficiency index) with the demographic and socioeconomic characteristics of the subjects. They work with a large sample of over 2,000 Dutch households. In their experiments, subjects are presented with 25 different budgets, each one chosen randomly. They find an average AEI of .88, and that almost half the population has an AEI above .95; so the population is quite close to satisfying GARP. The meat of their study lies in correlating AEI with the socioeconomic characteristics of the subjects. They find that men as well as highly educated and rich individuals score higher AEI than others. They also find that high AEI scores predict high levels of wealth: a standard deviation increase in AEI predicts 15–19% higher household wealth.

5.4 CHAPTER REFERENCES

A basic reference to matching in statistics is Rubin (1973). Famulari (1995) is an example of the use of matching in revealed preference analysis. Famulari (2006) uses a similar methodology to study labor supply from the viewpoint of revealed preference. She uses nonlinear budget sets to capture the effects of taxes on labor supply. A different methodological approach is taken by

Hoderlein and Stoye (2014), who focus on bounding the joint distribution of the population of consumer characteristics, and by Kitamura and Stoye (2013), who translate the problem into the framework analyzed in Chapter 7. Hoderlein (2011) should also be mentioned: he focuses on testing the implications of rationality for the Slutsky matrix of demand.

One issue we have not dealt with here is that consumption data usually reflect the decisions of households, not of single agents. We shall consider models of collective decision making in Chapter 9, 10, and 11, but the focus on those chapters will not be on consumption data. In the consumption setting, the issue is addressed by Cherchye, De Rock, and Vermeulen (2007, 2009), based on the model of Chiappori (1988). See also Browning and Chiappori (1998).

Afriat (1967) proposed Afriat's efficiency index. Varian (1990) extended the index as explained above, and gives it an interpretation in terms of consistency with rationality and errors in measurement (see also Varian, 1985 and Epstein and Yatchew, 1985). Afriat's index is also called the critical cost efficiency index, or CCEI in the literature. The critical cost efficiency index (CCEI) terminology was introduced by Varian (1991), based on Afriat (1972) (a paper on optimality in cost and production, see Chapter 6). It is used heavily in applied work: see Choi, Fisman, Gale, and Kariv (2007) and Choi, Kariv, Müller, and Silverman (2014).

The Money Pump Index is proposed by Echenique, Lee, and Shum (2011), who show that the MPI has an interpretation as a statistical test. Smeulders, Cherchye, De Rock, and Spieksma (2013) propose a variant of MPI that is computationally easy. An alternative measure of a violation of GARP results from computing the smallest set of observations one would need to delete from the data in order for it to satisfy GARP: see Houtman and Maks (1985), and more recently Dean and Martin (2013). An early related work in abstract choice theory is Basu (1984).

We have omitted a discussion of Varian's procedure for estimating demand responses by using revealed preference inequalities: see Varian (1982), Knoblauch (1992) and Blundell, Browning, and Crawford (2008). The discussion in Section 5.2.2 on the Engel-curve corrections approach to the problem of power is related to this procedure, and is taken from Blundell, Browning, and Crawford (2003).

Bronars' index was proposed in Bronars (1987). The model of random choice as a model of irrational behavior was proposed by Becker (1962). It is curious, however, that the point of Becker's paper is that random behavior is close to being rational. This point calls into question the idea of using random choices as a measure of the power of GARP. The "bootstrap" approach to power described in the text is due to Andreoni and Miller (2002).

There are alternative power indices formulated by Famulari (1995) and by Andreoni, Gillen, and Harbaugh (2013). Andreoni, Gillen, and Harbaugh's test, in particular, rests on a clever "reversion" of AEI to measure how far an observation that satisfies GARP is from not satisfying it. Beatty and Crawford

(2011) propose a measure of power that is related to Bronars', but based on the ideas in Selten (1991).

In addition to the evaluation of power based on a collection of budgets, it is sensible to use the data on actual choices to get an idea for the power of GARP. Andreoni, Gillen, and Harbaugh (2013) propose econometric methodologies for carrying out such evaluations of power.

The selection of empirical papers in Section 5.3 is obviously arbitrary. It is worth mentioning some papers that study the correlation between subjects' pass rates for GARP, and the presence of factors that may impede subjects' cognitive abilities. In particular, the paper of Burghart, Glimcher, and Lazzaro (2013) finds that subjects in experiments who have consumed substantial amounts of alcohol still pass GARP. The paper by Castillo, Dickinson, and Petrie (2014) in contrast compares subjects who are sleepy with those who are fully alert: again pass rates for GARP are the same across treated and non-treated subjects. It is important to note that both papers do find an effect of the treatment on agents' risk-taking behavior.

CHAPTER 6

Production

Production theory is another classical environment in which revealed preference theory is applied. The case of production is simpler than the case of demand treated in the previous chapters, mainly because firm output is a cardinally measurable and observable concept, whereas utility is not. In the case of production, we shall assume that firm output and prices are both observed, while the set of all feasible production vectors, that is the firm's technology, is not.

We will consider two approaches to production theory: the cost minimization model and the profit maximization model. In the first model, factor prices and factor demands are observed, and (single-dimensional) output is observed as well. This environment is very similar to the consumer case, but, as we have noted, simpler. We want to know whether the model is consistent with the cost minimization hypothesis, meaning that the cost of production is minimized for a given level of output.

In the second model, the model of profit maximization, we want to test the hypothesis that producers maximize profit. This model is in a sense "dual" to the consumer case. In the consumer case, we needed to solve for the function being maximized, but we know the budget set. In contrast, in the producer case, we know the function being maximized: it is a linear profit function; but we do not necessarily know the available technology (the constraint set faced by the firm).

6.1 COST MINIMIZATION

We take as primitive a dataset comprising the input–output decisions of a firm. The firm uses n factors, and produces a single good. An *input–output dataset* D consists of a collection (y^k, x^k, p^k), $k = 1, \ldots, K$, where $y^k \in \mathbf{R}$, $x^k \in \mathbf{R}^n_+$, and $p^k \in \mathbf{R}^n_{++}$. Each observation k consists of a quantity of output y^k, a vector of factor demands x^k, and factor prices p^k. Note that output can be negative, but inputs are always positive.

A *production function* is a mapping $f : \mathbf{R}^n_+ \to \mathbf{R}$. We say that a production function f *cost rationalizes* input–output dataset D if $f(x^k) = y^k$ for all k, and

$f(x) \geq f(x^k)$ implies that $p^k \cdot x \geq p^k \cdot x^k$. In other words, given prices p^k, x^k is a cost-minimizing bundle across all bundles which can, according to f, produce at least y^k.

Theorem 6.1 *The following statements are equivalent:*

I) *There is a continuous production function that cost rationalizes D.*
II) $y^j \leq y^k$ *implies* $p^j \cdot x^j \leq p^j \cdot x^k$ *and* $y^j < y^k$ *implies* $p^j \cdot x^j < p^j \cdot x^k$.
III) *There are real numbers* $U^k, \lambda^k > 0$ *for which* $y^j \leq y^k$ *implies* $U^j \leq U^k$ *and* $y^j < y^k$ *implies* $U^j < U^k$, *and for all* j, k,

$$U^j \leq U^k + \lambda^k p^k \cdot (x^j - x^k).$$

IV) *There is a continuous, monotonic, and quasiconcave production function that cost rationalizes D.*

Equation (II) plays the role of GARP in this context. If we were to define the revealed preference by $x^k \succeq^R x^j$ if $p^k \cdot x^j \leq p^k \cdot x^k$, and $x^k \succ^R x^j$ if $p^k \cdot x^j < p^k \cdot x^k$, then (II) guarantees that $\langle \succeq^R, \succ^R \rangle$ is acyclic.

The equivalence between (III) and (IV) in Theorem 6.1 is reminiscent of Afriat's Theorem. The statement in (III) gives the "Afriat inequalities" corresponding to the problem under consideration. Note, however, that (III) says more than in Afriat's Theorem. The reason is that we observe production output, the analogue of utility in demand theory, while utility is not observable.

Proof. To see that (I) implies (II), we first note that if $y^j \leq y^k$ then since f cost rationalizes D, we have $p^j \cdot x^j \leq p^j \cdot x^k$. If $y^j < y^k$, then we know that $p^j \cdot x^j \leq p^j \cdot x^k$, and if in fact $p^j \cdot x^j = p^j \cdot x^k$, we cannot have $x^k = 0$, as otherwise, $x^k = x^j = 0$, which would imply $y^k = f(x^k) = f(x^j) = y^j$, a contradiction. Since $f(x^k) = y^k > y^j = f(x^j)$, and f is continuous, there is $x < x^k$ for which $f(x) > f(x^j)$, yet $p^j \cdot x < p^j \cdot x^j$, a contradiction to the fact that f cost rationalizes D.

To see that (II) implies (III), we refer to Afriat's Theorem. We may define the revealed preference relations $\succeq^R$ and $\succ^R$ in the same way they are defined in Chapter 3, so that $x^j \succeq^R x^k$ if $p^j \cdot x^k \leq p^j \cdot x^j$, and $x^j \succ^R x^k$ if $p^j \cdot x^k < p^j \cdot x^j$.

By (II), $x^j \succeq^R x^k$ implies $y^j \geq y^k$ and $x^j \succ^R x^k$ implies $y^j > y^k$. It follows that the preference relation $\succeq$ on $X^0 = \{x^k : k = 1, \ldots, K\}$ defined by $x^j \succeq x^k$ iff $y^j \geq y^k$ is such that $x^j \succeq^R x^k$ implies $x^j \succeq x^k$ and $x^j \succ^R x^k$ implies $x^j \succ x^k$. The result then follows by the constructive proof of Afriat's Theorem, so that the desired numbers exist. It is easily verified that $y^j \leq y^k$ implies $U^j \leq U^k$ and $y^j < y^k$ implies $U^j < U^k$.

Finally, to see that (III) implies (IV), let $u : \mathbf{R}^n_+ \to \mathbf{R}$ be the utility function as constructed in Afriat's Theorem. Recall that u is strictly increasing and concave and that $u(x^k) = U^k$. Observe first that if $u(x) \geq u(x^k)$, then it follows that $U^k + \lambda^k p^k \cdot (x - x^k) \geq u(x) \geq U^k$, so that $p^k \cdot x^k \leq p^k \cdot x$.

We now let φ be any strictly increasing transformation of u for which $\varphi(u(x^k)) = y^k$ (that this is possible follows as $y^j \leq y^k$ implies $u^j \leq u^k$ and $y^j < y^k$ implies $u^j < u^k$). Then let $f = \varphi \circ u$, and note that f is strictly increasing and quasiconcave. Finally, it cost rationalizes the data: $f(x) \geq f(x^k)$ implies that $u(x) \geq u(x^k)$, which we have shown implies $p^k \cdot x^k \leq p^k \cdot x$.

Theorem 6.1 describes the datasets that are rationalizable by a quasiconcave production function. Unlike the demand context, concavity here will impose additional testable restrictions. For example, consider an environment with one input. Suppose three observations are given in D: $(y^1, x^1, p^1) = (0,0,1)$, $(y^2, x^2, p^1) = (1,1,1)$, and $(y^3, x^3, p^3) = (3,2,1)$. Note that D is cost rationalizable by a quasiconcave production function; for example, $f(x) = \max\{x, 2x-1\}$ cost rationalizes the data. However, any f which cost rationalizes D must satisfy $f(0) = 0, f(1) = 1$, and $f(2) = 3$. No such function can be concave.

To this end, we can also test when an input–output dataset can be cost rationalized by a *concave* production function.

Theorem 6.2 *The following are equivalent:*

I) *There is a concave production function that cost rationalizes D.*
II) *For each k, and all $\alpha^j \geq 0$ for which $\sum_{j \neq k} \alpha^j = 1$, if $p^k \cdot (\sum_{j \neq k} \alpha^j x^j) \leq p^k \cdot x^k$, then $\sum_{j \neq k} \alpha^j y^j \leq y^k$, and if $p^k \cdot (\sum_{j \neq k} \alpha^j x^j) < p^k \cdot x^k$, then $\sum_{j \neq k} \alpha^j y^j < y^k$.*
III) *There is a concave, monotonic, and continuous production function that cost rationalizes D.*

Proof. We first show that (I) implies (II). Suppose D can be cost rationalized by a concave production function f, and suppose that $p^k \cdot x^k \geq p^k \cdot \left(\sum_{j \neq k} \alpha^j x^j\right)$ for some α^j as in statement (II). Then suppose by way of contradiction that $\sum_{j \neq k} \alpha^j y^j > y^k$. In particular this implies that $\sum_{j \neq k} \alpha^j f(x^j) > f(x^k)$. By concavity, we know that $f\left(\sum_{j \neq k} \alpha^j x^j\right) \geq \sum_{j \neq k} \alpha^j f(x^j) > f(x^k)$. First, we show that $\sum_{j \neq k} \alpha^j x^j \neq 0$. Suppose, toward a contradiction, that $\sum_{j \neq k} \alpha^j x^j = 0$. Choose some j for which $\alpha^j > 0$ and $y^j > y^k$. We must have $x^j = 0$, as $\sum_{j \neq k} \alpha^j x^j = 0$, which allows us to conclude that $y^j = f(0) > f(x^k)$. By cost rationalization, we then have that $0 = p^k \cdot 0 \geq p^k \cdot x^k$, which implies that $x^k = 0$, contradicting $f(0) > f(x^k)$. This shows that $\sum_{j \neq k} \alpha^j x^j > 0$.

Next, on the interior of any one-dimensional subset of $\mathbf{R}^n$, f is continuous (as it is concave). In particular, except possibly at the origin, f is continuous on the ray passing through the origin and $\sum_{j \neq k} \alpha^j x^j$. So, consider $\beta < 1$ for which $f\left(\beta\left(\sum_{j \neq k} \alpha^j x^j\right)\right) > f(x^k)$. Then since $p^k \in \mathbf{R}^n_{++}$, we know that $p^k \cdot \left(\beta\left(\sum_{j \neq k} \alpha^j x^j\right)\right) < p^k \cdot x^k$, a contradiction to the cost rationalization hypothesis. This establishes that $\sum_{j \neq k} \alpha^j y^j \leq y^k$.

To complete the proof of (II), suppose that that $p^k \cdot x^k > p^k \cdot \left(\sum_{j \neq k} \alpha^j x^j\right)$. Suppose, toward a contradiction, that $\sum_{j \neq k} \alpha^j y^j \geq y^k$. Then $f(x^k) \leq \sum_{j \neq k} \alpha^j f(x^j) \leq f\left(\sum_{j \neq k} \alpha^j x^j\right)$, where the inequality follows by concavity. This is a direct contradiction to the cost rationalization hypothesis, as $\sum_{j\neq k}\alpha^j x^j$ can produce y^k at a lower cost than x^k.

Second, we prove that (II) implies (III). To that end, we show the existence of $\lambda^k > 0$ such that for all j,k,

$$y^k \leq y^j + \lambda^j p^j \cdot (x^k - x^j). \tag{6.1}$$

The existence of such λ^k is equivalent to the existence of $\lambda^k > 0$ and $\mu > 0$ such that for all j,k,

$$\mu(y^j - y^k) + \lambda^j p^j \cdot (x^k - x^j) \geq 0.$$

If we can solve these inequalities, we can renormalize, setting $\mu = 1$, and obtain a solution to (6.1). Now, by Lemma 1.12, there is no solution exactly when, for each (j,k) where $j \neq k$, there is $\alpha^{(j,k)} \geq 0$ for which $\sum_{(j,k)}\alpha^{(j,k)}(y^j - y^k) \leq 0$ and for all j, $\sum_{k\neq j}\alpha^{(j,k)}p^j \cdot (x^k - x^j) \leq 0$, and at least one of these inequalities is strict. Since for all j, $\sum_{k\neq j}\alpha^{(j,k)}p^j \cdot (x^k - x^j) \leq 0$, we get by (II) that for every j, $\sum_{k\neq j}\alpha^{(j,k)}(y^k - y^j) \leq 0$, with a strict inequality if the original inequality is strict. By summing across j, we have $\sum_{(j,k)}\alpha^{(j,k)}(y^k - y^j) \leq 0$, with a strict inequality if any of the inequalities corresponding to some j is strict, a contradiction.

The construction of a production function is the same as in Afriat's Theorem. Let $f(x) = \min_k y^k + \lambda^k p^k \cdot (x - x^k)$, a concave, continuous, and strictly monotonic function. Cost rationalization is verified as in Theorem 6.1. Finally, for all $k, f(x^k) = y^k$.

Often we want to ensure that $f(x) \geq 0$ for all x. A test for this is provided by weakening the equality $\sum_{j\neq k}\alpha^j = 1$ in Theorem 6.2.

Theorem 6.3 *The following are equivalent:*

I) *There is a non-negative concave production function that cost rationalizes D.*
II) *For each k, and all $\alpha^j \geq 0$ for which $\sum_{j\neq k}\alpha^j \leq 1$, if $p^k \cdot (\sum_{j\neq k}\alpha^j x^j) \leq p^k \cdot x^k$, then $\sum_{j\neq k}\alpha^j y^j \leq y^k$, and if $p^k \cdot (\sum_{j\neq k}\alpha^j x^j) < p^k \cdot x^k$, then $\sum_{j\neq k}\alpha^j y^j < y^k$.*
III) *There is a non-negative, concave, monotonic, and continuous production function that cost rationalizes D.*

Proof. We first establish that (I) implies (II). The only difference from the proof of Theorem 6.2 is that the equation $f\left(\sum_{j\neq k}\alpha^j x^j\right) > f(x^k)$ is established by observing that $f\left(\sum_{j\neq k}\alpha^j x^j\right) = f\left((1-\sum_{j\neq k}\alpha^j x^j)0 + \sum_{j\neq k}\alpha^j x^j\right) \geq (1 - \sum_{j\neq k}\alpha^j)0 + \sum_{j\neq k}\alpha^j f(x^j)$ follows from non-negativity and concavity instead of concavity alone.

To see that (II) implies (III), we add, for every j, an inequality of the form: $y^j + \lambda^j p^j \cdot (-x^j) \geq 0$ to the list of inequalities described in Theorem 6.2. Equivalently, in terms of the expression involving μ, this adds, for every j, an inequality of the form:

$$\mu y^j + \lambda^j p^j \cdot (-x^j) \geq 0.$$

Again, by Lemma 1.12, there is no solution exactly when, for each j, there is η^j and for each (j,k) where $j \neq k$, there is $\alpha^{(j,k)} \geq 0$ for which $\left(\sum_j \eta^j y^j\right) + \left(\sum_{(j,k)} \alpha^{(j,k)}(y^j - y^k)\right) \leq 0$ and for all j, $\eta^j p^j \cdot (-x^j) + \sum_{k \neq j} \alpha^{(j,k)} p^j \cdot (x^k - x^j) \leq 0$, and at least one of these inequalities is strict. Since for all j, $\eta^j p^j \cdot (-x^j) + \sum_{k \neq j} \alpha^{(j,k)} p^j \cdot (x^k - x^j) \leq 0$, we get by (II) that for every j, $\eta^j(-y^j) + \sum_{k \neq j} \alpha^{(j,k)}(y^k - y^j) \leq 0$, with a strict inequality if the original inequality is strict. By summing across j, we have $\left(\sum_j \eta^j\right) + \left(y^j \sum_{(j,k)} \alpha^{(j,k)}(y^k - y^j)\right) \leq 0$, with a strict inequality if any of the inequalities corresponding to some j is strict, a contradiction.

The construction of f used in the proof of Theorem 6.2 ensures non-negativity; indeed, observe that $f(0) = \min_k y^k + \lambda^k p^k \cdot (-x^k) \geq 0$. Non-negativity then follows from monotonicity.

6.2 PROFIT MAXIMIZATION

The previous section assumed a firm with a single output y using n factors of production. We now turn to a more flexible formulation in which a firm operates in n goods, choosing a net production vector $y \in \mathbf{R}^n$. If $y_i > 0$ then good i is produced in quantity y_i by the firm. If $y_i < 0$ then the firm uses good i as an input.

A *production dataset* D is a collection (y^k, p^k), $k = 1, \ldots K$, with $y^k \in \mathbf{R}^n$ and $p^k \in \mathbf{R}^n_{++}$.

We are interested in when a production dataset D is consistent with the hypothesis of profit maximization. A *production set* Y is a subset of $\mathbf{R}^n$. Production sets consist of all potential combinations of inputs and outputs which are feasible. We say that production set Y *rationalizes* production dataset D if for all k, $y^k \in Y$ and $p^k \cdot y^k \geq p^k \cdot y$ for all $y \in Y$. We say a production dataset D is rationalizable if it is rationalizable by a production set. We will say that Y is *comprehensive* if whenever $y \in Y$ and $y' \leq y$, then $y' \in Y$.

Given is a production dataset D.

Theorem 6.4 *The following statements are equivalent:*

I) *For all j,k, $p^k \cdot y^k \geq p^k \cdot y^j$.*
II) *D is rationalizable.*
III) *D is rationalizable by a closed, convex, and comprehensive production set.*

Proof. That (III) implies (II) and (II) implies (I) are obvious. To see that (I) implies (III), let Y be the convex and comprehensive hull of $\{y^k\}_{k=1}^K$.[1] Y is obviously closed, convex, and comprehensive. We claim that Y rationalizes D. To see this, it is first clear that $y^k \in Y$ for all k, by definition. Second, suppose that $y \in Y$. We want to show that for any j, $p^j \cdot y^k \geq p^k \cdot y$. By definition of the convex and comprehensive hull, there exists $y' = \sum_{k=1}^K \lambda_k y^k$, where $\lambda_k \geq 0$ for all k and $\sum_{k=1}^K \lambda_k = 1$, where $y \leq y'$ (this is an easy set-theoretic argument). Consequently,

$$p^j \cdot y \leq p^j \cdot y' = \sum_{k=1}^{K} \lambda_k (p^j \cdot y^k) \leq \sum_{k=1}^{K} \lambda_k (p^j \cdot y^j) = p^j \cdot y^j,$$

where the last inequality follows from (I).

It is usually assumed that $0 \in Y$, because a firm can always choose to do nothing. This adds the additional implication that profits must be non-negative.

Corollary 6.5 *Given is a production dataset D. Then the following are equivalent:*

I) *For all j,k, $p^k \cdot y^k \geq 0$ and $p^k \cdot y^k \geq p^k \cdot y^j$.*
II) *D is rationalizable by a production set containing* 0.
III) *D is rationalizable by a closed, convex, and comprehensive production set containing* 0.

Proof. Let Y be the convex hull of the elements of D and the origin, and proceed as above.

Theorem 6.4 illustrates an important distinction between the cases of production and demand. We can say that a dataset D satisfies the *weak axiom of production* if for all j,k, $p^k \cdot y^k \geq p^k \cdot y^j$; that is, if condition (I) in Theorem 6.4 is satisfied. The weak axiom of production is also called the *weak axiom of profit maximization*. Note that the weak axiom of production is a binary condition – that is, we only need to check *pairs* of data points to verify its satisfaction. In our analysis of rational demand, we found that WARP was too weak, and that rationalizability instead required GARP. The reason behind the sufficiency of the weak axiom of production lies in the simpler structure of the problem of production. In the case of demand, utility and the "shadow price" on utility are unknowns. The Afriat inequalities of Chapter 3 state that such unknowns must be extracted from the data. In contrast, in the case of production, profit is directly observable from the data.

An interesting and simple result on identification of production sets is possible. Given a rationalizable dataset D, we can define the *lower production set* $\underline{Y}(D)$ to be the set defined in the proof of Theorem 6.4: Let $\underline{Y}(D)$ be the

[1] This is the smallest convex and comprehensive set containing these points. See Figure 6.2(a) for an example.

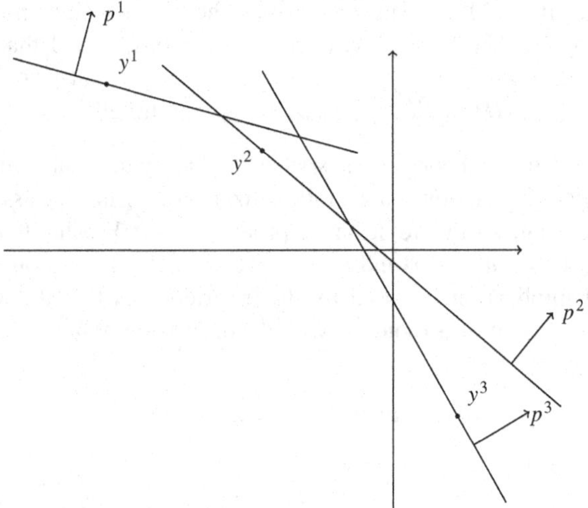

Fig. 6.1 A rationalizable production dataset.

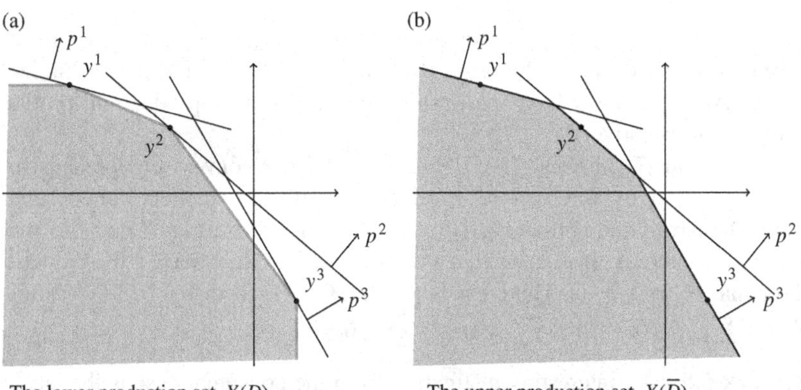

The lower production set, $\underline{Y}(D)$). The upper production set, $Y(\overline{D})$.

Fig. 6.2 Range of rationalizing production sets.

convex and comprehensive hull of the elements y^k of D. We can define the *upper production set* $\overline{Y}(D)$ to be the polyhedron generated by data D; that is, let

$$\overline{Y}(D) = \{y \in \mathbf{R}^n : p^j \cdot y \le p^j \cdot y^j \text{ for all } j\}.$$

These rationalizing production sets are illustrated in Figure 6.2, based on the example from Figure 6.1.

Theorem 6.6 *Let D be a rationalizable production dataset, and $Y \subseteq \mathbf{R}^n$ be convex and comprehensive. Then Y rationalizes D iff $\underline{Y}(D) \subseteq Y \subseteq \overline{Y}(D)$.*

Proof. It is clear that if Y rationalizes D, then the set inclusions must hold. Conversely, suppose that Y is convex and comprehensive and that the set inclusions hold. Let $y \in Y$. Because $\underline{Y}(D) \subseteq Y$, we know that $y^k \in Y$ for all k. And because $Y \subseteq \overline{Y}(D)$, we know that $p^k \cdot y \leq p^k \cdot y^k$ for all k.

As in the case of demand theory, if one wishes to place additional assumptions on Y, these may add restrictions on the rationalizable datasets. One assumption of interest is constant returns to scale: A production set Y exhibits *constant returns to scale* if for all $y \in Y$ and all $\lambda \in \mathbf{R}_+$, $\lambda y \in Y$. It turns out that the only additional implication imposed by this restriction is that the observed firm always earns zero profits (contrast with the discussion of homotheticity in 4.2.1).

Theorem 6.7 *The following statements are equivalent:*

I) *For all j,k, $0 = p^k \cdot y^k \geq p^k \cdot y^j$.*
II) *D is rationalizable by a production set satisfying constant returns to scale.*
III) *D is rationalizable by a closed, convex, and comprehensive production set satisfying constant returns to scale.*

Proof. That (III) implies (II) is obvious. To see that (II) implies (I), we must have $0 = p^j \cdot y^j$ for all j, otherwise, if $p^j \cdot y^j > 0$, then y^j could not maximize profits. And because a firm can always choose $0 \in Y$ as production, profits must be non-negative.

To see that (I) implies (III), define Y to be the convex, comprehensive cone generated by the vectors y^k of D; that is, the smallest convex and comprehensive cone containing $\{y^k : k = 1, \ldots, K\}$. Note that Y satisfies the required properties. It is clear that $y^k \in Y$ for all k. Now, let $y \in Y$. We will show that $p^j \cdot y^j \geq p^j \cdot y$. There exists $\lambda \in \mathbf{R}^n_+$ for which $y \leq \sum_{k=1}^K \lambda_k y^k$. Now, $p^j \cdot y \leq \sum_{k=1}^K \lambda_k (p^j \cdot y^k) \leq \sum_{k=1}^K \lambda_k (p^j \cdot y^j) = 0 = p^j \cdot y^j$.

Remark 6.8 An interesting distinction from the consumer case is that each of the results of this section could be proved with infinite datasets.

6.2.0.1 Nonlinear pricing

Just as in demand theory, we can consider an environment of nonlinear pricing. To this end, for each k, we suppose we have a *profit function* $g^k : \mathbf{R}^n \to \mathbf{R}$ which is weakly increasing (so that $x \leq y$ implies $g(x) \leq g(y)$) and continuous. In this context, we say that D is rationalizable if there exists Y for which $y^k \in Y$ for all k, and for all $y \in Y$, $g^k(y^k) \geq g^k(y)$.

Theorem 6.9 *For a given production dataset D, the following are equivalent:*

I) *For all j,k, $g^k(y^k) \geq g^k(y^j)$.*
II) *D is rationalizable.*
III) *D is rationalizable by a closed and comprehensive production set.*

Proof. That (III) implies (II) and (II) implies (I) are again obvious. To see that (I) implies (III), define $Y = \{x \in \mathbf{R}^n : g^k(x) \leq g^k(y^k) \text{ for all } k\}$. Note that Y is closed, as the intersection of a collection of closed sets (that is, $Y = \bigcap_{k=1}^K \{x \in \mathbf{R}^n : g^k(x) \leq g^k(y^k)\}$, each of which is closed by continuity). Further, it is comprehensive since each g^k is weakly increasing. By (I), for all k, $y^k \in Y$. And if $y \in Y$, then by definition, $g^k(y^k) \geq g^k(y)$.

Theorem 6.9 has an interesting connection with the theory of fairness. If each g^k is a utility function, and y^k is agent k's consumption, then the inequality $g^k(y^k) \geq g^k(y^j)$ states that the allocation $(y^1, \ldots, y^K)$ is *envy-free*. The result characterizes envy-free allocations as those for which there is some set Y from which each agent is allowed to maximize preference.

6.2.1 Unobserved factors of production

In contrast with demand theory (see 3.2.3), we can obtain restrictions from profit maximization even when the choices of some goods are unobserved.

Assume that production takes place in $\mathbf{R}^{m+n}$; prices and output of the first m goods are observed, while of the last n goods, only prices are observed. We shall define a *partial production dataset* to be a collection D of vectors $(y^k, (p^k, \pi^k))$, $k = 1, \ldots K$, with $y^k \in \mathbf{R}^m$ and $(p^k, \pi^k) \in \mathbf{R}^{m+n}_{++}$. Say that partial production dataset D is *rationalizable* if there exists $Y \subseteq \mathbf{R}^{m+n}$ and, for each k, $x^k \in \mathbf{R}^n$ such that for all k, $(y^k, x^k) \in Y$ and $(p^k, \pi^k) \cdot (y^k, x^k) \geq (p^k, \pi^k) \cdot (y, x)$ for all $(y, x) \in Y$.

By Theorem 6.4, we know that a partial production dataset is rationalizable iff it is rationalizable by a closed, convex, and comprehensive production set.

Theorem 6.10 *A partial production dataset is rationalizable iff for all $\Lambda = (\lambda_{j,k}) \in \mathbf{R}^{K \times K}_{+}$ such that for all k,*

$$\sum_{j \in K} \lambda_{(j,k)} \pi^k = \sum_{j \in K} \lambda_{(k,j)} \pi^j$$

and $\lambda_{(k,k)} = 0$, we have

$$\sum_{(j,k) \in K \times K} \lambda_{(j,k)} p^k \cdot (y^j - y^k) \leq 0.$$

Proof. By Theorem 6.4, rationalizability is equivalent to the existence of x^k solving the following inequalities, one for each pair j, k where $j \neq k$:

$$\pi^k \cdot x^k - \pi^k \cdot x^j \geq p^k \cdot (y^j - y^k).$$

By Lemma 1.14, this inequality has no solution iff there are non-negative real numbers $\lambda_{(j,k)}$ such that for all k,

$$\sum_{\{j \in K : j \neq k\}} \lambda_{(j,k)} \pi^k - \sum_{\{j \in K : j \neq k\}} \lambda_{(k,j)} \pi^j = 0$$

and

$$\sum_{\{(j,k)\in K\times K:j\neq k\}} \lambda_{(j,k)} p^k \cdot (y^j - y^k) > 0.$$

This is exactly what the statement of the theorem precludes (note that $\lambda_{(k,k)}$ is unconstrained so we can take $\lambda_{(k,k)} = 0$).

Theorem 6.10 has two immediate important corollaries. The first is the following negative result, which concerns prices of unobserved commodities that are *conically independent* across observations, in the sense that no such price vector is in the convex cone spanned by the remaining price vectors. For example, every linearly independent set of vectors is conically independent, but not conversely. In the case of conic independence, there are no testable implications to the profit maximization hypothesis. This is problematic if we do not know which factors may not be observed. As a practical matter, it seems likely that the larger the number of unobserved commodities, the more likely the price vectors are to be conically independent. In such an environment, the hypothesis of profit maximization is not falsifiable.

Corollary 6.11 *Suppose that the vectors $\{\pi^k\}_{k=1}^K$ have the property that for each j, π^j is not in the convex cone spanned by $\{\pi^k\}_{k\neq j}$. Then $(y^k, (p^k, \pi^k))$ is rationalizable.*

The second is the case in which for all j,k, we have $\pi^j = \pi^k$. The matrix Λ in Theorem 6.10 then satisfies the condition that, for all k, $\sum_{\{j:j\neq k\}} \lambda_{(j,k)} = \sum_{\{j:j\neq k\}} \lambda_{(k,j)}$. The diagonal of Λ is identically zero. Consider a modified matrix Λ' which differs only from Λ on the diagonals, and the diagonals are chosen to be non-negative and so that for all j,k, $\sum_{\{i\in K\}} \lambda_{(i,j)} = \sum_{\{i\in K\}} \lambda_{(i,k)}$. The matrix Λ' now has the feature that all columns and rows sum to the same number. In combinatorics, such a matrix is a non-negative multiple of a *bistochastic matrix*.[2] The reason this is of interest is that, by a theorem of Birkhoff and von Neumann (which can be found in Berge 1963, for example), a bistochastic matrix is known to be a convex combination of *permutation* matrices.[3]

It therefore follows that Λ' is a non-negative linear combination of permutation matrices. As a result of this, it is easily seen that the condition in Theorem 6.10 reverts to a cyclic monotonicity condition as in Theorem 1.9. However, the inequality here is of the opposite sign as the version in Theorem 1.9. This should not be a surprise, as the following corollary relates to profit maximization, and the profit function is well known to be convex, rather than concave.

[2] A matrix is bistochastic if it consists of only non-negative entries, and the row and column sums are equal to one.

[3] A permutation matrix is a matrix of ones and zeroes, with exactly one 1 in each row and each column.

Corollary 6.12 *Suppose that for all j,k, $\pi^j = \pi^k$. Then D is rationalizable iff for all sequences $i_1,...,i_k$,*

$$\sum_{j=1}^{k} p^{i_j} \cdot (y^{i_{j+1}} - y^{i_j}) \leq 0.$$

It is possible to give a "cyclic" version (one ruling out certain cycles, that is) of Theorem 6.10 in the general case, but this condition does not seem to be any more illuminating than the one stated in the theorem.

Similar exercises can be undertaken with partial production datasets, which can derive the testable implications of constant returns to scale and other such hypotheses. We shall not undertake such an exercise here.

6.2.2 Measuring violations from rationalizability

The most common approach to measuring deviations from rationalizability is to find an approximate technology which would have generated the observed data. There are generally two approaches: a most conservative, and a least conservative, corresponding to the ideas in Theorem 6.6. Given an approximate production set, a measure of efficiency as in Debreu (1951) or Farrell (1957) can be applied to the observed data given this production set.

Banker and Maindiratta (1988) suggest that one should construct a technology so that as many data points as possible are consistent with profit maximization. So, they ask that all observed vectors are feasible for the technology, and as many of possible maximize profits. They establish that $\underline{Y}(D)$ generates such a technology. The axiomatic approach of Banker, Charnes, and Cooper (1984) justifies $\underline{Y}(D)$.[4]

Varian (1990) describes a very similar idea. That is, if there is a pair (p^k,y^k) (p^j,y^j) for which $p^k \cdot y^k < p^k \cdot y^j$, Varian recommends that the measure of inefficiency for this violation should be $\frac{p^k \cdot y^j}{p^k \cdot y^k} - 1$. This measure is economically meaningful, in that it represents the percentage gain in profit that the firm could have obtained by producing y^j instead of y^k.

6.3 CHAPTER REFERENCES

Theorem 6.1 can be found in Hanoch and Rothschild (1972) and Varian (1984). Hanoch and Rothschild (1972) considers the case when the rationalizing production function is only required to be weakly monotonic.

Theorems 6.4 and 6.7 and Corollary 6.5 are also found in Hanoch and Rothschild (1972). Again, Varian (1984) also discusses this result.

[4] Their axioms are convexity, comprehensivity, $y^k \in Y$ for all k, and minimality with respect to set inclusion while satisfying these properties. That is, their axioms define the convex, comprehensive hull of y^k.

Theorems 6.2 and 6.3 are basically due to Afriat (1972) and Diewert and Parkan (1983). The idea behind Theorem 6.6 is due to Diewert and Parkan (1983) and Varian (1984).

The ideas of this section first appear in Afriat (1972) and Hanoch and Rothschild (1972). These papers also consider the case where no price data are observed; and the goal is simply to test whether there is a production function or production set consistent with the observed inputs and outputs being produced efficiently. Tests where there are data only on certain of the variables are considered in detail in Afriat (1972), Hanoch and Rothschild (1972), and Diewert and Parkan (1983). Theorem 6.10 is based on the linear programming ideas found in these works. Issues we have not discussed, which are discussed in detail in these papers, are the implications of assumptions on production when profits may be observable, or when no prices are observable, and so on. Färe, Grosskopf, and Lovell (1987), for example, talks about tests for non-monotonicity.

Many of the early results described in this chapter have evolved into the field of *data envelopment analysis* (DEA), which seeks to measure and test efficiency of productive units via linear programming and convex analytic techniques. See, for example, Cooper, Seiford, and Tone (2007). *Stochastic frontier analysis* studies similar questions from a stochastic production standpoint; see Kumbhakar and Lovell (2003) for an exposition.

The ideas on which production set to use for efficiency measurement are due to Banker, Charnes, and Cooper (1984) and Banker and Maindiratta (1988). These ideas are fundamental in DEA. The measure of inefficiency of observed data briefly discussed is due to Varian (1990).

One may be interested in studying particular properties of the unobserved technologies: The papers by Chambers and Echenique (2009a) and Dziewulski and Quah (2014) focus on supermodularity of the production function.

There is a large empirical literature testing the ideas in this chapter in a nonparametric fashion. A few such works which test the ideas in agricultural settings include Fawson and Shumway (1988), Färe, Grosskopf, and Lee (1990), Ray and Bhadra (1993), Featherstone, Moghnieh, and Goodwin (1995), and Tauer (1995).

The Birkhoff–von Neumann Theorem is an important result in graph theory, and is attributed to Birkhoff (1946) and Von Neumann (1953).

CHAPTER 7

Stochastic Choice

We now study the empirical content of individual rational choice when choice is stochastic. There are two possible interpretations of this exercise.

The first is that we lack data on individual choices. There is instead a population of agents, and we observe the *distribution* of choices in the population. For example we may know how many people purchased Italian wine in a wine store, and how many purchased French cheese in a cheese store, but we do not know if those who bought the French product in one store are the same people who bought Italian in the other. The theory to be tested is that of rational agents with stable preferences. Thus we want to know when an observed distribution of choices is consistent with a population of rational agents with potentially different, but stable, preferences.

The second interpretation is that we observe an individual who literally randomizes among different alternatives. We might observe this individual agent over time, enough to infer a stochastic rule that he uses to select an element at random when faced with a given set of available choices.

7.1 STOCHASTIC RATIONALITY

The model of stochastic choice can be described as follows. A *system of choice probabilities* is a pair (X,P), where X is a finite set of *alternatives* and P is a function with domain contained in $2^X\setminus\{\varnothing\} \times X$, where $P(A,x) = P_A(x)$ is a non-negative number for each nonempty $A \subseteq X$ and $x \in A$, and such that $\sum_{x\in A} P_A(x) = 1$. In other words, $P_A(x)$ defines a probability distribution over the set A.

In our first interpretation of stochastic choice, there would be an underlying large population of agents: $P_A(x)$ is the fraction of agents who choose x when the set A of possible alternatives is available. In the second interpretation of stochastic choice, an individual agent's choices really are random, and we know that $P_A(x)$ is her probability of choosing x from A.

We assume here that all nonempty $A \subseteq X$ are possible sets of alternatives to choose from (they are budgets in the terminology of Chapters 2 and 3). We explain below (Remark 7.5) which results hold true when this assumption is relaxed.

Given a finite set X, we consider the set Π of all strict preferences on X. We can identify each element of Π with a one-to-one function $\pi : X \to \{1, \dots, |X|\}$; such a function is a specific utility representation of the preference in question. It is convenient in what follows to describe preferences using utility functions.

We use the following notational simplification. Denote by $\pi(A)$ the set $\{\pi(x) : x \in A\}$ and write $\pi(x) \geq \pi(A)$ to mean that $\pi(x) \geq \pi(y)$ for all $y \in A$. Recall that the preferences in Π are strict, so if $x \in A$ then $\pi(x) \geq \pi(A)$ means that x gives the highest utility in A for utility function π.

A probability distribution on Π is a function $\nu : \Pi \to \mathbf{R}_+$ with $\sum_{\pi \in \Pi} \nu(\pi) = 1$. Denote by $\Delta(\Pi)$ the set of all probability distributions on Π. When $\nu \in \Delta(\Pi)$ and $E \subseteq \Pi$ then we write $\nu(E)$ for $\sum_{\pi \in E} \nu(\pi)$.

A system of choice probabilities (X, P) is *rationalizable* if there is $\nu \in \Delta(\Pi)$ such that for all nonempty $A \subseteq X$ and all $x \in A$,

$$P_A(x) = \sum_{\pi \in \Pi} \nu(\pi) \mathbf{1}_{\{\pi(x) \geq \pi(A)\}} = \nu(\{\pi \in \Pi : \pi(x) \geq \pi(A)\}).$$

Rationalizability has different interpretations, depending on how we interpret the stochastic choice and the system (X, P). If we interpret stochastic choice as the choices of a population of agents, and $P_A(x)$ as the fraction of agents that choose x from A, then rationalizability means that there is a population distribution ν over the possible preferences that agents can have. Then the fraction of agents choosing x is the fraction of agents for whom x is best in the set A. If, on the other hand, $P_A(x)$ is the result of individual random choices, then rationalizability means that the individual's preferences change. Given a choice problem A, the individual agent draws a utility at random from Π, and chooses x with probability equal to the probability of drawing a utility for which x is best in A. Given this interpretation, the model is often called a model of *random utility*.

Before we go any further, it is worth setting down a very basic implication of rationalizability:

Observation 7.1 *If (X, P) is rationalizable, then for any $x \in X$ and nonempty $A, A' \subseteq X$ such that $x \in A \subseteq A'$, we have*

$$P_A(x) \geq P_{A'}(x).$$

The monotonicity property in Observation 7.1 is the stochastic counterpart of Sen's α (discussed in Chapter 2). The property is called *regularity* in the literature on stochastic choice. Regularity is clearly too weak to characterize rationalizable systems of choice probabilities. We turn instead to two stronger properties: the axiom of revealed stochastic preference and the non-negativity of the Block–Marschak polynomials.

A system of choice probabilities (X, P) satisfies the *axiom of revealed stochastic preference* if, for all sequences $(x_1, A_1), \dots (x_n, A_n)$, with $x_i \in A_i$ for

$i = 1,\ldots,n$, we have that

$$\sum_{i=1}^{n} P_{A_i}(x_i) \le \max_{\pi \in \Pi} \sum_{i=1}^{n} \mathbf{1}_{\{\pi(x_i) \ge \pi(A_i)\}}.$$

Note that the sequence $(x_1,A_1),\ldots(x_n,A_n)$ may repeat the same term (x_i,A_i) many times. As a consequence, testing the satisfaction of the axiom of revealed stochastic preference is problematic because one must verify that an infinite number of sequences have the property above. This is never an issue when using other revealed preference axioms, for example when testing for SARP or GARP. It turns out, however, that there is an algorithm that infinitely many steps determines if the axiom is satisfied. The algorithm amounts to checking the existence of a solution of a system of linear inequalities.[1]

In addition to the axiom of revealed stochastic preference, a certain system of polynomials turns out to characterize stochastic rationality. For all $A \subsetneq X$ and $x \in A^c = X \setminus A$, define the number $K_{x,A}$ by

$$K_{x,A} = \sum_{i=0}^{|A|} (-1)^{|A|-i} \sum_{\{C \subseteq A : |C| = i\}} P_{C^c}(x).$$

The collection of all $K_{x,A}$ comprise the *Block–Marschak polynomials* for the system of choice probabilities (X,P).

The meaning of the Block–Marschak polynomials is made clear by Proposition 7.3 below. They are in principle difficult to interpret. Note, however, that a simple calculation gives:

$$K_{x,\{y\}} = P_{X \setminus \{y\}}(x) - P_X(x),$$

for $x \neq y$. So Observation 7.1 means that $K_{x,\{y\}} \geq 0$ is necessary for rationalizability. It turns out that, not only $K_{x,\{y\}}$, but all the Block–Marschak polynomials must be non-negative for rationalizability; and conversely that if they are all non-negative, then the system of choice probabilities is rationalizable.

The following result collects two theorems, one due to McFadden and Richter, and one due to Falmagne.

Theorem 7.2 *Let (X,P) be a system of choice probabilities, where X is a finite set. The following statements are equivalent:*

I) *(X,P) is rationalizable.*
II) *(X,P) satisfies the axiom of revealed stochastic preference.*
III) *The Block–Marschak polynomials for (X,P) are non-negative.*

The role of the Block-Marschak polynomials may seem obscure. The following result gives them a natural interpretation. We present this result

[1] The existence of such solutions lies at the heart of many problems studied in this book: see the discussion in Chapter 12.

before the proof of Theorem 7.2 because it turns out to play a crucial rule in the proof.

For $C \subseteq X$, and any $x \in C^c$, let

$$M_{x,C} = \{\pi \in \Pi : \pi(C) > \pi(x) \geq \pi(C^c)\}$$

be the set of all utilities in Π that rank any member of C above x, and x at the top of C^c. Proposition 7.3 says that, if (X,P) is rationalizable, then $K_{x,A}$ is the probability that all the elements in A are ranked above x, and that x is at the top of A^c; put differently, $K_{x,A}$ is the probability that A is the upper contour set of x.

Proposition 7.3 *The system of choice probabilities* (X,P) *is rationalized by* $\nu \in \Delta(\Pi)$ *iff* $K_{x,A} = \nu(M_{x,A})$ *for all* (x,A).

Proof. The proof is an application of a combinatorial technique called *Möbius inversion*; this specific type of Möbius inversion is called the *inclusion–exclusion principle*. The technique lets us invert variables which are defined by cumulative sums of real-valued functions defined on a lattice. For a set A and $x \in A$, ν rationalizes the system of choice probabilities iff $P_A(x)$ is the probability that the strict upper contour set of π at x is contained in A^c; formally

$$P_A(x) = \nu(\{\pi \in \Pi : \{y : \pi(y) > \pi(x)\} \subseteq A^c\}).$$

Moreover, $\nu(M_{x,B})$ is by definition the probability that the strict upper contour set of x is exactly B. Consequently, ν rationalizes the system of choice probabilities iff $P_A(x) = \sum_{B \subseteq A^c} \nu(M_{x,B})$, or inverting the role of A and A^c,

$$P_{A^c}(x) = \sum_{B \subseteq A} \nu(M_{x,B}). \tag{7.1}$$

Equation (7.1) shows that P_{A^c} is defined by a cumulative sum; namely, one defines it by summing $\nu(M_{x,B})$ across all $B \subseteq A$. Möbius inversion tells us that, conversely, if we know the value of the left-hand side of equation (7.1) for every A, we can recover $\nu(M_{x,B})$ for all B. An explicit formula for this inversion in this case is well known, and is called the inclusion–exclusion principle. The application of this principle in this environment gives exactly $\nu(M_{x,A}) = K_{x,A}$. (See Proposition 2 of Rota (1964) and the Corollary (Principle of Inclusion–Exclusion) on p. 345.)

7.1.1 Proof of Theorem 7.2

The proof requires the following technical lemma, which we state here without proof. Note that the first part of the lemma is an alternative inductive definition of the Block–Marschak polynomials.

Lemma 7.4 *For all* $A \subseteq X$:

I) $K_{x,A} = P_{A^c}(x) - \sum_{C \subsetneq A} K_{x,C}$ *if* $x \in A^c$;
II) $\sum_{x \in A^c} K_{x,A} = \sum_{x \in A} K_{x,A \setminus \{x\}}$.

We start by proving the equivalence of (I) and (III). The proof uses Proposition 7.3 in important ways. First, note that the implication (I) $\Longrightarrow$ (III) is immediate from Proposition 7.3. We shall prove that (III) $\Longrightarrow$ (I) by constructing a rationalizing $\nu \in \Delta(\Pi)$.

The structure of this proof is quite involved, so we divide it into steps. Here is the basic structure. Our ultimate goal is to construct $\nu \in \Delta(\Pi)$ which rationalizes P. We do this by first recursively constructing a set function ν^* on a collection of "cylinders" in Π. Let us consider $\pi^* \in \Pi$, and suppose x_1 is the π^*-maximal element, x_2 is the second highest ranked element, and so forth. We will first define ν^*, the probability of the set of all π for which x_1 is maximal. Using this number, we then find the probability of the set of all π for which x_1 is maximal and x_2 comes second. Ultimately, this will allow us to construct the probability of π^*.

We use the notation ν^* simply because the function is not defined on all subsets of Π, but rather on the set of cylinders described in the previous paragraph. But ν^* will then be defined on atoms (on each singleton $\{\pi\}$); and will thus have a natural extension from the set of atoms to a probability measure. This probability measure is ν. Of course, ν and ν^* will coincide on all cylinders. Along the way we will simply need to show that $\nu(\pi) \geq 0$ for every π, that the associated numbers add to one, and that we have rationalization. Note that the cylinders referred to in the previous paragraph will be exactly the type we need to consider in order to discuss rationalization.

Step 1: Defining the cylinders.

We use the term *d-sequence* for a sequence $(x_1,\ldots,x_k)$ such that all its terms are (pairwise) distinct. For any d-sequence $(x_1,\ldots,x_k)$ let

$$S_{(x_1,\ldots,x_k)} = \{\pi \in \Pi : \pi(x_1) > \pi(x_2) > \cdots > \pi(x_k) > \pi(X \setminus \{x_1,\ldots,x_k\})\}.$$

The set $S_{(x_1,\ldots,x_k)}$ is the *cylinder* associated to $(x_1,\ldots,x_k)$. Let $\mathcal{S}$ be the collection of all cylinders: the subsets of Π of the form $S_{(x_1,\ldots,x_k)}$, for some d-sequence $(x_1,\ldots,x_k)$. We shall define a function ν^* on $\mathcal{S}$.

Step 2: Constructing ν^*, and verifying two important additivity properties.

We want to define ν^* on $\mathcal{S}$ by induction. Let $A = \{x_1,\ldots,x_k\}$ for some d-sequence $(x_1,\ldots,x_k)$ and let R_A be the set of d-sequences of length k with elements in A. The key properties required of ν^* will be the following.

$$\sum_{(x'_1,\ldots,x'_k)\in R_A} \nu^*(S_{(x'_1,\ldots,x'_k,x)}) = K_{x,\{x_1,\ldots,x_k\}}. \tag{7.2}$$

and

$$\sum_{x\in A^c} \nu^*(S_{(x_1,\ldots,x_k,x)}) = \nu^*(S_{(x_1,\ldots,x_k)}) \tag{7.3}$$

We proceed to define ν^*. The guiding principle in the definition of ν^* is the interpretation of $K_{x,A}$ obtained from Proposition 7.3. We seek to construct ν so that $K_{x,A}$ is the probability that A is the strict upper contour set of x. The same guiding principle suggests properties (7.2) and (7.3).

First, for every $x \in X$, let $\nu^*(S_{(x)}) = K_{x,\varnothing}$. Second, for every $x,y \in X$, with $x \neq y$, let $\nu^*(S_{(y,x)}) = K_{x,\{y\}}$. Suppose now that $\nu^*(S_{(y_1,\ldots,y_l)})$ has been defined for all d-sequences $(y_1,\ldots,y_l)$ with $l \leq k$. Fix a d-sequence $(x_1,\ldots,x_k,x_{k+1})$. Let $A = \{x_1,\ldots,x_k\}$ and R_A be the set of all d-sequences in A. If $\sum_{(x'_1,\ldots,x'_k)\in R_A} \nu^*(S_{(x'_1,\ldots,x'_k)}) = 0$, let $\nu^*(S_{(x_1,\ldots,x_k,x_{k+1})}) = 0$. Otherwise, let

$$\nu^*(S_{(x_1,\ldots,x_k,x_{k+1})}) = \frac{\nu^*(S_{(x_1,\ldots,x_k)})K_{x_{k+1},\{x_1,\ldots,x_k\}}}{\sum_{(x'_1,\ldots,x'_k)\in R_A} \nu^*(S_{(x'_1,\ldots,x'_k)})}. \tag{7.4}$$

This defines ν^* on $\mathcal{S}$ by induction.

We shall prove that (7.2) and (7.3) are satisfied. The proof is by induction on the length of the d-sequence defining A. It is easy to see by a direct calculation that (7.2) and (7.3) are satisfied for all sequences of length 0 and 1, where a sequence of length 0 is associated to $A = \varnothing$, and we define $\nu^*(S_\varnothing) = 1$.

Suppose that (7.2) holds for all d-sequences of length $l \leq k-1$. Let $A = \{x_1,\ldots,x_k\}$ for some d-sequence $(x_1,\ldots,x_k)$, of length k. Then we know that

$$\sum_{(x'_1,\ldots,x'_k)\in R_A} \nu^*(S_{(x'_1,\ldots,x'_k)}) = \sum_{x\in A}\left(\sum_{(x'_1,\ldots,x'_{k-1})\in R_{A\setminus\{x\}}} \nu^*(S_{(x'_1,\ldots,x'_{k-1},x)})\right) \tag{7.5}$$

$$= \sum_{x\in A} K_{x,A\setminus\{x\}} \tag{7.6}$$

$$= \sum_{x\in A^c} K_{x,A}. \tag{7.7}$$

Here, (7.5) follows from the inductive hypothesis and (7.3) (by adding over the right-hand-side of (7.3)). Furthermore, (7.6) is a consequence of the inductive hypothesis and (7.2); and (7.7) follows from the second part of Lemma 7.4.

Step 2a: Verifying the two additivity properties ((7.2) and (7.3)) in the case $\sum_{(x'_1,\ldots,x'_k)\in R_A} \nu^*(S_{(x'_1,\ldots,x'_k)}) = 0$.

There are two cases to consider. Suppose first that $\sum_{(x'_1,\ldots,x'_k)\in R_A} \nu^*(S_{(x'_1,\ldots,x'_k)}) = 0$. Then (7.7) implies that for any $x \in A^c$, we have $K_{x,A} = 0$, as all Block-Marschak polynomials are non-negative (the hypothesis). Therefore, as by definition of ν^*, $\sum_{(x'_1,\ldots,x'_k)\in R_A} \nu^*(S_{(x'_1,\ldots,x'_k,x)}) = 0$, we have $\sum_{(x'_1,\ldots,x'_k)\in R_A} \nu^*(S_{(x'_1,\ldots,x'_k,x)}) = K_{x,A}$. This verifies (7.2).

Further, Equation (7.3) is clearly satisfied when $\sum_{(x'_1,\ldots,x'_k)\in R_A} \nu^*(S_{(x'_1,\ldots,x'_k)}) = 0$, because, by definition, $\nu^*(S_{(x_1,\ldots,x_k,x)}) = 0$.

Step 2b: Verifying the two additivity properties ((7.2) and (7.3)) in the case $\sum_{(x'_1,\ldots,x'_k)\in R_A} \nu^*(S_{(x'_1,\ldots,x'_k)}) > 0$.

The second case to consider is when $\sum_{(x'_1,\ldots,x'_k)\in R_A} \nu^*(S_{(x'_1,\ldots,x'_k)}) > 0$. By definition of $\nu^*(S_{(x_1,\ldots,x_k,x)})$, Equation (7.2) is always satisfied when

$\sum_{(x'_1,\dots,x'_k)\in R_A} \nu^*(S_{(x'_1,\dots,x'_k)}) > 0$. To see that (7.3) also holds, note that:

$$\sum_{x\in A^c} \nu^*(S_{(x_1,\dots,x_k,x)}) = \frac{\nu^*(S_{(x_1,\dots,x_k)}) \sum_{x\in A^c} K_{x,\{x_1,\dots,x_k\}}}{\sum_{(x'_1,\dots,x'_k)\in R_A} \nu^*(S_{(x'_1,\dots,x'_k)})}$$
$$= \frac{\nu^*(S_{(x_1,\dots,x_k)}) \sum_{x\in A} K_{x,A\setminus\{x\}}}{\sum_{(x'_1,\dots,x'_k)\in R_A} \nu^*(S_{(x'_1,\dots,x'_k)})}$$
$$= \nu^*(S_{(x_1,\dots,x_k)}).$$

The second equality above follows from the second property in Lemma 7.4; the third equality follows from Equation (7.6).

This finishes the proof that ν^* satisfies (7.2) and (7.3).

Step 3: Defining ν from the $\nu^*(\pi)$, and verifying that they coincide on cylinders.

Now, ν can be defined on Π in the following way. If we fix $\pi \in \Pi$ then $S_{(x_1,\dots,x_{|X|})} = \{\pi\}$, where $(x_1,\dots,x_{|X|})$ is the sequence defined by $\pi(x_l) > \pi(x_{l+1})$, for $l = 1\dots,|X|-1$. We write $\nu(\pi)$ for $\nu^*(S_{(x_1,\dots,x_{|X|})})$ and let ν be the obvious extension of this measure to all subsets of Π, namely $\nu(E) = \sum_{\pi\in E} \nu(\pi)$. Equation (7.3) establishes that $\nu^* = \nu$ on $\mathcal{S}$. Moreover, $\nu \geq 0$, and it is easily verified that $\sum_{\pi\in\Pi} \nu(\{\pi\}) = 1$, so it is a probability measure.[2] Finally, the fact that $\nu(M_{x,A}) = K_{x,A}$ is the content of Equation (7.2). By Proposition 7.3, the proof is complete.

We proceed to prove that (I) is equivalent to (II). The proof is a direct application of a version of Farkas' Lemma.

Note first that (I) implies (II) because, for any sequence $(x_1,A_1),\dots,(x_n,A_n)$, rationalizability implies $\sum_{i=1}^n P_{A_i}(x_i) \leq \max_{\nu\in\Delta(\Pi)} \sum_{i=1}^n \nu(\{\pi : \pi(x_i) \geq \pi(A_i)\})$. The latter expression exhibits a linear function being maximized over a compact and convex set. Hence, there is a maximizer at an extreme point; in this case, there is a maximizer at some $\delta_{\pi^*} \in \Delta(\Pi)$, where δ_{π^*} is the point mass on $\{\pi^*\}$. Then $\delta_{\pi^*}(\{\pi : \pi(x_i) \geq \pi(A_i)\}) = \mathbf{1}_{\{\pi^*(x_i)\geq\pi^*(A_i)\}}$, concluding this direction.

Conversely, let W be a matrix that has one column for every $\pi \in \Pi$ and one row for every pair (x,A) with $x \in A$. In the entry corresponding to row (x,A) and column π we have a zero if there is $y \in A$ with $\pi(y) > \pi(x)$ and a one otherwise; so the entry is $\mathbf{1}_{\{\pi(x)\geq\pi(A)\}}$. The matrix W can be represented as follows:

$$\begin{array}{c} \\ \vdots \\ (x,A) \\ \vdots \end{array} \begin{array}{c} \pi_1 \quad\quad \cdots \quad\quad \pi_{|X|!} \\ \left[\begin{array}{ccc} \vdots & \cdots & \vdots \\ \mathbf{1}_{\{\pi_1(x)\geq\pi_1(y)\forall y\in A\}} & \cdots & \mathbf{1}_{\{\pi_{|X|}(x)\geq\pi_{|X|!}(y)\forall y\in A\}} \\ \vdots & \cdots & \vdots \end{array}\right] \end{array}$$

[2] Indeed, using (7.6) we obtain that $(-1)\sum\nu(\pi) = \sum_{i=0}^{|X|-1}(-1)^{|X|-i}\binom{|X|}{i} = -1$, by the Binomial Theorem.

Let p be the vector with as many entries as there are pairs (x,A), whose entries of p are arranged in the same order as the rows of W, so that $P_A(x)$ is the entry in position (x,A) of the vector p.

Then we can represent a probability distribution $\nu \in \Delta(\Pi)$ as a vector with one entry for every $\pi \in \Pi$. The existence of a rationalizing ν is the same as the existence of a solution ν to the system

$$p = W \cdot \nu,$$

such that $\nu \geq 0$ and $\nu \cdot (1,\ldots,1) = 1$.

By Farkas' Lemma (Lemma 1.14), there is no solution to the system iff there is a vector η and a scalar θ such that

$$\eta \cdot W + \theta(1,\ldots,1) \leq 0 \tag{7.8}$$

$$\eta \cdot p + \theta > 0. \tag{7.9}$$

We proceed to show first that a violation of the axiom of revealed stochastic preference follows from the existence of a solution to (7.8)–(7.9) in which the entries of η are non-negative integers (in fact the two statements are equivalent).

Let η and θ be a solution to (7.8)–(7.9) in which the entries of η are non-negative integers. Define a sequence $(x_1,A_1),\ldots(x_n,A_n)$ by including (in any order) $\eta_{(x,A)}$ times the term (x,A); the sequence must have at least one term since a solution η to (7.8)–(7.9) cannot be the null vector. Then $\sum_{i=1}^n P_{A_i}(x_i) = \sum_{(x,A)} \eta_{(x,A)} P_A(x)$ and, for any π, $\sum_{i=1}^n \mathbf{1}_{\{\pi(x_i) \geq \pi(A_i)\}} = \sum_{(x,A)} \eta_{(x,A)} \mathbf{1}_{\{\pi(x) \geq \pi(A)\}}$. Since η and θ solve (7.8)–(7.9) we obtain that

$$\sum_{i=1}^n P_{A_i}(x_i) + \theta > 0 \geq \sum_{i=1}^n \mathbf{1}_{\{\pi(x_i) \geq \pi(A_i)\}} + \theta,$$

for all π. Thus the sequence $(x_1,A_1),\ldots(x_n,A_n)$ presents a violation of the axiom.

Finally, we prove that if there is a solution to (7.8)–(7.9) then we can take the entries of η to be non-negative integers. We show how to reduce the system to a collection of strict inequalities in η, by substituting out θ. Then we can take η to have rational entries and satisfy the system. After multiplying η by a large enough positive integer, we can assume that its entries are integers. We shall prove that they can be assumed to be non-negative.

To see how to substitute out θ, note that Equations (7.8) and (7.9) imply that, for every π,

$$\sum_{(x,A)} \eta_{(x,A)} \mathbf{1}_{\{\pi(x) \geq \pi(A)\}} + \theta \leq 0 < \sum_{(x,A)} \eta_{(x,A)} P_A(x) + \theta.$$

Hence for all π,

$$\sum_{(x,A)} \eta_{(x,A)} \mathbf{1}_{\{\pi(x) \geq \pi(A)\}} < \sum_{(x,A)} \eta_{(x,A)} P_A(x). \tag{7.10}$$

(In fact (7.10) being true for every π is necessary and sufficient for the existence of θ that satisfies Equations (7.8) and (7.9), by setting $\theta = -\max_{\pi\in\Pi}\sum_{(x,A)}\eta_{(x,A)}\mathbf{1}_{\{\pi(x)\geq\pi(A)\}}$ for a solution to (7.10).)

So it is without loss of generality to assume that η is integer-valued.

We show that we can take $\eta\geq 0$ in (7.10) by showing that whenever $\eta_{(\hat{x},\hat{A})}<0$ then Equation (7.10) holds for some η' with $\eta'_{(\hat{x},\hat{A})}=0$ and $\eta\leq\eta'$.

Suppose $\eta_{(\hat{x},\hat{A})}<0$. Note that for any $\pi\in\Pi$, $\mathbf{1}_{\{\pi(\hat{x})\geq\pi(\hat{A})\}} = 1-\sum_{z\in\hat{A}\setminus\{\hat{x}\}}\mathbf{1}_{\{\pi(z)\geq\pi(\hat{A})\}}$ and $P_{\hat{A}}(\hat{x}) = 1-\sum_{z\in\hat{A}\setminus\{\hat{x}\}}P_{\hat{A}}(z)$. Consequently we get

$$\eta_{(\hat{x},\hat{A})}\mathbf{1}_{\{\pi(\hat{x})\geq\pi(\hat{A})\}} = \eta_{(\hat{x},\hat{A})}+(-\eta_{(\hat{x},\hat{A})})\sum_{z\in\hat{A}\setminus\{\hat{x}\}}\mathbf{1}_{\{\pi(z)\geq\pi(\hat{A})\}}$$

and

$$\eta_{(\hat{x},\hat{A})}P_{\hat{A}}(\hat{x}) = \eta_{(\hat{x},\hat{A})}+(-\eta_{(\hat{x},\hat{A})})\sum_{z\in\hat{A}\setminus\{\hat{x}\}}P_{\hat{A}}(z).$$

So now find η' as follows. Add $-\eta_{(\hat{x},\hat{A})}$ to both sides of Equation (7.10) for all π and make the preceding substitutions. Hence, η' coincides with η everywhere except that $\eta_{(\hat{x},\hat{A})}=0$ and for all $z\in\hat{A}\setminus\{\hat{x}\}$ $\eta'_{(z,\hat{A})}=\eta_{(z,\hat{A})}-\eta_{(\hat{x},\hat{A})}$, we obtain that η' satisfies (7.10) for all $\pi\in\Pi$ while $\eta\leq\eta'$ and $\eta'_{(\hat{x},\hat{A})}=0$.

Remark 7.5 The proof that (I) is equivalent to (II) in the preceding does not rely on the ability to observe the entire system of choice probabilities. In particular, the axiom of revealed stochastic preference is also necessary and sufficient for rationalization by $\nu\in\Delta(\Pi)$ for environments as in Chapter 2, whereby we only observe P_A for A in some set of budgets $\Sigma\subseteq 2^X\setminus\{\varnothing\}$.

7.2 LUCE'S MODEL

We now analyze the special class of systems (X,P) introduced by Duncan Luce. The model is heavily used in applied work, and it lies at the foundation of statistical and econometric studies of discrete choice. We proceed to describe the model, and study its relation to stochastic rationality.

A system of choice probabilities (X,P) satisfies *Luce's independence of irrelevant alternatives (LIIA)* if for any A, and any $x,y\in A$, $P_A(x)P_{\{x,y\}}(y) = P_{\{x,y\}}(x)P_A(y)$. The LIIA axiom is easiest to interpret when the probabilities involved are non-zero, so we can divide and obtain

$$\frac{P_A(x)}{P_A(y)} = \frac{P_{\{x,y\}}(x)}{P_{\{x,y\}}(y)}.$$

So the LIIA axiom says that the likelihood of choosing x relative to y is independent of what other alternatives may be available in A.

An example illustrates that LIIA may be unreasonable. Consider an agent facing the set of alternatives {car, bus$_1$}, who chooses each with probability 1/2. If the agent faces instead the set {car, bus$_1$, bus$_2$}, where the two buses only differ in their color (they go to the same place at the same speed), then we might expect him to choose the car or *either* of the two buses with probability $1/2$. LIIA, however, implies that he must choose each alternative with probability $1/3$.

LIIA has a clear implication. For notational simplicity, write $q_{x,y}$ for $P_{\{x,y\}}(x)$. Suppose that $P_A(x) > 0$ for all $x \in A$, and for all nonempty A. Fix an element $z \in X$. Then we can define $u(x) = q_{x,z}/q_{z,x}$.

Note that LIIA implies that $1 = \sum_{x \in A} P_A(x) = P_A(y) \sum_{x \in A} \frac{q_{x,y}}{q_{y,x}}$. Note also that

$$\frac{q_{x,y}}{q_{y,x}} = \frac{P_{x,y,z}(x)}{P_{x,y,z}(y)} = \frac{P_{x,y,z}(z) q_{x,z}/q_{z,x}}{P_{x,y,z}(z) q_{y,z}/q_{z,y}} = \frac{u(x)}{u(y)}.$$

Then,

$$P_A(y) = \frac{u(y)}{\sum_{x \in A} u(x)}. \tag{7.11}$$

We say that (X, P) conforms to the *Luce model* if there is a function $u : X \to \mathbf{R}_+$ such that (7.11) holds for all A and y. We can make the interpretation of u a bit more precise. Say that $x \succeq^* y$ if $q_{x,y} \geq 1/2$. If (X, P) conforms to Luce's model then $x \succeq^* y$ iff $u(x) \geq u(y)$. So $\succeq^*$ is a preference relation represented by u.

The numbers $u(x)$ can be thought of as utility intensities. In previous chapters, the utility functions have played a purely ordinal role in choice. But in the Luce model, an alternative that has a higher utility than another alternative has a higher probability of being chosen. So the utility function u conveys a meaning above and beyond how it orders the different objects of choice.

The "revealed preference" problem of testing whether (X, P) conforms to Luce's model is very simple to solve: set $u(x) = P_X(x)$ and verify whether the resulting u satisfies the definition. Instead of testing Luce's model, we focus on the relation between the model and stochastic rationality, as described in Section 7.1.

Theorem 7.6 *If (X, P) conforms to Luce's model, then it is rationalizable.*

Before proving Theorem 7.6 we show that Luce's model does not exhaust all the rationalizable systems of choice probabilities. Consider the following example.

Let $X = \{a, b, c\}$. Suppose that the utility of a is given by a random variable $\tilde{a}$; and that there are random variables $\tilde{b}$ and $\tilde{c}$ that define the utilities of b and c. Suppose that the three random variables, $\tilde{a}$, $\tilde{b}$ and $\tilde{c}$, are independent and distributed on $\{1, \ldots, 6\}$ according to the following table:

	1	2	3	4	5	6
$\tilde{a}$	0	0	1/2	1/2	0	0
$\tilde{b}$	0	0.6	0	0	0	0.4
$\tilde{c}$	0.4	0	0	0	0.6	0.

The distributions of $\tilde{a}$, $\tilde{b}$, and $\tilde{c}$ describe a probability distribution on Π, as any specification of random utilities is equivalent to a probability distribution on Π.

Then $q_{a,b} = 0.6$, $q_{b,c} = 0.4 + 0.6 \times 0.4 = 0.64$, and $q_{c,a} = 0.6$. So $a \succ^* b$, $b \succ^* c$ and $c \succ^* a$. Then $\succeq^*$ cannot have any utility representation, let alone one that allows (X,P) to conform with the Luce model.

7.2.1 Proof of Theorem 7.6

Suppose that (X,P) conforms to Luce's model with a corresponding function u; by a normalization we can suppose that $\sum_{x \in X} u(x) = 1$. We use the same notation as in the proof of Theorem 7.2.

For any $\pi \in \Pi$ and j, let x_j^π denote the alternative in X with the jth highest value in π. Thus, $\pi(x_1^\pi) = |X|$, $\pi(x_2^\pi) = |X| - 1, \ldots \pi(x_{|X|}^\pi) = 1$.

The proof proceeds by constructing a probability space in which one can calculate the probability that a sequence of random draws will correspond to a preference π. Consider a probability space defined as follows. Draw infinite sequences in X at random by drawing independently (with replacement) elements from X such that each z is drawn with probability $u(z)$. Let μ be the associated probability measure on X. It should be clear that for any $A \subseteq X$ and $x \in A$, the probability that x is drawn *before* any other element in A is equal to $u(x)/\sum_{y \in A} u(y)$.[3]

For any sequence $j_1 < \ldots < j_{|X|}$ with $j_1 = 1$, let $D_{j_1,\ldots,j_{|X|}}(\pi)$ denote the event that x_k^π is drawn for the first time at draw number j_k. Then $\bigcup_{j_1 < \ldots < j_{|X|}} D_{j_1,\ldots,j_{|X|}}(\pi)$ is the event $C(\pi)$ that the draws will conform to π: so $C(\pi) = \bigcup_{j_1 < \ldots < j_{|X|}} D_{j_1,\ldots,j_{|X|}}(\pi)$ is the event where x_1^π is drawn first; followed by x_2^π (possibly after several repeated draws of x_1^π); followed by x_3^π (possibly after several repeated draws of x_1^π and x_2^π), and so on. The sets $D_{j_1,\ldots,j_{|X|}}(\pi)$ are disjoint, so the probability that the draws will conform to π is

$$\begin{aligned}\mu(C(\pi)) &= \sum_{j_1 < \ldots < j_{|X|}} \mu(D_{j_1,\ldots,j_{|X|}}(\pi)) \\ &= \sum_{j_1 < \ldots < j_{|X|}} u(x_1^\pi)^{j_2 - j_1} u(x_2^\pi) \left(u(x_1^\pi) + u(x_2^\pi)\right)^{j_3 - j_2 - 1} \\ &\quad \cdot u(x_3^\pi) \left(u(x_1^\pi) + u(x_2^\pi) + u(x_3^\pi)\right)^{j_4 - j_3 - 1} \cdots u(x_{|X|}^\pi).\end{aligned}$$

The events $C(\pi)$ form a partition. Define $\nu(\{\pi\})$ to be the probability of $C(\pi)$. We can explicitly calculate ν as follows. Let $h_k = j_{k+1} - j_k - 1$ and

[3] To see this: Let E be the event that x is drawn before any other element in A. Then E occurs if either x is obtained in the first draw, which has probability $u(x)$, or else an element of A^c is obtained in the first draw (which has probability $1 - \sum_{y \in A} u(y)$) and then E occurs. Then the probability q of E obeys the equation $q = u(x) + (1 - \sum_{y \in A} u(y))q$.

$v_k^\pi = \sum_{l=1}^k u(x_l^\pi)$. Then,

$$\begin{aligned}\nu(\pi) = \mu(C(\pi)) &= \prod_{z\in X} u(z) \sum_{h_1\geq 0,\ldots h_{|X|-1}\geq 0} (v_1^\pi)^{h_1}(v_2^\pi)^{h_2}\cdots(v_{|X|-1}^\pi)^{h_{|X|-1}} \\ &= \prod_{z\in X} u(z) \prod_{k=1}^{|X|-1} \frac{1}{1-v_k^\pi} \\ &= \prod_{z\in X} u(z) \prod_{k=1}^{|X|-1} \frac{1}{\sum_{l=k+1}^{|X|} u(x_l^\pi)} \\ &= \prod_{k=1}^{|X|-1} \frac{u(x_k^\pi)}{\sum_{l=k}^{|X|} u(x_l^\pi)};\end{aligned}$$

where the next-to-last equality follows by distributing the product $\prod_{z\in X} u(z)$ appropriately, and using that $\sum_{l=1}^{|X|} u(x_l^\pi) = 1$.

Finally, we have already observed that the probability of drawing x before any other alternative in A is equal to $u(x)/\sum_{y\in A} u(y) = P_A(x)$. Note that this probability also equals $\sum_{\{\pi:\pi(x)\geq\pi(A)\}} \mu(C(\pi)) = \nu(\{\pi : \pi(x) \geq \pi(A)\})$. Hence ν rationalizes (X,P).

7.2.2 Luce's model and the logit model

Luce's model can be interpreted as a random utility model in which the "average" utility of x is some known quantity $v(x)$, but where the actual utility is $v(x)+\varepsilon(x)$, where $\varepsilon(x)$ is unknown and random.

The following calculation shows a method of determining v, and motivates why we can think of Luce's model as the "logit model." Suppose that (X,P) conforms to Luce's model, with utility index u. Note that

$$q_{x,y} = \frac{u(x)}{u(x)+u(y)} = \frac{u(x)/u(y)}{u(x)/u(y)+1} = \frac{e^{v(x)-v(y)}}{1+e^{v(x)-v(y)}},$$

where $v(x) = \log(u(x))$. Then the probability of choosing x over y is $q_{x,y} = \varphi(v(x)-v(y))$. The function φ is the logistic distribution function. Then

$$P_A(x) = \frac{e^{v(x)}}{\sum_{y\in A} e^{v(y)}}. \tag{7.12}$$

In particular, Equation (7.12) alternatively derives from a particular random utility model specification, which is called the logit model. Suppose that $P_A(x)$ equals the probability that $v(y)+\varepsilon(y) \leq v(x)+\varepsilon(x)$ for all $y\in A$, $y\neq x$. That is, the probability that $\varepsilon(y)-\varepsilon(x) \leq v(x)-v(y)$ for all $y\in A$, $y\neq x$. Let $v : X \to \mathbf{R}$ be an arbitrary function, and let G be a cdf on $\mathbf{R}$, from which the terms $\varepsilon(x)$ are drawn independently across x. In particular, if G is a Gumbel distribution, then $q_{x,y}$, the probability of choosing x over y, is equal to the probability that a logistic random variable is below $v(x)-v(y)$. The choice of a Gumbel distribution is suggested by the function φ being logistic. The following proposition establishes that this specification implies the choice probabilities in Equation (7.12). It can therefore be viewed as a counterpart to Theorem 7.6.

Proposition 7.7 *Let $v : X \to \mathbf{R}$, and suppose that $G(\alpha) = \exp(-\exp(-\alpha))$. Let ε be a random vector drawn from $\mathbf{R}^X$ according to $|X|$ independent draws of G. Let (X,P) be defined by*

$$P_A(x) = Pr(v(y) + \varepsilon(y) \leq v(x) + \varepsilon(x) \text{ for all } y \in A^4).$$

Then (X,P) conforms to Luce's model with index $u(x) = e^{v(x)}$.

Proof. Fix A and $x \in A$. Let $u(y) = e^{v(y)}$ and $\delta(y) = e^{-\varepsilon(y)}$. Note that the form of G implies that the distribution function of $\delta(y)$ is $Pr(\delta(y) \leq \alpha) = 1 - e^{-\alpha}$ (the exponential distribution). Then, by the definition of (X,P),

$$\begin{aligned} P_A(x) &= Pr(u(x)/\delta(x) \geq u(y)/\delta(y) \text{ for all } y \in A) \\ &= \int_0^\infty Pr(\delta(y) \geq \bar{\delta}u(y)/u(x) \text{ for all } y \in A)e^{-\bar{\delta}}d\bar{\delta} \\ &= \int_0^\infty \left(\prod_{y \in A \setminus \{x\}} e^{-\bar{\delta}u(y)/u(x)} \right) e^{-\bar{\delta}}d\bar{\delta} \\ &= \int_0^\infty \exp\left\{ -\bar{\delta}\left(1 + \sum_{y \in A \setminus \{x\}} \frac{u(y)}{u(x)} \right) \right\} d\bar{\delta} \\ &= \frac{u(x)}{\sum_{y \in A} u(y)}. \end{aligned}$$

Proposition 7.7 relies on a particular distribution for the random utility term ε. One may ask if there are other distributions for ε that lead to the Luce model. We provide a partial answer in the next result (which is due to McFadden), where we show that if we insist on G being translation complete and the utility index being onto, then the distribution giving rise to the Luce model is unique.

Consider now a system of choice probabilities (X,P), where we depart from the assumptions in this chapter by allowing that X may be infinite. Suppose that $P_A(x)$ is only defined for finite sets A. As before, $x \mapsto P_A(x)$ is a probability distribution on A.

Assume that $P_A(x)$ is obtained from a random utility model, as above. Specifically, suppose that there is a utility v defined on A, and random variables $\varepsilon(x)$ such that x is chosen from A if $v(y) + \varepsilon(y) < v(x) + \varepsilon(x)$ for all $y \in A$. Suppose that the random variables $\varepsilon(x)$ are independent with identical distribution function G on $\mathbf{R}$. Say that (X,P) is *generated* from $v : X \to \mathbf{R}$ and G.

[4] Here, Pr is probability calculated according to independent draws from G.

The distribution function G is *translation complete* if, for any function f such that

$$0 = \lim_{x\to-\infty} f(x) = \lim_{x\to+\infty} f(x),$$

$\int f(x+t)dG(x) = 0$ for all t implies that $f = 0$ a.s. The property of translation completeness is shared by many common distribution functions.

Proposition 7.8 *Suppose that (X,P) is generated from v and G, and that (X,P) conforms to Luce's model with utility index $u(x) = e^{v(x)}$. Suppose that $v : X \to \mathbf{R}$ is such that $v(X) = \mathbf{R}$, and that G is translation complete. Then there is $\alpha > 0$ such that $G(x) = \exp(-\alpha \exp(-x))$.*

Proof. Fix $w \in \mathbf{R}$ and $x \in X$. Let $A = \{x, y_1, \ldots, y_K\}$, and let δ_i be such that $v(y_i) = w + \delta_i$ for $i = 1, \ldots, K$. Importantly, K is an arbitrary positive integer. Note that

$$P_A(x) = \frac{\exp(v(x))}{\exp(v(x)) + \sum_{i=1}^K \exp(w+\delta_i)} = \int \left[\prod_{i=1}^K (G(v(x)+t-w-\delta_i))\right] dG(t).$$

Because $v(X) = \mathbf{R}$, we can let all the $\delta_i \to 0$ from below to obtain that (using the right continuity of G)

$$\frac{\exp(v(x))}{\exp(v(x)) + K\exp(w)} = \int (G(v(x)+t-w))^K dG(t).$$

On the other hand, if we choose $z \in X$ such that $v(z) = w + \log(K)$ then $P_{\{x,z\}}(x) = \int G(v(x)+t-w-\log(K))dG(t)$. Now,

$$P_{\{x,z\}}(x) = \frac{\exp(v(x))}{\exp(v(x)) + \exp(v(z))} = \frac{\exp(v(x))}{\exp(v(x)) + K\exp(w)},$$

hence

$$\int (G(v(x)+t-w))^K dG(t) = \int (G(v(x)+t-w-\log(K)))dG(t).$$

Since, w and x were arbitrary, we obtain that for all w,

$$\int \left[(G(v(x)+t-w))^K - G(v(x)+t-w-\log(K))dG(t)\right] = 0.$$

Since x was arbitrary, we can choose $v(x) = 0$ and note that by translation completeness, $(G(t))^K = G(t-\log(K))$ for all t. We claim that there is $\alpha > 0$ such that $G(t) = \exp(-\alpha\exp(-t))$.

First, note that $G(t - \log(K)) = (G(t))^K$ implies, setting $t = 0$, that $G(-\log(K)) = (G(0))^K$ for any positive integer K. Likewise, for any positive integer L, we have, by setting $t = \log(K/L)$, $G(-\log(L)) = (G(\log(K/L)))^K$. But $G(-\log(L)) = (G(0))^L$, so $(G(0))^L = (G(\log(K/L)))^K$, or $G(\log(K/L)) = (G(0))^{\frac{L}{K}}$. $G \circ \log$ is therefore continuous on the strictly positive rational numbers, and by definition, it is right-continuous, so that for any strictly positive real number r, $G(\log(r)) = (G(0))^{1/r}$. Now, let $x \in \mathbf{R}$. We have

$G(x) = G(\log(\exp(x))) = (G(0))^{\exp(-x)}$. Finally, since $G(x)$ is a cumulative distribution function, we infer that $0 < G(0) < 1$, so we may set $\alpha = -\log(G(0)) > 0$, and obtain $G(x) = \exp(-\alpha \exp(-x))$.

7.3 RANDOM EXPECTED UTILITY

The previous discussion has not sought to limit the structure of rationalizing preferences in any way. We shall now study the random choice of lotteries, and consider only von Neumann–Morgenstern expected utility preferences.

Let Y be a finite set of "prizes." The objects of choice will be lotteries over Y. A lottery is a probability distribution over Y. Let X be the set of all lotteries over Y. An alternative x in X indicates the probability x_i of the ith element of Y.

In the present setting, a (von Neumann–Morgenstern) utility function is a vector $u \in \mathbf{R}^Y$. An expected utility maximizing agent with utility function u weakly prefers a lottery x over y iff $u \cdot x \geq u \cdot y$.

We have as before a system of choice probabilities, but where X is infinite and we define the choice only over finite nonempty sets. So a system of choice probabilities is a pair (X,P), where P_A is a probability distribution over A, for all finite nonempty sets A. More specifically, P_A is a Borel probability measure on X with $P_A(A) = 1$.

We say that (X,P) is *expected-utility rationalizable* if there is a probability measure μ on $\mathbf{R}^Y$ such that for every finite nonempty A and every $x \in A$,

$$P_A(x) = \mu\left(\{u \in \mathbf{R}^Y : u \cdot x \geq u \cdot y \text{ for all } y \in A\}\right).$$

The domain of μ is required to be the σ-algebra generated by all sets of the form $\{u \in \mathbf{R}^Y : u \cdot x \geq u \cdot y \text{ for all } y \in A\}$. Such sets are discussed in a bit more detail below. Further, μ is required to be *regular*, in the sense that for every possible A, with probability 1, u has a unique maximizer.

The system (X,P) is *monotonic* if $A \subseteq A'$ and $x \in A$, then $P_A(x) \geq P_{A'}(x)$. The property of monotonicity, or *regularity*, was discussed earlier in 7.1. By Observation 7.1, any rationalizable system of choice probabilities must be monotonic.

We say that the system (X,P) is *linear* if

$$P_{\lambda A+(1-\lambda)y}(\lambda x + (1-\lambda)y) = P_A(x).$$

The notion of linearity is analogous to the property of independence in expected-utility theory.[5]

The convex hull of a finite set A, denoted by conv(A) is the set of all convex combinations of the elements in A. Write ext(A) for the extreme points of the

[5] If $\succeq$ is a preference relation over lotteries, independence says that $x \succeq y$ iff $\lambda x + (1-\lambda)z \succeq \lambda y + (1-\lambda)z$, for all z and $\lambda \in (0,1)$. In the present setup, the probability of selecting x is unaffected by a mixture with y because any of the intended rationalizing preferences should be unaffected by the mixture.

convex hull of A: these are the points in the convex hull of A which cannot be written as a convex combination of other points in the convex hull of A.

A system (X,P) is *extreme* if $P_A(\text{ext}(A)) = 1$.

Finally, say that (X,P) is *mixture continuous* if $P_{\lambda A+(1-\lambda)A'}$ is continuous as a function of λ, for all finite nonempty sets A and A'.

The next result is due to Gul and Pesendorfer.

Theorem 7.9 *A system of choice probabilities is expected-utility rationalizable iff it is monotone, linear, extreme, and mixture continuous.*

We proceed to discuss the main ideas in the proof of Theorem 7.9. Let

$$N(A,x) = \{u \in \mathbf{R}^Y : u \cdot x \geq u \cdot y \quad \forall y \in A\}.$$

Thus $N(A,x)$ is the set of utilities rationalizing the choice of x from the set A. Note that the rationalizability of (X,P) by a probability measure μ means that $P_A(x) = \mu(N(A,x))$.

The proof of Theorem 7.9 uses basic ideas from convex analysis in Euclidean spaces. Part of the difficulty in the proof is due to the domain of P being subsets of the simplex, not more general subsets of a Euclidean space. So the first step is to recast the problem using finite subsets of $\mathbf{R}^n$ as the domain of P. The way to do that is to assume that Y has $n+1$ elements, and observe that the $(n+1)$-dimensional simplex is contained in an n-dimensional hyperplane. This hyperplane is isomorphic to $\mathbf{R}^n$. Then use linearity to extend P to the domain of all finite subsets of $\mathbf{R}^n$. We omit the details.

Suppose then that we have defined P_A for finite sets $A \subseteq \mathbf{R}^n$. Linearity can be more simply recast in this case as stating that $P_A(x) = P_{A+\{y\}}(x+y)$ for all $x \in A$.

For P to be rationalizable, we need a probability measure μ for which $P_A(x) = \mu(N(A,x))$. So one can define a function μ on all sets of the form $N(A,x)$ by setting $\mu(N(A,x)) = P_A(x)$. The proof proceeds by first showing that μ is well defined, and then that μ is additive on the family of sets of the form $N(A,x)$.

Note that if $u,v \in N(A,x)$ then $\alpha u + \beta v \in N(A,x)$ for any $\alpha, \beta \geq 0$. So $N(A,x)$ is a convex cone. In fact, $0 \in N(A,x)$ so it is a pointed cone, and A is finite so it is a polyhedral cone (one defined by the intersection of a finite number of halfspaces).

To see that μ is well defined on sets of this kind (pointed polyhedral cones), we need to establish two things. The first is a basic result from convex analysis: if K is any pointed cone, then there is always a finite set A and $x \in A$ such that $K = N(A,x)$. The result is geometrically intuitive, and illustrated in Figure 7.1. We do not provide a formal proof of the existence of A and x with $K = N(A,x)$, but hope that the figure suggests one. The dotted lines in the figure are obtained as perpendicular to the extreme rays of the cone.

The second fact we need to establish says that if $K = N(A,x) = N(A',x')$, then $P_A(x) = P_{A'}(x')$. To prove this fact, note first that linearity implies that $P_A(x) = P_{A-\{x\}}(0)$. In an abuse of notation, let A and A' denote $A - \{x\}$ and

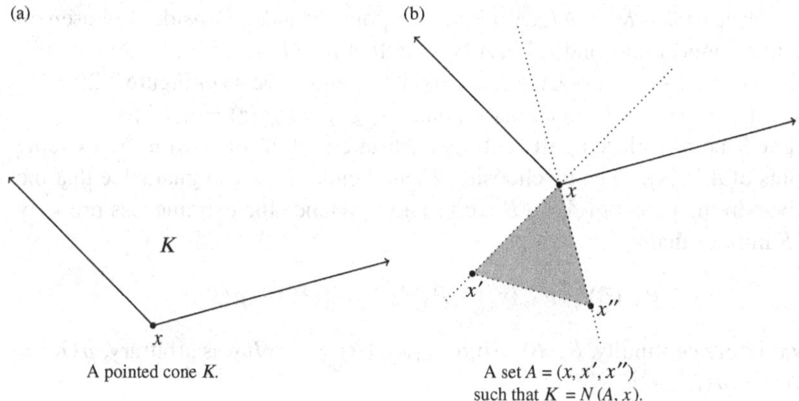

Fig. 7.1 Cones and decision problems.

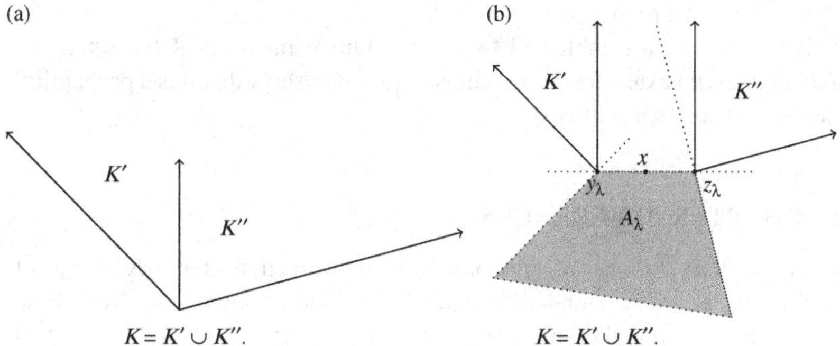

Fig. 7.2 Finite additivity.

$A' - \{x'\}$. Let $K = N(A,0) = N(A',0)$. Then we know that $\text{pos}(A) = N(K,0)$ and $\text{pos}(A') = N(K,0)$, so $A' \subseteq \text{pos}(A)$.[6] Since A' is finite and $0 \in A$, there is $\lambda > 0$ such that $\lambda A' \subseteq \text{conv}(A)$. Then monotonicity and linearity imply that

$$P_{A'}(0) = P_{\lambda A'}(0) \geq P_A(0).$$

The reverse argument establishes $P_{A'}(0) \leq P_A(0)$.

To show that μ is (finitely) additive we need to show that if K, K', and K'' are pointed polyhedral cones (meaning sets of the form $N(A,0)$) such that $K = K' \cup K''$, and the cones have disjoint interior, then $\mu(K) = \mu(K') + \mu(K'')$.[7] We give a sketch of the argument based on Figure 7.2. On the left of the figure we have a cone K that is the union of K' and K'', two cones with disjoint interior. By the previous graphical argument, one can find A' and A'' such that

6 The notation pos$A$ stands for the set of all positive linear combinations of elements in A.

7 The intersection of these cones must have probability zero, if we are to obtain a regular probability measure.

$K' = N(y,A')$ and $K'' = N(z,A'')$ for some points y and z. Consider x chosen on the line connecting y and z. Let A be such that $K = K' \cup K'' = N(x,A)$.

Let $A_\lambda = (1-2\lambda)A + \lambda A' + \lambda A''$, and let y_λ and z_λ be as in Figure 7.2(a). By linearity, $P_{A_\lambda}(y_\lambda) = P_{A'}(y) = \mu(K')$ and $P_{A_\lambda}(z_\lambda) = P_{A''}(z) = \mu(K'')$.

Let B be any closed ball such that the intersection of B with the extreme points of A is $\{x\}$. Then by choosing λ small enough we can guarantee that the only extreme points of A_λ in B are y_λ and z_λ. Hence the extremeness property of P implies that

$$P_{A_\lambda}(B) = P_{A_\lambda}(y_\lambda) + P_{A_\lambda}(z_\lambda) = \mu(K') + \mu(K'').$$

By mixture continuity, $P_A(B) = \lim_{\lambda \to 0} P_{A_\lambda}(B)$. Since B was arbitrary, $\mu(K) = P_A(x) = \mu(K') + \mu(K'')$.

The general argument for additivity is more sophisticated. It relies on basic results from convex analysis and the idea that $N(\sum_i \beta_i D_i, \sum_i \beta_i y_i)$ is independent of β_i so long as they are positive (think of the set of all rectangles with sides parallel to the axes).

Once μ has been established to be an additive measure of the set of all pointed cones, an extension argument is required to show that it is a probability measure on vectors u (utility indices).

7.4 CHAPTER REFERENCES

The two interpretations of random choice outlined at the beginning of the chapter are very standard. Many econometric applications of these models assume a population distribution of preferences (so-called individual unobserved heterogeneity). There is also substantial evidence that agents choose different alternatives when faced with the same choice problem: see, for example, Mosteller and Nogee (1951), Papandreou (1953), and Chipman (1960) for early discussions of this fact. Agranov and Ortoleva (2013) conduct an experiment in which subjects seem to deliberately randomize.

Theorem 7.2 is due to McFadden and Richter (1971, 1990) and Falmagne (1978). In particular, the equivalence between (I) and (II) is due to McFadden and Richter, while the equivalence between (I) and (III) is due to Falmagne. The earlier work of Block and Marschak (1960) had established that the non-negativity of the Block-Marschak polynomials was necessary for rationalization. Lemma 7.4 is from Falmagne (1978) (see his Theorem 3). Proposition 7.3 appears in Barberá and Pattanaik (1986). The idea of applying Möbius inversion to these problems first appears in Colonius (1984), see also Fiorini (2004) and Billot and Thisse (2005). Rota (1964) provides a classic discussion of Möbius inversion and the inclusion–exclusion principle.

Luce's model is presented in Luce (1959). The example of the buses and the car is due to Debreu (1960b), while a related example attributed to Savage is presented in Luce and Suppes (1965). This example motivates a model in which objects are first categorized before applying a Luce-style model, see Gul, Natenzon, and Pesendorfer (2014). There is plenty of experimental evidence where subjects exhibit violations of LIIA. One of the best-known such experiments is reported in Huber, Payne, and Puto (1982): it is called the attraction effect.

Theorem 7.6 is due to Block and Marschak (1960). The proof presented here follows Debreu (1960a). The example showing that there are rationalizable systems that do not conform to Luce's model is attributed by Block and Marschak (1960) to Paul Halmos.

Propositions 7.7 and 7.8 appear in McFadden (1974). He attributes Proposition 7.7 to Holman and Marley, who never published their result. Proposition 7.8 is part of a collection of uniqueness results regarding models of random utility: see Yellott (1977). Hausman and Wise (1978) investigate the related random utility model where error terms are normally distributed.

Theorem 7.9 is due to Gul and Pesendorfer (2006). Our informal discussion of the proof is largely taken from their paper.

There are other natural approaches to stochastic choice which we have not discussed here. For example, Machina (1985) suggests that the choice probabilities attributed to any set may be generated by maximizing a convex preference relation on the space of lotteries over that set.

CHAPTER 8

Choice Under Uncertainty

In this chapter we turn to models of choice under uncertainty. We consider an agent who makes choices without fully knowing the consequences of those choices, and focus on models in which uncertainty can be quantified and formulated probabilistically. The most important such model is, of course, expected utility.

8.1 OBJECTIVE PROBABILITY

There are times when probabilities can be thought to be objective and known, or observable. This is the case, for example, when outcomes are randomized according to some known physical device—such as a game in a casino, or a randomization device used by an experimenter in the laboratory.

We consider two basic environments. In one the primitive objects of choice are lotteries. In the other, the objects of choice are state-contingent consumption.

8.1.1 Notation

Let X be a finite set. We denote by $\Delta(X) = \{p \in \mathbf{R}^X : p \geq 0; \sum_{x \in X} p(x) = 1\}$ the set of all probability distributions over X.

8.1.2 Choice over lotteries

Given is a finite set X of possible *prizes*. $\Delta(X)$ is the set of all *lotteries* over X. We imagine an agent who chooses a lottery. The agent understands that there is uncertainty over the realization of the lottery: over which prize the lottery will result in. But the probabilities specified in the lottery are accurate (or at least useful) representations of that uncertainty.

We investigate a very basic result on revealed preference in this environment.

An *expected utility preference* $\succeq$ is a binary relation for which there exists $u : X \to \mathbf{R}$ such that for all $p, q \in \Delta(X)$,

$$p \succeq q \text{ iff } \sum_{x \in X} p(x)u(x) \geq \sum_{x \in X} q(x)u(x).$$

The classical axiomatization of expected utility preferences relies on the *independence axiom* of decision theory; namely, that for all $p, q, r \in \Delta(X)$ and all $\alpha \in (0,1]$, $p \succeq q$ iff $\alpha p + (1-\alpha)r \succeq \alpha q + (1-\alpha)r$.

Most experimental studies refuting the expected utility model are direct refutations of the independence axiom. The best-known such refutation is through a thought experiment, known as the Allais paradox. Instead of setting up a thought experiment, we are going to assume that we are given data on choices among pairs of lotteries.

The data can be organized into a revealed preference pair $\langle \succeq^R, \succ^R \rangle$, where each of $\succeq^R$ and $\succ^R$ are finite sets. The idea is that an agent makes "binary choices:" choices from budgets with two alternatives, and these choices define $\langle \succeq^R, \succ^R \rangle$. We ask when there exists an expected utility preference $\succeq$ such that for all $p, q \in \Delta(X)$, $p \succeq^R q$ implies $p \succeq q$ and $p \succ^R q$ implies $p \succ q$.

The following example demonstrates that observed data can be incompatible with the expected utility model without directly violating the independence axiom.

Example 8.1 *Let $X = \{x,y,z\}$, and consider the rankings: $(1,0,0) \succ^R (1/3,1/3,1/3)$, $(0,1,0) \succ^R (1/3,1/3,1/3)$, $(0,0,1) \succ^R (1/3,1/3,1/3)$. This is clearly incompatible with the expected utility model: namely, the rankings would imply that $u(x), u(y), u(z) > \frac{u(x)+u(y)+u(z)}{3}$, which is impossible. However, there is no direct refutation of the independence axiom. There is, instead, a refutation of the joint hypotheses of the independence axiom and transitivity. (Note, incidentally, that the example is not a direct refutation of transitivity either.) Our aim is to uncover all implications of the joint hypotheses of independence and transitivity for finite datasets.*

Theorem 8.2 *Suppose that each of $\succeq^R$ and $\succ^R$ are finite, and without loss of generality let $\succeq^R = \{(p_i, q_i)\}_{i=1}^K$ and $\succ^R = \{(p_i, q_i)\}_{i=K+1}^L$. There is an expected utility preference $\succeq$ such that for all $p, q \in \Delta(X)$, $p \succeq^R q$ implies $p \succeq q$ and $p \succ^R q$ implies $p \succ q$ iff there is no $\lambda \in \Delta(L)$ for which $\lambda(\{K+1, \ldots, L\}) > 0$ and $\sum_{i=1}^L \lambda_i p_i = \sum_{i=1}^L \lambda_i q_i$.*

It is worth remarking on what Theorem 8.2 says. The $\lambda \in \Delta(L)$ can be understood as a lottery over lotteries (a "first stage" lottery), which is compounded either with the lotteries $\{p_i\}_{i=1}^L$ or the lotteries $\{q_i\}_{i=1}^L$. When λ is compounded with the lotteries $\{p_i\}_{i=1}^L$, the reduced lottery is $\sum_{i=1}^L \lambda_i p_i$, and when compounded with $\{q_i\}_{i=1}^L$, it is $\sum_{i=1}^L \lambda_i q_i$. The condition in Theorem 8.2 requires that, for weights λ, it is impossible that the corresponding p lotteries are preferred *ex-post*, yet *ex-ante* the two compound lotteries are identical. Figure 8.1 illustrates the condition in Theorem 8.2.

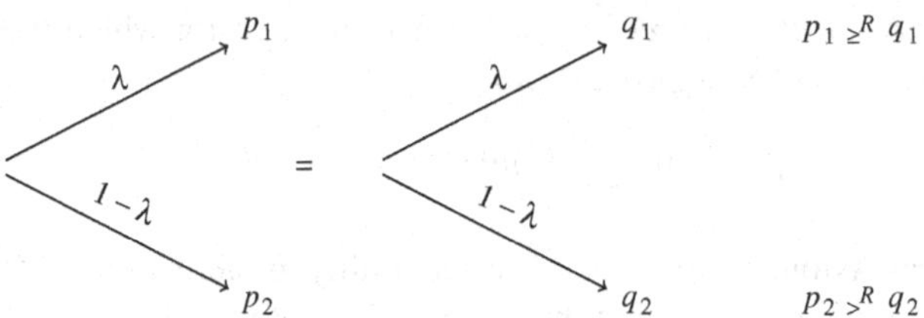

Fig. 8.1 An illustration of Theorem 8.2.

Proof. The proof is almost a direct translation of Lemma 1.12 to this environment. Namely, we seek the existence of $u \in \mathbf{R}^X$ such that for all $i = 1,\ldots,K$, $(p_i - q_i)\cdot u \geq 0$, and for all $i = K+1,\ldots,L$, $(p_i - q_i)\cdot u > 0$. Non-existence of u is therefore equivalent to existence of $\lambda \in \mathbf{R}^L_+$ such that for some $i \in \{K+1,\ldots,L\}$, $\lambda_i > 0$ and $\sum_{i=1}^L (p_i - q_i) = 0$. Since $\sum_{i=1}^L \lambda_i > 0$, we can normalize λ so that $\sum_{i=1}^L \lambda_i = 1$.

8.1.3 State-contingent consumption

Many applications of choice under uncertainty in economic models involve a state-contingent environment. Suppose that there is a finite set Ω of *states of the world*. A state-contingent consumption bundle is modeled as a vector in $\mathbf{R}^\Omega_+$. An agent chooses $x \in \mathbf{R}^\Omega_+$: If the state of the world is $\omega \in \Omega$ then the agent obtains a monetary payment of x_ω. The vectors $x \in \mathbf{R}^\Omega_+$ are referred to as *monetary acts* in decision theory.

The focus of our discussion will be expected utility theory with risk aversion. Consider an agent with a known *prior probability measure* $\pi \in \Delta(\Omega)$ describing her beliefs over the possible states of the world. We suppose that for all $\omega \in \Omega$, $\pi_\omega > 0$. The prior is known. This means that it is observable; possibly it has been induced by some experimental design (for example, experiments in economics often use a randomization device).

Expected utility theory says that the choice of $x \in \mathbf{R}^\Omega_+$ is determined by maximizing a utility function of the form

$$U(x) = \sum_{\omega\in\Omega} \pi_\omega u(x_\omega),$$

where $u : \mathbf{R}_+ \to \mathbf{R}$ is a strictly monotonically increasing and concave function. The function u is a utility function over money, and the concavity of u means that the agent in question is risk averse.

Suppose we are given data on the behavior of our agent in the market. When faced with prices $p = (p_\omega)_{\omega\in\Omega} \in \mathbf{R}^\Omega_{++}$ and an income $I > 0$, the agent chooses x to maximize $U(x)$ over the x that she can afford. It is important to emphasize what the meaning of prices are here. In the development of the theory, we take prices for state-contingent consumption as given, but to have access to such prices in real data requires the relevant financial markets to be complete.[1]

A dataset is a collection $(x^k, p^k)_{k \in K}$ of pairs of a consumption $x^k \in \mathbf{R}^{\Omega}_{+}$ chosen at prices $p^k \in \mathbf{R}^{\Omega}_{++}$ and budget $p^k \cdot x^k$. Here K denotes the set $\{1, \ldots, K\}$, an instance of inconsequential notational abuse.

We are given a probability distribution $\pi \in \Delta(\Omega)$. A function $u : \mathbf{R}_{+} \to \mathbf{R}$ *weakly expected-utility rationalizes* a dataset $(x^k, p^k)_{k \in K}$ if u is strictly increasing and concave, and if $p^k \cdot y \leq p^k \cdot x^k$ implies that

$$\sum_{\omega \in \Omega} \pi_{\omega} u(y_{\omega}) \leq \sum_{\omega \in \Omega} \pi_{\omega} u(x^k_{\omega})$$

for all $k \in K$. We should emphasize that:

I) The prior π is given and known. We are interested in testing whether the agent behaves according to expected utility with respect to prior π, rather than any other (possibly subjective) prior.

II) The exercise is restricted to concave utility functions. Concavity means that the agent is risk averse.

The existence of a known prior π allows us to compute *risk-neutral prices*, defined as follows: for $k \in K$ and $\omega \in \Omega$, let

$$\rho^k_{\omega} = \frac{p^k_{\omega}}{\pi_{\omega}}.$$

Risk-neutral prices turn out to be the relevant prices one needs to use to test for expected utility theory.

We can gain some intuition for how the problem can be solved by considering the case when $u : \mathbf{R}_{+} \to \mathbf{R}$ is differentiable. The first-order condition for utility maximization demands that, for any k and ω, we have $\pi_{\omega} u'(x^k_{\omega}) = \lambda^k p^k_{\omega}$, where λ^k is the Lagrange multiplier for the maximization problem in which x^k is chosen, and we have assumed an interior optimum. Using the definition of risk-neutral prices, we obtain that $u'(x^k_{\omega}) = \lambda^k \rho^k_{\omega}$. It follows from concavity of u, then, that $x^k_{\omega} > x^k_{\omega'}$ implies $\rho^k_{\omega} / \rho^k_{\omega'} \leq 1$. This property can be thought of as *downward-sloping demand*.

More generally, if we have $x^k_{\omega} > x^{k'}_{\omega'}$ and $x^{k'}_{\omega''} > x^k_{\omega'''}$ then we obtain that

$$1 \geq \frac{u'(x^k_{\omega})}{u'(x^{k'}_{\omega'})} \cdot \frac{u'(x^{k'}_{\omega''})}{u'(x^k_{\omega'''})} = \frac{\rho^k_{\omega}}{\rho^{k'}_{\omega'}} \cdot \frac{\rho^{k'}_{\omega''}}{\rho^k_{\omega'''}},$$

as u is concave, and Lagrange multipliers cancel out. The implication is not that two pairs of quantities and prices are inversely related, but in some sense that $(x^k_{\omega}, x^{k'}_{\omega'})$ and $(x^{k'}_{\omega''}, x^k_{\omega'''})$ are "inversely related" to $(\rho^k_{\omega}, \rho^{k'}_{\omega'})$ and $(\rho^{k'}_{\omega''}, \rho^k_{\omega'''})$.

The preceding calculation suggests that one should consider sequences of pairs $(x^{k_i}_{\omega_i}, x^{k'_i}_{\omega'_i})_{i=1}^n$ for which each k appears in k_i (on the left of the pair) the

[1] Prices p can be calculated (uniquely) from an array of asset prices under two assumptions: that the markets are complete and that there is no arbitrage.

same number of times it appears in k'_i (on the right). Such sequences will be called *balanced.*

A dataset $\{(x^k,p^k)\}_{k=1}^K$ satisfies the *Strong Axiom of Revealed Objective Expected Utility (SAREU)* if, for any balanced sequence of pairs $(x^{k_i}_{\omega_i}, x^{k'_i}_{\omega'_i})_{i=1}^n$ with the property that $x^{k_i}_{\omega_i} > x^{k'_i}_{\omega'_i}$ for all i, the product of relative risk-neutral prices satisfies

$$\prod_{i=1}^n \frac{\rho^{k_i}_{\omega_i}}{\rho^{k'_i}_{\omega'_i}} \leq 1.$$

It is possible to write SAREU so that it rules out certain kinds of cycles. We use the syntax above to make the comparison with subjective probabilities in Section 8.2.2 (below) easier.

Theorem 8.3 *The following statements are equivalent:*

I) $\{(x^k,p^k)\}_{k=1}^K$ *is weakly expected-utility rationalizable.*
II) *For all* $k \in K$ *and* $s \in S$ *there exist* $\lambda^k > 0$ *and* $v^k_\omega > 0$ *such that*

$$\pi_\omega v^k_\omega = \lambda^k p^k_\omega$$

and $x^k_\omega > x^{k'}_{\omega'}$ *implies that* $v^k_\omega \leq v^{k'}_{\omega'}$.
III) $\{(x^k,p^k)\}_{k=1}^K$ *satisfy SAREU.*

Remark 8.4 Statement (II) asserts the existence of Afriat inequalities for this problem. The numbers v^k_ω are meant to be the marginal utilities (for money) at the quantity x^k_ω, and λ^k is meant to be the Lagrange multiplier.

We could equivalently have written Statement (II) as: For all $k \in K$ and $\omega \in \Omega$ there exist $\lambda^k > 0$ and $u^{k,\omega}$ such that

$$u^{k,\omega'} \leq u^{l,\omega} + \lambda^l \frac{p^l_\omega}{\pi_\omega}[x^k_{\omega'} - x^l_\omega],$$

for all $k,l \in K$ and all $\omega, \omega' \in \Omega$.

Proof. To begin with, we establish the equivalence between statements (II) and (III), the more interesting aspect of the proof of Theorem 8.3. The reader should note the similarities between the construction in the proof that (III) implies (II), and the construction in Theorem 1.9. The proof of the equivalence of (I) and (II) is standard, and is included below for completeness' sake.

Let $Y = \{x^k_\omega : k \in K; \omega \in \Omega\}$; enumerate the elements of Y in increasing order, as follows:

$$y_1 < y_2 < \ldots < y_n.$$

First we show that (III) implies (II). Suppose that $\{(x^k,p^k)\}_{k=1}^K$ satisfies SAREU. We shall construct a solution to the system

$$\pi_\omega v^k_\omega = \lambda^k p^k_\omega \tag{8.1}$$

$$x^k_\omega > x^{k'}_{\omega'} \Longrightarrow v^k_\omega \leq v^{k'}_{\omega'}, \tag{8.2}$$

where $\lambda^k > 0$ and $v^k_\omega > 0$ for each k, thereby proving (II).

Let k_0 be such that $x^{k_0}_\omega = y_n$ for some ω, and such that

$$\rho^{k_0}_\omega = \max\{\rho^{k'}_{\omega'} : x^{k'}_{\omega'} = y_n\}.$$

For $k,l \in K$, define $\eta(k,l)$ as follows. Let

$$\eta(k,l) = \max\left\{\frac{\rho^k_\omega}{\rho^l_{\omega'}} : x^k_\omega > x^l_{\omega'}\right\}$$

if there is $\omega,\omega' \in \Omega$ such that $x^k_\omega > x^l_{\omega'}$, and $\eta(k,l) = 0$ otherwise.

Note that SAREU implies that

$$\eta(k_1,k_2)\eta(k_2,k_3)\cdots\eta(k_m,k_1) \leq 1.$$

Therefore, for any sequence $k_1,\ldots,k_m \in K$, in which $k_i = k_j$ for $i < j$, we have that

$$\begin{aligned}&\eta(k_0,k_1)\eta(k_1,k_2)\cdots\eta(k_{i-1},k_i)\eta(k_i,k_{i+1})\cdots\eta(k_{j-1},k_j)\eta(k_j,k_{j+1})\cdots\\ &\eta(k_{m-1},k_m) \leq \eta(k_0,k_1)\eta(k_1,k_2)\cdots\eta(k_{i-1},k_i)\eta(k_j,k_{j+1})\cdots\eta(k_{m-1},k_m).\end{aligned} \tag{8.3}$$

Let $\lambda^l = 1$ whenever l is such that there is $\omega \in \Omega$ such that $x^l_\omega = y_n$. For any other l, let

$$\lambda^l = \max\{\eta(k_0,k_1)\eta(k_1,k_2)\cdots\eta(k_m,l) : k_1,\ldots,k_m \in K \text{ and } m \geq 0.\}$$

Observe that λ^l is well defined, as Equation (8.3) implies that one can restrict attention to a finite set of sequences $k_1,\ldots,k_m$; observe also that $\lambda^l > 0$.

The definition of $(\lambda^l)_{l\in K}$ implies that, when $y_n > x^k_\omega > x^l_{\omega'}$ we have

$$\lambda^l \geq \eta(k,l)\lambda^k \geq \frac{\rho^k_\omega}{\rho^l_{\omega'}}\lambda^k; \tag{8.4}$$

and when $y_n = x^k_\omega > x^l_{\omega'}$ we have that, for some $\hat{\omega}$,

$$\lambda^l \geq \eta(k_0,l) \geq \frac{\rho^{k_0}_{\hat{\omega}}}{\rho^l_{\omega'}} \geq \frac{\rho^k_\omega}{\rho^l_{\omega'}}\lambda^k;$$

where the first inequality is by definition of λ^l; the second by definition of η (as $y_n = x^{k_0}_{\hat{\omega}} > x^l_{\omega'}$); the third by definition of k_0, and where we have used that $\lambda^k = 1$ in this case. Therefore we have that $\lambda^l \geq \frac{\rho^k_\omega}{\rho^l_{\omega'}}\lambda^k$ holds whenever $x^k_\omega > x^l_{\omega'}$, regardless of whether $x^k_\omega = y_n$ or $x^k_\omega < y_n$.

If we let $v^l_\omega = \lambda^l\rho^l_\omega$ for all $l \in K$ and $\omega \in \Omega$, then we have solutions to system (8.1)–(8.2).

Conversely, suppose that (II) is true. Let there be strictly positive numbers v^k_ω, λ^k, for $\omega \in \Omega$ and $k = 1,\ldots,K$, solving system (8.1)–(8.2).

Let $(x^{k_i}_{\omega_i}, x^{k'_i}_{\omega'_i})_{i=1}^n$ be a sequence of pairs under the assumptions of SAREU. Since $x^{k_i}_{\omega_i} > x^{k'_i}_{\omega'_i}$ we have that $v^{k_i}_{\omega_i} \leq v^{k'_i}_{\omega'_i}$. Hence

$$1 \leq \prod_{i=1}^{n} \frac{v^{k'_i}_{\omega'_i}}{v^{k_i}_{\omega_i}} = \prod_{i=1}^{n} \frac{\lambda^{k'_i} \rho^{k'_i}_{\omega'_i}}{\lambda^{k_i} \rho^{k_i}_{\omega_i}} = \prod_{i=1}^{n} \frac{\rho^{k'_i}_{\omega'_i}}{\rho^{k_i}_{\omega_i}},$$

as each k appears as k_i the same number of times it appears as k'_i in the sequence, and therefore the λ^{k_i} and $\lambda^{k'_i}$ cancel out. So the data satisfy SAREU, and thus we establish (III).

We shall now prove that (I) implies (II). Let $(x^k, p^k)_{k=1}^K$ be weakly rationalizable by an expected utility preference with prior π. Let $u : \mathbf{R}_+ \to \mathbf{R}$ be a strictly increasing and concave rationalizing utility function. We can then consider the first-order conditions for a maximizing utility: see, for example, Theorem 28.3 of Rockafellar (1997) for a formulation that does not require u to be smooth. The first-order conditions say that there are numbers $\lambda^k \geq 0$, $k = 1, \ldots, K$ such that if we let

$$v^k_\omega = \frac{\lambda^k p^k_\omega}{\pi_\omega}$$

then $v^k_\omega \in \partial u(x^k_\omega)$ if $x^k_\omega > 0$, and there is $\underline{w} \in \partial u(x^k_\omega)$ with $v^k_\omega \geq \underline{w}$ if $x^k_\omega = 0$. In fact, since u is strictly increasing it is easy to see that $\lambda^k > 0$, and therefore $v^k_\omega > 0$.

By the concavity of u, and the consequent monotonicity of $\partial u(x^k_\omega)$ (Theorem 1.9), if $x^k_\omega > x^{k'}_{\omega'} > 0$, $v^k_\omega \in \partial u(x^k_\omega)$, and $v^{k'}_{\omega'} \in \partial u(x^{k'}_{\omega'})$, then $v^k_\omega \leq v^{k'}_{\omega'}$. If $x^k_\omega > x^{k'}_{\omega'} = 0$, then $\underline{w} \in \partial u(x^{k'}_{\omega'})$ with $v^{k'}_{\omega'} \geq \underline{w}$. So $v^k_\omega \leq \underline{w} \leq v^{k'}_{\omega'}$.

Next, we show that (II) implies (I). Suppose that the numbers v^k_ω, λ^k, for $s = 1, \ldots, S$ and $k = 1, \ldots, K$, are as in (II).

Let

$$\underline{y}_i = \min\{v^k_\omega : x^k_\omega = y_i\} \text{ and } \bar{y}_i = \max\{v^k_\omega : x^k_\omega = y_i\}.$$

Let $z_i = (y_i + y_{i+1})/2$, $i = 1, \ldots, n-1$; $z_0 = 0$, and $z_n = y_n + 1$. Let f be a correspondence defined as follows:

$$f(z) = \begin{cases} [\underline{y}_i, \bar{y}_i] & \text{if } z = y_i, \\ \max\{\bar{y}_i : z < y_i\} & \text{if } y_n > z \text{ and } \forall i (z \neq y_i), \\ \underline{y}_n / 2 & \text{if } y_n < z. \end{cases}$$

By the assumptions placed on v^k_ω, and by construction of f, $y < y'$, $v \in f(y)$ and $v' \in f(y')$ imply that $v' \leq v$. Then the correspondence f is monotone, and there exists a concave function u for which $f(z) \subseteq \partial u(z)$ (see Corollary 1.10 of Theorem 1.9). Given that $v^k_\omega > 0$ for all k and ω, all the elements in the range of f are positive, and therefore u is a strictly increasing function.

Finally, for all (k,s), $p^k_\omega/\pi_\omega = v^k_\omega \in \partial u(v^k_\omega)$ and therefore the first-order conditions to a maximum choice of x hold at x^k_ω. Since u is concave the first-order conditions are sufficient. The data are therefore rationalizable.

8.2 SUBJECTIVE PROBABILITY

The expected utility model of Section 8.1 assumes that an agent's behavior can be represented probabilistically, and in Section 8.1 probabilities are in fact observable. However, in most situations of interest to economists, probabilities are not observable. Economic agents are assumed that assign subjective probabilities to the states of the world. It is important to understand when agents' behavior is consistent with the use of subjective probabilities.

8.2.1 The Epstein Test

One of the most basic questions in the theory of choice under uncertainty is whether individuals perceive uncertainty probabilistically. One way of formalizing this idea is due to Machina and Schmeidler (1992), and is called probabilistic sophistication. A preference $\succeq$ over $\mathbf{R}^\Omega_+$ is said to be *probabilistically sophisticated* if there is a probability measure π on Ω such that for all $x,y \in \mathbf{R}^\Omega$, if the random variable x first-order stochastically dominates y on the probability space (Ω,π), then $x \succeq y$; and $x \succ y$ when the first-order stochastic dominance is strict.[2]

Consider a dataset $\{(x^k,p^k)\}_{k=1}^K$, as in 8.1. The dataset is *weakly rationalizable by a probabilistically sophisticated preference* if there is a probabilistically sophisticated preference $\succeq$ such that $x^k \succeq y$, for all $y \in \mathbf{R}^\Omega_+$ with $p^k \cdot y \leq p^k \cdot x^k$.

The following test of the probabilistic sophistication hypothesis is due to Larry Epstein. The idea is as follows. For two states, ω and ω', what type of behavior could reveal that $\pi_\omega \geq \pi_{\omega'}$? Epstein's idea was that if prices in state ω are higher than they are in state ω', and the individual demands more in state ω, then if the probabilistic sophistication hypothesis were true, the only reason this could occur would be if $\pi_\omega > \pi_{\omega'}$.

Theorem 8.5 *Suppose the dataset $\{(x^k,p^k)\}_{k=1}^K$ contains observations l,m for which $p^l_\omega > p^l_{\omega'}$ and $p^m_\omega \leq p^m_{\omega'}$, and $x^l_\omega > x^l_{\omega'}$ and $x^m_{\omega'} > x^m_\omega$. Then there is no probabilistically sophisticated preference which weakly rationalizes the data.*

Proof. Suppose by way of contradiction that there is a probabilistically sophisticated rationalization with associated probability π. We know that either $\pi_\omega > \pi_{\omega'}$ or $\pi_{\omega'} \geq \pi_\omega$. In the first case, because $p^m_\omega \leq p^m_{\omega'}$, we know that

$$p^m_\omega x^m_{\omega'} + p^m_{\omega'} x^m_\omega \leq p^m_\omega x^m_\omega + p^m_{\omega'} x^m_{\omega'}.$$

[2] We say a random variable x first-order stochastically dominates y on probability space (Ω,π) if for all $a \in \mathbf{R}$, $\pi(\{\omega \in \Omega : X(\omega) \geq a\}) \geq \pi(\{\omega \in \Omega : Y(\omega) \geq a\})$.

But the bundle which results by switching consumption in states ω and ω' in x^m strictly first-order stochastically dominates x^m, a contradiction. So it must be the case that $\pi_{\omega'} \geq \pi_{\omega}$. Now, we have

$$p^l_{\omega} x^l_{\omega'} + p^l_{\omega'} x^l_{\omega} < p^l_{\omega} x^l_{\omega} + p^l_{\omega'} x^l_{\omega'},$$

so the bundle which results from switching consumption in states ω and ω' for bundle x^l first-order stochastically dominates x^l, and is strictly cheaper. By increasing consumption in every state, there is a bundle which strictly first-order stochastically dominates x^l and is feasible at prices p^l, a contradiction to the fact that x^l is demanded.

8.2.2 Subjective expected utility

The benchmark model of decisions under uncertainty is the model of *subjective expected utility* (SEU). This model postulates that agents' choices are governed by expected utility calculations, as in Section 8.1.3, but where the prior π is not given, or observable. Instead, the agents' choices are *as if* there were some prior, and some utility function, that could explain them.

As in Section 8.1.3, a dataset is a collection $\{(x^k, p^k)_{k\in K}\}$ of pairs of a consumption $x^k \in \mathbf{R}^{\Omega}_{+}$ chosen at prices $p^k \in \mathbf{R}^{\Omega}_{++}$ and income $p^k \cdot x^k$.

A utility function $u : \mathbf{R}_+ \to \mathbf{R}$, together with a prior $\pi \in \Delta(\Omega)$, *weakly subjective expected-utility rationalizes* a dataset $(x^k, p^k)_{k\in K}$ if u is strictly increasing and concave, and if $p^k \cdot y \leq p^k \cdot x^k$ implies that

$$\sum_{\omega\in\Omega} \pi_{\omega} u(y_{\omega}) \leq \sum_{\omega\in\Omega} \pi_{\omega} u(x^k_{\omega}),$$

for all $k \in K$. We say that such a dataset is weakly SEU rationalizable.

Viewed in this light, it is clear that the SEU model is a special case of both the additive separable model considered in Section 4.2.2, and the probabilistically sophisticated model of Section 8.2.1.

Now one can reason along the same lines of 8.1.3 to obtain an implication from quantities on prices. The complication is that, since the prior π is not observable, one cannot subsume probabilities into risk-neutral prices. Instead, unknown probabilities need to be accounted for in the analysis. The details are omitted; but suffice it to say that we need the same notion of balancedness as in 8.1.3. In fact, we need more: say that a sequence of pairs $(x^{k_i}_{\omega_i}, x^{k'_i}_{\omega'_i})^n_{i=1}$ is *doubly balanced* if it is balanced and if, moreover, each $\omega \in \Omega$ appears as ω_i (on the left of the pair) the same number of times it appears as ω'_i (on the right).

A dataset $\{(x^k, p^k)\}^K_{k=1}$ satisfies the *Strong Axiom of Revealed Subjective Expected Utility (SARSEU)* if, for any sequence of pairs $(x^{k_i}_{\omega_i}, x^{k'_i}_{\omega'_i})^n_{i=1}$ for which

$x^{k_i}_{\omega_i} > x^{k'_i}_{\omega'_i}$ for all i, the product of relative prices satisfies

$$\prod_{i=1}^{n} \frac{p^{k_i}_{\omega_i}}{p^{k'_i}_{\omega'_i}} \leq 1.$$

SAREU in 8.1.3 can be written as ruling out certain kinds of cycles. With SARSEU this is not possible because the axiom involves, in a sense, pairs of cycles (one cycle in k's and one in ω's).

Theorem 8.6 *The following statements are equivalent:*

I) $\{(x^k, p^k)\}_{k=1}^{K}$ *is weakly SEU rationalizable.*
II) *For all* $k = \{1, \ldots, K\}$, *there exist* $\lambda^k > 0$ *and* $\pi \in \Delta(\Omega)$ *such that for all* $\omega \in \Omega$, $\pi_\omega > 0$, *and for each pair* k, ω, *there exists* $u^{k,\omega}$ *such that for all* k, l *and all* ω, ω',

$$u^{k,\omega'} \leq u^{l,\omega} + \lambda^l \frac{p^l_\omega}{\pi_\omega}[x^k_{\omega'} - x^l_\omega].$$

III) $\{(x^k, p^k)\}_{k=1}^{K}$ *satisfies SARSEU.*

We will not offer a proof of Theorem 8.6, but note that it rests on familiar ideas. Basically, (II) in Theorem 8.6 are the relevant Afriat inequalities for the problem at hand. We only care to construct a utility index for a single commodity, which should be the same across states after rescaling; π_ω here acts as a scaling factor. Importantly, these Afriat inequalities define a nonlinear polynomial system in the variables u, λ, π, which presents a significant complication. The proof that SARSEU characterizes SEU rationalizability rests on linearizing the Afriat inequalities, and then using an approximation argument.

8.3 COMPLETE CLASS RESULTS

The above discussion has focused on consumption data, but one could ask the same type of question in an abstract environment of choice. We now assume as given a single observation of a choice in an abstract environment: the set X is some abstract payoff space; Ω is a finite set of states; and the objects of choice are *acts*, mappings $f : \Omega \to X$. The set of all acts is X^Ω.

Choice is modeled by a preference relation $\succeq$ over acts. The important aspect of $\succeq$ will be that it has a maximal element in some "budget," or set of available acts, $\mathcal{F}$; so we know that there is $f^* \in \mathcal{F}$ such that $f^* \succ g$ for all $g \in \mathcal{F} \setminus \{f^*\}$. The existence of f^* can be obtained from a single observation of a choice at $\mathcal{F}$.[3]

[3] Of course, information on the other comparisons contained in $\succeq$ would have to entail additional observations.

A *constant act* is one whose payoff is independent of the state. We identify an element $x \in X$ with the constant act that takes the value x for all states.

A *null state* is a state ω with the property that the agent does not care about what obtains on ω. Formally, $\omega \in \Omega$ is *null* if for all $x, y \in X$ and $f \in X^{\Omega}$, $x\omega f \sim y\omega f$, where $x\omega f$ denotes the act which pays x if ω obtains and f otherwise.

A preference $\succeq$ on X^{Ω} satisfies *monotonicity* if for all $f, g \in X^{\Omega}$, $f(\omega) \succeq g(\omega)$ for all $\omega \in \Omega$ implies $f \succeq g$, with strict preference if there is non-null $\omega \in \Omega$ for which $f(\omega) \succ g(\omega)$.

In this context, a preference $\succeq$ is a *subjective expected utility preference* if there is a function $u : X \to \mathbf{R}$ and a probability measure π on Ω for which $f \succeq g$ iff $\sum_{\omega} u(f(\omega))\pi_{\omega} \geq \sum_{\omega} u(g(\omega))\pi_{\omega}$.

The following result (due to T. Börgers) is related to the results in statistical decision theory known as "complete class theorems," except that no convexification via randomization is required.

Theorem 8.7 *Suppose that $\mathcal{F} \subseteq X^{\Omega}$ is finite and that $\succeq$ satisfies monotonicity. If $f^* \in \mathcal{F}$ satisfies $f^* \succ g$ for all $g \in \mathcal{F}\backslash\{f^*\}$, then there exists a subjective expected utility preference $\succeq^*$ for which $f^* \succ^* g$ for all $g \in \mathcal{F}\backslash\{f^*\}$.*

Proof. Because $f^* \in \mathcal{F}$ is strictly better than all $g \neq f^*$ where $g \in \mathcal{F}$, it follows that there must exist at least one non-null state. In the rest of the proof we ignore null states; it is easy to assign them probability zero at the end.

The proof is by induction on the size of Ω. We actually prove the slightly stronger induction hypothesis: if $\mathcal{G}$ is a finite set of acts, $\succeq$ is a preference on $\mathcal{G}$, and $g^* \in \mathcal{G}$ has the property that for all $g \in \mathcal{G}\backslash\{g^*\}$, there is $\omega \in \Omega$ for which $g^*(\omega) \succ g(\omega)$, then there is $u : X \to \mathbf{R}$ and π on $(\Omega, 2^{\Omega})$ for which $\sum_{\omega} u(g^*(\omega))\pi_{\omega} > \sum_{\omega} u(g(\omega))\pi_{\omega}$ for all $g \in \mathcal{G}\backslash\{g^*\}$. (The proof of Theorem 8.7 will then be done, as monotonicity implies that for all $f \in \mathcal{F}\backslash\{f^*\}$, there is $\omega \in \Omega$ for which $f^*(\omega) \succ f(\omega)$.)

The result is trivial if $|\Omega| = 1$. Suppose then that $|\Omega| > 1$, and that the result is true whenever the size of the state space is strictly smaller than $|\Omega|$. Let $X^* = \{x \in g^*(\Omega) : g^*(\omega) \succeq x \text{ for all } \omega \in \Omega\}$; that is, X^* is the set of worst possible outcomes occurring with g^* (recall that $g^*(\Omega)$ is finite). Consider $\Omega^* = \{\omega \in \Omega : g^*(\omega) \in X^*\}$ and $\mathcal{G}^* = \{g \in \mathcal{G} : \exists \omega \in \Omega \text{ such that for all } x \in X^*, x \succ g(\omega)\}$: Ω^* is the set of states which lead to one of the worst outcomes, and $\mathcal{G}^*$ is the set of acts which realize outcomes worse than any in X^*.

Suppose that $\Omega\backslash\Omega^* \neq \varnothing$. Clearly, $|\Omega\backslash\Omega^*| < |\Omega|$. Further, $g^* \in \mathcal{G}\backslash\mathcal{G}^*$. Finally, there is no $g \in \mathcal{G}\backslash\mathcal{G}^*$ for which $g(\omega) \succeq g^*(\omega)$ for all $\omega \in \Omega\backslash\Omega^*$. If there were, then by definition, since $g \notin \mathcal{G}^*$, g never realizes a worse outcome than an outcome in X^*; consequently, we would have $g(\omega) \succeq g^*(\omega)$ for all $\omega \in \Omega^*$ as well, so that $g(\omega) \succeq g^*(\omega)$ for all $\omega \in \Omega$, contradicting the hypothesis.

Therefore, by the induction hypothesis, there exists $u^* : X \to \mathbf{R}$ and π^* on $\Omega \setminus \Omega^*$ for which $\sum_{\omega \in \Omega\setminus\Omega^*} u^*(g^*(\omega))\pi^*_{\omega} > \sum_{\omega \in \Omega\setminus\Omega^*} u^*(g(\omega))\pi^*_{\omega}$ for all $g \in \mathcal{G} \setminus \mathcal{G}^*$. For $\delta > 0$, let $u^*_{\delta} : X \to \mathbf{R}$ be defined by $u^*(x)$ if $x \succeq x^*$ for some $x^* \in X^*$, and $u^*_\delta(x) = u^*(x) - \delta$ otherwise. Further, for $\varepsilon > 0$, define $\pi^*_\varepsilon(\{\omega\}) = \frac{\varepsilon}{|\Omega^*|}$ if $\omega \in \Omega^*$, otherwise, $\pi^*_\varepsilon(\{\omega\}) = (1-\varepsilon)\pi^*(\{\omega\})$.

For ε small enough, g^* satisfies $\sum_{\omega\in\Omega} u^*(g^*(\omega))\pi^*_\varepsilon(\{\omega\}) > \sum_{\omega\in\Omega} u^*(g(\omega))\pi^*_\varepsilon(\{\omega\})$ for all $g \in \mathcal{G}\backslash\mathcal{G}^*$. Now, for all $\delta > 0$, and for all $g \in \mathcal{G}\backslash\mathcal{G}^*$, we have $\sum_{\omega\in\Omega} u^*(g(\omega))\pi^*_\varepsilon(\{\omega\}) = \sum_{\omega\in\Omega} u^*_\delta(g(\omega))\pi^*_\varepsilon(\{\omega\})$. By choosing $\delta > 0$ large, we can ensure that for any $g \in \mathcal{G}^*$, $\sum_{\omega\in\Omega} u^*_\delta(g(\omega))\pi^*_\varepsilon(\{\omega\})$ can be made arbitrarily small. This completes the induction step.

On the other hand, if $\Omega\backslash\Omega^* = \varnothing$, we know that $g^*(\omega) \sim g^*(\omega')$ for all ω, ω'. In this case, let π be arbitrary, and let $u^* : X \to \mathbf{R}$ so that for any $x \in X^*$ and $g \in \mathcal{G}$, if $x \succ g(\omega)$, then $u^*(x) > u^*(g(\omega))$. Again by considering u^*_δ for $\delta > 0$ large, the result follows.

Theorem 8.7 establishes that, with one observation, the empirical content of monotonicity coincides with the empirical content of subjective expected utility maximization. With more than one observation, such a result does not hold in general.

Given the conclusion of Theorem 8.7, it is useful to have an understanding of the empirical content of monotonicity. We shall explain this empirical content in the case of one observation.

Proposition 8.8 *Suppose that $\mathcal{F} \subseteq X^\Omega$ is finite, and let $f^* \in \mathcal{F}$. Then there exists a monotonic preference relation $\succeq$ for which $f^* \succ g$ for all $g \in \mathcal{F} \backslash \{f^*\}$ iff $\omega_g \in \Omega$ can be chosen for all $g \in \mathcal{F}\backslash\{f^*\}$ such that the binary relation $\{(f^*(\omega_g), g(\omega_g))\}_{g\in\mathcal{F}\backslash\{f^*\}}$ on X is acyclic.*

Proof. If there exists a monotonic and rational $\succeq$, we know that for each $g \in \mathcal{F}\backslash\{f^*\}$, there is ω_g for which $f^*(\omega_g) \succ g(\omega_g)$; if not, then $g(\omega) \succeq f^*(\omega)$ for all $\omega \in \Omega$, whereby monotonicity dictates that $g \succeq f^*$, contradicting $f^* \succ g$. The relation $\{(f^*(\omega_g), g(\omega_g))\}_{g\in\mathcal{F}\backslash\{f^*\}}$ is clearly acyclic, as it is a subrelation of $\succ$ defined on X.

On the other hand, suppose that there are states $\omega_g \in \Omega$ for which the relation $\{(f^*(\omega_g), g(\omega_g))\}_{g\in\mathcal{F}\backslash\{f^*\}}$ on X is acyclic. By Szpilrajn's Theorem (Theorem 1.4) there is an extension of this binary relation to a linear order $\succeq^*$ on X. Define $\succeq'$ on $\mathcal{F}$ by $f \succeq' g$ if and only if $f(\omega) \succeq^* g(\omega)$ for all $\omega \in \Omega$: note that by definition $\succeq'$ is reflexive, transitive, and antisymmetric. Further, if $g \succeq' f^*$, then $g = f^*$. Let

$$\succeq'' = \succeq' \cup \bigcup_{g\in\mathcal{F}\backslash\{f^*\}} \{(f^*, g)\}.$$

There can be no $\langle \succeq'', \succ'' \rangle$ cycles as, by construction, if $g \succeq' f^*$, then $g = f^*$. As there are no $\succeq''$ cycles, we can use Theorem 1.5 again to extend $\succeq''$ to a preference relation $\succeq$ on $\mathcal{F}$ such that for all $g \in \mathcal{F}\backslash\{f^*\}, f^* \succ g$. The preference relation is, by construction, monotonic.

8.4 SUBJECTIVE EXPECTED UTILITY WITH AN ACT-DEPENDENT PRIOR

Many modern theories of decisions under uncertainty are predicated on an assumption that probability can depend on the act chosen; for example, the theory of maxmin expected utility supposes a utility of the form $U(f) = \sum_{\omega\in\Omega} u(f(\omega))\pi_f(\{\omega\})$, where π_f is chosen from $\arg\min_{\pi\in\Pi} \sum_{\omega\in\Omega} u(f(\omega))\pi_f(\{\omega\})$ for some $\Pi \subseteq \Delta(\Omega)$.

We end the chapter by considering the testable implications of the notion that choices are guided by an expected utility calculation in which the probability measure over states can depend on the act chosen. The notion of a dataset will correspond to that in Chapter 2, namely abstract choice.

Let X and Ω be finite sets. Say that a preference $\succeq$ on X^Ω is an *act-dependent probability representation* if there is $u : X \to \mathbf{R}$ and, for all $f \in X^\Omega$, there is $\pi_f \in \Delta(\Omega)$ such that the function $U(f) = \sum_{\omega\in\Omega} u(f(\omega))\pi_f(\{\omega\})$ represents $\succeq$.

It is quite easy to characterize act-dependent probability preferences. Say that a preference $\succeq$ satisfies *uniform monotonicity* if $f \succeq g$ whenever $f, g \in X^\Omega$ are such that for all $\omega, \omega' \in \Omega, f(\omega) \succeq g(\omega')$.[4]

Proposition 8.9 *If X^Ω is finite, a preference $\succeq$ has an act-dependent probability representation iff it satisfies uniform monotonicity.*

Proof. Suppose $\succeq$ is a preference satisfying uniform monotonicity. Since X^Ω is finite and $\succeq$ is a preference relation, there exists $U : X^\Omega \to \mathbf{R}$ which represents $\succeq$. Define $u(x) = U(x)$, where $U(x)$ is the value of U applied to the constant act taking outcome x. Note that for every f, by uniform monotonicity,

$$\min_{\omega\in\Omega} u(f(\omega)) \leq U(f) \leq \max_{\omega\in\Omega} u(f(\omega)).$$

Therefore, $U(f)$ can be expressed as a convex combination of $\min_{\omega\in\Omega} u(f(\omega))$ and $\max_{\omega\in\Omega} u(f(\omega))$. Choose the probability π_f so as to obtain the result of this convex combination.

The other direction is equally simple; suppose that for all $\omega, \omega' \in \Omega, f(\omega) \succeq g(\omega')$: $U(f) = \sum_{\omega\in\Omega} u(f(\omega))\pi_f(\{\omega\}) \geq \min_{\omega\in\Omega} u(f(\omega)) \geq \max_{\omega\in\Omega} u(g(\omega)) \geq \sum_{\omega\in\Omega} u(f(\omega))\pi_g(\{\omega\}) = U(g)$.

We can now speak of a choice function defined on a collection of "budgets," or sets of feasible acts Σ, each element of Σ being a subset of X^Ω. We assume that Σ is *certainty inclusive*, in the sense that for all $x, y \in X$, $\{x, y\} \in \Sigma$. Thus, choice from every pair of certain outcomes can be observed. According to this choice function, we have our standard revealed preference pair, $\langle \succeq^c, \succ^c \rangle$, as defined in Chapter 2. We introduce a new relation $\succeq'$ defined by $f \succeq' g$ if $f(\omega) \succeq^c g(\omega')$ for all $\omega, \omega' \in \Omega$.

With the property of certainty inclusiveness, the empirical content of uniform monotonicity is quite easy to describe using previous results.

[4] With a slight abuse of notation, an element of X is identified with a constant act returning that element.

Theorem 8.10 *A choice function on a certainty inclusive domain is strongly rationalized by a preference relation satisfying uniform monotonicity iff* $\langle \succeq^c \cup \succeq', \succ^c \rangle$ *is acyclic.*

Proof. Follows easily from Corollary 1.6 and Theorem 2.5.

8.5 CHAPTER REFERENCES

Allais' paradox is due to Allais (1953). He presents a classic test of the expected utility hypothesis. Typical choices in Allais' experiment directly violate the independence axiom. Theorem 8.2 appears in Fishburn (1974), among other related results. Bar-Shira (1992) also investigates the set of linear inequalities arising in this problem, and uses it to bound risk aversion in the context of monetary lotteries. Border (1992) extends this idea to a choice-theoretic approach, assuming monetary lotteries and a strictly increasing utility index. Border's approach is closer to the ideas in Afriat's Theorem. Kim (1996) also provides a generalization of this result.

The equivalence between (I) and (III) in Theorem 8.3 is essentially taken from Kubler, Selden, and Wei (2014). The equivalence between (I) and (II) in Theorem 8.3 is a version of Afriat inequalities for this problem: it appears in Green and Srivastava (1986), Varian (1983b), Varian (1988b), Bayer, Bose, Polisson, Renou, and Quah (2012), and Diewert (2012). The recent paper by Chambers, Liu, and Martinez (2014) provides a revealed preference axiom for the case of multiple goods in each state (the setup of Green and Srivastava, 1986). Green and Osband (1991) study a version of the objective probability problem in which the probability measure over states is changing, and "demand" as a function of the objective probability measure over states is observed. Park (1998) conducts a related investigation of the weighted expected utility model of Hong (1983).

The Epstein Test is due to Epstein (2000), who viewed his test as a market counterpart of Ellsberg's paradox (Ellsberg, 1961). Theorem 8.6 is based on the work of Green and Srivastava (1986), who take π as an observable, and also provide a cyclic monotonicity-style test; Kim (1991) presents related results in this direction. Bayer, Bose, Polisson, Renou, and Quah (2012) investigate related conditions which arise in the context of ambiguity models.

Axiomatizations of subjective expected utility have a long history, but the most important are due to Savage (1954) and Anscombe and Aumann (1963). The latter of these provides an axiomatization for finite states of the world. Theorem 8.6 is due to Echenique and Saito (2013), which also presents a characterization of state-dependent utility (i.e. additively separable utility across states). The equivalence between rationalizability and the version of Afriat inequalities in Theorem 8.6 is the same as obtained by Green and Srivastava (1986) (presented in Theorem 8.3 for the case of objective expected utility, only existentially quantified over the prior). The papers by Bayer, Bose, Polisson, Renou, and Quah (2012), Ahn, Choi, Gale, and Kariv (2014), and

Hey and Pace (2014) apply revealed preference tests to experimental data on uncertainty and subjective probabilities.

Polisson, Renou, and Quah (2013) also develop a system of Afriat inequalities for the model of subjective expected utility, and for other models. One important difference between the work of Polisson and Quah and other papers is that they do not require the utility over money to be concave.

Chambers, Echenique, and Saito (2015) give revealed preference axioms for translation invariant and homothetic models of choice under uncertainty, including the maxmin model of Gilboa and Schmeidler (1989), and the expected utility model when the utility function takes the specific "constant absolute risk aversion" (CARA) or "constant relative risk aversion" (CRRA) form.

The paper by Richter and Shapiro (1978) should be mentioned as well. They study the design of a set of pairwise comparisons so that, given the outcome of such a pair of comparisons, a definitive statement can be made about the agents' subjective probabilities. An example of such a statement is whether the probability of state ω_1 is at least twice that of state ω_2.

Theorem 8.7 is due to Börgers (1993), and the interpretation offered here is due to Lo (2000). It can be shown that for the primitive $\succeq$, one can choose $\succeq^*$ to have the same null states and the same ranking over constant acts as $\succeq$. This result is related to a class of results in statistical decision theory known as "complete class theorems," which establish related results when the outcome space has a convex structure due to randomization and linearity of payoffs in randomization. These results are originally due to Wald (1950, 1947a,b); Dvoretzky, Wald, and Wolfowitz (1951) use the fact that the range of a nonatomic vector measure is convex and compact to establish a similar result without any required randomization. A classic reference on these topics is Ferguson (1967).

Bossert and Suzumura (2012) establish Theorem 8.10. The question of the empirical content of preferences satisfying uniform monotonicity on domains which do not satisfy certainty inclusiveness is open, as is the same question for monotonic preferences.

Finally, there is a literature investigating the empirical content of different updating rules for probabilistic beliefs. Shmaya and Yariv (2012) characterize the empirical content of Bayes' rule, and show that it is equivalent to many apparently more general classes of updating rules.

CHAPTER 9

General Equilibrium Theory

The previous chapters deal with theories of individual agents' behavior. In the rest of the book, we turn to economic theories that predict group or societal outcomes. We first turn our attention to general equilibrium theory.

General equilibrium theory can often be studied through a reduced-form model, the excess demand function of an economy. The equilibrium outcomes of the economy are given as zeroes of the excess demand function. There are two immediate questions about the scope of the model: What is the class of excess demand functions that can arise from a well-behaved economy? And which sets of prices can be equilibrium prices?

The answers to these questions carry a largely negative message about general equilibrium theory. The Sonnenschein–Mantel–Debreu Theorem (as we shall refer to it) shows that, roughly speaking, any continuous function that satisfies Walras' law can be the aggregate excess demand function of a very well-behaved economy. The result implies that any compact set of strictly positive prices can be the set of Walrasian equilibrium prices of a well-behaved economy. No additional constraints are obtained by insisting on basic regularity properties of the equilibria.

Considered as data on an economy, an excess demand function, or a set of putative equilibrium prices, may seem odd. The next set of questions under study is much more similar to the approach in Chapter 3. If we assume that we can observe equilibria for different vectors of endowments (in a sense, we can sample from the "equilibrium manifold"), then the theory of general equilibrium can be refuted: There are nonrationalizable datasets. The theory is testable if we can observe prices from different endowment vectors. The nature of the testable implications follow from a very general principle, the Tarski–Seidenberg Theorem, which we shall also review here.

We focus on a model of an economy where all economic activity takes the form of exchange. There are I consumers; each consumer i is described by a pair $(\succeq_i, \omega_i)$, where $\succeq_i$ is a preference relation on $\mathbf{R}^n_+$, and $\omega_i \in \mathbf{R}^n_+$ is an *endowment vector*. An *exchange economy* is a tuple $\mathcal{E} = (\succeq_i, \omega_i)_{i=1}^I$.

When $\succeq_i$ is continuous, strictly convex, and locally nonsatiated, the *demand function* of agent i is well defined as $d^i(p,M) = \arg\max_{\succeq_i}\{x \in \mathbf{R}^n_+ : p \cdot x \leq M\}$, for $p \in \mathbf{R}^n_{++}$ and $M > 0$. The *excess demand function* of agent i is $Z^i(p) = d^i(p, p \cdot \omega_i) - \omega_i$. Finally, the *aggregate excess demand function* of the economy $\mathcal{E}$ is $Z = \sum_{i=1}^I Z^i$. The function Z is continuous and satisfies $p \cdot Z(p) = 0$ for all p in its domain, a property called *Walras' Law*. A vector $p \in \mathbf{R}^n_{++}$ is a *Walrasian equilibrium price* if $Z(p) = 0$.

One can define the weak axiom of revealed preference for excess demand functions. Indeed, note that WARP for individual demand functions says that there cannot exist prices p and q such that $q \cdot d^i(p, p \cdot \omega_i) < q \cdot \omega_i$ and $p \cdot d^i(q, q \cdot \omega_i) \leq p \cdot \omega_i$. So we say that an individual excess demand function Z^i satisfies WARP if there are no p and q such that $q \cdot Z^i(p) < 0$ and $p \cdot Z^i(q) \leq 0$. Moreover, Z^i satisfies a version of the strong axiom of revealed preference, which states that there is no sequence of prices $p_1, \ldots p_K$ with $p_k \cdot Z^i(p_{k+1}) \leq 0$, $k = 1, \ldots,$ $K-1$ and $p_K \cdot Z^i(p_1) < 0$.

9.1 THE SONNENSCHEIN–MANTEL–DEBREU THEOREM

We know that the aggregate excess demand function of an exchange economy satisfies Walras' Law and has homogeneity of degree zero. We ask here whether there are any other properties which are systematically satisfied by excess demand. Let $S = \{p \in \mathbf{R}^n_+ : \|p\| = 1\}$ be the intersection of the unit sphere with the non-negative orthant, and let $\Delta = \{p \in \mathbf{R}^n_+ : \sum_i p_i = 1\}$. By homogeneity, one can, without loss of generality, restrict attention to prices either in S or Δ, as demand functions and excess demand functions are homogeneous of degree zero. Depending on the context, it is easier to work with S or Δ. The relative interior of S is denoted by int S. Likewise the relative interior of Δ is denoted by int Δ.

Sonnenschein–Mantel–Debreu Theorem *Suppose $Z : S \to X$ is a continuous function satisfying Walras' Law and let $K \subseteq$ int S be compact. Then there exists an exchange economy $\mathcal{E} = (\succeq_i, \omega_i)_{i=1}^n$, in which each $\succeq_i$ is continuous, strictly convex, and monotonic, such that the sum of individuals agents' excess demand functions in $\mathcal{E}$ coincides with Z on K.*

The Sonnenschein–Mantel–Debreu (SMD) Theorem has a complicated proof, but we present the gist of it in Section 9.1.1. Note that the economy $\mathcal{E}$ in the SMD Theorem has a number of agents that is equal to the number of goods. The next result shows that the conclusion of the theorem does not hold with fewer consumers.

Proposition 9.1 *There is a function Z satisfying the hypotheses of the SMD Theorem, and a nonempty compact set $K \subseteq$ int S such that Z cannot be written as the sum of fewer than n individual agents' excess demand functions on K.*

Proof. For any $p \in S$, let $T(p)$ denote the subspace that is orthogonal to p in $\mathbf{R}^n_+$. Choose $p^0 \in \text{int}\, S$ arbitrarily, and let $\varepsilon > 0$ be such that $p^0_i > \varepsilon$ for all i. Let K be the set of $p \in \text{int}\, S$ with $p_i \geq \varepsilon$ for all i. The set K is compact.

Define the function $Z : S \to \mathbf{R}^n_+$ by letting $Z(p)$ be the projection of the vector $(p - p^0)$ on to $T(p)$.[1] Note that Z is continuous and satisfies Walras' Law, as $p \cdot Z(p) = 0$ because $Z(p)$ is orthogonal to p. Observe that, for any $p \in S \backslash \{p^0\}$,

$$(p - p^0) \cdot Z(p) > 0, \tag{9.1}$$

because $p - p^0$ can never be orthogonal to p, as both p and p^0 are in the unit sphere. This is a basic property of projections.

Suppose, toward a contradiction, that there are $k < n$ individual excess demand functions such that $Z(p) = \sum_{i=1}^k Z^i(p)$ for all $p \in K$. Walras' Law implies that $Z^i(p^0) \in T(p^0)$. The vectors $Z^i(p^0)$, $i = 1, \ldots, k$, form a linearly dependent set, as $0 = Z(p^0) = \sum_{i=1}^k Z^i(p^0)$. Let Λ be the linear subspace of $T(p^0)$ spanned by the vectors $Z^i(p^0)$, $i = 1, \ldots, k$.

The dimension of Λ is strictly smaller than the dimension of $T(p^0)$, because $\dim \Lambda < k \leq n - 1 = \dim T(p^0)$. Then the orthogonal complement $\Lambda^\perp$ of Λ in $T(p^0)$ is nontrivial. Since p^0 projects to 0 in $T(p^0)$, one can choose $\eta \in \Lambda^\perp$ small enough so that there is $\bar{p} \in K$ such that $\bar{p} \neq p^0$, and $\bar{p} - p^0$ projects to η in $T(p^0)$.

Choose an arbitrary i. Then

$$(\bar{p} - p^0) \cdot Z^i(p^0) = (\bar{p} - p^0 - \eta) \cdot Z^i(p^0) + \eta \cdot Z^i(p^0) = 0.$$

This follows because we know $(\bar{p} - p^0 - \eta) \cdot Z^i(p^0) = 0$ as $Z^i(p^0) \in T(p^0)$ and $(\bar{p} - p^0 - \eta)$ is the orthogonal projection of $(\bar{p} - p^0)$ onto p^0. Further, we know $\eta \cdot Z^i(p^0) = 0$ as $Z^i(p^0) \in \Lambda$ and $\eta \in \Lambda^\perp$. The function Z^i satisfies the weak axiom of revealed preference, because it is an individual agent's excess demand function. Then by Walras' Law, $(\bar{p} - p^0) \cdot Z^i(p^0) = 0$ implies that $\bar{p} \cdot Z^i(p^0) \leq 0$. By the weak axiom then, $p^0 \cdot Z^i(\bar{p}) \geq 0 = \bar{p} \cdot Z^i(\bar{p})$. Thus $(\bar{p} - p^0) \cdot Z^i(\bar{p}) \leq 0$. Since this holds for all i, we obtain that $(\bar{p} - p^0) \cdot Z(\bar{p}) \leq 0$, in contradiction of (9.1).

The SMD Theorem talks about the behavior of Z on a compact subset of the sphere; but students of general equilibrium theory know that many results rely on the behavior of Z close to the boundary of its domain, when some prices are close to zero. The next theorem says that one can decompose Z on all of its domain as the sum of individual excess demand functions. The decomposition is of a weaker nature, though.

Theorem 9.2 *Suppose $Z : S \to X$ is a function satisfying Walras' Law that is bounded below. Then there are functions $Z^i : S \to X$, $i = 1, \ldots, n$, satisfying Walras' Law and the Strong Axiom of Revealed Preference, for which $Z = \sum_{i=1}^n Z^i$.*

[1] Formally, $Z(p) = p - p^0 - pp'(p - p^0) = pp'p^0 - p^0$, since $||p|| = 1; p'$ is the transpose of p.

A proof of Theorem 9.2 can be obtained with arguments similar to those in Section 9.1.1.

The SMD Theorem says that general equilibrium theory does not restrict aggregate excess demand functions. It may not seem natural to assume that someone could "observe" an excess demand function. It makes more sense that one could observe a set of putative equilibrium prices. The theorem implies, however, that any compact set of prices can be Walrasian equilibrium prices:

Corollary 9.3 *Let $K \subseteq \text{int}\, S$ be compact. For any compact set $K' \subseteq \text{int}\, S$ with $K \subseteq K'$, there exists an exchange economy $\mathcal{E} = (\succeq_i, \omega_i)_{i=1}^n$, in which each $\succeq_i$ is continuous, strictly convex, and monotonic, for which K is the set of Walrasian equilibrium prices of $\mathcal{E}$ in K'.*

Proof. Let $g(p) = (\mathbf{1}_1 - pp'\mathbf{1}_1)$ (one of the projections in the proof of the SMD Theorem in Section 9.1.1, below),

$$f(p) = \inf_{q \in K} \|p - q\|,$$

and set $Z(p) = f(p)g(p)$. Note that Z is continuous, $p \cdot Z(p) = f(p)(p \cdot g(p)) = 0$, and $Z(p) = 0$ iff $p \in K \cup \{\mathbf{1}_1\}$. So for $p \in \text{int}\, S$, $Z(p) = 0$ iff $p \in K$. The result follows from the SMD Theorem applied to Z and K'.

Some classic results of Mas-Colell strengthen Corollary 9.3. First, he shows that any compact set in the interior of the price sphere can be the equilibrium price set of a well-behaved economy (even taking the boundary into consideration). Further, if there are at least three commodities, then for any finite set $A \subseteq \text{int}\, S$ with an odd number of elements, and any function $d : A \to \{-1, 1\}$ such that $\sum_{p \in A} d(p) = 1$, there is a well-behaved exchange economy with a smooth excess demand function such that A is its set of Walrasian equilibrium prices, and $d(p)$ is the index (see Mas-Colell, Whinston, and Green, 1995) of equilibrium p.

9.1.1 Sketch of the proof of the Sonnenschein–Mantel–Debreu Theorem

Consider first the excess demand function of a single consumer, $Z(p) = d(p, p \cdot \omega) - \omega$. As discussed at the beginning of the chapter, the excess demand function Z satisfies WARP if there are no p and q such that $q \cdot Z(p) < 0$ and $p \cdot Z(q) \leq 0$. Observe that if Z satisfies the weak axiom of revealed preference, and $g : S \to \mathbf{R}_+$ is a strictly positive function, then $p \mapsto g(p)Z(p)$ also satisfies the weak axiom of revealed preference.

In preparation for the proof, we need to consider the function $\tilde{Z}^i(p) = \mathbf{1}_i - p_i p$. We intend for $\tilde{Z}^i$ to be the excess demand function of an individual consumer. Recall that $\mathbf{1}_i$ is the unit vector with a one in the ith coordinate. Recall that $\|p\| = 1$ for $p \in S$; thus for any vector $x \in X$, $pp'x$ is the orthogonal projection of x onto the subspace defined by the vector p. To see this, note that

pp' satisfies $(pp')(pp') = pp'$, so that for any x, if $y = pp'x$, then $y = pp'y$ (a property called idempotence). Moreover, for any x, $pp'(x - pp'x) = 0$. So

$$\tilde{Z}^i(p) = \mathbf{1}_i - pp'\mathbf{1}_i = \mathbf{1}_i - p_i p$$

is the "residual" of projecting $\mathbf{1}_i$ on the linear subspace spanned by p. In other words, it is the projection of $\mathbf{1}_i$ on the subspace of vectors orthogonal to p. Observe that $\tilde{Z}^i$ is continuous and satisfies Walras' Law, as $p \cdot \tilde{Z}^i(p) = p_i - p_i p \cdot p = 0$.

Note that $\tilde{Z}^i$ is obtained as the result of a maximization program because $\tilde{Z}^i(p)$ is the projection of $\mathbf{1}_i$ on to a subspace. (The projection results from maximizing the negative of the distance of $\mathbf{1}_i$ to the subspace of vectors orthogonal to p.) As a consequence of being the solution to a maximization program, $\tilde{Z}^i$ will satisfy the weak axiom of revealed preference.

So we see that $\tilde{Z}^i$ is continuous, and satisfies Walras' law and WARP. The idea in the rest of the proof is to use the functions $\tilde{Z}^i$ as a "basis" on which one can decompose the function Z.

The set K from the hypothesis of the theorem is a compact set in the interior of the sphere. Let $f : S \to \mathbf{R}$ be a continuous function for which

$$Z_i(p) + f(p)p_i > 0$$

for all $p \in K$.[2] There is such a function because K is compact and $p_i > 0$. Note that the function

$$p \mapsto (Z_i(p) + f(p)p_i)\tilde{Z}^i(p) = (Z_i(p) + f(p)p_i)(\mathbf{1}_i - p_i p)$$

satisfies the weak axiom of revealed preference on K by the observation made above. Define then $Z^i(p) = (Z_i(p) + f(p)p_i)(\mathbf{1}_i - p_i p)$.

We are not going to prove that $Z^i(p)$ on K can be generated by preferences $\succeq_i$ which are continuous, strictly convex, and monotonic. This proof is quite involved and depends on the fact that K is a compact subset of the relative interior of the unit sphere. One can see that it is "almost" generated by preferences satisfying these properties (since it is based on a maximization problem). We hope that having established that $Z^i(p)$ satisfies the weak axiom is instructive enough.

Finally, we must verify that $Z = \sum_{i=1}^n Z^i$. Observe that

$$\begin{aligned}
&\sum_{i=1}^{n} (Z_i(p) + f(p)p_i)(p_i p) \\
&= \sum_{i=1}^{n} (p_i Z_i(p) + p_i^2 f(p))p \\
&= (p \cdot Z(p) + p \cdot p f(p))p = f(p)p.
\end{aligned}$$

[2] Note that Z_i is the ith component of the function Z, not to be confused with Z^i.

Likewise,

$$\sum_{i=1}^{n}(Z_i(p)+f(p)p_i)\,\mathbf{1}_i$$
$$=Z(p)+f(p)p.$$

Thus,

$$\sum_{i=1}^{n}(Z_i(p)+f(p)p_i)\,(\mathbf{1}_i-p_ip)=Z(p).$$

9.2 HOMOTHETIC PREFERENCES

We now turn to a different (and simpler) construction than the one in SMD. It requires that Z be smooth, but it delivers a rationalizing economy in which all agents' preferences are homothetic.

Homotheticity has, generally speaking, strong implications. For example, it is a crucial ingredient in aggregation theorems, from which the existence of a representative consumer follows. It is therefore striking that there is a version of the SMD Theorem even when we ask that agents' preferences be homothetic.

For convenience, we now take the domain of Z to be Δ. The next result is due to Rolf Mantel.

Theorem 9.4 *Suppose that $Z:\Delta\to X$ is a C^2 function satisfying Walras' Law, and let $K\subseteq \operatorname{int}\Delta$ be compact. Then there exists an exchange economy $\mathcal{E}=(\succeq_i,\omega_i)_{i=1}^n$, in which each $\succeq_i$ is continuous, convex, homothetic, and monotonic, such that the sum of individuals agents' excess demand functions in $\mathcal{E}$ coincides with Z on K.*

Proof. Let Z be as in the hypothesis of the theorem. We construct an exchange economy with n agents, each one endowed with m units of one good: the endowment of agent i is $m\mathbf{1}_i$. As we shall see, the parameter m plays an important role in this construction because it scales up an economy in which all prices are equilibrium prices.

Let A be an $n\times n$ matrix and denote by a_i the vector formed from its ith column. We choose A such that the a_i vectors are linearly independent and $a_i\cdot\mathbf{1}=1$ (we use the notation $\mathbf{1}$ for a vector of ones). For an n-vector x, $\log(x)$ denotes the vector whose entries are the logarithms of the entries of x.

Define the following functions:

$$g^i(p)=\frac{1}{m}Z_i\left(\frac{1}{\sum_j p_j}p\right)-a_i\cdot\log(Ap),$$

on the domain consisting of $p\in\mathbf{R}^n_{++}$ with $\frac{1}{\sum_j p_j}p\in K$. Denote by K' this domain of prices. We intend g^i to be the indirect utility function of agent i in our construction, when her income is 1.

Observe now that $a_i \log(Ap)$ is a concave function of p, and that the second derivatives of Z are bounded on K. Then by choosing m large enough we know that $g^i(p)$ is a convex function on K.

Define the utility function of agent i to be

$$u^i(x) = \inf\{g^i(p) : p \cdot x \leq 1, p \in K'\}.$$

It is routine to verify that u^i is monotonic, continuous, and quasiconcave. To see that the preferences represented by u^i are homothetic, note that u^i is log-homogeneous:

$$\begin{aligned} u^i(\lambda x) &= \inf\{g^i(p) : \lambda p \cdot x \leq 1, p \in K'\} \\ &= \inf\{g^i((1/\lambda)q) : q \cdot x \leq 1, q \in K'\} \\ &= \inf\{\frac{1}{m} Z_i\left(\frac{1}{\sum_j q_j} q\right) - a_i \cdot \log(Aq(1/\lambda)) : q \cdot x \leq 1, q \in K'\}, \end{aligned}$$

but

$$a_i \cdot \log(Aq(1/\lambda)) = a_i \cdot \log(Aq) - a_i \cdot \mathbf{1} \log(\lambda) = a_i \cdot \log(Aq) - \log(\lambda),$$

so that $u^i(\lambda x) = u^i(x) + \log(\lambda)$. This means that a monotonic transformation of u^i is homogeneous, and therefore that the preferences represented by u^i are homothetic.

As a result, if we let $v^i(p,M)$ be the indirect utility function derived from u^i, then

$$v^i(p,M) = g^i(p) + \log(M),$$

for $M > 0$.

Using Roy's identity we obtain the demand of agent i as

$$d_i(p, p \cdot m\mathbf{1}_i) = -\frac{\nabla_p v^i(p, p \cdot m\mathbf{1}_i)}{\nabla_M v^i(p, p \cdot m\mathbf{1}_i)} = -p \cdot m\mathbf{1}_i \nabla_p g^i(p).$$

Now,

$$\nabla_p g^i(p) = \frac{1}{m} \nabla Z_i(p) - A' L(p)^{-1} a_i,$$

where $L(p)$ is the $n \times n$ diagonal matrix which has $\sum_{j=1}^n a_{ji} p_j$ in its ith row and column. So

$$d_i(p, p \cdot m\mathbf{1}_i) = -p \cdot m\mathbf{1}_i \nabla g^i(p) = -p_i \nabla Z_i(p) + (p_i m) A' L(p)^{-1} a_i.$$

Then aggregate excess demand for this economy is

$$\begin{aligned} \sum_{i=1}^n d_i(p, p \cdot m\mathbf{1}_i) - m\mathbf{1} &= -\sum_{i=1}^n p_i \nabla Z_i(p) + \sum_{i=1}^n (p_i m) A' L(p)^{-1} a_i - m\mathbf{1} \\ &= Z(p) + m A' L(p)^{-1} A p - m\mathbf{1} \\ &= Z(p) + m A' \mathbf{1} - m\mathbf{1} = Z(p), \end{aligned}$$

where we have used the facts that $Z(p) + \sum_{i=1}^n p_i \nabla Z_i(p) = 0$ (which follows from Walras' Law) and that $A'\mathbf{1} = \mathbf{1}$.

Remark 9.5 The proof of Theorem 9.4 uses an interesting construction. It uses an economy in which agents' preferences are homothetic and all prices are equilibrium prices. One can verify that if g^i in the proof is defined to be $a_i \cdot \log(Ap)$, and agents' endowments are as above, then the construction used in the proof gives an economy in which all prices are zero.

The proof works by adding a scaled-down version of $Z(p)$ to the excess demand function, and rationalizes such a "perturbed" excess demand by a perturbation of the original homothetic preferences. The new economy has the zeroes of Z as equilibrium prices, but its excess demand function is a scaled-down version of Z. Now homotheticity guarantees that by scaling up endowments we obtain an economy in which Z is the excess demand function.

9.3 PRICES AND ENDOWMENTS

We have looked at the implications of general equilibrium theory when one is given either a set of prices or an aggregate excess demand function. We now turn to a different set of givens.

We assume that we observe a finite collection of prices and endowments (or, equivalently, of aggregate endowment and individual agents' incomes). Under the assumption that one can observe prices and endowments, we are going to show that general equilibrium theory is testable. This observation is due to Brown and Matzkin, as is most of the discussion in Section 9.3.

Consider an exchange economy $\mathcal{E} = (\succeq_i, \omega_i)_{i=1}^I$, where each pair $(\succeq_i, \omega_i)$ describes one consumer; as before, each agent i is described by a preference relation $\succeq_i$ and a vector of endowments $\omega_i \in \mathbf{R}^n_+$. I is a positive integer specifying the number of consumers. An *allocation of* $\sum_i \omega_i$ is a vector $(x_i)_{i \in I} \in \mathbf{R}^{nI}_+$ such that $\sum_i x_i = \sum_i \omega_i$. A *Walrasian equilibrium* is a pair $((x_i), p)$ such that (x_i) is an allocation and $p \in \mathbf{R}^l_{++}$ satisfies that x_i is maximal for $\succeq_i$ in the set

$$\{z \in \mathbf{R}^n_+ : p \cdot z \leq p \cdot \omega_i\}.$$

We assume that we have data on prices, incomes, and resources. Specifically, an *economy-wide dataset* is a collection $D_W = (p^k, (\omega_i^k)_{i=1}^I)_{k=0}^K$. If it seems unreasonable to assume that individual endowments are observable, note that one can instead work with individual incomes and aggregate endowment. The results will be the same.

A dataset D_W is *Walras rationalizable* if there are locally nonsatiated preference relations $\succeq_i$ and, for each k an allocation (x_i^k) of $\sum_i \omega_i^k$ such that $((x_i^k), p^k)$ is a Walrasian equilibrium of the exchange economy $(\succeq_i, \omega_i^k)_{i=1}^I$.

There are economy-wide datasets that are not Walras rationalizable. Consider for example the dataset represented in Figure 9.1. In the figure, there are two observations $(p^k, (\omega_1^k, \omega_2^k))$, $k = 1, 2$. For each k, $\bar{\omega}^k = \omega_1^k + \omega_2^k$ defines an Edgeworth box. Suppose that $k = 1$ gives the taller box, while $k = 2$ defines the wider of the two boxes. The boxes are represented so that the consumption space of agent 1 is the same in the two boxes (the $(0,0)$ consumption vector

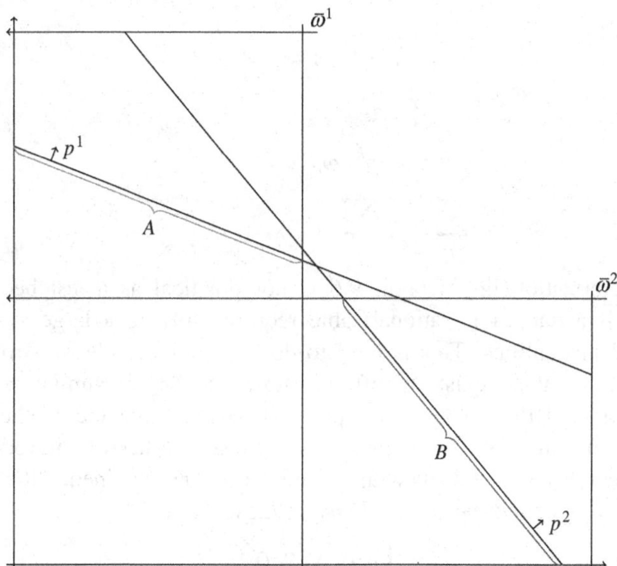

Fig. 9.1 Two Edgeworth boxes representing a non-rationalizable dataset.

for agent 1 is the same in the two boxes). Note that p^k and ω_i^k define a budget set for each consumer.

If the data in Figure 9.1 were Walras rationalizable, there would need to exist some (unobserved) allocation of $\bar{\omega}^k$, for $k = 1,2$. These allocations must lie inside each Edgeworth box. Then, if the dataset in Figure 9.1 were Walras rationalizable, the allocation of $\bar{\omega}^1$ would have to lie on the segment A of the budget line for consumer 1, while the allocation of ω^2 would have to lie on the segment B of the budget line for consumer 1 at prices p^2. Any such allocation would imply that consumer 1 violates WARP. So the allocation could not be part of a Walrasian equilibrium, as the resulting choices by consumer 1 would be incompatible with any preference relation for consumer 1.

The observation that the theory of Walrasian equilibrium is testable is subtle, and in sharp contrast with the message of the SMD Theorem, but it is not different in nature than the idea that there are individual observations that violate WARP. One would ideally want to characterize all datasets that are Walras rationalizable: such a test exists, but a "closed form" test is not known.

The following theorem (due to Brown and Matzkin) is a direct consequence of Afriat's Theorem. It is useful because it sets up the problem of Walras-rationalizing data as a system of polynomial inequalities.

Theorem 9.6 *A dataset $D_W = (p^k, (\omega_i^k)_{i=1}^I)_{k=0}^K$ is rationalizable iff there are numbers $(U_i^k, \lambda_i^k)_{i=1}^I$ for $k = 1,\dots,K$, and vectors $(x_i^k)_{i=1}^I \in X^I$ for $k = 1,\dots,K$,* *such that*

$$U_i^k \leq U_i^l + \lambda_i^l p^l \cdot (x_i^k - x_i^l)$$
$$\lambda_i^k > 0$$
$$p^k \cdot x_i^k = p^k \cdot \omega_i^k$$
$$\sum_i x_i^k = \sum_i \omega_i^k.$$

The characterization in Theorem 9.6 is not practical as a test because to determine if a dataset is rationalizable requires solving a large system of polynomial inequalities. This is hard to do. The point made by Brown and Matzkin is that there exists a different test: one that is similar in nature to checking GARP or SARP. We proceed to introduce the mathematical framework in which we can express such a test. We need to introduce the mathematical theory that deals with systems of polynomial inequalities.

Consider a system of *polynomial inequalities:*

$$I : \begin{cases} p_1(a,x)\; S_1\; 0 \\ \vdots \\ p_k(a,x)\; S_k\; 0, \end{cases}$$

where $a \in \mathbf{R}^m$ and $x \in \mathbf{R}^n$, so that p_i is a polynomial of $m+n$ variables and $S_i \in \{\geq, =, >, \neq\}$. Here we interpret $a \in \mathbf{R}^m$ as a parameter, and the variables $x \in \mathbf{R}^n$ as unknowns: We want to know whether, for given a, there is x such that (a,x) solves system I.

The following is a celebrated theorem due to Tarski and Seidenberg.

Theorem 9.7 *There are systems of polynomial inequalities $J_1, \ldots, J_L$ in m variables with the following property: For all $a \in \mathbf{R}^m$, there is $x \in \mathbf{R}^n$ for which (a,x) solves system I iff there is l such that a solves system J_l.*

Remark 9.8 The theorem actually says more. It says that if we fix a real closed field F, then there is a solution to I in F iff the coefficients of I are a solution to some J_l in F. Perhaps more importantly, the theorem is not just an existence result. It is also associated with an algorithm which can be used, in principle, to derive the systems $J_1, \ldots, J_L$ from the system I. The algorithm is, however, not computationally efficient. It is known that the problem of eliminating quantifiers for real closed fields in general is computationally complex. We discuss related ideas in Chapter 12.

We present two examples to illustrate the theorem. The first is an example in elementary algebra. Consider the second-degree polynomial of one variable: $p(x) = ax^2 + bx + c$. Suppose that $a \neq 0$. The equation $p(x) = 0$ has a solution (in $\mathbf{R}$) iff the inequality $b^2 - 4ac \geq 0$ is satisfied. The example is an instance of *quantifier elimination* since the statement $\exists x(p(x) = 0)$, which involves an existential quantifier over x, is seen to be equivalent (when $a \neq 0$)

to the statement $b^2 - 4ac \geq 0$.[3] We can call the statement $\exists x(p(x) = 0)$ an *existential* statement because it is preceded by an existential quantifier; while $b^2 - 4ac \geq 0$ is non-existential. As a statement that describes the empirical content of a theory, $\exists x(p(x) = 0)$, or any other existential statement, is very problematic because its verification requires checking all possible real numbers. By eliminating quantifiers we can go from an existential statement to a statement that can be directly verified on the data. Chapter 13 discusses this issue in more depth.

The second example is familiar from our discussion of demand theory in Chapter 3. Let $D = \{(x^k, p^k)\}_{k=1}^K$ be a consumption dataset. Afriat's Theorem says that there is a solution $(U^1, \ldots, U^K, \lambda^1, \ldots, \lambda^K)$ to the (linear) system of Afriat inequalities

$$U^k \leq U^l + \lambda^l p^l \cdot (x^k - x^l), k \neq l$$

and $\lambda^k > 0$ iff the data satisfy GARP. Afriat's Theorem is an example of elimination of quantifiers: The statement that there is a solution to the system of Afriat inequalities is existential. And Afriat's Theorem says that such an existential system is equivalent to GARP – observe that GARP is the statement that for any sequence $x^{h_1}, \ldots, x^{h_H}$ of distinct observations $p^{h_1} \cdot x^{h_1} \geq p^{h_1} \cdot x^{h_2}, \ldots, p^{h_{H-1}} \cdot x^{h_{H-1}} \geq p^{h_{H-1}} \cdot x^{h_H}$ implies that $p^{h_H} \cdot x^{h_H} \leq p^{h_H} \cdot x^{h_1}$. Saying that a dataset satisfies GARP is not an existential statement.

We can formulate the satisfaction of GARP as the satisfaction of a system of polynomial inequalities. To write down this system, let s denote a sequence $x^{h_1^s}, \ldots, x^{h_{H^s}^s}$ of distinct observations in D. Let Σ be the set of all such sequences. For each $s \in \Sigma$ we need to check that there is not a cycle $x^{h_1^s} \succeq^R \ldots \succeq^R x^{h_{H^s}^s} \succ^R x^{h_1^s}$. Satisfaction of GARP is the same as saying that no sequence $s \in \Sigma$ gives rise to a cycle.

Let r_s^i be the inequality $p^{h_i^s} \cdot x^{h_i^s} < p^{h_i^s} \cdot x^{h_{i+1}^s}$, $i = 1, \ldots H^s - 1$, and q_s the inequality $p^{h_{H^s}^s} \cdot x^{h_{H^s}^s} \leq p^{h_{H^s}^s} \cdot x^{h_1^s}$. Note that, for a sequence s, the satisfaction of any one of these inequalities rules out the potential cycle $x^{h_1^s} \succeq^R \ldots \succeq^R x^{h_{H^s}^s} \succ^R x^{h_1^s}$.

Define $L = \prod_{s \in \Sigma} \{r_s^1, \ldots, r_s^{H^s}, q_s\}$. Note that each $l \in L$ selects, for every sequence s, one inequality: either one of the r_s^i, or q_s. If we satisfy the inequality selected by l for s then we rule out the cycle indicated by sequence s. Let J_l be the system of inequalities obtained by collecting the inequalities selected by l. Satisfaction of just one system J_l rules out all potential cycles.

We know from Afriat's Theorem that there is a solution to the system of Afriat inequalities iff there is l such that the observed data (which are the coefficients of the system of Afriat inequalities) satisfy the corresponding J_l. Thus Afriat's Theorem illustrates an instance of quantifier elimination, as formalized in Theorem 9.7.

[3] Formally, to apply the theorem, we need to treat $a \neq 0$ as an inequality in the original system, although the existentially quantified x does not appear there. The inequality $a \neq 0$ then also appears in the system in which x has been eliminated.

9.4 THE CORE OF EXCHANGE ECONOMIES

We finalize the discussion of exchange economies by briefly looking instead into the core of Walrasian equilibrium. Much less is known about the core than about equilibrium, and we need to restrict attention to the case of two agents. The material here is due to Bossert and Sprumont.

Consider an exchange economy with two consumers. Suppose that there is an aggregate endowment $\bar{\omega} \in \mathbf{R}^n_{++}$. In any allocation, consumption of agent 2 is determined by the consumption of agent 1. The set of possible endowments and consumptions of agent 1 is $E = \{x \in \mathbf{R}^n_+ : x \leq \bar{\omega}\}$ (either agent is permitted to have zero endowment). For a set of preferences $\succeq_1$ and $\succeq_2$, we define the *core*

$$\begin{aligned}&\mathcal{C}(\succeq_1, \succeq_2, \omega) = \\ &\{x \in E : x \succeq_1 \omega_1 \text{ and } (\bar{\omega} - x) \succeq_2 (\bar{\omega} - \omega_1)\} \\ &\cap \{x \in \mathbf{R}^n_+ : \nexists y \in E \text{ such that } y \succ_1 x \text{ and } (\bar{\omega} - y) \succ_2 (\bar{\omega} - x)\}.\end{aligned}$$

The first part of this equation specifies the usual individual rationality constraint. The second expresses Pareto optimality. In fact, it expresses weak Pareto optimality, but note that for strictly convex preferences, the notions coincide.

The question is, given a correspondence $c : E \rightrightarrows E$, when do there exist preferences $\succeq_1$ and $\succeq_2$, satisfying natural properties, such that for all $e \in E$, $c(e) = \mathcal{C}(\succeq_1, \succeq_2, e)$? The properties under consideration are continuity, strict monotonicity, and strict convexity.

We say that a set $S \subseteq E$ is *connected* if it is connected in the usual topological sense; that is, the set cannot be partitioned into nontrivial disjoint open sets. Viewing c as a correspondence, we can also define continuity in the usual sense (of the joint hypotheses of lower and upper hemicontinuity). We say that the correspondence c is *regular* if it is continuous in e, and for all e, $c(e)$ is connected.

For the core with strictly convex and monotone preferences, if some vector e is ever selected for an endowment e', then e must be the uniquely chosen element when e' is the endowment. We say that c satisfies *persistence* if for all $e, e' \in E$, if $e \in c(e')$, then $c(e) = \{e\}$.

Two more technical conditions are specified. The conditions are a method of "identifying" the best and worst elements in the correspondence, and postulating that they behave naturally with respect to the usual order on $\mathbf{R}^n$.

Define, for $e \in E$,

$$\mathcal{S}_0(e) = \{S \subseteq E : c(e) \cup \{0\} \subseteq S, S \text{ path connected }\}$$

and

$$\mathcal{S}_\omega(e) = \{S \subseteq E : c(e) \cup \{\omega\} \subseteq S, S \text{ path connected }\}.$$

We say that c satisfies *strict path monotonicity* if for all $e,e' \in E$ for which $e \geq e'$ and $e \neq e'$, we have

$$\bigcap_{S \in \mathcal{S}_0(e)} S \subsetneq \bigcap_{S \in \mathcal{S}_0(e')} S$$

and

$$\bigcap_{S \in \mathcal{S}_\omega(e')} S \subsetneq \bigcap_{S \in \mathcal{S}_\omega(e)} S.$$

Finally, we define $\mathcal{S}(e,e') = \{S \subseteq E : c(e) \cup c(e') \subseteq S, S \text{ path connected }\}$. Say that c satisfies *strict averaging reduction* if for all $e,e' \in E$ for which $e \neq e'$ and all $\lambda \in (0,1)$, $c(\lambda e + (1-\lambda)e')$ is contained in the interior of $\bigcap_{S \in \mathcal{S}(e,e')} S$ relative to $\bigcup_{e \in E} c(e)$.

Theorem 9.9 *There exist strictly convex, strictly monotonic, and continuous $\succeq_1$ and $\succeq_2$ for which $c(e) = \mathcal{C}(\succeq_1, \succeq_2, e)$ for all $e \in E$ iff $c : E \rightrightarrows E$ satisfies regularity, persistence, strict path monotonicity, and strict averaging reduction.*

9.5 CHAPTER REFERENCES

The Sonnenschein–Mantel–Debreu Theorem was first established for the case when Z is a polynomial in Sonnenschein (1972). Mantel (1974) proved a decomposition of Z as in the statement of the theorem, but using $2n$ agents. The final statement was obtained by Debreu (1974). Proposition 9.1 is due to Debreu (1974). Corollary 9.3 is proved in Mas-Colell (1977); a much more general statement appears there: that any compact subset of the interior of the price sphere can be the equilibrium price set of a well-behaved economy. The strengthening follows from a strengthening of the SMD Theorem. The result pertaining to indices can also be found in this work; see also Mas-Colell, Whinston, and Green (1995). Geanakoplos (1984) constructs an explicit utility function to rationalize the individual excess demand functions constructed in Debreu's proof. Theorem 9.2 is from McFadden, Mas-Colell, Mantel, and Richter (1974).

Theorem 9.4 is due to Mantel (1976). Mantel shows more. The endowments in the construction in the theorem can be chosen arbitrarily, as long as they are linearly independent. In particular, they can be close to proportional: when they are exactly proportional (and preferences homothetic) we know that the economy admits a representative consumer, which of course strongly limits the excess demand function. A graphical illustration of the proof of Theorem 9.4 can be found in Shafer and Sonnenschein (1982) (attributed to Mas-Colell).

The SMD Theorem has a host of important implications. Uzawa (1960b) has shown that Brouwer's Fixed-Point Theorem is equivalent to the existence theorem of the zeroes of a continuous function satisfying the properties usually obtained from exchange economies. The SMD Theorem implies that the Fixed-Point Theorem is equivalent to a standard equilibrium existence theorem. In recent years, this has been exploited by computer scientists studying the computational complexity of finding competitive equilibria (see Papadimitriou and Yannakakis (2010); this possibility was anticipated by Mantel (1977)).

Theorem 9.6, the example in 9.3, and the idea of using the Tarski–Seidenberg result appear in Brown and Matzkin (1996). The Tarski–Seidenberg result is due to Tarski (1951), and was popularized by Seidenberg (1954). The computational complexity of quantifier elimination in this environment was described in Davenport and Heintz (1988). Brown and Shannon (2000) show that, in the setting assumed by Brown and Matzkin, certain regularity conditions of equilibria (that all equilibria are locally stable, and that the equilibrium correspondence is monotone) have no testable implications in addition to Walrasian rationalizability.

The discussion in 9.4, and in particular, Theorem 9.9, is due to Bossert and Sprumont (2002).

We have not discussed the literature on public goods. Snyder (1999) provides a discussion of the relevant ideas.

The survey paper by Carvajal, Ray, and Snyder (2004) covers in depth some of the same material as this chapter.

CHAPTER 10

Game Theory

In this chapter we continue the study of the testable implications of models of collective behavior. We focus here on game-theoretic models. Our first results use a version of the abstract choice environments from Chapter 2, and discuss testing Nash equilibrium as the prediction of the choices made by a collection of agents. We then turn to models of bargaining and two-sided matching.

10.1 NASH EQUILIBRIUM

Let N be a finite set of agents of cardinality n. For each $i \in N$, consider some finite set $\bar{S}_i$. The idea is that $\bar{S}_i$ is some "global" set of strategies that may be available to agent i. In a specific (observable) instance, player i is restricted to choosing a strategy from $S_i \subseteq \bar{S}_i$, a "budget" of possible strategies. Consider the nonempty product subsets of $\prod_{i \in N} \bar{S}_i$, denoted by $\mathcal{S}$. A typical element of $\mathcal{S}$ has the form $S_1 \times S_2 \times \cdots \times S_n$; where each S_i is a nonempty subset of $\bar{S}_i$. These sets are called *game forms*.

An element of $\prod_{i \in N} \bar{S}_i$ is called a *strategy profile*. As usual in game theory we use (s_i, s_{-i}) to denote a strategy profile in which s_i is i's strategy and $s_{-i} \in \prod_{j \in N \setminus \{i\}} \bar{S}_j$ is a strategy profile for players in $N \setminus \{i\}$.

A *joint choice function* is a mapping $c : \Sigma \subseteq \mathcal{S} \to 2^{\prod_{i \in N} \bar{S}_i} \setminus \{\varnothing\}$ satisfying $c(S) \subseteq S$. Note that $c(S)$ need not have a product structure, but it is required to be nonempty. In particular, every joint choice function is a choice function in the sense of Chapter 2. We will be interested in notions of rationalization that reflect the product structure of $\mathcal{S}$.

Let $\{\succeq_i\}_{i \in N}$ be a family of preference relations, each over $\prod_{i \in N} \bar{S}_i$. Note that these preferences define a (normal-form) *game* $(N, (S_i, \succeq_i|_S)_{i \in N})$ for each $S = S_1 \times S_2 \times \cdots \times S_n \in \mathcal{S}$. By $\succeq_i|_S$ we mean the restriction of preferences $\succeq_i$ to S. A *strategy profile* $s = (s_i)_{i \in N} \in S$ is a *Nash equilibrium* of $(N, (S_i, \succeq_i|_S)_{i \in N})$ if $(s_i, s_{-i}) \succeq_i (s_i', s_{-i})$ for all $s_i' \in S_i$ and all $i \in N$.

We say that the family of preference relations $\{\succeq_i\}_{i \in N}$ *strongly Nash rationalize* a choice function c if for all $S = \prod_{i \in N} S_i \in \mathcal{S}$, $c(S)$ coincides with the set of Nash equilibria of the game $(N, (S_i, \succeq_i|_S)_{i \in N})$:

$$c(S) = \{(s_i)_{i \in N} : \text{ for all } j \in N \text{ and all } s'_j \in S_j, (s_j, s_{-j}) \succeq_j (s'_j, s_{-j})\}.$$

We say that c is *strongly Nash rationalizable* by a class of preference relations if there exist preference relations $\succeq_i$ in that class which strongly Nash rationalize c.

We say that a family of binary relations $\succeq_i$ *weakly Nash rationalize* c if for all $S \in \mathcal{S}$, $c(S) \subseteq \{(s_i)_{i \in N} : \text{ for all } j \in N \text{ and all } s'_j \in S_j, (s_j, s_{-j}) \succeq_j (s'_j, s_{-j})\}$. We will say c is *weakly Nash rationalizable* by a class of preference relations if there exist preference relations $\succeq_i$ in that class which weakly Nash rationalize c.

Clearly, weak Nash rationalizability by weak orders has no empirical content; thus, when we speak of weak Nash rationalization, we shall take interest in weak Nash rationalization by strict preference relations.

10.1.1 Choice from all game forms

We shall assume that we observe the outcomes of the strategic interaction of the agents in N for each possible game form. That is, $\Sigma = \mathcal{S}$.[1] The results in this subsection are due to Yves Sprumont.

The set $\mathcal{S}$ forms a lattice under the set inclusion relation; its meet is given by $S \wedge S' = S \cap S'$. Writing $S = \prod_{i \in N} S_i$ and $S' = \prod_{i \in N} S'_i$, the join $S \vee S'$ is given by $S \vee S' = \prod_{i \in N} (S_i \cup S'_i)$.

Say that a joint choice function c satisfies *persistence under expansion* if for all $S, S' \in \mathcal{S}$, $c(S) \cap c(S') \subseteq c(S \vee S')$. It is obvious from the definition of Nash equilibrium that persistence under expansion is a necessary condition for c to be strongly Nash rationalizable.

We will say that $S \in \mathcal{S}$ is a *line* if there exists $i \in N$ such that for all $j \neq i$, S_i is a singleton. A line can be understood as a single-agent decision problem. We say that a joint choice function c satisfies *persistence under contraction* if the following two properties are satisfied:

- for all $S, S' \in \mathcal{S}$ with $S \subseteq S'$, $c(S') \cap S \subseteq c(S)$.
- If S' is a line, $S \subseteq S'$, and $c(S') \cap S \neq \varnothing$, then $c(S) \subseteq c(S')$.

Note that the first property of persistence under contraction is condition α of Chapter 2. The second property, which is only required to hold for lines, is similar to condition β.

The following theorem characterizes strongly Nash rationalizable joint choice functions.

[1] This assumption is analogous to assuming that the choices from all possible budgets are observed in Chapter 2.

Theorem 10.1 *A joint choice function c is strongly Nash rationalizable by preference relations iff it satisfies persistence under expansion and persistence under contraction.*

Proof. It is easy to verify that if c is strongly Nash rationalizable by preference relations, then it satisfies persistence under expansion and persistence under contraction. Conversely, suppose c satisfies these two properties.

We first define a basic revealed preference, $\succeq_i^c$. For any pair (s_i, s_{-i}) and (s_i', s_{-i}), we define $(s_i, s_{-i}) \succeq_i^c (s_i', s_{-i})$ in the natural way; that is, $(s_i, s_{-i}) \succeq_i^c (s_i', s_{-i})$ iff $(s_i, s_{-i}) \in c\left(\{s_i, s_i'\} \times \prod_{j \neq i}\{s_j\}\right)$. Each $\succeq_i^c$ is clearly reflexive. Transitivity is also straightforward and follows similarly to the proof of Theorem 2.9. Hence, each $\succeq_c^i$ has an extension (by Theorem 1.5) to a weak order $\succeq_i$.

We claim that the orders $\succeq_i$ strongly Nash rationalize c. So, suppose we have given $S \in \mathcal{S}$ and $s \in S$ such that for all $i \in N$ and all $s_i' \in S_i$, $(s_i, s_{-i}) \succeq_i (s_i', s_{-i})$. Hence, for all $i \in N$ and all $s_i' \in S_i$, $(s_i, s_{-i}) \succeq_i^c (s_i', s_{-i})$, so that $(s_i, s_{-i}) \in c\left(\{s_i, s_i'\} \times \prod_{j \neq i}\{s_j\}\right)$. Now, $S = \bigvee_{i \in N} \bigvee_{s_i' \in S_i}\left(\{s_i, s_i'\} \times \prod_{j \neq i}\{s_j\}\right)$, so that by persistence under expansion (applied inductively), we have $s \in c(S)$. Conversely, suppose that $s \in c(S)$. Then it follows by persistence under contraction that $s \in c\left(\{s_i, s_i'\} \times \prod_{j \neq i}\{s_j\}\right)$ for all i and all s_i', so that $(s_i, s_{-i}) \succeq_i^c (s_i', s_{-i})$, or $(s_i, s_{-i}) \succeq_i (s_i', s_{-i})$.

The following result characterizes weak rationalizability by strict preference relations. We omit its proof, which is simple.

Theorem 10.2 *A joint choice function c is weakly rationalizable by strict preference relations iff for all $S \in \mathcal{S}$, all $s \in c(S)$, all $i \in N$, and all $s_i' \in S_i$, $c\left(\{s_i', s_i\} \times \prod_{j \neq i}\{s_j\}\right) = \{s\}$.*

The notion of Nash rationalizability is based on individual agents' incentives to choose strategies. We can instead consider what the group of agents N would jointly decide to do. One natural property is that the chosen strategy profiles should not be dominated: A joint choice function c is *Pareto rationalizable* by preference relations iff there are preference relations $\succeq_i$ on $\prod_{i \in N} \bar{S}_i$ such that for all $S \in \mathcal{S}$, $s \in c(S)$ iff there is no $s' \in S$ for which $s' \succeq_i s$ for all i, with at least one preference strict. Say it is *team rationalizable* if there exists a preference $\succeq$ over $\prod_{i \in N} \bar{S}_i$ such that for all $S \in \mathcal{S}$, $c(S)$ is the set of $\succeq$-maximal elements of S.

Theorem 10.3 *Suppose a joint choice function c satisfies $|c(S)| = 1$ for all $S \in \mathcal{S}$. Then c is Pareto rationalizable iff it is team rationalizable.*

Proof. If c is team rationalizable, it is clearly Pareto rationalizable. Conversely, suppose c is Pareto rationalizable, and let $\{\succeq_i\}_{i \in N}$ be the rationalizing relations. Define $s \succeq^* s'$ if it is not the case that $s \succeq_i s'$ for all $i \in N$ with at least one preference strict. Clearly then, $s \succ^* s'$ iff $s \succeq_i s'$ for all $i \in N$ and there is $j \in N$ for which $s \succ_j s'$. Hence, $\succeq^*$ is quasitransitive. By definition, for every S, $c(S)$ coincides with the $\succeq^*$ maximal elements of S. The result now follows from Proposition 2.7.

In fact, Theorem 10.3 does not rely on the product structure of $\mathcal{S}$ and could be proved more generally.

The following theorem establishes that the implications of Nash rationalizability are stronger than those of Pareto rationalizability. We omit its proof, which is technical.

Theorem 10.4 *Suppose that $|N| = 2$, and that a joint choice function c satisfies $|c(S)| = 1$ for all $S \in \mathcal{S}$. Then if c is Nash rationalizable, it is Pareto rationalizable.*

10.1.2 Choice from a subset of game forms

We now discuss results in the revealed preference approach to game theory when not all possible game forms in $\mathcal{S}$ are observable.

We will say a collection $\Sigma \subseteq \mathcal{S}$ is *line-closed* if for all $S \in \Sigma$, all $s \in S$, and all $i \in N$, $S_i \times \prod_{i \neq j \in N} \{s_j\} \in \Sigma$. Line-closedness is enough to allow us to generate a meaningful revealed preference relation. A joint choice function can now be defined on Σ, and it is meaningful to discuss strong rationalizability by preferences.

The following idea is due to Galambos. We define the following revealed preference pair. Define $\succeq_i^c$ by $s \succeq_i^c s'$ if for all $j \neq i$, $s_j = s'_j$, and there exists $S \in \Sigma$ for which $s, s' \in S$ and $s \in c(S)$. We say a joint choice function c defined on Σ satisfies *N-congruence* if for all $i \in N$ and all S, if for $s \in S$ we have $s \left(\succeq_i^c\right)^T (s'_i, s_{-i})$ for all i and all $s'_i \in S_i$, then $s \in c(S)$.[2]

Theorem 10.5 *Suppose that Σ is a line-closed domain. Then a joint choice function is strongly rationalizable by preference relations iff it satisfies N-congruence.*

Proof. Suppose a joint choice function is strongly Nash rationalizable by weak orders $\succeq_i$. Clearly, $\left(\succeq_i^c\right)^T \subseteq \succeq_i$. Consequently, if $s \in S$ satisfies $s \left(\succeq_i^c\right)^T (s'_i, s_{-i})$ for all $s'_i \in S_i$, it follows that $s \succeq_i (s'_i, s_{-i})$ for all $s'_i \in S_i$, so that $s \in c(S)$, since the $\{\succeq_i\}_{i \in N}$ strongly Nash rationalize c.

Conversely, suppose that choice function c satisfies N-congruence. If we define $\succ_i^c$ by $(s_i, s_{-i}) \succ_i^c (s'_i, s_{-i})$ if there exists S for which $s, (s'_i, s_{-i}) \in S$ and $s \in c(S)$ but $(s'_i, s_{-i}) \notin c(S)$, then by N-congruence, order pair $\langle \succeq_i^c, \succ_i^c \rangle$ is acyclic, so that by Theorem 1.5, there is a weak order $\succeq_i$ for which $\succeq_i^c \subseteq \succeq_i$ and $\succ_i^c \subseteq \succ_i$.

We claim that the $\{\succeq_i\}_{i \in N}$ strongly Nash rationalize c. Suppose that $s \in c(S)$. We claim that for all i and all $s'_i \in S_i$, $(s_i, s_{-i}) \succeq_i (s'_i, s_{-i})$. This follows as

2 Recall that for a binary relation $\succeq$, $\succeq^T$ denotes the transitive closure.

$(s_i, s_{-i}) \succeq_i^c (s'_i, s_{-i})$ and $\succeq_i^c \subseteq \succeq_i$. On the other hand, suppose that $s \in S$ satisfies $(s_i, s_{-i}) \succeq_i (s'_i, s_{-i})$ for all i and all $s'_i \in S_i$. We claim that $s \in c(S)$. Since Σ is line-closed, it follows that $S_i \times \prod_{j \neq i}\{s_j\} \in \Sigma$. Then $s \in c\left(S_i \times \prod_{j \neq i}\{s_j\}\right)$. Otherwise, since c is nonempty-valued, there exists $s'_i \in S_i$ for which $(s'_i, s_{-i}) \in \left(S_i \times \prod_{j \neq i}\{s_j\}\right)$, from which it follows that $(s'_i, s_{-i}) \succ_i^c s$, contradicting the definition of $\succeq_i$. Consequently, we know that $s \succeq_i^c (s'_i, s_{-i})$ for all $i \in N$, so that by N-congruence, $s \in c(S)$.

10.1.3 Zero-sum games

The preceding results impose no structure on the rationalizing games, but one may want to investigate the joint implications of Nash behavior and some properties of the strategic environment. One of the most natural restrictions is the property that the game be a zero-sum game. Zero-sum games are the subject of intense study in game theory; they also arise naturally if one believes that players care about relative, not absolute, payoffs.[3]

Fix $N = \{1,2\}$. Suppose that $\Sigma = \mathcal{S}$ again, so that we are given choice from all possible game forms. A choice function c is *strongly Nash rationalizable by a zero-sum game* if there is a preference relation $\succeq$ on $\bar{S}_1 \times \bar{S}_2$ such that, for all $S \in \mathcal{S}$, $c(S)$ is the set of Nash equilibria of $(\{1,2\}, (S_1, \succeq|_S), (S_2, \preceq|_S))$; where we denote by $\preceq$ the dual binary relation defined from $\succeq$, i.e. $x \preceq y$ iff $y \succeq x$.

It turns out that to characterize strong zero-sum rationalizability, all we need is one additional restriction on c. Say that c is *interchangeable* if, for all $S \in \mathcal{S}$, and all $s, s' \in c(S)$, $\{s\} \vee \{s'\} \subseteq c(S)$. Our next result is due to SangMok Lee.

Theorem 10.6 *A choice function is strongly Nash rationalizable by a zero-sum game iff it satisfies persistence under expansion, persistence under contraction, and it is interchangeable.*

We omit the proof of Theorem 10.6, which is somewhat technical.

10.2 BAYESIAN NASH EQUILIBRIUM

The next class of problems we tackle are motivated by mechanism design. Given a function from agents' types to outcomes, we want to know if the function could be an incentive-compatible direct revelation mechanism, for some preferences of the agents.

Formally, let N be a set of agents, and X a finite set of *outcomes*. For each agent $i \in N$, suppose we are given a finite *type space* T_i. A *direct revelation mechanism* is a function $g : T = \prod_{i \in N} T_i \to X$. The question we ask here is simple. Suppose we observe N, $T = \prod_{i \in N} T_i$, and g. Can we rationalize g as a strongly incentive-compatible direct revelation mechanism for some list

[3] For example, suppose that "material" payoffs are p_i and there are two players; $i = 1,2$. If each player i cares about the difference $p_i - p_{3-i}$, then the sum of payoffs will be zero.

of preferences? In particular, is it possible that these mappings could be the unique Bayesian Nash equilibrium for some preferences in the direct revelation game? This answer and its question are due to John Ledyard.

Formally, let us define a *Bayesian environment* to be a pair of functions, one for each agent, denoted by $u_i : X \times T \to \mathbf{R}$ and $p_i : T_i \to \Delta(T_{-i})$. The function u_i is meant to be i's utility function over outcomes. The function p_i gives i's beliefs about other agents' types.

Two points are worth mentioning here. First, we allow agent i's utility to depend on the entire profile of types. Second, p_i carries each type to a probability measure over the others' types. We denote the probability of type profile t_{-i} by $p_i(t_{-i}|t_i)$. Note, however, that we are not making any common prior assumption.

A Bayesian environment *strongly rationalizes* direct revelation mechanism g if for all $t_i, t_i' \in T_i$, if $g(t) \neq g(t_i', t_{-i})$ for some t_{-i}, then

$$\sum_{t_{-i} \in T_{-i}} u_i(g(t_i, t_{-i}), t) p(t_{-i}|t_i) > \sum_{t_{-i} \in T_{-i}} u_i(g(t_i', t_{-i}), t) p(t_{-i}|t_i). \tag{10.1}$$

Theorem 10.7 *For any direct revelation mechanism, there exists a Bayesian environment strongly rationalizing it.*

Proof. Rewrite Equation (10.1), so that we have:

$$\sum_{t_{-i} \in T_{-i}} \sum_{x \in X} u_i(x,t) p(t_{-i}|t_i) \mathbf{1}_{g(t_i,t_{-i})=x} > \sum_{t_{-i} \in T_{-i}} \sum_{x \in X} u_i(x,t) p(t_{-i}|t_i) \mathbf{1}_{g(t_i',t_{-i})=x};$$

equivalently:

$$\sum_{t_{-i} \in T_{-i}} \sum_{x \in X} u_i(x,t) p(t_{-i}|t_i) [\mathbf{1}_{g(t_i,t_{-i})=x} - \mathbf{1}_{g(t_i',t_{-i})=x}] > 0. \tag{10.2}$$

First, observe that given any t_i, we can find u_i and p_i (depending on t_i) which satisfy equation (10.2) iff there is a function $w_{t_i} : X \times T_{-i} \to \mathbf{R}$ such that for all t_i' for which $g(t_i, t_{-i}) \neq g(t_i', t_{-i})$ for some t_{-i}, then

$$\sum_{t_{-i} \in T_{-i}} \sum_{x \in X} w_{t_i}(x, t_{-i}) [\mathbf{1}_{g(t_i,t_{-i})=x} - \mathbf{1}_{g(t_i',t_{-i})=x}] > 0. \tag{10.3}$$

This follows because it is simple to then find $u_i(x,t)$ and $p_i(t_{-i}|t_i)$ for which $u_i(x,t) p_i(t_{-i}|t_i) = w_{t_i}(x, t_{-i})$ (for example, define $p_i(t_{-i}|t_i) > 0$ arbitrarily so that $\sum_{t_{-i}} p_i(t_{-i}|t_i) = 1$, and then define $u_i(x,t) = \frac{w_{t_i}(x,t_{-i})}{p_i(t_{-i}|t_i)}$). Hence, we turn to equation (10.3). For every t_i, there is a list of such equations.

If we can solve the corresponding list of equations for each t_i, then we have proved that the direct revelation mechanism is strongly rationalizable. So, fix t_i. For each t_i' for which there exists t_{-i} such that $g(t_i, t_{-i}) \neq g(t_i', t_{-i})$, there is an equation of type (10.3). Denote the set of such t_i' by $T_i'(t_i)$.

In equation (10.3), view w as a vector in $\mathbf{R}^{X \times T_{-i}}$. The quantities $[\mathbf{1}_{g(t_i,t_{-i})=x} - \mathbf{1}_{g(t_i',t_{-i})=x}]$ play the role of coefficients. Applying Lemma 1.12, if for some t_i, a solution to the system described by equation (10.3) does not exist, then there exists, for each $t_i' \in T_i'(t_i)$, $\eta_{t_i'} \geq 0$, not all of which are zero, such that for all t_{-i}, x,

$$\sum_{t_i' \in T_i'(t_i)} \eta_{t_i'} [\mathbf{1}_{g(t_i,t_{-i})=x} - \mathbf{1}_{g(t_i',t_{-i})=x}] = 0. \tag{10.4}$$

By assumption, for any $t_i'' \in T_i'(t_i)$, there are t_{-i} and x for which $g(t_i,t_{-i}) = x \neq g(t_i'',t_{-i})$. Pick such t_{-i} and x. Because $\mathbf{1}_{g(t_i,t_{-i})=x} = 1$, we then have that $[\mathbf{1}_{g(t_i,t_{-i})=x} - \mathbf{1}_{g(t_i'',t_{-i})=x}] = 1$, and further, for any $t_i' \in T_i'(t_i)$, we have $[\mathbf{1}_{g(t_i,t_{-i})=x} - \mathbf{1}_{g(t_i',t_{-i})=x}] \geq 0$. Hence, equation 10.4 implies $\eta_{t_i'} = 0$. We conclude that $\eta = 0$, a contradiction.

10.3 BARGAINING THEORY

We now turn to a formulation of the revealed preference problem for bargaining theory. We can work out the empirical consequences of the most commonly used cooperative theories of bargaining.

Suppose n agents bargain over a fixed quantity of a single-dimensional resource: think of bargaining over a fixed monetary amount, which needs to be allocated among n agents. There is a given disagreement point, a point that specifies monetary outcomes for all the agents in the event that there is no agreement. We imagine that we observe similar agents bargaining in different circumstances, for example workers and firms in wage bargaining. The question is when observed outcomes can be rationalized as consistent with standard bargaining theory.

We shall first describe the theories under consideration, then define the kinds of data we might use to test them. Then, we present a result that characterizes the observable implications of these theories in the case where the disagreement points are fixed and the same for all agents. The surprising implication is that all of these theories are observationally equivalent. Each theory tries to capture a distinct economic phenomenon or criterion, but they turn out to have rather weak empirical consequences, to the point that they are all equivalent.

In fact, we uncover a particularly striking form of observational equivalence. We find preferences (utility functions) that serve to rationalize the data as coming from *any* of the theories. We might expect that two theories are observationally equivalent because a given dataset can be rationalized by one theory or by the other, but normally each rationalization will involve different values for the unobservable variables in the theories (preferences in our case). In the case of bargaining theory, it turns out that we can choose the unobservables so that they work for all rationalizations.

The model is as follows. We assume some quantity $m \in \mathbf{R}_+$ of money, and a vector $d = (d_1, \ldots, d_n)$ that represents the disagreement point. The set

$$B(m,d) = \{(x_1, \ldots, x_n) \in \mathbf{R}^n_+ : \sum_{i=1}^{n} x_i \leq m \text{ and, for all } i, x_i \geq d_i\}$$

is the set of all allocations of m amongst n agents, in which everyone gets at least their disagreement outcomes. The set B is therefore a set of feasible and "individually rational" allocations.

A bargaining theory uses information on agents' preferences to predict an outcome in $B(m,d)$. Suppose that each agent i is described by a strictly increasing and concave utility function $u_i : \mathbf{R}_+ \to \mathbf{R}$. We shall focus on three theories: *utilitarianism, Nash bargaining*, and *egalitarianism.*

The *utilitarian* theory calls for maximizing the sum of agents' utilities. It predicts that m is allocated so as to maximize the sum $\sum_{i=1}^n u_i(x_i)$ over $B(m,d)$. In fact, for reasons that will become clear later, we consider a generalization of the utilitarian theory, where for some function $g : A \subseteq \mathbf{R} \to \mathbf{R}$, the sum $\sum_{i=1}^n g(u_i(x_i) - u_i(d_i))$ is maximized over $B(m,d)$.

The *Nash bargaining* theory predicts a choice in $B(m,d)$ that maximizes

$$\prod_{i=1}^{n} [u_i(x_i) - u_i(d_i)] .$$

The expression being maximized is termed the *Nash product*. Note that the Nash bargaining theory is a special case of our generalization of the utilitarian theory, letting $g = \log$.

Finally, the *egalitarian* (or maxmin) theory says that $x \in B(m,d)$ should be chosen to maximize

$$\min_{i \in N} [u_i(x_i) - u_i(d_i)] .$$

We assume a set of K observations of bargaining outcomes. Each outcome represents a split of some monetary quantity. We assume that the disagreement points are fixed and the same for all agents: we can, for all intents and purposes, take the disagreement outcome to be zero for all agents. A *dataset* is then a set $D = \{x^k : k = 1, \ldots, K\}$. Each observation k specifies an allocation $x^k = (x^k_1, \ldots, x^k_n) \in \mathbf{R}^n_+$ of the total amount of money $\sum_{i=1}^n x^k_i$. Let $N = \{1, \ldots, n\}$.

Let $g : \mathbf{R}_+ \to \mathbf{R} \cup \{-\infty\}$ be a strictly increasing, smooth, and concave function. We say that data $\{x^k\}_{k=1}^K$ are *g-rationalizable* if there exist strictly increasing, smooth, and strictly concave functions u_i for which $u_i(0) = 0$ and $u'_i(0) = \infty$ (*Inada conditions*), and for which $\sum_{i \in N} g(u_i(x^k_i)) \geq \sum_{i \in N} g(u_i(y_i))$ for all allocations $(y_1, \ldots, y_n) \in B(\sum_i x^k_i, 0)$ and $k = 1, \ldots, K$. The utilitarian and Nash models are special cases of g-rationalizability. Note that the assumption of rationalizability already reflects our assumption that the disagreement point is fixed and the same for all agents.

On the other hand, data $\{x^k\}_{k=1}^K$ are *maxmin rationalizable* if there exist strictly increasing and strictly concave u_i, normalized so that $u_i(0) = 0$, for which $\min_{i\in N} u_i(x_i^k) \geq \min_{i\in N} u_i(y_i)$ for all $(y_1,\ldots,y_n) \in B(\sum_i x_i^k, 0)$ and $k = 1,\ldots,K$.

We say that data $\{x^k\}_{k=1}^K$ are *comonotonic* if for all $i,j \in N$ and all k,l, $x_i^k < x_i^l$ implies $x_j^k < x_j^l$, and for all $i,j \in N$, $x_i^k = 0$ iff $x_j^k = 0$. Comonotonicity requires that outcomes are perfectly strictly ordinally correlated (when 0 is also considered an outcome).

The following result characterizes the data that are g-rationalizable or maxmin rationalizable.

Theorem 10.8 *Given data $\{x^k\}_{k=1}^K$ and a strictly increasing concave g, the following are equivalent:*

I) *The data are comonotonic.*
II) *The data are g-rationalizable.*
III) *The data are maxmin rationalizable.*

The proof shows more than is stated here. In the proof we construct rationalizing utilities that work for any function g, as well as for the maxmin model. The resulting observational equivalence is therefore unusually strong. We can find unobservable preferences that rationalize the data using any of the models under consideration.

Proof. It follows from the first-order conditions that if the data are either g-rationalizable or maxmin rationalizable, then they are comonotonic.

For the other direction, we show something slightly stronger: If the data are comonotonic, then there exist strictly concave, continuous, and increasing functions u_i such that, if $\varphi : [0,\infty) \to \mathbf{R} \cup \{-\infty\}$ is an increasing, symmetric, and quasiconcave function, then $\varphi(u_1(x_1^k),\ldots,u_n(x_n^k)) \geq \varphi(u_1(y_1),\ldots,u_n(y_n))$ for all allocations $(y_1,\ldots,y_n)$ satisfying $\sum_{i\in N} x_i^k = \sum_{i\in N} y_i$.[4] As a special case, we have $\varphi(z_1,\ldots,z_n) = \sum_{i=1}^n g(z_i)$. Note the order of the quantifiers used above: the same profile of utility functions $u_1,\ldots,u_n$ works across all φ.

To this end, we suppose the data are comonotonic, and ignore replications as well as points where every agent consumes 0. Without loss of generality, let us suppose that $x_i^1 < x_i^2 < \ldots < x_i^K$ for all $i \in N$ (that this is possible follows from comonotonicity). Below we construct a profile of utility functions $u_1,\ldots,u_n$ with the property that for all $k = 1,\ldots,K$, $\sum_{i\in N} u_i(x_i^k)$ is maximal across all allocations $y_1,\ldots,y_n$ for which $\sum_{i\in N} x_i^k = \sum_{i\in N} y_i$, and $\min_{i\in N} u_i(x_i^k)$ is also maximal across all such allocations; it follows that, since each u_i is strictly increasing, $u_i(x_i^k) = u_j(x_j^k)$ for all $i,j \in N$.

We first argue that such a construction suffices to establish the result: Let φ be as above, and suppose by way of contradiction that there is a k and a feasible allocation $(y_1,\ldots,y_n)$ for which $\varphi(u_1(y_1),\ldots,u_n(y_n)) > \varphi(u_1(x_1^k),\ldots,u_n(x_n^k))$. Note then, by symmetry of φ, that for any permutation of the agents $\sigma : N \to N$,

[4] Symmetry means that if σ is a permutation on $\{1,\ldots,n\}$ then $\varphi(x_{\sigma(1)},\ldots,x_{\sigma(n)}) = \varphi(x_1,\ldots,x_n)$. Increasing here means that if $x_i > y_i$ for all i, then $\varphi(x_1,\ldots,x_n) > \varphi(y_1,\ldots,y_n)$.

$\varphi(u_{\sigma(1)}(y_{\sigma(1)}),\dots,u_{\sigma(n)}(y_{\sigma(n)})) = \varphi(u_1(y_1),\dots,u_n(y_n))$. Quasiconcavity of φ then implies that

$$\varphi\left(\sum_{i\in N}\frac{u_i(y_i)}{n},\dots,\sum_{i\in N}\frac{u_i(y_i)}{n}\right) > \varphi(u_1(x_1^k),\dots,u_n(x_n^k)).$$

By the strictly increasing property of φ, and using the fact that $u_i(x_i^k) = u_j(x_j^k)$ for all $i,j \in N$, this implies that

$$\sum_{i\in N}\frac{u_i(y_i)}{n} > \sum_{i\in N}\frac{u_i(x_i^k)}{n},$$

contradicting

$$\sum_{i\in N} u_i(x_i^k) \geq \sum_{i\in N} u_i(y_i)$$

for all feasible allocations $y_1,\dots,y_n$.

We finish the proof by constructing, for each i, a strictly decreasing, continuous, and positive function f_i, with the property that if we set u_i to be the integral of f_i, then the profile of utility functions $(u_1,\dots,u_n)$ works as required by the first part of the proof.

We proceed by induction. We ensure that, for each $i \in N$ and each k, the following are true:

I) $\int_0^{x_i^k} f_i(x)dx = \int_0^{x_j^k} f_j(x)dx$

II) $f_i(x_i^k) = f_j(x_j^k)$.

In the first place, for $k = 1$, we define for each agent j, $f_j(0) = +\infty$. The construction is done in a series of steps, labeled (I) to (VI).

I) For K, define $f_i(x_i^K) = 1$ for all $i \in N$;

II) for $x > x_i^K$, we define $f_i(x)$ to be any strictly decreasing function, taking values everywhere less than 1 and making f_i continuous.

III) We proceed by induction. Let $k > 1$ be arbitrary, and suppose that $f_i(x)$ has been defined for all $x \geq x_i^k$. We assume that for all $k' \geq k$, $f_i(x_i^{k'}) = f_j(x_j^{k'})$ and

$$\int_{x_i^k}^{x_i^K} f_i(x)dx = \int_{x_j^k}^{x_j^K} f_j(x)dx \text{ for all } i,j \in N.$$

Recall that we have $x_i^1 < x_i^2 < \dots < x_i^K$. We choose a finite $f_j(x_j^{k-1})$ but we must choose it to be sufficiently large. Specifically, let z be large enough so that there is $\varepsilon > 0$ for which $z(x_j^k - x_j^{k-1}) - \varepsilon > \max_{i\in N} f_i(x_i^k)(x_i^k - x_i^{k-1}) + \varepsilon$ for all j. We can then set $f_j(x_j^{k-1}) = z$ for all j.

IV) Observe that, given $f_j(x_j^{k-1})$ and $f_j(x_j^k)$, for any $\varepsilon > 0$ and any

$$y \in \left(f_j(x_j^k)(x_j^k - x_j^{k-1}) + \varepsilon, f_j(x_j^{k-1})(x_j^k - x_j^{k-1}) - \varepsilon\right),$$

we may define f_j continuous and decreasing on $x \in (x_j^{k-1}, x_j^k)$ so that

$$\int_{x_j^{k-1}}^{x_j^k} f_j(x)dx = y.$$

This follows as we may choose the integral as close as possible to $f_j(x_j^{k-1})(x_j^k - x_j^{k-1})$ by taking a sequence of decreasing continuous functions approaching the constant value $f_j(x_j^{k-1})$ pointwise in (x_j^{k-1}, x_j^k); likewise we may choose the integral as close as possible to $f_j(x_j^k)(x_j^k - x_j^{k-1})$.

V) Complete $f_j(x)$ on $x \in (x_j^{k-1}, x_j^k)$ so that

$$\int_{x_j^{k-1}}^{x_j^k} f_j(x)dx$$

is equalized across all agents, by picking

$$y \in \bigcap_{i \in N} \left(f_i(x_i^k)(x_i^k - x_i^{k-1}) + \varepsilon, f_i(x_i^{k-1})(x_i^k - x_i^{k-1}) - \varepsilon\right)$$

and choosing $f_j(x)$ on $x \in (x_j^{k-1}, x_j^k)$ so that

$$\int_{x_j^{k-1}}^{x_j^k} f_j(x)dx = y.$$

VI) In the case of $k = 1$, we must also maintain that

$$\int_0^{x_j^1} f_j(x)dx < +\infty.$$

The functions f_j so constructed satisfy the conditions we ask for: that for all k, $f_j(x_j^k)$ is equalized across j, and

$$\int_0^{x_j^k} f_j(x)dx$$

is equalized across j. By setting

$$u_j(x) = \int_0^x f_j(x)dx,$$

we have the required u_j.

10.4 STABLE MATCHING THEORY

We now turn to stable matching theory. Stable matchings find very important normative applications in economics, but the theory provides a basic predictive framework as well. Many markets, such as labor markets and the marriage "market," have two sets of agents who pair up and who may have preferences over who they form a pair with. We describe the basic notion of a stable matching, and carry out a simple revealed preference exercise.

Our version of the model assumes a set M of *types of men* and a set W of *types of women*. The sets M and W are finite and disjoint. We assume a number K_m of men of type m, and K_w of women of type w. The primitives of the model are then given by a tuple $\langle M, W, P, K\rangle$, in which M and W denote sets as before, $K = (K_i)_{i\in M\cup W}$ is a list of non-negative integers, and P is a *preference profile*: a list of preferences $>_m$ for every $m \in M$ and $>_w$ for every $w \in W$. Each $>_m$ is a linear order over W, and each $>_w$ is a linear order over M.[5]

The standard prediction concept, or theory of which matchings to expect, is the notion of stable matching. A *matching* is an $|M| \times |W|$ matrix $X = (x_{m,w})$ such that $x_{m,w} \in \mathbf{Z}_+$, $\sum_w x_{m,w} = K_m$ for all m, and $\sum_m x_{m,w} = K_w$ for all w. The number $x_{m,w}$ is the number of men of type m matched to women of type w.

Stability requires the definition of blocking. A pair $(m,w) \in M \times W$ is a *blocking pair for* X if there are m' and w' such that $m >_w m'$, $w >_m w'$, $x_{m,w'} > 0$, and $x_{m',w} > 0$. The matching X is *stable* if there are no blocking pairs for X. To keep the presentation simple, we ignore individual rationality and single (non-matched) agents.

A matching X is *stable-rationalizable* if there exists a preference profile $P = ((>_m)_{m\in M}, (>_w)_{w\in W})$ such that X is a stable matching in $\langle M, W, P, K\rangle$.

A (undirected) *graph* is a pair $G = (V, L)$, where V is a set and $L \subseteq V \times V$ is a non-reflexive and symmetric binary relation on V. Elements of V are referred to as *vertices* and elements of L as *edges*. A *path* in G is a sequence $p = \langle v_0, \ldots, v_N\rangle$ such that $(v_n, v_{n+1}) \in L$ for all $n \in \{0, \ldots, N-1\}$. We denote by $v \in p$ that v is a vertex in p. A path $\langle v_0, \ldots, v_N\rangle$ *connects* the vertices v_0 and v_N. A path $\langle v_0, \ldots, v_N\rangle$ is *minimal* if there is no proper subsequence of $\langle v_0, \ldots, v_N\rangle$ which also connects v_0 and v_N.

A *cycle* in G is a path $c = \langle v_0, \ldots, v_N\rangle$ with $v_0 = v_N$. A cycle is *minimal* if for any two vertices v_n and $v_{n'}$ in c, the paths in c from v_n to $v_{n'}$ and from $v_{n'}$ to v_n are distinct and minimal. If c and c' are two cycles, and there is a path from a vertex in c to a vertex in c', then we say that c and c' are *connected*.

For a matching X, we consider the graph defined by letting the vertices be all the nonzero elements of X; and by letting there be an edge between two vertices when they lie on the same row or column of X. Formally, to each matching X we associate a graph (V, L) defined as follows. The set of vertices V is $\{(m,w) : m \in M, w \in W \text{ such that } x_{m,w} > 0\}$, and an edge $((m,w),(m',w')) \in L$ is formed for every pair of vertices (m,w) and (m',w') with $m = m'$ or $w = w'$ (but not both).

[5] The most basic model assumes that there is only one agent of each type, but the revealed preference question is more interesting with many agents of each type.

Theorem 10.9 *A matching is stable-rationalizable iff its associated graph does not contain two connected distinct minimal cycles.*

We omit the proof of Theorem 10.9, but the intuition behind the necessity direction is simple, and worth conveying here. Consider for example the matching on the left below:

$$\begin{array}{ccc} 11 & 9 & 10 \\ 0 & 22 & 41 \\ 13 & 91 & 0 \end{array} \qquad \begin{array}{ccccc} 11 & — & 9 & & 10 \\ | & & | & & \\ 0 & & 22 & & 41 \\ | & & | & & \\ 13 & — & 91 & & 0 \end{array}$$

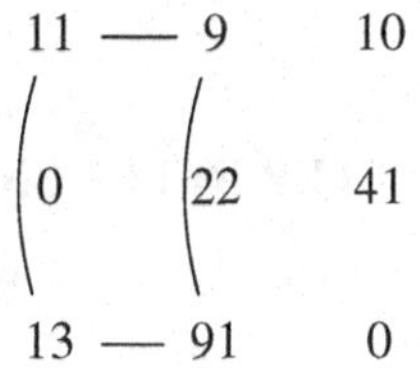

The matching has three types of men and three types of women. There are 11 men of type 1 matched to women of type 1, 9 men of type 1 are matched to women of type 2, and so on. The graph associated to this matching contains a cycle, shown on the right. In fact, it has more than one cycle, and they are connected, but focus now on the cycle depicted.

If we are to find rationalizing preferences, we need to decide how men of type 1 rank women of type 1 and 2. Say that women of type 2 are preferred to 1; we can denote this preference by orienting the horizontal edge on the graph as pointing from 11 to 9. Now consider the preferences of women of type 2. Is it possible for them to rank men of type 1 above men of type 3? The answer is negative, as there are type 2 women matched to type 3 men, and, simultaneously, type 1 men matched to type 2 women. If women of type 3 were to prefer type 1 men, then some of the latter would form blocking pairs with type 1 men who are matched to type 1 women. Thus the vertical edge from 9 to 91 must point down, *away* from the direction of the first edge, which points from 11 to 9. In fact, the important implication of stability is that for any two consecutive edges which form a right angle in the graph, one must be oriented to point away from the other.

The reasoning above extends to the horizontal edge between 91 and 13, and then to the vertical edge between 13 and 11. The former must point to the left, and the latter must then point up. As a result, a cycle must be oriented as a "flow." If we start, as we did, by having type 1 men prefer type 2 to type 1 women, then we obtain a clockwise flow. If we instead had started with the opposite preference, then we would have obtained a counterclockwise flow.

Now, we can consider a path leaving the cycle, for example the horizontal edge between 11 and 10 in the graph. An orientation of this edge amounts to specifying type 1 men's preferences between women of type 1 and 3. Recall that we have oriented the cycle in a clockwise fashion, so that the edge between 13 and 11 points up. Then the edge leaving the cycle, and going from 11 to 10, cannot be oriented to the left. The reason is that we would then have a blocking pair using some of the 10 men of type 1 who are matched with women of type

3, and some women of type 1 who are matched to men of type 3. The general principle is that any path leaving a cycle must point away from the cycle.

It should now be clear that we cannot have two cycles connected by a minimal path. Such a path would have to point away from both cycles. Then there would be two consecutive edges on the path, such that each edge point to their common vertex. This situation would imply the existence of some blocking pair, just as in the examples we discussed above.

10.5 CHAPTER REFERENCES

Persistence under expansion was introduced by Yanovskaya (1980), while Theorem 10.1 is a generalization of her result due to Sprumont (2000). Persistence under expansion and persistence under contraction are closely related to the consistency concepts discussed by Peleg and Tijs (1996). Persistence under expansion is clearly related to condition γ from social choice theory (see, e.g., Sen, 1971). The first part of persistence under contraction is similar to condition α for single-agent choice functions, while the second part is related to condition β. Theorems 10.2, 10.3, and 10.4 are also from Sprumont (2000). Ray and Zhou (2001) establishes related results for extensive-form games and subgame perfection. Xu and Zhou (2007), Bossert and Sprumont (2013), Rehbeck (2014), and Xiong (2013) study the extensive-form question when the game itself is not observable. Instead, the primitive is a classical choice function.

Theorem 10.5 and the notion of N-congruence are due to Galambos (2010). Galambos (2010) describes a more sophisticated version of Theorem 10.5 which appears in his dissertation. It need not rely on the assumption of a line-closed domain.

Theorem 10.6 is due to Lee (2011). Interchangeability is a well-known property of the Nash equilibria of zero-sum games. The contribution in Lee's work is to show that it is *all* that the property of zero-sum adds, from the revealed preference perspective.

Theorem 10.7 is due to Ledyard (1986). More complicated theorems appear there, dealing with certain restrictions on the forms of the u_i and p_i functions. For example, he obtains the necessary and sufficient conditions required for a direct revelation mechanism to be strongly rationalized by a Bayesian environment when the ordinal, but not cardinal, structure of each u_i is known conditional on each type profile t (as would be the case in standard private-valued single-dimensional consumption environments). Such characterizations are based on Lemma 1.12. However, a few important questions seem to remain unresolved. More importantly, the results described here consist of a single observation. It is not terribly surprising that anything is rationalizable in this case. For an analogy with choice theory, a choice function defined only on one budget is always rationalizable, unless there is sufficient structure on the class of rationalizing relations. An interesting idea would be to understand what happens when multiple observations are possible, possibly when some parameters of the environment change, but others remain fixed. In fact, a simple method of doing this would be to consider strategy spaces S_i, one for each agent, and consider Bayesian strategies $\sigma_i : T_i \to S_i$. It is then meaningful to discuss notions of strict Bayesian Nash equilibrium, and by varying the spaces of strategies, one may come up with interesting testable implications.

Section 10.3 is based on Chambers and Echenique (2014b). The paper includes results for the cases where disagreement points may vary in an observable way (when disagreement points are unobservable the theories become non-testable). The proof of Theorem 10.8 and the observation that the same list of utility functions works to rationalize each environment, taken here from Chambers and Echenique (2014b), were suggested to us by an anonymous referee. For a continuous version of the problem, see Chiappori, Donni, and Komunjer (2012). We discuss other approaches in Chapter 12.

Theorem 10.9 and the discussion in Section 10.4 is taken from Echenique, Lee, Shum, and Yenmez (2013). That paper also includes results on which matchings are rationalizable as optimal for one side of the market, and rationalizable with transfers. These notions turn out to be observationally equivalent: a matching is rationalizable using monetary transfers iff it is rationalizable as stable and optimal for one side of the market (men or women).

We have assumed that observed matches consist of matrices of non-negative integers. We can instead suppose that multiple matching among the same individuals (or types of individuals) are observed. Then we can insist on rationalizing preferences that make all of them stable. This exercise is carried out in Echenique (2008). The same problem for a model with transfers is worked out in Chambers and Echenique (2014a).

CHAPTER 11

Social Choice and Political Science

This chapter deals with models of collective choice in which individual agents' preferences are aggregated into collective behavior. The first class of models use some fixed method to aggregate preferences. We assume that collective choices can be observed, but that individual agents' preferences are unobserved. The second class of models are more structured models of voting in political economy and political science. A common idea in political science is that voters' preferences are "Euclidean"; we present the testable implications of this notion. Finally, we consider models of individual voter behavior and work out the corresponding observable implications.

11.1 TESTABLE IMPLICATIONS OF PREFERENCE AGGREGATION FUNCTIONS

The main questions in this section take the following form. Suppose that a group preference (or choice) is observable. Is this group preference consistent with a collection of rational agents whose preferences are aggregated according to some rule? We may, for example, wonder when a group's collective behavior is consistent with majority rule.

There are three ways to interpret the material that we are about to present. First, if we know the aggregation rule that the agents use, we may want to test the hypothesis that a society of agents behave rationally as individuals, when the only observable data come in the form of aggregate preference. Second, when the aggregation rule is unknown, we may want to test the *joint* hypotheses that a group of agents use a certain aggregation rule, and that they each behave rationally as individuals. Finally, a different interpretation of these results is that we might want to characterize all possible "paradoxes" that we might expect from using a given aggregation rule. Condorcet's paradox (a cycle on three alternatives) illustrates the problems that can arise from using majority rule. The results in this section describe all possible paradoxes of this type.

The model is as follows. Let X be a set of possible alternatives. We shall assume that we observe all possible binary comparisons of elements in X; that is, we observe a complete binary relation $\succeq$ on X. This assumption is similar in spirit to our assumption in Chapter 2 that all choice behavior is observable. The set of all complete binary relations will be denoted $\mathcal{C}(X)$. Individual agents' preferences will be strict preferences (linear orders) over X. Denote the set of linear orders over X by $\mathcal{L}(X)$.

We now describe two classical aggregation methods. We fix a finite set N, which we interpret as a set of agents. An *aggregation rule* is a function $f : \mathcal{L}(X)^N \to \mathcal{C}(X)$ mapping *profiles* of strict preferences $(\succeq_i)_{i\in N}$ into a complete binary relation $f((\succeq_i)_{i\in N})$.

The *majority rule* is the aggregation rule f_m defined by

$$(x,y) \in f_m((\succeq_i)_{i\in N}) \text{ iff } |\{i \in N : (x,y) \in \succeq_i\}| \geq \frac{|N|}{2}.$$

Note that, if we let $\succeq = f_m((\succeq_i)_{i\in N})$, then $x \succ y$ iff there is a strict majority of agents who strictly prefer x over y (defining the strict part of $\succeq$ in the usual way).

The *unanimity rule* is the function f_u defined by $(x,y) \in f_u((\succeq_i)_{i\in N})$ if there is $i \in N$ for which $x \succeq_i y$. Note that, if we let $\succeq = f_u((\succeq_i)_{i\in N})$, then $x \succ y$ iff all agents strictly prefer x over y (defining the strict part of $\succeq$ in the usual way).

We can now turn the above definitions into a revealed-preference exercise. Assuming that a complete binary relation $\succeq$ is observed, and given a rule f, we want to know when there is a set of agents N and a preference profile for the agents in N such that $\succeq$ is the image of the profile under f. Say that $\succeq_0 \in \mathcal{C}(X)$ is *majority rationalizable* if there exist a finite N and $(\succeq_i)_{i\in N}$ for which $f_m((\succeq_i)_{i\in N}) = \succeq_0$. Similarly, we will say that $\succeq_0 \in \mathcal{C}(X)$ is *unanimity rationalizable* (or *Pareto rationalizable*) if there exist a finite N and $(\succeq_i)_{i\in N}$ for which $f_u((\succeq_i)_{i\in N}) = \succeq_0$.

Remark 11.1 Note that we allow the freedom of choosing the cardinality of N when we construct a rationalization. Below we turn to problems in which the cardinality of N is fixed.

The first and most important result here is a negative result stating that any $\succeq_0 \in \mathcal{C}(X)$ is majority rationalizable. Therefore, the hypothesis that a social preference arises from application of majority rule to some unknown society is untestable.

McGarvey's Theorem *Any $\succeq_0 \in \mathcal{C}(X)$ is majority rationalizable.*

The negative message in McGarvey's Theorem is not affected by our assumption that all binary comparisons are observable. If one's observations were less complete, then, of course, majority rule would remain non-testable. The conclusion in McGarvey's Theorem carries over to cases in which our observations are poorer than a complete binary relation.

Proof. The proof is constructive. Let $\succeq_0 \in \mathcal{C}(X)$. If $\succeq_0$ is complete indifference, simply let N consist of two agents with exactly opposed preferences. Suppose then that there is at least one pair $x, y \in X$ with $x \succ_0 y$.

First, let us write $X = \{x_1, ..., x_m\}$ (this is possible as X is finite). Given any pair $x, y \in X$ for which $x \succ_0 y$, we define two linear-order relations. The first, $\succeq^0_{(x,y)}$ ranks $x \succ^0_{(x,y)} y$, and ranks x and y (strictly) above every element of $X \backslash \{x,y\}$; otherwise, for $x_i, x_k \in X \backslash \{x,y\}$, $x_i \succ^0_{(x,y)} x_k$ iff $i > k$. The second, $\succeq^1_{(x,y)}$, ranks $x \succ^1_{(x,y)} y$, and ranks x and y (strictly) below every element of $X \backslash \{x,y\}$; otherwise, for $x_i, x_k \in X \backslash \{x,y\}$, $x_k \succ^1_{(x,y)} x_i$ iff $i > k$. By defining N to be a set of cardinality $2|\{(x,y) \in X^2 : x \succ_0 y\}|$ and assigning, for each $(x,y) \in \succ_0$, one agent with preference $\succeq^0_{(x,y)}$ and one with preference $\succeq^1_{(x,y)}$, we arrive at $(\succeq_i)_{i \in N}$ for which $f_m((\succeq_i)_{i \in N}) = \succeq_0$.

We now turn to a revealed preference question for the unanimity rule. Our second result states that any quasitransitive relation is unanimity rationalizable.

Theorem 11.2 *A binary relation $\succeq_0 \in \mathcal{C}(X)$ is unanimity rationalizable iff it is quasitransitive.*

Proof. It is easy to see that any unanimity rationalizable relation is quasitransitive. Conversely, let $\succeq_0 \in \mathcal{C}(X)$ be quasitransitive.

We shall show that, for every x, y which are unranked in $\succ_0$, there is a linear order extending $(\succ_0 \cup \{(x,y)\})$. Then let N have a cardinality of

$$2 \times |\{(x,y) \in X^2 : x, y \text{are unranked}\}|.$$

Assign, for each such pair, one agent with a linear order extending $\succ_0 \cup \{(x,y)\}$ and one with a linear order extending $\succ_0 \cup \{(y,x)\}$. Then it is easy to see that $f_u((\succeq_i)_{i \in N}) = \succeq_0$.

Let, then, $x, y \in X$ be unranked according to $(\succ_0 \cup =)$. That is, $x \sim_0 y$ and $x \neq y$. The relation $(\succ_0 \cup =)$ is a partial order. Let $\succeq'$ be the transitive closure of $(\succ_0 \cup = \cup \{(x,y)\})$. We claim that $\succeq'$ is also a partial order. It is clearly antisymmetric and reflexive; it remains to show that it is transitive. But this kind of argument is familiar from Theorem 1.5, so we omit it here. By Theorem 1.4, we know that there is a linear order which extends $\succeq'$.

The previous results deal with groups of unknown size: the size of the group is as unknown as the agents' preferences (see Remark 11.1). Therefore, in constructing a rationalization, one has the freedom of using a group of any size. The construction in each of the proofs illustrates that the groups can be quite large.

It so happens, though, that we frequently know the size of the group, or at least an upper bound. For example one may want to rationalize the behavior of a given committee (such as a faculty meeting, Congress, or the United Nations) when the number of members is known, but not their individual preferences.

It turns out that when we restrict the cardinality of the set of agents, the problem of determining whether a binary relation is majority (or unanimity) rationalizable is much more difficult, and there are far fewer known results.

For an integer n, we say that $\succeq_0$ is *n-unanimity rationalizable* if there exists a set N of cardinality n for which there are $(\succeq_i)_{i \in N}$ such that $f_u((\succeq_i)_{i \in N}) = \succeq_0$.

We could similarly define a related concept for majority rule, but as far as we know there are no results in this direction.

Almost most all results for n-unanimity rationalization concern $n = 2$. The next result is due to Dushnik and Miller.

Theorem 11.3 *A binary relation $\succeq_0 \in \mathcal{C}(X)$ is 2-unanimity rationalizable iff $\succeq_0$ is quasitransitive, and there exists a partial order $\succeq^*$ such that $x \sim_0 y$ iff either $x \succeq^* y$ or $y \succeq^* x$.*

Proof. Suppose that $\succeq_0$ is 2-unanimity rationalizable, say by $(\succeq_1, \succeq_2)$. Clearly $\succ_0$ is quasitransitive. Now, define $x \succeq^* y$ if $x \succeq_1 y$ and $y \succeq_2 x$. Note that $\succeq^*$ is a partial order which satisfies the property in the statement of the theorem.

Conversely, suppose that $\succeq^*$ satisfying the property in the statement of the theorem exists. Define a binary relation $\succeq_1$ as follows. Let $x \succeq_1 y$ if either $x \succ_0 y$, or if $x \sim_0 y$ and $x \succeq^* y$. We claim that $\succeq_1$ is a linear order. Completeness is a consequence of the completeness of $\succeq_0$ and the property of $\succeq^*$. To see that it is antisymmetric, suppose that $x \succeq_1 y$ and $y \succeq_1 x$. It cannot be that $x \succ_0 y$, as that would rule out $y \succeq_1 x$. Thus we can assume that $x \sim_0 y$; then $x \succeq_1 y$ implies $x \succeq^* y$, and $y \succeq_1 x$ implies $y \succeq^* x$. It follows that $x = y$, as $\succeq^*$ is a partial order.

Finally, $\succeq_1$ is transitive. Let $x \succeq_1 y$ and $y \succeq_1 z$. There is only something to show when one of these comparisons is due to $\succeq_0$ and the other to $\succeq^*$. These cases are $x \succ_0 y \succeq^* z$ and $x \succeq^* y \succ_0 z$. In the first case, by completeness, if we do not have $x \succeq_1 z$, then we must have $z \succeq_1 x$: (a) If $z \succeq_1 x$ is due to $z \succ_0 x$, we have a contradiction because the transitivity of $\succ_0$ implies that $z \succ_0 y$, which contradicts $y \succeq^* z$; (b) If $z \succeq_1 x$ is due to $z \succeq^* x$, we have a contradiction because the transitivity of $\succeq^*$ implies that $y \succeq^* x$, a contradiction of $x \succ_0 y$. We can derive a similar contradiction in the case $x \succeq^* y \succ_0 z$.

Similarly, we can define the binary relation $\succeq_2$ by $x \succeq_2 y$ if $x \succ_0 y$ or $y \succeq^* x$. Then $\succeq_2$ is a linear order as well.

The linear orders $\succeq_1$ and $\succeq_2$ thus defined provide a rationalization of $\succ_0$. If $x \neq y$, then $x \succ_0 y$ iff $x \succ_1 y$ and $x \succ_2 y$; and $x \sim_0 y$ iff $\succeq_1$ and $\succeq_2$ disagree in how they compare x and y.

In light of Theorem 11.2, Theorem 11.3 gives the property of $\succeq_0$ that, *in addition* to being unanimity rationalizable, it is rationalizable by a group of two agents. This condition, that $\sim_0$ can be "oriented" to form a transitive $\succeq^*$, is difficult to falsify. One would need to check all possible orientations of $\sim_0$. A falsifiable characterization of when such an orientation is possible is provided in the next result.

We first need a simple definition. We will say $x_1, ..., x_k$ is an *odd $\sim_0$ cycle* if k is odd, and for all i, $x_i \sim_0 x_{i+1}$ (as usual, addition is modulo k, and we allow repetitions of vertices). We say the cycle is *triangulated* if there is $i \in \{1, ..., k\}$ for which $x_i \sim_0 x_{i+2}$.

Theorem 11.4 *A binary relation $\succeq_0 \in \mathcal{C}(X)$ is 2-unanimity rationalizable iff it is quasitransitive and every odd $\sim_0$ cycle is triangulated.*

Proof. We will establish necessity of the condition only. Sufficiency, while not conceptually difficult, is tedious. Therefore, let us suppose that $\succeq_1$ and $\succeq_2$ are linear orders which 2-unanimity rationalize $\succeq_0$.

To see that any odd $\sim_0$ cycle is triangulated, suppose, by way of contradiction, that there exists an odd $\sim_0$ cycle $x_1,...,x_k$ which is not triangulated. First, it is the case that for all i, $x_i \neq x_{i+1}$; otherwise since $x_{i-1} \sim_0 x_i = x_{i+1}$, we have $x_{i-1} \sim_0 x_{i+1}$, contradicting the fact that the cycle is not triangulated.

Suppose, without loss of generality, that $x_1 \succ_1 x_2$ and $x_2 \succ_2 x_1$. Now, because $x_1,...,x_k$ is not triangulated, it follows that $x_2 \succ_2 x_3$ and $x_3 \succ_1 x_2$; because, if instead $x_2 \succ_1 x_3$ and $x_3 \succ_2 x_2$, we would have $x_1 \succ_1 x_3$ and $x_3 \succ_2 x_1$, contradicting the fact that $x_1,...,x_k$ is not triangulated. By continuing this argument and using the fact that k is odd, we establish that $x_2 \succ_1 x_1$ and $x_1 \succ_2 x_2$, a contradiction.

These results more or less exhaust the known characterizations of unanimity rationalizable relations for fixed and finite numbers of agents in abstract environments. As far as we know, there are no such results for majority rationalizable relations (or for other simple voting rules). Characterizing such relations should be an important goal for future research. There is reason to believe that such characterizations will be, in general, difficult to come by. A classical result in computer science states that, given a quasitransitive relation, determining whether or not n agents suffice to rationalize that relation by unanimity rule is NP-complete for any $n \geq 3$.

11.1.1 Utilitarian rationalizability

Suppose we have given a family of preference relations $\succeq_1,...,\succeq_n$ on a finite set X. Further, let $\succeq_0$ be an arbitrary transitive relation on X. We will say that $\succeq_0$ is *utilitarian rationalizable* by $\succeq_1,...,\succeq_n$ if there exists, for each i, a utility representation $u_i : X \to \mathbf{R}$ for which $x \succeq_i y \leftrightarrow u_i(x) \geq u_i(y)$ such that

- $x \succ_0 y$ implies $\sum_{i=1}^n u_i(x) > \sum_{i=1}^n u_i(y)$
- $x \sim_0 y$ implies $\sum_{i=1}^n u_i(x) = \sum_{i=1}^n u_i(y)$.[1]

If $\succeq_0$ is complete, these conditions are equivalent to the function $u_0 = \sum_{i=1}^n u_i$ being a utility representation for $\succeq_0$.

Our goal is to characterize utilitarian rationalizable relations $\succeq_0$. That is, we want to test the hypothesis that society ranks alternatives according to a utilitarian criterion, where the ordinal content of individual preference is known, but not the cardinal content. The next result is due to Peter Fishburn.

Theorem 11.5 *A transitive relation $\succeq_0$ is utilitarian rationalizable by $\succeq_1$ $,...,\succeq_n$ iff for all finite disjoint sequences $x_1,...,x_K$ and $y_1,...,y_K$ (*i.e. *there is no k,l for which $x_k = y_l$, but possibly allowing repetitions), and for all collections*

[1] See our discussion in 10.3 of utilitarianism in the context of bargaining.

of permutations $\sigma_i : K \to K$ *(one for each* $i = 1,\ldots,n$*), such that for all* $j = 1,\ldots,K$, $x_j \succeq_0 y_j$ *and for all* $i = 1,\ldots,n$, $y_j \succeq_i x_{\sigma_i(j)}$, *it follows that for all* $j = 1,\ldots,K$, $x_j \sim_0 y_j$ *and for all* $i = 1,\ldots,n$, $y_j \sim_i x_{\sigma_i(j)}$.

Proof. The relation $\succeq_0$ is utilitarian rationalizable iff there exists, for each i and each $x \in X$ a number $u_i^x \in \mathbf{R}$, for which the following inequalities are satisfied:

I) If $x \succeq_0 y$, then $\sum_i u_i^x \geq \sum_i u_i^y$.
II) If $x \succ_0 y$, then $\sum_i u_i^x > \sum_i u_i^y$.
III) If $x \succeq_i y$, then $u_i^x \geq u_i^y$.
IV) If $x \succ_i y$, then $u_i^x > u_i^y$.

We can easily write this in matrix form. Let B be a matrix with $|X \times N|$ columns, and with one row for each constraint listed above. Rows of type (I) and (II) will be specified by the vector $\mathbf{1}_{N\times\{x\}} - \mathbf{1}_{N\times\{y\}}$, while rows of type (III) and (IV) will be of the form $\mathbf{1}_{(i,x)} - \mathbf{1}_{(i,y)}$. We search for the existence of a real-valued vector $u \in \mathbf{R}^{X\times N}$ with the property that for rows m of type (I) or (III), $B_m \cdot u \geq 0$, and for rows m of type (II) or (IV), $B_m \cdot u > 0$. By Lemma 1.13, the non-existence of such a u is equivalent to the existence of an integer-valued vector $\eta \geq 0$, such that for some row m of either type (II) or (IV), $\eta_m > 0$, and $\eta \cdot B = 0$. Rows are indexed by their associated relation; so a row of type (I) will be written $B_{x\succeq_0 y}$, for example.

It cannot be that only constraints of type (III) or (IV) are associated with $\eta_m > 0$, as we know there always exists a utility representation for a weak order on a finite set. So, let us consider two sequences of length $K = \sum_{\{m:m \text{ is of type (I) or (II)}\}} \eta_m$, say $x_1,\ldots,x_K$ and $y_1,\ldots,y_K$, where for fixed $(x,y) \in X \times X$, $|\{k : x_k = x, y_k = y\}| = \eta_{x\succeq_0 y} + \eta_{x\succ_0 y}$.

Since $\succeq_0$ is transitive, we may assume these two sequences are disjoint (that is, there is no j,k for which $x_j = y_k$), as the rows can be canceled to remove overlapping elements. Similarly, since each $\succeq_i$ is transitive, we can assume that there is no triple x,y,z and $i \in N$ for which the rows corresponding to $x \, R_i \, y$ and $y \, Q_i \, z$ each have positive weight, where R and Q can be either $\succeq$ or $\succ$.

Similarly, we may also assume that for any $i = 1,\ldots,n$, and any x, it cannot be the case that there are y,z for which both a row corresponding to $y \succeq_i x$ or $y \succ_i x$ and a row corresponding to $x \succeq_i z$ or $x \succ_i z$ each have positive weight. This we may assure by simply summing such rows to get a row involving only y and z. We will call this assumption (*).

Now, it follows that since $\eta \cdot B = 0$, and since the $x_1,\ldots,x_K$ and $y_1,\ldots,y_K$ sequences are disjoint, it must be that rows of type (I) or (II) can only be eliminated by a collection of rows of type (III) or (IV). That is, every instance of x_j contributes a positive term $\mathbf{1}_{(i,x_j)}$, so in order for $\eta \cdot B = 0$, this positive term must be canceled by a negative term. This negative term must come from a constraint of type (III) or type (IV), so there must exist, for agent i, a row of type $y \succeq_i x$ or a row of type $y \succ_i x$ with positive weight. And by our assumption (*), this introduces a positive term on $\mathbf{1}_{(y,i)}$, which must be matched by some y_k.

What we have shown is that there exists, for each agent, a bijection $\sigma_i : K \to K$ such that $y_j \succeq_i x_{\sigma_i(j)}$. And since one of the rows corresponds to type (II) or (IV), $\eta_m > 0$, it follows that either there exists $x_j \succ_0 y_j$, or there exists $i \in 1,\ldots,n$ such that $y_j \succ_i x_{\sigma_i(j)}$. This is exactly what is precluded by the statement of the theorem.

11.2 MODELS IN FORMAL POLITICAL SCIENCE

It is interesting and fruitful to analyze formal models in political science from the perspective of revealed preference theory. There is a wealth of data on which to test theories of political competition and voters' behavior. Here we shall discuss two different models, and investigate their empirical content under different assumptions about what can be observed.

We first discuss the standard model of "spatial" preference and investigate circumstances where it lacks testable implications, even when we have rich data (we observe a full preference relation). We then turn to more general models of voter behavior, and consider more limited data.

11.2.1 Refuting Euclidean preferences

Many models in political science are based on voters having a special kind of "spatial" preference. We consider here the testable implications of such models of voter behavior. The idea is that policy positions can be represented as points in some Euclidean space, $\mathbf{R}^d$. We can view a vector $x \in \mathbf{R}^d$ as representing a position in each of d issues. We can then model a voter's behavior using a preference relation on $\mathbf{R}^d$.

The standard benchmark model in political science is that of *Euclidean preferences,* where each agent is endowed with an ideal point, and a vector of policy positions is preferred to another iff it is closer to the voter's ideal point. Formally, for each agent i, let $y_i \in \mathbf{R}^d$ be i's *ideal point*. Then i's preference relation, $\succeq_i$, is defined by $x \succeq_i z$ iff $\|x - y_i\| \leq \|z - y_i\|$, where $\|x\| = (\sum_{i=1}^d x_i^2)^{1/2}$ is the Euclidean norm on $\mathbf{R}^d$ (hence the term Euclidean preferences).

The theory is simple, but when we observe data on voter behavior, we do not observe choices among vectors in $\mathbf{R}^d$. One basic problem is then to identify alternatives with vectors in some Euclidean space, in a way that is consistent with the theory.

Given are a finite set X of alternatives and a finite set of agents N. Agents are endowed with preference relations over X, $\succeq_i$, one for each $i \in N$. A preference profile $(\succeq_i)_{i \in N}$ is *Euclidean rationalizable* if there exist a mapping $\rho : X \to \mathbf{R}^d$, and ideal points $y_i \in \mathbf{R}^d$, so that for all $x, z, \in X$ and all $i \in N$, $x \succeq_i z$ iff $\|\rho(x) - y_i\| \leq \|\rho(z) - y_i\|$. Note that we make no requirement that ρ be one-to-one.

In revealed preference theory, we often try to understand the properties of data that refute a given theory. Here we shall instead ask if the theory is at all refutable, without trying to understand the morphology of refutations. So we ask, when is it the case that all preference profiles are Euclidean rationalizable?

The answer to this question will clearly depend on at least three things: $|X|$, $|N|$, and d. If, for some triple $(|X|,|N|,d)$, all preference profiles are Euclidean rationalizable, then the model has, in some sense, no empirical content. If instead there are profiles that are not Euclidean rationalizable, then the theory may have some empirical bite. The following two results are due to Bogomolnaia and Laslier.

Theorem 11.6 *All profiles* $(\succeq_i)_{i\in N}$ *of preference relations are Euclidean rationalizable iff* $d \geq \min\{|X|-1,|N|\}$.

Proof. We first demonstrate that if $d \geq \min\{|X|-1,|N|\}$, then the Euclidean model has no empirical content. To this end, first suppose that $d \geq |X|-1$. In particular, let us consider the case $d = |X|-1$; the other cases follow trivially from this. We shall carry out a construction for which we do not actually need to know the profile of preferences $\succeq_i$.

We let the set of policy alternatives be the set in $\mathbf{R}^{d+1}$ given by $\{x \in \mathbf{R}^{d+1} : \sum_{j=1}^{d+1} x_i = 1\}$. This set is isomorphic to $\mathbf{R}^d$. Now, we can write $X = \{1,...,d+1\}$. Consider the mapping ρ which carries each m to the vector $\mathbf{1}_m$ (as usual, $\mathbf{1}_m$ denotes the unit vector with a 1 in entry m, and zeros in all other entries). The simplex defined by $\Delta(d) = \{x \in \mathbf{R}^{d+1} : x \geq 0 \text{ and } \sum_{j=1}^{d+1} = x\}$ can be used to choose the ideal points, y_i. In particular, for $m,l \in X$, we can consider the set $H(m,l) = \{x \in \Delta(d) : x_m \geq x_l\}$, and the set $H^+(m,l) = \{x \in \Delta(d) : x_m > x_l\}$. If $y \in H(m,l)$, then $\|\mathbf{1}_m - y\| \leq \|\mathbf{1}_l - y\|$, and if $y \in H^+(m,l)$, then $\|\mathbf{1}_m - y\| < \|\mathbf{1}_l - y\|$. So, given a preference $\succeq_i$, we need $y_i \in H(m,l)$ for all $m \succeq_i l$ and $y_i \in H^+(m,l)$ for all $m \succ_i l$. It is easy to see that this can always be done. For example, take any utility representation $u_i : X \to \mathbf{R}$ of $\succeq_i$ and consider $-u_i$. Consider the function $v_i(x) = -u_i(x) + \lambda$, where $\lambda > 0$ is chosen large enough so that $v_i(x) > 0$ for all x. Then renormalize by $\alpha > 0$ so that $\sum_{x\in X} \alpha(-u_i(x) + \lambda) = 1$. Then the vector $y_i \in \mathbf{R}^{d+1}$ defined by letting $y_{il} = \alpha(-u_i(l) + \lambda)$ for each l satisfies the desired property.

On the other hand, suppose that $d \geq |N|$. We can suppose that $d = |N|$. The case where $d > |N|$ will easily follow from the argument given here. For each $i \in N$, let $u_i : X \to \mathbf{R}$ be a utility function representing $\succeq_i$. Consider the point $\rho^*(x) \in \mathbf{R}^d$ whose ith coordinate is given by $\rho^*(x)_i = u_i(x)$. Now, consider the function $F : \mathbf{R}^{d+1} \to \mathbf{R}^d$ given by

$$F_i(\alpha, z) = -\alpha(z \cdot z) + z_i;$$

with $\alpha \in \mathbf{R}$ and $z \in \mathbf{R}^d$.

Note that $\nabla_z F(0,z) = I$ for all z (where $\nabla_z F$ here stands for the Jacobian matrix), and that $F_i(0,\rho^*(x)) = u_i(x)$ for $x \in X$. By the implicit function theorem (for example, see Rudin, 1976), for each $x \in X$, there is a neighborhood U_x of 0 such that for all $\alpha \in U_x$, there is a point $\rho^\alpha(x)$ for which $F_i(\alpha,\rho^\alpha(x)) = u_i(x)$. By choosing $\overline{\alpha}$ such that $\overline{\alpha} \in \bigcap_{x\in X} U_x$ and $\overline{\alpha} > 0$, we have for each x a point $\rho^{\overline{\alpha}}(x)$ for which $F_i(\overline{\alpha}, \rho^{\overline{\alpha}}(x)) = u_i(x)$. Thus, $x \mapsto F_i(\overline{\alpha}, \rho^{\overline{\alpha}}(x))$ represents $\succeq_i$ on X. Finally, we claim that for each $i \in N$, $z \mapsto F_i(\overline{\alpha}, z)$ represents a Euclidean preference. We have

$$F_i(\overline{\alpha}, z) = -(\overline{\alpha}(z \cdot z) - z_i),$$

which is ordinally equivalent to

$$-\left(z - \frac{\mathbf{1}_i}{2\overline{\alpha}}\right) \cdot \left(z - \frac{\mathbf{1}_i}{2\overline{\alpha}}\right),$$

which represents a Euclidean preference with ideal point $\frac{\mathbf{1}_i}{2\overline{\alpha}}$. Let $\rho(x) = \rho^{\overline{\alpha}}(x)$, and we are done.

To show the converse, for every d, we will consider an environment with $d+1$ individuals and $d+2$ alternatives which is not consistent with the Euclidean model. We will demonstrate a list of preferences which cannot be represented. Let us write out the alternatives as $\{x_0, x_1, ..., x_{d+1}\}$. Individual $i \in N$ will have a preference which ranks x_i strictly above all other alternatives, and ranks the remaining alternatives as indifferent. We will argue by contradiction.

The first point to mention is that, by virtue of the preference profile under consideration, it follows that for all $j \neq k$, $\rho(x_j) \neq \rho(x_k)$. That is, ρ is one-to-one.

Though the following proof will hold for arbitrary d, it helps to establish it first in the special case of $d = 1$.

First, for $d = 1$, it is simple to show that there is no representation of this environment. We have two individuals, and $\rho(x_0), \rho(x_1)$, and $\rho(x_2)$ all lie on a straight line. Since $i = 1$ is indifferent between $\rho(x_0)$ and $\rho(x_2)$, $\rho(x_1)$ must be in between $\rho(x_0)$ and $\rho(x_2)$. And since $i = 2$ is indifferent between $\rho(x_0)$ and $\rho(x_1)$, it follows that $\rho(x_1)$ must be in between $\rho(x_0)$ and $\rho(x_1)$. This is clearly impossible.

The proof for $d \geq 2$ relies on an interesting geometric fact. Consider the function $\psi : \mathbf{R}^d \backslash \{0\} \to \mathbf{R}^d$ given by

$$\psi(x) = \frac{x}{\|x\|^2}.$$

This function, known as an *inversion* function in geometry, has two very interesting properties. First, it satisfies $\psi(\psi(x)) = x$ for all $x \in \mathbf{R}^d \backslash \{0\}$. Second, it maps every sphere containing the origin (on its boundary, and of course excluding the origin) to a hyperplane which does not intersect the origin, and of course, therefore maps every hyperplane not containing the origin to a sphere containing the origin (on its boundary). Every hyperplane which passes through the origin is mapped to itself. Lastly, for any point in the interior of any sphere containing the origin, this point is mapped to the opposite side of the origin from the hyperplane which is the image of this sphere. For more on the interesting geometry behind this function, one should consult Coxeter (1969), Chapter 6.

So, now suppose that $d \geq 2$. It is clear that without loss of generality, we may assume that $\rho(x_0) = 0$.

We know that any $(d+1)$-tuple of elements of $\{0, \rho(x_1), \rho(x_2), ..., \rho(x_{d+1})\}$ containing 0 must lie on some sphere (as there is some agent who is indifferent between them all and 0). As a consequence, any set of $\{\psi(\rho(x_1)), ..., \psi(\rho(x_{d+1}))\} \backslash \{\psi(\rho(x_i))\}$ lies on some hyperplane which does not intersect the origin (the image of i's indifference surface), and having the property that $\psi(\rho(x_i))$ lies on the opposite side of the origin from this hyperplane.

We will study the intersection of all hyperplanes containing $\{\psi(\rho(x_1)), ..., \psi(\rho(x_{d+1}))\}$, namely $\mathcal{H} = \{\sum_{i=1}^{d+1} \lambda_i \psi(\rho(x_i)) : \sum_i \lambda_i = 1\}$.[2] We will also make use of the affine set generated by the set $\{\psi(\rho(x_1)), ..., \psi(\rho(x_{d+1}))\} \backslash \{\psi(\rho(x_i))\}$, call this $\mathcal{H}_i$. $\mathcal{H}_i$ lies in a hyperplane which does not pass through the origin, on the other side of which is $\psi(\rho(x_i))$.

We have two possibilities: either $\mathcal{H} = \mathcal{H}_i$ for some i, or not.

Suppose $\mathcal{H} = \mathcal{H}_i$ for some i. Without loss of generality, assume that $\mathcal{H} = \mathcal{H}_{d+1}$. This implies that on any sphere on which $0, \rho(x_1), ..., \rho(x_d)$ all lie, $\rho(x_{d+1})$ must also lie, so that the preference $\succeq_{d+1}$ cannot be represented. This is a contradiction.

For the second case, we note that we may conclude that $0 \in \mathcal{H}$.[3] In particular, there are λ_i for which $\sum_{i=1}^{d+1} \lambda_i = 1$ such that $0 = \sum_{i=1}^{d+1} \lambda_i \psi(\rho(x_i))$. We claim that each $\lambda_i \leq 0$, which will be a contradiction.

We illustrate the case of $i = d+1$. To see this, remember we said that each $\mathcal{H}_{d+1}$ lies on a hyperplane (the image of the indifference surface for agent $d+1$), the other side of the origin from which is $\psi(\rho(x_{d+1}))$. Let the normal of this hyperplane be p_{d+1}. Formally, we have that there is $\alpha_{d+1} > 0$ such that for all $j = 1, \ldots, d$, $p_{d+1} \cdot \psi(\rho(x_j)) = \alpha_{d+1} > 0$, and $p_{d+1} \cdot \psi(\rho(x_{d+1})) > \alpha_{d+1}$. We know that $\sum_{j=1}^{d+1} \lambda_j \psi(\rho(x_j)) = 0$; consequently, $\sum_{j=1}^{d+1} \lambda_j p_{d+1} \cdot \psi(\rho(x_j)) = 0$. However, $\sum_{j=1}^{d+1} \lambda_j p_{d+1} \cdot \psi(\rho(x_j)) = \alpha_{d+1}(\sum_{j=1}^{d} \lambda_j) + \lambda_{d+1} p_{d+1} \cdot \psi(\rho(x_{d+1}))$. If $\lambda_{d+1} \geq 0$, then we have $\alpha_{d+1}(\sum_{j=1}^{d} \lambda_j) + \lambda_{d+1} p_{d+1} \cdot \psi(\rho(x_{d+1})) \geq \alpha_{d+1} \sum_{j=1}^{d+1} \lambda_j = \alpha_{d+1} > 0$, a contradiction. Consequently, $\lambda_{d+1} \leq 0$.

[2] That all hyperplanes containing $\{\psi(\rho(x_i)), \ldots, \psi(\rho(x_{d+1}))\}$ also contain $\mathcal{H}$ is obvious. That each $w \in \mathcal{H}$ is contained in all such hyperplanes can be proved via Lemma 1.12. That is, for vectors $y_1, \ldots, y_m$, $p \cdot y = 0$ is a consequence of $p \cdot y_i = 0$ for all i iff there is $\lambda \in \mathbf{R}^m$ for which $y = \sum_{i=1}^{m} y_i$. Now w is in every hyperplane containing each $\psi(\rho(x_i))$ if for all $p \in \mathbf{R}^{d+1}$ and $\alpha \in \mathbf{R}$, $p \cdot \psi(\rho(x_i)) - \alpha(1) = 0$ implies $p \cdot w - \alpha(1) = 0$. So apply this result to the vectors $(\psi(\rho(x_i)), -1)$ and $(w, -1)$, so that there is $\lambda \in \mathbf{R}^{d+1}$ for which $\sum_{i=1}^{d+1} \lambda_i = 1$ and $w = \sum_{i=1}^{d+1} \lambda_i \psi(\rho(x_i))$.

[3] To see this, note that by dimensionality of the space, there is $\mu \in \mathbf{R}^{d+1} \backslash \{0\}$ for which $\sum_{i=1}^{d+1} \mu_i \psi(\rho(x_i)) = 0$ (the vectors $\psi(\rho(x_i))$ cannot be linearly independent). We must show that $\sum_{i=1}^{d+1} \mu_i \neq 0$. But, since $\mu \neq 0$, the converse would imply that there exists some i for which $\mu_i \neq 0$ and $-\mu_i = \sum_{j \neq i} \mu_j$. Then $-\mu_i \psi(\rho(x_i)) = \sum_{j \neq i} \mu_j \psi(\rho(x_j))$. Dividing each side by $-\mu_i$ now results in $\psi(\rho(x_i)) \in \mathcal{H}_i$, a contradiction.

Theorem 11.6 says that rationalization by Euclidean preferences may require many dimensions. Our next result deals with a weaker theory: voters have convex preferences over policies, but they do not need to be Euclidean. It turns out that two dimensions suffice in this case.

Formally, we say that a profile $(\succeq_i)_{i\in N}$ is *convex rationalizable* if there exists a mapping $\rho : X \to \mathbf{R}^d$, and a convex preference relation $\succeq_i^*$ on $\mathbf{R}^d$ for all $i \in N$, such that for all $x, y \in X$, $x \succeq_i y$ iff $\rho(x) \succeq_i^* \rho(y)$.

Theorem 11.7 *If $d > 1$, $|X| = 2$, or $|N| = 1$, then any profile $(\succeq_i)_{i\in N}$ of preference relations is convex rationalizable.*

We omit the proof of Theorem 11.7, but the basic idea is to let $\rho : X \to \mathbf{R}^d$ be any mapping carrying each X to a distinct vertex of some regular polytope. Then, for each preference $\succeq_i$, we let $U(x) = \text{conv}\{\rho(y) : y \succeq_i x\}$, where conv denotes the convex hull. These are nested. The preferences $\succeq_i^*$ to be constructed must be such that their upper contour sets at x contain $U(x)$. It is always possible to construct such $\succeq^*$.

11.2.2 Rational voting when policy positions are known

We now turn to the case when policy alternatives are already given by vectors in $\mathbf{R}^d$. A voter has preferences over $\mathbf{R}^d$; we are going to consider convex and Euclidean preferences.

Suppose that we observe the behavior of a single voter. A *voting record V* is a finite collection of pairs, $\{(y^k, n^k)\}_{k=1}^K$, where each $y^k, n^k \in \mathbf{R}^d$ and $y^k \neq n^k$. The interpretation is that out of the pair (y^k, n^k), $y^k \in \mathbf{R}^d$ was chosen (voted "yes") while $n^k \in \mathbf{R}^d$ was not.

The environment is a special case of choice theory, as described in Chapter 2. For each k, y^k is chosen over (or "revealed preferred" to) n^k. The set of "budgets" consist of pairs; and we assume that we observe the entire choice function over those budgets (which happens to be single-valued).

By our results in Chapters 2 and 3, we know that any voting record is weakly rationalizable by some utility function (namely, complete indifference). And a voting record is strongly rationalizable iff its revealed preference pair admits no cycles. In this case, we know the revealed preference pair is given by $y^k \succeq^c n^k$ for all k, and $y^k \succ^c n^k$ for all k; that is, $\succeq^c = (\succ^c \cup =)$, so acyclicity of the order pair is the same as acyclicity of $\succ^c$.[4] The first result highlights a reformulation of acyclicity.

A voting record is *strongly pair rationalizable* if there is a utility function $u : \mathbf{R}^d \to \mathbf{R}$ such that, for all k, $u(y^k) > u(n^k)$. The word "pair" in "strongly pair rationalizable" is meant to remind us that data come in the form of pairwise comparisons.

[4] Of course, we also have $y^k \succeq^c y^k$ for all k.

For any $V' \subseteq V$, we define $Y(V') = \{y^k : (y^k, n^k) \in V'\}$ and $N(V') = \{n^k : (y^k, n^k) \in V'\}$. These are the sets of elements that were chosen from V' and rejected from V' respectively. Finally, $X(V') = Y(V') \cup N(V')$.

Proposition 11.8 *A voting record V is strongly pair rationalizable iff for all nonempty $V' \subseteq V$, $Y(V') \neq N(V')$.*

Proof. Suppose that V is strongly rationalizable, and suppose, toward a contradiction, that there is some $V' \subseteq V$ for which $Y(V') = N(V')$. We will show how to construct a $\succ^c$ cycle. Let $n^{k_1} \in N(V')$ be arbitrary; we know that $y^{k_1} \succ^c n^{k_1}$. Moreover, $y^{k_1} \in N(V')$, so there is $(y^{k_2}, n^{k_2}) \in V'$ for which $n^{k_2} = y^{k_1}$. But then we have $y^{n_2} \succ^c n^{k_2} = y^{k_1} \succ^c n^{k_1}$. By continuing this construction inductively, and since V' is finite, we must eventually construct a cycle.

Conversely, suppose that we have $Y(V') \neq N(V')$ for all nonempty $V' \subseteq V$, but that V is not strongly rationalizable. Then we know there is a cycle

$$y^{k_l} \succ^c n^{k_l} = y^{k_{l-1}} \succ^c n^{k_{l-1}} \dots n^{k_1} = y^{k_l}.$$

By setting $V' = \{(y^{k_i}, n^{k_i})\}$, we have $Y(V') = N(V')$, a contradiction.

An *extreme point* of a set $X \subseteq \mathbf{R}^d$ is a point $x \in X$ which cannot be written as a convex combination of points in $X \backslash \{x\}$. The set of extreme points of X will be denoted $E(X)$. The following theorem is due to Tasos Kalandrakis (as was Proposition 11.8).

Theorem 11.9 *Let V be a voting record. The following conditions are equivalent:*

I) *For all nonempty $V' \subseteq V$, there is $x \in E(X(V')) \backslash Y(V')$.*
II) *There exists a concave utility function strongly pair rationalizing V.*
III) *There exists a strictly concave utility function strongly pair rationalizing V.*
IV) *There exists a quasiconcave utility function strongly pair rationalizing V.*

The main interest is in condition (I). Notice that it is a stronger condition than acyclicity. In fact, we included Proposition 11.8 to highlight the difference between Condition (I) and acyclicity as formulated in Proposition 11.8. If for all nonempty $V' \subseteq V$ there is $x \in E(X(V')) \backslash Y(V')$, then, of course, it is impossible that $Y(V') = N(V')$. The following is a simple example of a strongly pair rationalizable voting record which is not rationalizable by a concave, or a quasiconcave, utility function.

Example 11.10 *Suppose $X = \mathbf{R}$, and that the voting record consists of $V = \{(0,1),(2,1)\}$. Then this voting record can never be strongly rationalized by a concave utility function. This is obvious, but to see this via Theorem 11.9, note that $E(X(V)) = \{0,2\}$, and $Y(V) = \{0,2\}$, a contradiction to condition* (I).

Hence, in the voting model, concavity imposes testable restrictions over and above the restrictions contained in strong rationalizability by a utility function. Contrast this with Afriat's Theorem of Chapter 3, which says that concavity has no testable implications above rationality alone. The difference arises from the kind of data we have assumed here. In the demand theory environment of Chapter 3, we could never directly compare two arbitrary consumption bundles. In the present environment, such comparisons are not only possible, they are the only types of comparisons allowed.

Proof. That the existence of a concave strict rationalization implies Equation (I) is well known, as at least one minimizer of a concave function always occurs at an extreme point. And the minimizer cannot occur at a point $y^k \in Y(V')$, as the corresponding point $n^k \in N(V')$ is ranked strictly lower.

We will show that Equation (I) implies the existence of a concave utility function strictly rationalizing V. To see this, consider the set X. We will show that for each $x \in X(V)$, there is $u_x \in \mathbf{R}$ and $p_x \in \mathbf{R}^d$ such that for all $(x,y) \in V$, $u_x > u_y$, and for all $x,y \in X(V)$, $u_y \leq u_x + p_x \cdot (y-x)$. By defining $u : \mathbf{R}^d \to \mathbf{R}$ by $u(z) = \min_{x \in X(V)} u_x + p_x \cdot (z-x)$, we will have a rationalization. This is the typical Afriat construction; see Chapter 3.

In fact, we shall set up a system like that in the proof of Afriat's Theorem. Define a matrix B as follows. The matrix has $|X(V)| + d\,|X(V)|$ columns. First are $|X(V)|$ columns, one labeled with each element of $X(V)$. Then a second collection of $d\,|X(V)|$ columns, these come in groups of d columns, each group is labeled with an element of $X(V)$.

For each pair $(x,y) \in V$, we have a row with a zero in each entry, with the exception of a 1 in the first column labeled with x and a -1 in the first column devoted to y. For each distinct pair $(x,y) \in X(V) \times X(V)$, we have a row with a zero in each entry, with the exception of 1 in the first column labeled with x, -1 in the first column devoted to y, and in the second set of d columns labeled with x we include the vector $(y-x)$. That is, in the first such column we write $y_1 - x_1$; in the second column $y_2 - x_2$, and so on.

We are looking for a utility function $u : X \to \mathbf{R}$ and vector p_x for each $x \in X$ that solve the system of inequalities we described above. We can view a utility function as a vector $u \in \mathbf{R}^{X(V)}$, and stack the d-dimensional vectors p_x in a way that is congruent with the columns of B. Let P be the vector $(p_x)_{x \in X}$ stacked in a manner congruent with the columns of B. Then we can write the system of linear inequalities as

$$B \cdot \begin{bmatrix} u \\ P \end{bmatrix} \geq 0,$$

where the first V inequalities corresponding to u must be strict.

Now suppose that there is no solution to the system of inequalities. By Lemma 1.12, we conclude that for each $(x,y) \in V$, there exists $\lambda_{(x,y)} \geq 0$ and for each $(x,y) \in X(V) \times X(V)$, there is $\mu_{(x,y)} \geq 0$, where at least one λ is strictly positive, and such that for each $x \in X(V)$,

$$\sum_{y \in X(V):(x,y) \in V} \lambda_{(x,y)} - \sum_{y \in X(V):(y,x) \in V} \lambda_{(y,x)} + \sum_{y \in X(V)} \mu_{(x,y)} - \sum_{y \in X(V)} \mu_{(y,x)} = 0 \quad (11.1)$$

and

$$\sum_{y \in X(V)} \mu_{(x,y)}(y - x) = 0. \quad (11.2)$$

Consider all pairs (x,y) for which either $\lambda_{(x,y)} > 0$ or $\mu_{(x,y)} > 0$. Call this set M, and consider $X(M)$. The set M is nonempty; it is not necessarily a subset of V. Note that Equation (11.1) implies that, for any $x \in X(M)$, there is y with $\lambda_{(z,y)} > 0$ or $\mu_{(z,y)} > 0$ (or both).

Next, consider an extreme point z of the set $X(M)$. There is at least one extreme point because $X(M)$ is finite. As $z \in X(M)$, there is y with $\lambda_{(z,y)} > 0$ or $\mu_{(z,y)} > 0$. Now, we cannot have $\mu_{(z,y)} > 0$ for any y because equation (11.2) would imply that z is not an extreme point of $X(M)$.

Therefore, z is associated with a positive $\lambda_{(z,y)}$, for some y. But this implies, in fact, that $(z,y) \in V$. Define $V' \subseteq V$ by $(x,y) \in V'$ iff $\lambda_{(x,y)} > 0$. We know that all extreme points of $X(M)$ are therefore elements of $Y(V')$. But as a consequence, all extreme points of $X(V')$ are also elements of $Y(V')$, which is a contradiction.

Going back to the model discussed in Section 11.2.1, we can ask when a voting record V is rationalizable by a preference relation that is not only convex, but Euclidean. Data $V = \{(y^k, n^k)\}_{k=1}^K$ are rationalizable by the Euclidean model if there is $y \in \mathbf{R}^d$ such that, for all k, $\|y^k - y\| < \|n^k - y\|$.

The following result provides an answer. It states that whenever a weighted average of the y^k vectors and the n^k vectors coincide, it must be the case that the weighted average of the squared lengths of the y^k vectors is strictly less than the weighted average of squared lengths of the n^k vectors.

Theorem 11.11 *Let $V = \{(y^k, n^k)\}_{k=1}^K$ be a voting record. Then there is a Euclidean preference strongly rationalizing V iff for all $\lambda \in \mathbf{R}^k$ for which $\lambda \geq 0$ and $\sum_{k=1}^K \lambda_k = 1$, if $\sum_k \lambda_k y^k = \sum_k \lambda_k n^k$, then $\sum_k \lambda_k \left(y^k \cdot y^k\right) < \sum_k \lambda_k \left(n^k \cdot n^k\right)$.*

Proof. The proof is based on an application of a lemma related to Lemma 1.14. V is rationalizable by a Euclidean preference iff there exists $b \in \mathbf{R}^d$ such that for all $(y^k, n^k) \in V$,

$$-(y^k - b) \cdot (y^k - b) > -(n^k - b) \cdot (n^k - b).$$

Rewriting this equation, we seek the existence of $b \in \mathbf{R}^d$ such that for all k,

$$b \cdot \left(y^k - n^k\right) > \frac{(y^k \cdot y^k) - (n^k \cdot n^k)}{2}.$$

By introducing a variable $\alpha \in \mathbf{R}$, we see that there exists such a $b \in \mathbf{R}^d$ iff there exists $(b,\alpha) \in \mathbf{R}^{d+1}$ for which

$$b \cdot (y^k - n^k) - \alpha \left[\frac{(y^k \cdot y^k) - (n^k \cdot n^k)}{2} \right] > 0$$

and $\alpha > 0$. By Lemma 1.12, it can be shown that there is a solution to these inequalities iff for all $\lambda \in \mathbf{R}^k$ where $\lambda \geq 0$ and $\sum_{k=1}^{K} \lambda_k > 0$, we have $\sum_{k=1}^{K} \lambda_k (y^k - n^k) = 0$ implies $\sum_{k=1}^{K} \lambda_k \left[(y^k \cdot y^k) - (n^k \cdot n^k) \right] < 0$. Note that we may simply renormalize so that $\sum_k \lambda_k = 1$.

Remark 11.12 It can be similarly shown that a voting record V is strongly rationalizable by a *linear* preference iff for all $\lambda \in \mathbf{R}^k$ for which $\lambda \geq 0$ and $\sum_{k=1}^{K} \lambda_k = 1$, we have $\sum_{k=1}^{K} \lambda_k y^k \neq \sum_{k=1}^{K} \lambda_k n^k$. Thus, the condition of Euclidean rationalizability is strictly weaker than the condition of linear rationalizability. This should not be surprising, as a linear preference is like a Euclidean preference with an ideal point "at infinity." The situation would, of course, change if we allowed indifference into a voting record.

Section 11.2.1 also addressed the question of when the Euclidean model has no testable implications whatsoever. Instead of trying to describe the rationalizable datasets, we found properties on the parameters of the problems such that no data could refute the Euclidean model.

In the present context, we can ask a similar question. The difference compared to the environment in 11.2.1 is that now the policy positions are observed as vectors in $\mathbf{R}^d$. Let us define an *election* to be a binary set $\mathcal{E} = \{x,z\} \subseteq \mathbf{R}^d$, where $x \neq z$. For any finite collection of elections $\mathcal{E}_1, ..., \mathcal{E}_k$, a voting record V is *consistent* with this collection if for all $(x,z) \in V$, $\{x,z\} \in \mathcal{E}_i$ for some i, and for all i, if $\{x,z\} = \mathcal{E}_i$, then either $(x,z) \in V$ or $(z,x) \in V$. That is, a voting record is consistent with a sequence of elections iff it describes a sequence of possible votes over those elections. The next result is due to Degan and Merlo.

Theorem 11.13 *Suppose $k \leq d$. Then there is an open and dense set of election sequences of length k such that any consistent voting record is rationalizable by Euclidean preferences. If $d < k$, then for all election sequences there are voting records that are not rationalizable by Euclidean preferences.*

Proof. Let $\mathcal{E}$ be an election $\{x,z\}$. Let $\lambda \in \mathbf{R}^d$ be defined by $\lambda = x - z$ and let $c \in \mathbf{R}$ be defined by $c = \frac{(x \cdot x - z \cdot z)}{2}$. A simple calculation reveals that a Euclidean preference with ideal point y ranks $x \succ z$ if and only if $\lambda \cdot y > c$ and ranks $z \succ x$ iff $\lambda \cdot y < c$.

Each election $\mathcal{E}_i = \{x_i, z_i\}$ is identified with a pair (λ_i, c_i), defined as above. Given a voting record V, there is y such that the Euclidean preferences with ideal point y rationalize V iff there is $y \in \mathbf{R}^d$ such that $\lambda_i \cdot y > c_i$ if $(x_i, z_i) \in V$, and $\lambda_i \cdot y < c_i$ if $(z_i, x_i) \in V$. We may write in matrix form $\Lambda \in \mathbf{R}^{k \times d}$, where Λ collects the vectors λ_i, and $c \in \mathbf{R}^k$.

Now, with $k \leq d$, for an open and dense set of Λ, the range of the function $y \mapsto \Lambda \cdot y - c$ is k-dimensional. And by the preceding discussion, for any such Λ and c, and any V, there is y rationalizing V.

Suppose instead that $d < k$. We know then that $\lambda_1, ..., \lambda_k$ cannot be linearly independent; without loss of generality, let us suppose that $\lambda_k = \sum_{i=1}^{k-1} \alpha_i \lambda_i$, and let us suppose again without loss that $\alpha_i \geq 0$ for all i (we can always relabel x_i as z_i and z_i as x_i). Now consider the value $\overline{c} = \sum_{i=1}^{k-1} \alpha_i c_i$. There are two cases. Either $\overline{c} \leq c_k$ or $\overline{c} > c_k$. In the first case, whenever $\lambda_i \cdot y \leq c_i$ for all $i \leq k-1$, it follows that $\lambda_k \cdot y \leq c_k$. In the second case, whenever $\lambda_i \cdot y \geq c_i$ for all $i \leq k-1$, it follows that $\lambda_k \cdot y > c_k$. Either way, there are voting records that cannot be rationalized.

The message of Theorem 11.13 is similar to that of Theorem 11.6; it characterizes the environments where the Euclidean model is empirically vacuous.

11.3 CHAPTER REFERENCES

Theorem 11.1 is due to McGarvey (1953). Theorems 11.2 and 11.3 are due to Dushnik and Miller (1941). Theorem 11.4 is due to Ghouila-Houri (1962) and Gilmore and Hoffman (1964). The NP-completeness result is due to Yannakakis (1982). Results generalizing McGarvey's Theorem for other choice rules include Deb (1976) and Kalai (2004). Sprumont (2001) describes necessary and sufficient conditions for 2-unanimity rationalization by weak orders in certain economic environments. Theorem 11.5 appears in Fishburn (1969) without proof; a much more general statement can be found in Fishburn (1973a). Related to these results is the paper of Knoblauch (2005), which implicitly uses model-theoretic ideas (see Chapter 13) to describe the length of potential axiomatizations of Pareto rationalizability.

The results and proofs in Section 11.2.1 are due to Bogomolnaia and Laslier (2007). Bogomolnaia and Laslier (2007) actually establish a slightly different result than Theorem 11.6, that even when one admits linear preferences (preferences represented by a linear function), the result does not change.

Note that the function ρ described in the proof of Theorem 11.6 is allowed to depend on the profile $\succeq_1, ..., \succeq_n$. In general, we may not wish this to be the case. Bogomolnaia and Laslier (2007) discuss this issue.

As for a proof of Theorem 11.7, the construction of preferences $\succeq^*$ we suggest can be established as in Richter and Wong (2004).

Some related papers are useful to mention. Knoblauch (2010) provides a polynomial-time algorithm (and construction) for understanding when a profile is Euclidean rationalizable for $d = 1$. Azrieli (2011) studies Euclidean preferences with a "valence" dimension. Ballester and Haeringer (2011) describes conditions ensuring that a preference profile is rationalizable as a single-peaked profile for some ordering of the alternatives.

The discussion in Section 11.2.2 draws on Kalandrakis (2010) and Degan and Merlo (2009). Most of the technical ideas in this section can be ascribed to Richter and Wong (2004); we have followed Richter and Wong in the proof of Theorem 11.9, which appears in Kalandrakis (2010) with a different proof. Theorem 11.13 is due to Degan and Merlo (2009).

Richter and Wong (2004) deal with the following problem. Suppose we have a finite subset $K \subseteq \mathbf{R}^d$, and a complete and transitive binary relation $\succeq$ on K. When is it the case that there exists a complete, transitive, extension of $\succeq$ which can be represented by a concave utility function? (One difference with Kalandrakis (2010) is that he discards the completeness condition.)

Finally, Gomberg (2011, 2014) presents the testable implications of group behavior when the group can vary, and is assumed to be composed of rational individuals choosing according to a scoring rule.

CHAPTER 12

Revealed Preference and Systems of Polynomial Inequalities

It should be apparent by now that systems of linear inequalities emerge naturally in revealed preference theory. They constitute the essence of Afriat's Theorem, for example; and we formulated revealed preference problems using systems of linear inequalities in Chapters 3, 6, 7, and 8. In this chapter, we describe how revealed preference problems can generally be understood as a system of inequalities. From a purely computational perspective, one can very often solve a revealed preference problem by algorithmically solving the corresponding system of inequalities.

When the system of inequalities is linear, the problem is easy to solve both computationally and analytically. Here we develop a GARP-like acyclicity test (similar to the ones in Chapters 2 and 3). The test will follow from the linearity of the system of inequalities embodied in the revealed preference question.

We shall discuss an extension of the linear theory to systems of polynomial inequalities. The theory of polynomial inequalities will be seen to be very relevant for revealed preference theory (but harder to work with compared to the theory of linear inequalities).

12.1 LINEAR INEQUALITIES: THE THEOREM OF THE ALTERNATIVE AND REVEALED PREFERENCE

We start by revisiting the Theorem of the Alternative, or Farkas' Lemma from Chapter 1. It is easy to see why it is useful in revealed preference theory. We then discuss some sources of linear systems for popular models in economics. The following is a bit weaker than Lemma 1.13. It is written so as to emphasize that the lemma can be used to "remove existential quantifiers;" it states that an existential statement (one that start with "there is...") is equivalent to a universal statement (one that starts with "for all..."). Note that the discussion of the Tarski–Seidenberg Theorem in Chapter 9 is also about removing existential quantifiers.

Lemma 1.13′ *(Integer–Real Farkas) Let $\{A_i\}_{i=1}^M$ be a finite collection of vectors in $\mathbf{Q}^K$. The following statements are equivalent:*

I) *There exists* $y \in \mathbf{R}^K$ *such that for all* $i = 1, \ldots, M$, $A_i \cdot y > 0$.
II) *For all* $z \in \mathbf{Z}^M_+ \setminus \{0\}$, *it holds that* $\sum_{i=1}^M z_i A_i \neq 0$.

The vector y represents some unknown quantities. The vectors A_i encode some properties we want y to have. Typically, y is an unobservable theoretical object, such as a utility function. The properties in A_i can be theoretical (for example requiring utility to be monotonic) or come from the data, for example requiring the utility function to rationalize the data. In the example that we expand on below, M is the number of observations, and K is the number of possible alternatives from which an agent chooses. Then every observation corresponds to a vector A_i. For example, suppose that we observe object h chosen over object l. Then there is an A_i of the form $\mathbf{1}_h - \mathbf{1}_l$. See Section 12.1.2 below for more details. The existence of $y \in \mathbf{R}^K$ satisfying the inequalities then translates into the existence of a utility function rationalizing the data.

System I corresponds to the revealed preference formulation of a problem: A dataset is "rationalizable" if *there exists* a value for the theoretical object y that satisfies the right properties and explains the data. We call this an *existential* formulation of a theory. As stated, it is not falsifiable: If one is given a candidate solution y, it is easy to check whether System I is satisfied. If the candidate is a solution then we are done, but if the candidate y fails to satisfy System I then we have essentially no clue as to whether System I is solvable because there are infinitely many other potential solutions to the system. So when System I has no solution, and the dataset is "not rationalizable," then there is no way that checking individual vectors y one by one can tell us that the system is not solvable.

In contrast II is a *universal* statement. It says that something has to be true *for all* vectors z. Given a single $z \in \mathbf{Z}^M_+ \setminus \{0\}$ with $\sum_{i=1}^M z_i A_i = 0$, we know by Lemma 1.13′ that there cannot exist y solving System I. Despite the existential formulation of the theory, the theory is falsifiable. When System I has no solution, and the dataset is "not rationalizable," then no single y can certify that the theory has been falsified, but thanks to Lemma 1.13′, a single z can do that.

Lemma 1.13′ says a bit more about z. It says that it is a vector of integers. This is very often useful in finding a "combinatorial" revealed preference axiom, such as GARP or SARP.

Note that *verification* is, in some sense, a dual property to falsification. The existential formulation System I means that an individual y cannot certify that the system has no solution. But when the system does have a solution, a single vector y is enough to certify that a solution exists.

12.1.1 Linear systems from first-order conditions

First-order conditions are a common source of systems of inequalities in revealed preference theory. For example, in the revealed preference problem of rational demand theory, we obtain the system described in Afriat's Theorem from the first-order conditions in the consumer's maximization problem. The following is a heuristic derivation of the system of linear inequalities in Afriat's Theorem.

Recall the setup in Chapter 3. We observe a dataset (x^k, p^k), $k = 1, \ldots, K$. We want to know when there is a function $u : \mathbf{R}^n_+ \to \mathbf{R}$ such that x^k is a maximizer of u in the budget set $B(p^k, m^k) = \{x \in \mathbf{R}^n_+ : p^k \cdot x \leq m^k\}$, where $m^k = p^k \cdot x^k$.

If such a u exists, and if it is smooth and concave, then the first-order condition must be satisfied at the choices x^k:

$$\nabla u(x^k) - \lambda^k p^k = 0, \tag{12.1}$$

where $\nabla u(x^k)$ denotes the gradient of u at x^k, and λ^k is the Lagrange multiplier associated to this maximization problem. The unknowns here are the numbers $\nabla u(x^k)$ and λ^k.

We need to find values for these unknowns that are compatible with a concave u. Essentially we can solve for another set of numbers, *utility values*, $U^k = u(x^k)$, which can be extended to a function defined on all of $\mathbf{R}^n_+$. Concavity demands the following inequality be satisfied for all k and l:

$$U^l - U^k \leq \nabla u(x^k) \cdot (x^l - x^k). \tag{12.2}$$

Putting the equations of type (12.1), which result from the first-order conditions, together with inequalities of type (12.2) yields the linear system we solve for in Afriat's Theorem. By using Lemma 1.13 with this system one obtains GARP: see 3.1.1.

Another example can be obtained from Cournot oligopoly theory. Suppose that there are n firms in a market for a homogeneous good. The theory says that market price is determined as if each firm i has a cost function $c_i : \mathbf{R}_+ \to \mathbf{R}$, with $c_i(0) = 0$, and chooses quantity q_i to maximize

$$q_i P\left(\sum_{j=1}^{n} q_j\right) - c_i(q_i),$$

where $P : \mathbf{R}_+ \to \mathbf{R}_+$ is the market *inverse demand function*. The quantity $q_i P\left(\sum_{j=1}^{n} q_j\right)$ is the revenue of firm i, so the expression reflects that i maximizes profits.

Suppose that we observe K instances in which these firms were engaged in quantity competition. The data we observe are of the form:

$$(q_1^k, \ldots, q_n^k, p^k) : k = 1, \ldots K;$$

where $q_i^k \geq 0$ is the quantity chosen by firm i in instance k, and p^k is the prevailing market price. The functions c_i and P are *not* observable.

Now, say that a dataset is *Cournot rationalizable* if there are convex functions c_i and a smooth and decreasing function P such that q_i^k maximizes the profits of firm i, given that all other firms choose the quantities in the vector (q_j^k).

Now, the first-order condition for firm i is:

$$q_i^k P'\left(\sum_{j=1}^n q_j^k\right) + P\left(\sum_{j=1}^n q_j^k\right) - c_i'(q_i^k) = 0.$$

Recall that price p^k is observed as part of the data, so the unknowns are the numbers $P'(\sum_{j=1}^n q_j^k)$ and $c_i'(q_i^k)$. One needs to find cost and demand functions such that $p^k = P(\sum_{j=1}^n q_j^k)$, and derivatives behave properly. As with Afriat's Theorem, it is enough to do so by finding certain real numbers: in our case the numbers $P'(\sum_{j=1}^n q_j^k)$ and $c_i'(q_i^k)$, such that certain inequalities are satisfied.

We use the notation δ_i^k for the number $c'(q_i^k)$. The first-order condition implies that

$$\frac{\delta_j^k - p^k}{q_j^k} = \frac{\delta_i^k - p^k}{q_i^k} < 0, \tag{12.3}$$

for all i, j, and k, as $P'(\sum_j q_j^k)$ does not depend on i and must be negative for demand to slope down.

It is possible to show that data are Cournot rationalizable iff there are numbers δ_i^k, $i = 1,\ldots,N$, $k = 1,\ldots,K$ such that the linear inequalities (12.3) are satisfied, and such that when $q_i^k < q_i^l$ then $\delta_i^k < \delta_j^k$; the latter requirement captures that marginal cost must be monotone increasing for cost functions to be convex.

12.1.2 The existence of a rationalizing utility

We shall illustrate the role of linear inequalities with a very basic example, dealing with the simplest version of revealed preference for individual decision making.

Suppose that we are given a finite set X of alternatives. Suppose we are given a dataset in the form of an observed revealed preference relation $\succeq^R$. That is, we observe a set of binary comparisons, where an agent has chosen x over y iff $x \succeq^R y$. We want to know when R is rationalizable using a utility function $u : X \to \mathbf{R}$. Suppose that the relation R encompasses only strict comparisons, so $x \succeq^R y$ and $x \neq y$ implies that $x \succ^R y$. Then a utility function u rationalizes $\succeq^R$ if $u(x) > u(y)$ whenever $x \succ^R y$.

The problem can be set up as follows. A utility function is a vector in Euclidean space $\mathbf{R}^X$. Define a matrix B with $|X|$ columns. For every pair $(x,y) \in \succ^R$, include a row in B which has zeroes in all entries except for a 1 in the column for x and a -1 in the column for y. So the row is the vector $\mathbf{1}_x - \mathbf{1}_y$. Then there is a utility function that rationalizes the data if and only if there is a vector $u \in \mathbf{R}^X$ that solves the system $B \cdot u \gg 0$ of linear inequalities.[1]

[1] The matrix B is like the upper left submatrix of the matrix constructed in the proof of Afriat's Theorem.

By Lemma 1.13′ there is no rationalizing u (that is, no u such that $B \cdot u \gg 0$) if and only if there is $z > 0$ such that $z \cdot B = 0$. So suppose that that is the case, and let z be the vector promised by Lemma 1.13′. Let $(x,y) \in X \times X$ correspond to a row r for which $z_r > 0$; so $x \succ^R y$. There is at least one such pair because $z > 0$. There is a 1 in the column for x in row r. Now, no entry of z is negative, and $z \cdot B = 0$, so there must be some row r' with $z_{r'} > 0$ in which we have a -1 in the column for x. So there must exist x' with $x' \succ^R x$; the row r' corresponds to (x',x). Note that now x' is in the position that x was in when we started to make this argument. So there must exist $x'' \in X$ with

$$x'' \succ^R x' \succ^R x \succ^R y.$$

Since X is a finite set, by repeating the argument we must reach a cycle of $\succeq^R$. The argument shows that the order pair $\langle \succeq^R, \succ^R \rangle$ is not acyclic.

In conclusion, the non-existence of a solution to the system $u \cdot B \gg 0$ is equivalent to the existence of a cycle of $\succeq^R$. The standard result on acyclicity therefore emerges as a consequence of Lemma 1.13.

The same reasoning can be applied to many of the results in Chapter 2. We sketch proofs of Theorems 2.6, 2.8, 2.16, and 2.17 using this device. In fact, the Theorem of the Alternative is often a useful way of "guessing" the appropriate concept of rationalization specified by a particular choice-theoretic axiom.

Consider Theorem 2.6. Suppose that X is a finite set. Rationalizability in the sense of Theorem 2.6 is equivalent to the existence of a function $u : X \to \mathbf{R}$ for which $x \succeq^c y$ implies $u(x) \geq u(y)$ and $x \succ^c y$ implies $u(x) > u(y)$. One can then proceed almost exactly as we did in the previous paragraphs to obtain the acyclicity result. The only difference is that we now have weak revealed preference comparisons. Let the order pair $\langle \succeq^c, \succ^c \rangle$ be as defined in Chapter 2. Construct a matrix B with $|X|$ columns, and a row for each $\succeq^c$ or $\succ^c$ comparison. For comparisons of the type $x \succeq^c y$, we add a row to the matrix of form $\mathbf{1}_x - \mathbf{1}_y$; likewise for comparisons of type $x \succ^c y$. We want to find a solution $u \in \mathbf{R}^X$ such that for rows B_i of type $\succeq^c$, we have $B_i \cdot u \geq 0$, and for rows of type $\succ^c$, we have $B_i \cdot u > 0$. Applying Lemma 1.13 and using similar techniques as in the preceding proof for removing cycles, we come up with congruence as the necessary and sufficient condition.

Theorem 2.8 is a bit different. We can no longer work with a utility function, as it is clear that not every complete binary relation can be so encoded (unless it is transitive, of course). Instead, we encode the preference via a function $\varphi : X^2 \to \mathbf{R}$ for which $\varphi(x,y) = -\varphi(y,x)$. The interpretation here is that $x \succeq y$ iff $\varphi(x,y) \geq 0$. This suggests a matrix B, whose rows are indexed by X^2, and for each pair x, y, there is a row $\mathbf{1}_{(x,y)} + \mathbf{1}_{(y,x)}$. Now, we also add a row for each comparison of the type $x \succeq^c y$; namely, this row consists of $\mathbf{1}_{(x,y)}$; likewise, we add a row for each comparison of the type $x \succ^c y$, and again, this row consists of $\mathbf{1}_{(x,y)}$. We want to find a solution $\varphi \in \mathbf{R}^{X^2}$ such that for rows B_i of the first type, we have $B_i \cdot \varphi = 0$, for rows B_i of the second type, we have $B_i \cdot \varphi \geq 0$, and for rows B_i of the third type, we have $B_i \cdot \varphi > 0$. Again, a simple application of the Theorem of the Alternative leads to the weak axiom of revealed preference.

Theorems 2.16 and 2.17 can be proved using similar techniques to the preceding – the distinction is that in the case of Theorem 2.16, we search for a $u \in \mathbf{R}^X$ for which $x \succ^c y$ implies $u(x) > u(y)$ (no requirement is made for $x \succeq^c y$), and in the case of Theorem 2.17, we search for a $\varphi \in \mathbf{R}^{X^2}$ for which $x \succ^c y$ implies $\varphi(x,y) > 0$ (again no requirement is made for $x \succeq^c y$).

The general form of the requirement in these theorems is something along the following lines: "*There exists* some function such that *for all* pairs, the function is related to revealed preference in some way." The existential statement quantifies an unobservable object. The universal (for all) statement quantifies observable objects. The Theorem of the Alternative is used to show that these statements are logically equivalent to a statement which is universal and stated only in terms of observable objects; for example, Theorem 2.6 states that existence of such a utility is equivalent to the statement: "For all $x_1, \ldots, x_n$, it is not the case that for $i = 1, \ldots, n-1$, $x_i \succeq^c x_{i+1}$ and $x_n \succ^c x_1$." Though existential statements are in principle problematic from the viewpoint of falsifiability, we see that in general this might not be true when the existential operator quantifies unobservable objects. Existential operators operating on unobservables can sometimes be "removed," and turned into an equivalent universal statement involving only observables.

12.2 POLYNOMIAL INEQUALITIES: THE POSITIVSTELLENSATZ

Some revealed preference problems give rise to nonlinear, specifically polynomial, systems of inequalities. Below we give a detailed example taken from Nash bargaining theory (see Chapter 10). For polynomial systems of inequalities, there is a result like the Theorem of the Alternative; it is called the *Positivstellensatz*.

In order to state the Positivstellensatz, we need a bit of notation. Given is a collection of variables, say $\{x_1, ..., x_n\}$. We assume that the notion of a polynomial is understood. We will describe one version of the Positivstellensatz.

Given a collection of polynomials $\{f_1, ..., f_m\}$ over the variables $\{x_1, ..., x_n\}$, we define the *ideal* of $\{f_1, ..., f_m\}$ to be the collection of all polynomials which can be written in the form:

$$\sum_{i=1}^{m} g_i f_i,$$

where g_i is a polynomial. We define the *cone* generated by $f_1, ..., f_m$ to be the smallest set of polynomials that (1) includes all sums of squares of polynomials, (2) includes all polynomials $f_1, ..., f_m$, and (3) is closed under addition and multiplication. It is easy to see that any such element can be written as

$$\sum_{S \subseteq \{1,...,m\}} \left(g_S \prod_{i \in S} f_i \right),$$

where g_S is a sum of squares of polynomials. Finally, we define the *multiplicative monoid* generated by $f_1,...,f_m$ to be the collection of polynomials of the form $\prod_{i=1}^{m} f_i^{a_i}$, where each a_i is a non-negative integer.

Let f_i, g_j, and h_l be polynomials over $\{x_1,\ldots,x_n\}$, for $i = 1,...,m$, $j = 1,...,k$, and $l = 1,...,q$.

Theorem 12.1 (Positivstellensatz). *A collection of inequalities $f_i(x) = 0$, $i = 1,...,m$, $g_i(x) \geq 0$, $i = 1,...,k$, $h_l(x) \neq 0$, $i = 1,...,q$ has no solution iff there exist polynomials f in the ideal of $\{f_1,...,f_m\}$, g in the cone generated by $\{g_1,...,g_k\}$, and h in the multiplicative monoid generated by $\{h_1,...,h_q\}$ for which $f + g + h = 0$.*

The Positivstellensatz thus provides an alternative system of polynomial inequalities, such that the first system has no solution iff the second system has a solution. The statement is similar in spirit to the Theorem of the Alternative, but the unknowns in the second system are polynomials, not real numbers. From a computational perspective, the problem is clearly harder to deal with. Conceptually, the Positivstellensatz has implications that are similar to those we highlighted for the Theorem of the Alternative in Section 12.1: it turns an existential, verifiable theory into a universal, falsifiable statement. Thus, if a system of polynomial inequalities cannot be satisfied, it is possible to demonstrate, or certify, its infeasibility.

To actually find a falsification is challenging computationally. One practical approach is to search for a solution to the second system of inequalities among polynomials of bounded degree. This approach is common in the engineering literature (see the references in Section 12.3). So one would look for f in the ideal of $\{f_1,...,f_m\}$, g in the cone generated by $\{g_1,...,g_k\}$, and h in the multiplicative monoid generated by $\{h_1,...,h_q\}$ for which $f + g + h = 0$; but restricting such a search to polynomials of degree smaller than some given bound. The search for a solution among polynomials of bounded degree can be formulated as a semidefinite program, and thus there are efficient algorithms for solving the problem.

Of course, the approach only works when one finds a solution: when one finds polynomials certifying a solution $f + g + h = 0$, thus certifying that the first system of inequalities (the one we are really interested in) has no solution. If one does not find a solution among polynomials of bounded degree, then it is possible that there is a solution of a higher degree, or that the original system in fact has a solution.

12.2.1 Application: Nash bargaining

To get a sense for how these ideas might be applied in economics, let us consider the problem of testing Nash bargaining theory, as in Section 10.3 of Chapter 10. In Chapter 10, we assumed that the disagreement point was fixed across observations, and that it was the same for all agents. If we relax that assumption then things get more complicated. We can still formulate the problem as a polynomial system of inequalities and use the Positivstellensatz to obtain an answer. The alternative, or dual, system from the Positivstellensatz gives a test for Nash bargaining theory.

Assume a finite set N of agents is given. Generalizing the setup from Section 10.3, suppose that a dataset is a set $D = \{(x^k, d^k) : k = 1, \ldots, K\}$; where for each k, x^k and d^k are vectors in $\mathbf{R}^N_+$ such that $x^k \gg d^k \geq 0$. These are observations of K bargaining instances; in the kth instance, agent i received x^k_i dollars, while his disagreement outcome was d^k_i.

A dataset is *Nash bargaining rationalizable* if there are concave and monotonic functions $u_i : \mathbf{R}_+ \to \mathbf{R}$, $i \in N$, such that

$$\prod_{i=1}^{n} \left[u_i(x^k_i) - u_i(d^k_i)\right] \geq \prod_{i=1}^{n} \left[u_i(x_i) - u_i(d^k_i)\right],$$

for all $x \in \mathbf{R}^N_+$ such that $x_i \geq d^k_i$ and $\sum_{i \in N} x_i \leq \sum_{i \in N} x^k_i$.

Proposition 12.2 *A dataset D is Nash rationalizable if and only if for all $i \in N$, there are numbers $U_i(d^k_i), U_i(x^k_i), M_i(d^k_i)$, and $M_i(x^k_i)$ for $k = 1, \ldots, K$ which solve the following equations: for all $z \in \{x^k_i\}$, $z' \in \{x^k_i, d^k_i\}$, and all i, j, and k,*

$$\frac{M_i(x^k_i)}{U_i(x^k_i) - U_i(d^k_i)} = \frac{M_j(x^k_j)}{U_j(x^k_j) - U_j(d^k_j)}$$

and for all $z, z' \in \bigcup_{i=1}^{K} \{d^k_i, x^k_i\}$

$$\begin{cases} U_i(z) - U_i(z') > 0 & \text{if } z < z', \\ M_i(z')(z - z') \geq U_i(z) - U_i(z'). \end{cases}$$

Proposition 12.2 is straightforward. We simply ask for numbers $U_i(z)$ to signify levels of utility, and $M_i(z)$ for supergradients, or marginal utilities. The first system of equalities ensures that the first-order conditions for the maximization of the Nash product hold. The second set of inequalities make sure that utility is monotonic and that marginal utilities are a supergradient of the utility.

Proof. We first show that if we are given increasing and concave utility functions u_i, then $x^k_1, \ldots, x^k_n$ is a solution to $\max_{\sum_{i \in N} x_i = M} \prod_{i \in N} [u_i(x_i) - u_i(d^k_i)]$ if and only if for each i, there is a supergradient μ_i of u_i at x^k_i for which

$$\frac{\mu_i}{U_i(x^k_i) - U_i(d^k_i)} = \frac{\mu_j}{U_j(x^k_j) - U_j(d^k_j)}.$$

To this end, define $\mathcal{U} = \{(u_1(x_1) - u_1(d^k_1), \ldots, u_n(x_n) - u_n(d^k_n)) : \sum_{i \in N} x_i = M, x_i \geq d^k_i\}$, and consider maximizing the function $f(y) = \prod_{i \in N} y_i$ subject to $y \in \mathcal{U}$. A point $u \in \mathcal{U}$ maximizes f if and only if $\left(\prod_{i \neq 1} u_i, \ldots, \prod_{i \neq n} u_i\right)$ supports $\mathcal{U}$ at u (by definition). Because f is strictly convex, and since $\mathcal{U}$ is convex and compact, there is a unique such maximizer u^*. It is clear that $u_i^* > 0$ for all $i \in N$.

This states that there is a unique solution $x_1^k, \ldots, x_n^k$ to the Nash problem for which $u_i(x_i^k) - u_i(d_i^k) = u_i^*$. We define $\lambda_j = \prod_{i \neq j}[u_i(x_i^k) - u_i(d_i^k)]$. We know that $\sum_{i \in N} \lambda_i u_i(x_i)$ is maximized at $x_1^k, \ldots, x_n^k$ across all x_i for which $\sum_{i \in N} x_i = M$. Our next step is to show that this can happen if and only if the vector $(1/\lambda_1, \ldots, 1/\lambda_n)$ is proportional to a vector of supergradients.

Since the constraints $x_i \geq d_i^k$ are not binding, we can set up the Lagrangian for the problem, say $L(x, \mu) = \sum_{i \in N} \lambda_i u_i(x_i) + \mu(M - \sum_{i \in N} x_i)$, and note that it is equal to $L(x, \mu) = \sum_{i \in N}[\lambda_i u_i(x_i) - \mu x_i] + \mu M$. We know the constraint $\sum_{i \in N} x_i = M$ is binding, so that the solution to the maxmin problem features $\mu^* > 0$. For μ^*, we know that $\max_x L(x, \mu^*)$ is equal to the maximum Nash product subject to the constraint, and has the same solution. This is equivalent to saying that $(\lambda_i/\mu^*)u_i(x_i^k) - x_i^k \geq (\lambda_i/\mu^*)u_i(x_i) - x_i$ for all x_i, or, rewriting:

$$u_i(x_i) + (\mu^*/\lambda_i)(x_i^k - x_i) \leq u_i(x_i^k).$$

This is equivalent to saying that μ^*/λ_i is a supergradient, or that the vector $(1/\lambda_1, \ldots, 1/\lambda_n)$ is proportional to a supergradient.

Another way of saying that $(1/\lambda_1, \ldots, 1/\lambda_n)$ is proportional to a vector of supergradients is saying that for all $i \in N$, there is a supergradient $M_i(x_i^k)$ of u_i at x_i^k such that for all i,j, $\frac{\lambda_i}{\lambda_j} = \frac{M_j(x_j^k)}{M_i(x_i^k)}$. Writing out the explicit form of λ and eliminating terms, this is equivalent to saying that $\frac{M_i(x_i^k)}{u_i(x_i^k) - u_i(d_i^k)} = \frac{M_j(x_j^k)}{u_j(x_j^k) - u_j(d_j^k)}$, which is precisely the condition in the theorem. The other conditions simply say that M_i is a supergradient, and that u_i is strictly increasing.

Conversely, the details of how to construct a utility function from these numbers essentially follow from Afriat, defining $u_i(x) = \inf_{z \in \bigcup_{k=1}^K \{x_i^k, d_i^k\}} U_i(z) + M_i(z)(x - z)$, where the infimum is taken over all data points. It is then simple to verify by construction that for all $z \in \bigcup_{k=1}^K \{x_i^k, d_i^k\}$, $M_i(z)$ is a supergradient of u_i at z. From this, the fact that the equality in the statement of the theorem is solved implies that the Nash product is maximized for this collection of utility functions (by the previous argument).

From Proposition 12.2 and the Positivstellensatz we can obtain a test for Nash bargaining. The conditions in the proposition involve polynomials in $4|N|K$ variables, namely $U_i(d_i^k), U_i(x_i^k), M_i(d_i^k)$, and $M_i(x_i^k)$. We have the system of polynomial equalities

$$\frac{M_i(x_i^k)}{U_i(x_i^k) - U_i(d_i^k)} = \frac{M_j(x_j^k)}{U_j(x_j^k) - U_j(d_j^k)}$$

and the inequalities for all $z, z' \in \bigcup_{i=1}^K \{d_i^k, x_i^k\}$,

$$\begin{cases} U_i(z) - U_i(z') > 0 & \text{if } z < z', \\ M_i(z')(z - z') \geq U_i(z) - U_i(z'). \end{cases}$$

12.3 CHAPTER REFERENCES

In general, Lemma 1.13 allows us to find the exact empirical content of many linear models. Scott (1964) is a classic reference. The issue with Lemma 1.13 is that the universal quantifier does not typically operate on observables (here, z is simply a vector – but in our example, observed data were revealed preference comparisons). It turns out though, that since z is integer-valued, this universal quantifier can be translated directly into observables. For example, in the revealed preference example in Section 12.1.2, the fact that for all for all $z \in \mathbf{Z}_+^K$ with $\sum_{i=L+1}^K z_i > 0$, we have $\sum_{i=1}^K z_i A_i \neq 0$ is the same as saying there are no preference cycles. In fact, it is often the case that one can require the universal quantifier on z to operate over a *finite* number of z.

The discussion of the Cournot model in Section 12.1.1 borrows from the paper of Carvajal, Deb, Fenske, and Quah (2013). These authors prove that the condition we have stated (the existence of a solution to the system of inequalities) is equivalent to Cournot rationalizability.

The discussion of existential and universal axioms is inspired by the work of Popper (1959). Popper claimed famously that existential theories are not falsifiable: consider the theory that claims that there is a black swan. No matter how many non-black swans one observes, they do not disprove the theory. Universal theories are falsifiable, for example the theory that claims that all swans are white. The observation of a single non-white swan would disprove the theory. The papers by Van Benthem (1976) and Chambers, Echenique, and Shmaya (2012) present a general result on how existential quantifiers over theoretical objects can be removed, and a theory may be shown to be falsifiable. See also Craig and Vaught (1958), Lemma 3.4 for a related result in a more restrictive environment.

The Positivstellensatz as formulated in Theorem 12.1 can be found, for example, in Bochnak, Coste, and Roy (1998), Theorem 4.4.2. It is originally due to Krivine (1964) and rediscovered by Stengle (1974). It is interesting that, while many economists know and apply the Theorem of the Alternative, there are almost no applications of the Positivstellensatz (Richter, 1975 is a notable exception, which itself builds on the work of Tversky, 1967). The theorem is potentially useful to applied economists, who would use the algorithms in Parrilo (2004) to carry out tests on actual datasets.

The Positivstellensatz is closely related to, but distinct from, the Tarski–Seidenberg Theorem; see our discussion in Chapter 9. Brown and Matzkin (1996) (see also Brown and Kubler (2008)) exploit this technique to find testable implications of equilibrium behavior. They also explain how the well-known equivalence of the strong axiom of revealed preference and rationality is a special case of Tarski–Seidenberg.

The approach of searching among polynomials of bounded degree is described in Parrilo (2003). Indeed, it can be shown to revert to a classical semidefinite programming problem. This approach is outlined in Parrilo (2003), a shorter introduction is provided in Parrilo (2004); see especially

Example 1 there. Marshall (2008), Chapter 10 provides a detailed explanation. Also see Sturmfels (2002).

Proposition 12.2 is from Chambers and Echenique (2014b). There are similar results in Carvajal and González (2014) and Cherchye, Demuynck, and De Rock (2013). Cherchye, Demuynck, and De Rock (2013) propose a different computational approach than the one we have emphasized here. They propose instead using integer programming to obtain a test for Nash bargaining.

CHAPTER 13

Revealed Preference and Model Theory

In this book, we have studied the concept of empirical content in disparate environments. To conclude our study, we wish to suggest that there is a unifying theme behind these exercises. The idea of the empirical content of a theory as *the set of all falsifiable predictions of the theory* is generally applicable, and subject to formal study.

A theory can make predictions which are non-falsifiable. A case in point is the theory of representation by a utility function. Recall Theorem 1.1. The theorem implies that if a preference relation $\succeq$ over $\mathbf{R}^n_+$ possesses a utility representation, then there is a countable set $Z \subseteq \mathbf{R}^n_+$ such that for all $x, y \in X$ for which $x \succ y$, there exists $z \in Z$ for which $x \succeq z \succeq y$. This implication of the theory of utility is not falsifiable. To demonstrate that the theory has been falsified, one would need to establish the non-existence of such a set Z. Doing so involves checking, one-by-one, every possible countable subset Z of $\mathbf{R}^n_+$, a task which can never be completed.

A first and basic issue in understanding empirical content has to do with universal vs. existential axiomatizations. The idea was already introduced in Chapters 9 and 12, where we saw the removal of existential quantifiers as a source of testable implications. The issue of universal and existential axioms goes back to Popper (1959), who thought that a theory with a *universal* description is falsifiable, while an *existential* theory is not.

Popper offers the example of the theory that claims "all swans are white." This theory is universal, in the sense that it states a property of all swans, or "universally quantifies over swans." It is easy to see that, in principle, such a theory can be falsified by finding a single swan that is not white. Contrast with Popper's example of an *existential* theory: that "there exists a black swan." The existential theory cannot be falsified. Falsifying the theory would involve collecting all possible swans and verifying that each one is not black. We could only do this if we could somehow be sure to have exhaustively checked all the swans in the universe.

Universality is clearly important for falsifiability, but there is a second component that is particularly relevant for the subject of this book. Popper's idea captures the notion of empirical content and falsifiability very well in many environments. However, economic theories and data are often burdened by *partial observability*. Implicit in Popper's examples is the idea that when we observe a swan, we observe its color. And indeed, in the swans example, this is entirely natural. With economic choice data, on the other hand, it is perfectly reasonable to observe objects but not all their properties. It is common, for example, to observe a pair of alternatives and not be able to observe which of the pair an individual chooses, or would choose. Think of choice from a budget B. When $x \in B$ is chosen this reveals something about the pairs (x,y) for $y \in B$, but nothing about the pairs (z,y) for $z \neq x$. This issue has been important in many of the results we have established. It lies behind the non-testability of concave utility in Afriat's Theorem, for example.[1]

Thus, in contrast to the theories that Popper had in mind, economic theories have the feature that we may be able to observe objects without observing the properties these objects enjoy. The phenomenon of partial observability will be very important for our discussion.

The considerations of universality and partial observability will be reflected in the kinds of axioms that capture the empirical content of a theory. Recall GARP, which states that the revealed preference pair $\langle \succeq^R, \succ^R \rangle$ is acyclic. Acyclicity of a revealed preference pair is a universal theory, but it is more. Using the universal quantifier $\forall$ and the negation symbol $\neg$, we can write acyclicity succinctly as for all n,

$$\forall x_1 \ldots \forall x_n \neg \left(\bigwedge_{i=1}^{n-1} (x_i \succeq^R x_{i+1}) \wedge (x_n \succ^R x_1) \right). \tag{13.1}$$

The structure of Equation (13.1) explains its falsifiability: it begins with universal quantification, followed by a negation, followed by a conjunction $\wedge$ (meaning "and"), followed by basic properties about observables. Specifically, such "basic" properties amount to *observable* relations among observables. This mathematical equation is therefore a Universal Negation of Conjunction of Atomic Formulas: it is an *UNCAF* formula. Negating atomic formulas means that one rules out that a particular (observable) relation holds among observable entities or quantities.

Contrast GARP with the hypothesis that $\succeq^R$ is a preference relation (a weak order) and $\succ^R$ is its strict part. This hypothesis has a universal axiomatization, but *not* of the UNCAF form. We shall see that this distinction matters. The hypothesis that $\succeq^R$ is a weak order and $\succ^R$ is its strict part has the following axiomatization:

I) $\forall x \forall y (x \succeq^R y) \vee (y \succeq^R x)$
II) $\forall x \forall y \forall z (x \succeq^R y) \wedge (y \succeq^R z) \rightarrow (x \succeq^R z)$
III) $\forall x \forall y (x \succ^R y) \leftrightarrow (x \succeq^R y) \wedge \neg (y \succeq^R x)$.

[1] If one could observe comparisons between all pairs of alternatives, then concavity would clearly be testable.

Some claims made by this theory are falsifiable. For example if we observe that $x \succ^R y$, $y \succ^R z$, and $z \succ^R x$ (a violation of transitivity), then obviously we have falsified the theory. But not *all* claims made by the theory are falsifiable. A pair x,y could be observed without observing any relation between them for example: this is common in the consumption datasets analyzed in Chapters 3–5. Therefore, in the presence of partial observability, completeness cannot be falsified.[2] Interestingly, GARP is usually understood as forming the empirical content of axioms (I), (II), and (III). We demonstrate below the formal sense in which this is true.

13.1 A MODEL FOR OBSERVABLES, DATA, AND THEORIES

There are three important concepts we need to explain. The first is the primitive of the model: the things we can observe are the primitive, and these things will be specified through a *language.* The second is what we mean by a dataset: datasets are finite and consist of partial observations. The third is our notion of a theory: a theory is a formal way of hypothesizing that certain relationships hold between objects of interest.

A first-order *language* $\mathcal{L}$ is given by a finite set of *relation symbols* and, for each relation symbol R, a positive integer n_R, the *arity of* R.

Let $\mathcal{L}$ be a language. An $\mathcal{L}$*-dataset* $\mathcal{D}$ is given by:

I) A finite non-empty set D (the *domain* of $\mathcal{D}$).
II) An n-ary relation $R^{\mathcal{D}}$ over D for every n-ary relation symbol R of $\mathcal{L}$.

Each element $(x_1^*,\ldots,x_{n_R}^*) \in R^{\mathcal{D}}$ is intended to represent the *observation* that $(x_1^*,\ldots,x_n^*)$ stand in relation R. The notion of a dataset is intended to capture the idea that there can only be a finite number of observations.

As an example, consider the language $\mathcal{L}$ that has two binary relation symbols, $\succeq$ and $\succ$. We mean the former to signify revealed weak preference observations, and the latter to signify revealed strict preference observations. Consider a dataset $\mathcal{D}^1$, with domain $D^1 = \{a,b,c\}$, and where we observe that a is revealed weakly preferred to b, and b to c, but we do not observe any strict comparisons. In symbols, $\mathcal{D}^1 = (D^1, \succeq^{\mathcal{D}^1}, \succ^{\mathcal{D}^1})$; $\succeq^{\mathcal{D}^1}$ is the relation given by $a \succeq^{\mathcal{D}^1} b$ and $b \succeq^{\mathcal{D}^1} c$, while $\succ^{\mathcal{D}^1}$ is empty. The example illustrates partial observability: We might theorize that $a \succeq^{\mathcal{D}^1} b$ implies either $b \succeq^{\mathcal{D}^1} a$ or $a \succ^{\mathcal{D}^1} b$, but often data will not contain this kind of information. In fact partial observability is very prominent in economics, for example in the consumption datasets used by the papers described in Chapter 5.

[2] In an environment of full observability (meaning, not partial) and strong rationalization, Eliaz and Ok (2006) investigate choice functions based on maximization of a relation that retains transitivity, but which need not be complete. In such a context, they show that completeness adds real content. They also show how indifference can often be distinguished from incompleteness in such an environment.

We will now define a notion of theory. We are interested in investigating a notion of empirical content, so from this perspective, we imagine that all of the relevant aspects of a theory can be captured by describing the relations among potential observables that we hypothesize hold. To this end, define an *$\mathcal{L}$-structure* $\mathcal{M}$ to consist of the following objects:

I) A nonempty set M (the *domain* of $\mathcal{M}$).
II) An n-ary relation $R^{\mathcal{M}}$ over M for every n-ary relation symbol R of $\mathcal{L}$.

A structure forms a hypothesis about the relations which we might expect to observe, but we never expect to see the entire structure. Rather, we imagine that a dataset is consistent with a structure when all of the observations are members of the structure.

With this in mind, we say that an $\mathcal{L}$-structure $\mathcal{M}$ *rationalizes* an $\mathcal{L}$-dataset $\mathcal{D}$ if the following conditions are satisfied:

I) $D \subseteq M$, where D and M are the domains of $\mathcal{D}$ and $\mathcal{M}$.
II) $R^{\mathcal{D}} \subseteq R^{\mathcal{M}}$.

The definition of rationalization requires that $R^{\mathcal{D}} \subseteq R^{\mathcal{M}}$ rather than that $R^{\mathcal{D}}$ is the restriction of $R^{\mathcal{M}}$ to D. The idea is again simply that we do not imagine that all existing relations are necessarily observed. This is the nature of partial observability: observing only a weak preference for coffee over tea does not refute the possibility that coffee is strictly preferred to tea.

We say that two structures are *isomorphic* if we can relabel the objects across the two structures so that all relations are maintained. Let $\mathcal{M}$ and $\mathcal{N}$ be $\mathcal{L}$-structures with domains M and N respectively. Formally, an *isomorphism from $\mathcal{M}$ to $\mathcal{N}$* is a bijective map $\eta : M \to N$ that preserves the interpretations of all symbols of $\mathcal{L}$: $(a_1, ..., a_{n_R}) \in R^{\mathcal{M}}$ iff $(\eta(a_1), ..., \eta(a_{n_R})) \in R^{\mathcal{N}}$ for every relation symbol R of $\mathcal{L}$ and $a_1, ..., a_{n_R} \in M$.

Informally, two structures are isomorphic if there is no way to use our language to distinguish between them.

Finally, we define a theory to be a class of structures. Formally, an *$\mathcal{L}$-theory* T is a class of structures that is closed under isomorphism. A dataset $\mathcal{D}$ is *T-rationalizable* if there is a structure in T that rationalizes $\mathcal{D}$. Otherwise, $\mathcal{D}$ *falsifies* T.

As an example, consider again the language with two binary symbols, $\succeq$ and $\succ$. We have the theory T_{wo} consisting of the class of triples $(M, \succeq^M, \succ^M)$ such that $\succeq^M$ is a preference relation on M (a weak order), and $\succ^M$ is the strict preference derived from $\succeq^M$. The theory T_{wo} can be thought of as the theory of rational choice. Note that T_{wo} rationalizes the dataset $\mathcal{D}^1$ described above: $\mathcal{D}^1$ has observed objects $D^1 = \{a, b, c\}$, where a is revealed weakly preferred to b, and b to c. The data $\mathcal{D}^1$ is T_{wo}-rationalizable because it can be rationalized, for example, by the set M of all letters in the English alphabet, with $\succeq^M$ being the lexicographic order on M. Of course, there are many other structures in T_{wo} that could rationalize $\mathcal{D}^1$.

We emphasized that $\mathcal{D}^1$ is silent on some aspects of the relationship between a, b, and c; these aspects are not observed, but we do not view this partial observability as a conflict with T_{wo}. Some "theoretically true" relations are simply not observed in the dataset. The structure of all the letters in the English alphabet is a possible rationalization of $\mathcal{D}^1$ in T_{wo}. In this structure a is strictly preferred to c, a property that has not been observed in $\mathcal{D}^1$.

In contrast with data $\mathcal{D}^1$, consider the dataset $\mathcal{D}^2$; where $D^2 = \{a,b,c\}$ (the same as D^1), but where we observe no weak comparisons, and instead observe that

$$a \succ^{\mathcal{D}^2} b \succ^{\mathcal{D}^2} c \succ^{\mathcal{D}^2} a.$$

No structure in T_{wo} could rationalize $\mathcal{D}^2$ because the "theoretical" strict preference $\succ^M$ in such a structure would need to exhibit the cyclic comparisons $a \succ^M b \succ^M c \succ^M a$. This is impossible for a weak order.

Another example of a theory is the theory of utility maximization, denoted T_u, which is the set of triples $(M, \succeq^M, \succ^M)$ in T_{wo} such that there is $u : M \to \mathbf{R}$ with $x \succeq^M y$ iff $u(x) \geq u(y)$. Note that

$$T_u \subsetneq T_{wo}.$$

The theory of utility maximization is more stringent than T_{wo}. But T_u can also rationalize $\mathcal{D}^1$ (but not $\mathcal{D}^2$). In fact, it is easy to see that any dataset that is T_{wo}-rationalizable is also T_u-rationalizable, even though utility maximization is more stringent than rational choice. Put differently, one can weaken T_u to T_{wo} *without observable consequences*. When that happens we shall say that the two theories have the same empirical content.

13.1.1 Empirical content

We want the empirical content of a theory to capture all of the observable consequences of that theory, but no other consequences. To this end, we want to weaken the theory as much as possible without changing the observable consequences of the theory, removing all non-observable consequences. For example, we can obtain a new theory by adding structures to T_u (thus weakening T_u) without changing the datasets that falsify the new theory. The empirical content of T_u is the most one can weaken T_u in this fashion.

Hence we define the *empirical content* of a theory T, denoted $\mathrm{ec}(T)$, to be the class of all structures $\mathcal{M}$ that do not rationalize any dataset that falsifies T. The main result of this chapter is that the empirical content of a theory is captured by the UNCAF axioms that are true in that theory.

Given a language $\mathcal{L}$, we can write formulas using the symbols in $\mathcal{L}$. In addition to the relation symbols specified by $\mathcal{L}$, we shall use standard logical symbols: the *quantifiers* "exists" ($\exists$) and "for all" ($\forall$); "not" ($\neg$); the *logical connectives* "and" ($\wedge$) and "or" ($\vee$); a countable set of *variable symbols* $x, y, z, u, v, w, \ldots$; parentheses "(" and ")"; and equality and inequality symbols "$=$" and "$\neq$".

Strings of symbols are put together to form *axioms*. Rules for the formation of axioms can be found, for example, in Marker (2002).

We are primarily concerned with a special class of axioms, the UNCAF axioms. These are defined as follows. First we must define the notion of an *atomic formula*.

An *atomic formula* φ of a language $\mathcal{L}$ consists of either

I) $t_1 = t_2$ or $t_1 \neq t_2$, where t_1, t_2 are variable symbols or
II) $R(t_1, \ldots, t_{n_R})$ where R is a relation symbol of $\mathcal{L}$ and $t_1, \ldots, t_{n_R}$ are variable symbols.

Atomic formulas are closely related to the notion of observation discussed above. Let us consider again the language with two binary relation symbols, $\succeq$ and $\succ$. In this example, all atomic formulas use at most two variable symbols. For example, the string $x \succeq y$ is an atomic formula, as is $x \succ y$. These strings are unquantified and as such do not yet form axioms. But one can imagine that an observation might consist of some pair a and b for which a is observed to stand in relation $\succeq$ to b.

We will form axioms out of the atomic formulas. The axioms are intended to be statements precluding the existence of certain finite collections of observations from holding. To this end, let $\mathcal{L}$ be a language. A *universal negation of a conjunction of atomic formulas (UNCAF)* axiom is a string of the form

$$\forall v_1 \forall v_2 \ldots \forall v_n \neg (\varphi_1 \wedge \varphi_2 \cdots \wedge \varphi_m)$$

where $\varphi_1, \varphi_2, \ldots, \varphi_m$ are atomic formulas with variables from $v_1, \ldots, v_n$.

As an example, consider again the language that has two binary relation symbols, $\succeq$ and $\succ$. An example of an UNCAF axiom in this language is:

$$\forall x \forall y \neg (x \succeq y \wedge y \succ x);$$

which we might call the weak axiom of revealed preference (WARP). Similarly, GARP can be seen to be an UNCAF axiom. In a different language, congruence (recall Chapter 2) is UNCAF.

Let Γ be a set of UNCAF axioms of $\mathcal{L}$. Let $\mathcal{T}(\Gamma)$ consist of the structures for which all axioms in Γ are true; thus, $\mathcal{T}(\Gamma)$ is a theory. If $T = \mathcal{T}(\Gamma)$ for some set Γ of axioms, we say that Γ is an UNCAF *axiomatization* of T.

Given a theory T, let uncaf(T) be the set of UNCAF axioms that are true in all members of T. The following result establishes that the empirical content of a theory always has an UNCAF axiomatization. This is true whether or not the theory itself does. Moreover, one such UNCAF axiomatization consists of the UNCAF axioms true for every structure in the theory.

Theorem 13.1 *For every theory T, ec(T) is the theory axiomatized by the UNCAF axioms that are true in T: ec(T) $= \mathcal{T}$ (uncaf(T)).*

Thus, in the presence of partial observability, UNCAF axioms, not universal ones, properly describe the empirical content of the model. In the context of the examples we have been using, Theorem 13.1 presents the formal sense in which GARP is the empirical content of completeness and transitivity.

Theories that coincide with their empirical content are in some sense special. They cannot be weakened in any way without adding falsifying datasets. We shall see in 13.2 an example of a theory with $T = \mathrm{ec}(T)$.

13.1.2 Relative theories

In economics, a researcher often wants to take certain hypotheses as being given. For example, economic theorists often view continuity axioms as a technical assumption. By itself, continuity has no empirical content. Hence, they are not interested in testing for this property, though it is often useful for providing a representation. Even though continuity by itself usually has no empirical content, the axiom may have empirical content when imposed with other axioms. So what we really care about are the empirical implications of a preference in the presence of the hypothesized continuity.

Moreover, there are often obvious constraints imposed on us by the structure of the model. We can imagine an individual with preferences over bundles of coffee and tea. Bundles of coffee and tea are elements in a linear space. It would not be interesting to "test" the axioms for a vector space. One can then talk about the empirical content of the economically meaningful theory, relative to the theory of linear spaces.

Consider two theories, T and T', where $T \subseteq T'$. We can define the *empirical content of T relative to T'*, written $\mathrm{ec}_{T'}(T)$, as the class of all structures $\mathcal{M} \in T'$ that do not rationalize any dataset that falsifies T, i.e.,

$$\mathrm{ec}_{T'}(T) = \mathrm{ec}(T) \cap T'. \tag{13.2}$$

The following is an immediate consequence of Theorem 13.1.

Corollary 13.2 *For any theories T and T' such that $T \subseteq T'$, $\mathrm{ec}_{T'}(T) = \mathcal{T}(\mathrm{uncaf}(T)) \cap T'$.*

We say that a collection of UNCAF axioms Λ is an UNCAF axiomatization of T relative to T' if $T = \mathcal{T}(\Lambda) \cap T'$. Corollary 13.2 implies that the empirical content of T relative to T' admits an UNCAF axiomatization relative to T'.

13.2 APPLICATION: *STATUS QUO* PREFERENCES

As mentioned above, theories that satisfy $T = \mathrm{ec}(T)$ are particularly interesting. As an application, we discuss a recent theory of choice in the presence of *status quo* due to Masatlioglu and Ok. There is a sense in which their theory makes no non-falsifiable claims.

Let $\mathcal{L}$ be a language including the binary relation $\in$ and the ternary relations $c, \tilde{c}$. The latter two are meant to express "chosen" and "not chosen." We define the theory of choice with *status quo* T_{csq} to be the class of structures $(M, \in^{\mathcal{M}},$

$c^{\mathcal{M}}, \tilde{c}^{\mathcal{M}})$ whereby there is some set X, a collection $\Sigma \subseteq 2^X \backslash \{\varnothing\} \times X$ satisfying $(E,b) \in \Sigma$ implies $b \in E$, and a nonempty valued function $c^* : \Sigma \to 2^M \backslash \{\varnothing\}$ for which $c^*(E,b) \subseteq E$ for all $(E,b) \in \Sigma$ for which the following are satisfied:

I) $M = X \cup \Sigma$
II) $\in^{\mathcal{M}}$ is the usual set theoretic relation
III) $c^{\mathcal{M}}(a,b,E)$ if and only if $a \in c^*(E,b)$
IV) $\tilde{c}^{\mathcal{M}}(a,b,E)$ if and only if $a \notin c^*(E,b)$;

as well as all structures isomorphic to these. The idea here is that each budget set E possesses a *status quo* b. We observe the choices made (and not made) from budget sets.

The theory of *status quo* rationalizable choice is the subtheory $T_{sq} \subseteq T_{csq}$ whereby there exists a function $Q : X \to 2^X \backslash \{\varnothing\}$ such that for all $x \in X$, $x \in Q(x)$, and a complete and transitive binary relation $\succeq$ for which the corresponding function c^* can be expressed as $c^*(E,b) = \arg\max_{\succeq} Q(b) \cap E$. The idea is that the *status quo* alternative determines a "reference set" from which the agent will choose.[3]

Theorem 13.3 $ec_{T_{csq}}(T_{sq}) = T_{csq}$.

Proof. We provide an explicit syntactic characterization. The formula

$$(x \in E) \wedge (y \in E) \wedge c(x,d,E)$$

is abbreviated $x \succeq (E)_d\, y$, and the formula

$$(x \in E) \wedge (y \in E) \wedge c(x,d,E) \wedge \tilde{c}(y,d,E)$$

is abbreviated $x \succ (E)_d\, y$. Note that each of these formulas is a conjunction of atomic formulas.

Similarly, we define, for a structure $(M, \in^{\mathcal{M}}, c^{\mathcal{M}}, \tilde{c}^{\mathcal{M}}) \in T_{csq}$, the ternary relations $x \succeq_d^{\mathcal{M}} y$ to mean that there is E for which $x, y \in E$ and $x \in c^*(d,E)$, and $x \succ_d^{\mathcal{M}} y$ means there is E for which $x, y \in E$ and $x \in c^*(d,E)$ and $y \notin c^*(d,E)$ (here, we suppress the dependence of the relation on E as it is not needed).

Now, a *cycle* for a structure $\mathcal{M} \in T_{csq}$ is a collection $x_1, \ldots, x_n$, $y_1, \ldots, y_n$, and $z_1, \ldots, z_n$ all in M such that $x_{i+1} \neq y_i$ and $x_i \succeq_{z_i}^{\mathcal{M}} x_{i+1}$ with at least one strict part, and for each z_i, $x_{i+1} \succeq_{z_i}^{\mathcal{M}} y_i$ *or* $x_{i+1} = z_i$.

Note that the collection of axioms which rule out all cycles is UNCAF, as each formula $x \succeq (E)_d\, y$ is a conjunction of atomic formulas, as is the formula $x \succ (E)_d\, y$. In other words, the UNCAF list of axioms given by

$$\forall x_1 \ldots \forall z_n \forall E_1 \ldots \forall E_n \forall F_1 \ldots \forall F_n \neg \left(\bigwedge_{i=1}^{n} (x_i R_i (E_i)_{z_i} x_{i+1}) \wedge (Q_i(x_{i+1}, y_i, z_i, F_i)) \right),$$

[3] Masatlioglu and Ok (2014) also allow there to be no *status quo*, which they represent with a *status quo* "alternative" of $\diamondsuit$. We could accommodate this easily by introducing a constant symbol for $\diamondsuit$, and none of the results would change. However, the analysis would become notationally much more burdensome.

where each R_i is either $\succ$ or $\succeq$ and at least one is $\succ$, and each $Q_i(x_{i+1}, y_i, z_i, F_i)$ is either the expression $x_{i+1} \succeq (F_i)_{z_i}\ y_i$ or the expression $x_{i+1} = z_i$, is the appropriate collection of sentences.

Finally, given $\mathcal{M} \in T_{csq}$, we have its associated ternary relations $\succeq^{\mathcal{M}}$ and $\succ^{\mathcal{M}}$. We claim that $\mathcal{M} \in T_{sq}$ if and only if it has no cycles.

To this end, suppose that $\mathcal{M} \in T_{sq}$. Then $\mathcal{M}$ is isomorphic to a triple (X, Σ, c^*). There is a binary relation R and a function Q as stated in the definition. Suppose for a contradiction that there is a cycle. Each $x_{i+1} \in Q(z_i)$, since $x_{i+1} \succeq_{z_i}^{\mathcal{M}} y_i$ (implying it is chosen at some point when z_i is the *status quo*) or $x_{i+1} = z_i$, which again implies that $x_{i+1} \in Q(z_i)$. Therefore, $x_i \succeq_{z_i}^{\mathcal{M}} x_{i+1}$ implies $x_i\, R\, x_{i+1}$ and $x_i \succ_{z_i}^{\mathcal{M}} x_{i+1}$ implies $x_i\, R\, x_{i+1}$ but not $x_{i+1}\, R\, x_i$, contradicting transitivity.

Conversely, suppose $\mathcal{M} \in T_{csq}$ and that there are no cycles. Without loss of generality, we may assume that $\mathcal{M}$ is specified by a triple (X, Σ, c^*). We define $Q(d) = \{y : \exists E \in \Sigma \text{ such that } y \in c^*(d,E)\}$. Define $\overline{\succeq}_d = \{(x,y) \in \succeq_d : y \in Q(d)\}$ and $\overline{\succ}_d = \{(x,y) \in \succ_d : y \in Q(d)\}$. Finally, define $\overline{\succeq} = \bigcup_{d \in X} \overline{\succeq}_d$ and $\overline{\succ} = \bigcup_{d \in X} \overline{\succeq}_d$. Then because there are no cycles, there exist no $x_1, \ldots, x_n$ for which $x_1 \overline{\succeq} \ldots \overline{\succeq} x_n$, where at least one $\overline{\succeq}$ is $\overline{\succ}$. By Theorem 1.5, there is a complete and transitive R for which $x \overline{\succeq} y$ implies $x\, R\, y$ and $x \overline{\succ} y$ implies $x\, R\, y$. The pair Q, R then *status quo* rationalizes c^*.

13.3 CHOICE THEORY AND EMPIRICAL CONTENT

As mentioned earlier in the chapter, theories that coincide with their empirical content are in some sense special. We shall here consider the structure of such theories relative to a theory of choice.

The theory of rationalizable choice functions enjoys a very interesting property. Recall Chapter 2 and, in particular, Theorem 2.6. The theorem characterizes the empirical content of a preference relation by the congruence axiom. Congruence is a collection of first-order axioms precluding the existence of certain types of revealed preference cycles. Importantly, congruence can be described in a very parsimonious language: the language is able to express the relations $\in$, $\notin$, as well as the properties of being chosen or not. This means that the data the economist must possess in order to falsify the model are quite simple.

In this section, we demonstrate a very simple result claiming that most choice theories do not share this property. As motivation, consider the following simple example.

Example 13.4 *An economist asks whether a given individual maximizes a preference relation (a weak order). She observes three budget sets, A, B, and D, and three potential choices, x, y, and z. She sees that each of x and y are feasible in A, y and z are feasible in B, and x and z are feasible in D. She also sees that x is chosen from A, y is chosen from B, and z is chosen from D, while x* *is never chosen from D. These data clearly refute the hypothesis of preference maximization.*

To establish this refutation, the economist did not see every feasible option from each of the three budget sets or any "global set" on which the choice function might potentially be defined, nor did she need to see what the individual would choose from an unrelated budget E.

Consider two languages. The first, $\mathcal{L} = \{\in, \notin, c, \tilde{c}\}$, includes four binary predicates. The predicates $\in$ and $\notin$ are to be understood in their usual way, while $c(a,B)$ means a is chosen from B, and $\tilde{c}(a,B)$ means a is not chosen from B. The second language is more expressive: $\mathcal{L}' = \{\in, \notin, c, \tilde{c}, \subseteq, \nsubseteq\}$. The binary relations $\subseteq$ and $\nsubseteq$ are given their usual interpretation.

A choice function consists of a triple (X, Σ, c), where X is a set, $\Sigma \subseteq 2^X \backslash \{\varnothing\}$, and $c : \Sigma \to 2^X \backslash \{\varnothing\}$, so that for all $E \in \Sigma$, $c(E) \subseteq E$. Each choice function is naturally identified with a structure in either language.

In either language, $\mathcal{L}$ or $\mathcal{L}'$, a choice theory T is a class of choice functions and all structures isomorphic to an element of this class. The choice theory which consists of all choice functions is written T_{choice} in language $\mathcal{L}$ and T'_{choice} in language $\mathcal{L}'$, respectively.

Say that the $\mathcal{L}$-theory T is *rich* if for all (X, Σ, c) in T, there is $z \notin X$ and a choice function $(X \cup \{z\}, \Sigma', c') \in T$, where $\Sigma = \{E \cap X : E \in \Sigma'\}$ and for all $E \in \Sigma'$, $c'(E) = c(E \cap X)$. Intuitively, a rich choice theory is one with the property that, for any of its structures, we can add an alternative that is never chosen to the domain. Say that a choice theory satisfies condition α if all choice functions in the theory satisfy condition α.

When a theory satisfies $\text{ec}(T) \cap T_{choice} = T$, then we say that it makes no non-falsifiable claims relative to the theory of choice. We are now in a position to show that, under some conditions, the property of not making non-falsifiable claims can imply WARP.

Theorem 13.5 *Suppose that T is rich, satisfies condition α, and that $ec(T) \cap T_{choice} = T$. Then every $(X, \Sigma, c) \in T$ satisfies WARP. Further, the class of choice functions satisfying WARP is the maximal T which is rich, satisfies condition α, and $ec(T) \cap T_{choice} = T$.*

Proof. Suppose by way of contradiction that $(X, \Sigma, c) \in T$ violates WARP. Thus, there are $x, y \in X$ and $E, F \in \Sigma$ for which $x, y \in E \cap F$, $x \in c(E)$, $y \in c(F)$, and $x \notin c(F)$. Appeal to richness and consider $z \notin X$. Let Σ^* consist of all budgets of Σ, with the exception that z has been added to E. The choice function c^* then coincides with c, and $c^*(E \cup \{z\}) = c(E)$.

Now consider the following choice function: $X' = \{x, y, z\}$, $\Sigma' = \{E' = \{x, y, z\}, F' = \{x, y\}\}$, and $c'(\{x, y, z\}) = c(E) \cap \{x, y, z\}$, $c'(\{x, y\}) = \{y\}$. This choice function is clearly not a member of T as it violates condition α: $x \in c'(\{x, y, z\})$, but $x \notin c'(\{x, y\})$. However, every dataset consistent with (X', Σ', c') can be rationalized by $(X \cup \{z\}, \Sigma^*, c^*)$. This is a contradiction.

Clearly, the class of choice functions satisfying WARP has the desired property (WARP is an UNCAF axiom, so the result follows from Corollary 13.2).

A special example of choice theories are choice theories rationalizable by some binary relation. Let $\mathcal{R}$ be a class of complete binary relations. We define the theory of $\mathcal{R}$-rationalizable choice, $T_{\mathcal{R}}$, to be the class of choice functions (X,Σ,c) for which there exists $R\in\mathcal{R}$ such that for all $E\in\Sigma$, $c(E)=\{x\in E: x\,R\,y \text{ for all } y\in E\}$.

Let the relation $\succeq^*$ on $\mathbf{Z}_+\cup\{\omega\}$ be defined so that for all $n,m\in\mathbf{Z}_+$, we have $n\succeq^* m$ if and only if $n\geq m$, and otherwise, $\omega\sim^* n$ for all $n\in\mathbf{Z}_+$.

A simple corollary follows.

Corollary 13.6 *For the following $\mathcal{R}$, $ec(T_{\mathcal{R}})\cap T_{choice}\neq T_{\mathcal{R}}$:*

- *$\mathcal{R}$ is the set of all complete binary relations.*
- *$\mathcal{R}$ is the set of all quasitransitive and complete binary relations.*
- *$\mathcal{R}$ is the set of all complete binary relations for which there exists a pair of linear orders $\succeq_1$ and $\succeq_2$ for which $\succ=\succ_1\cap\succ_2$. These are the set of 2-Pareto rationalizable choice functions.*

Proposition 13.7 *If $\succeq^*\in\mathcal{R}$, then $ec(T_{\mathcal{R}})\cap T'_{choice}\neq ec(T_{\mathcal{R}})$.*

Proof. Let $X=\mathbf{Z}_+\cup\{\omega\}$ and let us consider the collection Σ which includes all binary subsets, as well as the set X itself. The choice function is specified by $c(X)=\{\omega\}$, $c(\{i,\omega\})=\{i,\omega\}$ for all $i\in\mathbf{Z}_+$, and finally, $c(\{i,j\})=\{j\}$ when $j>i$. Then $(X,\Sigma,c)\in T_{\mathcal{R}}$, and has the feature that ω is uniquely chosen from X, but it beats no $i\in\mathbf{Z}_+$.

Consider the following choice function: (X',Σ',c'), where $X'=\{1,2,\omega\}$, $\Sigma'=\{\{1,2\},\{2,\omega\},\{1,2,\omega\}\}$, and $c'(\{1,2\})=\{2\}$, $c'(\{2,\omega\})=\{2,\omega\}$, and $c'(\{1,2,\omega\})=\{\omega\}$. Clearly $(X',\Sigma',c')\notin T_{\mathcal{R}}$ as if it were, any R which rationalizes c' must have that $2\;R\;1$ and $2\;R\;\omega$, which would imply that $2\in c'(\{1,2,\omega\})$, a contradiction.

However any dataset contained in (X',Σ',c') can be rationalized by (X,Σ,c), a contradiction.

Proposition 13.7 demonstrates that none of the choice theories mentioned in Corollary 13.6 are equivalent to their empirical content, even when we can express set containment.

13.4 CHAPTER REFERENCES

Theorem 13.1 and Corollary 13.2 are due to Chambers, Echenique, and Shmaya (2014). This result is related to a theorem of Tarski (1954), which characterizes those theories that are universally axiomatizable. Tarski's result relies on the axiom of choice, while Theorem 13.1 does not. The working paper version of Chambers, Echenique, and Shmaya (2014) has results for languages with constants and function symbols. A collection of papers apply Tarski's result to the issue of falsifiability; see Simon and Groen (1973); Simon (1979, 1983); Rynasiewicz (1983); Simon (1985); Shen and Simon (1993).

Popper (1959) is a seminal reference in the philosophy of science, viewing falsifiable theories as those that admit universal axiomatizations. Much early literature in philosophy of science was concerned with whether the restrictions on observable relations imposed by axioms involving unobservable relations could be expressed in terms of observable relations alone. Craig (1956) provides a seminal result in this direction.

Adams, Fagot, and Robinson (1970) seem to be the first social scientists to discuss empirical content in a formal sense (see also Pfanzagl, Baumann, and Huber, 1971, and Adams, 1992). This work defines two theories to be empirically equivalent if the set of all axioms (of a certain type) consistent with one theory is equivalent to the set of all axioms consistent with the other. These works do not provide a general characterization of the axiomatic structure of empirical content, but rather focus on characterizing the empirical content of specific theories. Finally, there is an approach in philosophy of science called *structuralism*, which also comes close to the approach we have taken here. These works also adopt a model-theoretic perspective to investigating theories. Sneed (1971) is a classic reference as applied to physics. Stegmüller, Balzer, and Spohn (1982) present a collection applications of these ideas to economics.

Schipper (2009) has a notion of theory that is similar to ours.

The theory discussed in Section 13.2 is due to Masatlioglu and Ok (2014). The analysis of this section appeared in a working version of Chambers, Echenique, and Shmaya (2014).

References

Adams, E. (1992). "On the Empirical Status of Measurement Axioms: The Case of Subjective Probability," in *Philosophical and Foundational Issues in Measurement Theory*, edited by C. W. Savage and P. Erlich, pp. 53–73. Hillsdale, NJ: Lawrence Erlbaum Associates.

Adams, E., R. Fagot, and R. Robinson (1970). "On the Empirical Status of Axioms in Theories of Fundamental Measurement," *Journal of Mathematical Psychology*, 7(3), 379–409.

Afriat, S. N. (1967). "The Construction of Utility Functions from Expenditure Data," *International Economic Review*, 8(1), 67–77.

——— (1972). "Efficiency Estimation of Production Functions," *International Economic Review*, 13(3), 568–598.

Agranov, M., and P. Ortoleva (2013). "Stochastic Choice and Hedging," Discussion paper, California Institute of Technology.

Ahn, D., S. Choi, D. Gale, and S. Kariv (2014). "Estimating Ambiguity Aversion in a Portfolio Choice Experiment," *Quantitative Economics*, 5(2), 195–223.

Aleskerov, F., D. Bouyssou, and B. Monjardet (2007). *Utility Maximization, Choice and Preference*. Berlin *et al.*: Springer-Verlag.

Allais, M. (1953). "Le Comportement de l'Homme Rationnel Devant le Risque: Critique des Postulats et Axiomes de l'École Américaine," *Econometrica*, 21(4), 503–546.

Ambrus, A., and K. Rozen (2014). "Rationalising Choice with Multi-Self Models," *The Economic Journal*, forthcoming.

Andreoni, J., B. J. Gillen, and W. T. Harbaugh (2013). "Power Indices for Revealed Preference Tests," working paper, UC San Diego.

Andreoni, J., and J. Miller (2002). "Giving According to GARP: An Experimental Test of the Consistency of Preferences for Altruism," *Econometrica*, 70(2), 737–753.

Anscombe, F. J., and R. J. Aumann (1963). "A Definition of Subjective Probability," *Annals of Mathematical Statistics*, 34(1), 199–205.

Arrow, K. (1951). *Social Choice and Individual Values*. New Haven, CT: Yale University Press.

——— (1959). "Rational Choice Functions and Orderings," *Economica*, 26(102), 121–127.

Asplund, E. (1970). "A Monotone Convergence Theorem for Sequences of Nonlinear Mappings," in *Proceedings of Symposia in Pure Mathematics*, Vol. 18, pp. 1–9.

Azrieli, Y. (2011). "Axioms for Euclidean Preferences with a Valence Dimension," *Journal of Mathematical Economics*, 47(4–5), 545–553.

Azrieli, Y., C. P. Chambers, and P. J. Healy (2012). "Incentives in Experiments: A Theoretical Analysis," working paper.

Ballester, M. A., and G. Haeringer (2011). "A Characterization of the Single-Peaked Domain," *Social Choice and Welfare*, 36(2), 305–322.

Bandyopadhyay, T., I. Dasgupta, and P. Pattanaik (1999). "Stochastic Revealed Preference and the Theory of Demand," *Journal of Economic Theory*, 84(1), 95–110.

——— (2004). "A General Revealed Preference Theorem for Stochastic Demand Behavior," *Economic Theory*, 23(3), 589–599.

Banerjee, S., and J. H. Murphy (2006). "A Simplified Test for Preference Rationality of Two-Commodity Choice," *Experimental Economics*, 9(1), 67–75.

Banker, R., A. Charnes, and W. Cooper (1984). "Some Models for Estimating Technical and Scale Inefficiencies in Data Envelopment Analysis," *Management Science*, 30(9), 1078–1092.

Banker, R., and A. Maindiratta (1988). "Nonparametric Analysis of Technical and Allocative Efficiencies in Production," *Econometrica*, 56(6), 1315–1332.

Bar-Shira, Z. (1992). "Nonparametric Test of the Expected Utility Hypothesis," *American Journal of Agricultural Economics*, 74(3), 523–533.

Barberá, S., and P. K. Pattanaik (1986). "Falmagne and the Rationalizability of Stochastic Choices in Terms of Random Orderings," *Econometrica*, 54(3), 707–715.

Bartz, S., H. Bauschke, J. Borwein, S. Reich, and X. Wang (2007). "Fitzpatrick Functions, Cyclic Monotonicity and Rockafellar's Antiderivative," *Nonlinear Analysis*, 66(5), 1198–1223.

Basu, K. (1984). "Fuzzy Revealed Preference Theory", *Journal of Economic Theory*, 32(2), 212–227.

Battalio, R., J. Kagel, W. Winkler, E. Fischer, R. Basmann, and L. Krasner (1973). "A Test of Consumer Demand Theory Using Observations of Individual Consumer Purchases," *Western Economic Journal*, 11(4), 411–428.

Bayer, R., S. Bose, M. Polisson, L. Renou, and J. Quah (2012). "Ambiguity Revealed," Mimeo, University of Essex.

Beatty, T. K. M., and I. A. Crawford (2011). "How Demanding Is the Revealed Preference Approach to Demand?" *The American Economic Review*, 101(6), 2782–2795.

Becker, G. M., M. H. DeGroot, and J. Marschak (1964). "Measuring Utility by a Single-Response Sequential Method," *Behavioral Science*, 9(3), 226–232.

Becker, G. S. (1962). "Irrational Behavior and Economic Theory," *The Journal of Political Economy*, 70(1), 1–13.

Berge, C. (1963). *Topological Spaces*. Edinburgh and London: Oliver & Boyd.

Berge, C. (2001). *Theory of Graphs*. Mineola, NY: Dover.

Bernheim, B. D., and A. Rangel (2007). "Toward Choice-Theoretic Foundations for Behavioral Welfare Economics," *The American Economic Review*, 97(2), 464–470.

——— (2009). "Beyond Revealed Preference: Choice-Theoretic Foundations for Behavioral Welfare Economics," *The Quarterly Journal of Economics*, 124(1), 51–104.

Billot, A., and J.-F. Thisse (2005). "Stochastic Rationality and Möbius Inverse," *International Journal of Economic Theory*, 1(3), 211–217.

Birkhoff, G. (1946). "Tres Observaciones Sobre el Álgebra Lineal," *Univ. Nac. Tucumán Rev. Ser. A*, 5, 147–151.

Blackorby, C., W. Bossert, and D. Donaldson (1995). "Multi-Valued Demand and Rational Choice in the Two-Commodity Case," *Economics Letters*, 47(1), 5–10.

Block, H., and J. Marschak (1960). "Random Orderings and Stochastic Theories of Responses," in *Contributions to Probability and Statistics*, edited by I. Olkin, S. Ghurye, W. Hoeffding, W. G. Madow, and H. B. Mann, Vol. 2, pp. 97–132. Palo Alto, CA: Stanford University Press.

Blundell, R. W., M. Browning, and I. A. Crawford (2003). "Nonparametric Engel Curves and Revealed Preference," *Econometrica*, 71(1), 205–240.

——— (2008). "Best Nonparametric Bounds on Demand Responses," *Econometrica*, 76(6), 1227–1262.

Bochnak, J., M. Coste, and M. Roy (1998). *Real Algebraic Geometry*. Berlin *et al.*: Springer-Verlag.

Bogomolnaia, A., and J. Laslier (2007). "Euclidean Preferences," *Journal of Mathematical Economics*, 43(2), 87–98.

Border, K. C. (1992). "Revealed Preference, Stochastic Dominance, and the Expected Utility Hypothesis," *Journal of Economic Theory*, 56(1), 20–42.

Börgers, T. (1993). "Pure Strategy Dominance," *Econometrica*, 61(2), 423–430.

Bossert, W. (1993). "Continuous Choice Functions and the Strong Axiom of Revealed Preference," *Economic Theory*, 3(2), 379–385.

Bossert, W., and Y. Sprumont (2002). "Core Rationalizability in Two-Agent Exchange Economies," *Economic Theory*, 20(4), 777–791.

——— (2013). "Every Choice Function is Backwards-Induction Rationalizable," *Econometrica*, 81(6), 2521–2534.

Bossert, W., Y. Sprumont, and K. Suzumura (2005). "Maximal-Element Rationalizability," *Theory and Decision*, 58(4), 325–350.

Bossert, W., and K. Suzumura (2010). *Consistency, Choice, and Rationality*. Harvard University Press.

——— (2012). "Revealed Preference and Choice Under Uncertainty," *SERIEs: Journal of the Spanish Economic Association*, 3(1), 247–258.

Bronars, S. G. (1987). "The Power of Nonparametric Tests of Preference Maximization," *Econometrica*, 55(3), 693–698.

Brown, D., and F. Kubler (2008). *Computational Aspects of General Equilibrium Theory: Refutable Theories of Value*. New York *et al.*: Springer.

Brown, D. J., and C. Calsamiglia (2007). "The Nonparametric Approach to Applied Welfare Analysis," *Economic Theory*, 31(1), 183–188.

Brown, D. J., and R. L. Matzkin (1996). "Testable Restrictions on the Equilibrium Manifold," *Econometrica*, 64(6), 1249–1262.

Brown, D. J., and C. Shannon (2000). "Uniqueness, Stability, and Comparative Statics in Rationalizable Walrasian Markets," *Econometrica*, 68(6), 1529–1539.

Browning, M. (1989). "A Nonparametric Test of the Life-Cycle Rational Expectations Hypothesis," *International Economic Review*, 30(4), 979–992.

Browning, M., and P. A. Chiappori (1998). "Efficient Intra-Household Allocations: A General Characterization and Empirical Tests," *Econometrica*, 66(6), 1241–1278.

Burghart, D. R., P. W. Glimcher, and S. C. Lazzaro (2013). "An Expected Utility Maximizer Walks into a Bar...," *Journal of Risk and Uncertainty*, 46(3), 215–246.

Cantor, G. (1895). "Beiträge zur Begründung der transfiniten Mengenlehre," *Mathematische Annalen*, 46(4), 481–512.

Carvajal, A., R. Deb, J. Fenske, and J. K.-H. Quah (2013). "Revealed Preference Tests of the Cournot Model," *Econometrica*, 81(6), 2351–2379.

Carvajal, A., and N. González (2014). "On Refutability of the Nash Bargaining Solution," *Journal of Mathematical Economics*, 50, 177–186.

Carvajal, A., I. Ray, and S. Snyder (2004). "Equilibrium Behavior in Markets and Games: Testable Restrictions and Identification," *Journal of Mathematical Economics*, 40(1–2), 1–40, Aggregation, Equilibrium and Observability in Honor of Werner Hildenbrand.

Castillo, M., D. Dickinson, and R. Petrie (2014). "Sleepiness, Choice Consistency, and Risk Preferences," Mimeo, George Mason University.

Chalfant, J. A., and J. M. Alston (1988). "Accounting for Changes in Tastes," *Journal of Political Economy*, 96(2), 391–410.

Chambers, C. P., and F. Echenique (2009a). "Profit Maximization and Supermodular Technology," *Economic Theory*, 40(2), 173–183.

——— (2009b). "Supermodularity and Preferences," *Journal of Economic Theory*, 144(3), 1004–1014.

——— (2014a). "Core Matchings of Markets with Transfers," *AEJ Microeconomics*, forthcoming.

——— (2014b). "On the Consistency of Data with Bargaining Theories," *Theoretical Economics*, 9(1), 137–162.

Chambers, C. P., F. Echenique, and K. Saito (2015). "Testable Implications of Translation Invariance and Homotheticity: Variational, Maxmin, CARA and CRRA Preferences," working paper, California Institute of Technology.

Chambers, C. P., F. Echenique, and E. Shmaya (2010). "On Behavioral Complementarity and its Implications," *Journal of Economic Theory*, 145, 2332–2355.

——— (2011). "Testable Implications of Gross Substitutes in Demand for Two Goods," *American Economic Journal: Microeconomics*, 3(1), 129–136.

——— (2012). "General Revealed Preference Theory," working paper.

——— (2014). "The Axiomatic Structure of Empirical Content," *American Economic Review*, 104(8), 2303–2319.

Chambers, C. P., and T. Hayashi (2012). "Choice and Individual Welfare," *Journal of Economic Theory*, 147(5), 1818–1849.

Chambers, C. P., C. Liu, and S.-K. Martinez (2014). "A Test for Risk-Averse Expected Utility," Mimeo, UC San Diego.

Cherchye, L., I. Crawford, B. De Rock, and F. Vermeulen (2009). "The Revealed Preference Approach to Demand," in *Quantifying Consumer Preferences: Estimating Demand Systems*, edited by D. Slottje, Contributions to Economic Analysis. Bingley, UK: Emerald Group Publishing.

Cherchye, L., T. Demuynck, and B. De Rock (2013). "Nash Bargained Consumption Decisions: A Revealed Preference Analysis," *Economic Journal*, 123(567), 195–235.

——— (2014). "Revealed Preference Analysis for Convex Rationalizations on Nonlinear Budget Sets," *Journal of Economic Theory*, 152, 224–236.

Cherchye, L., T. Demuynck, P. Hjertstrand, and B. De Rock (2014). "Revealed Preference Tests for Weak Separability: An Integer Programming Approach," *Journal of Econometrics*, forthcoming.

Cherchye, L., B. De Rock, and F. Vermeulen (2007). "The Collective Model of Household Consumption: A Nonparametric Characterization," *Econometrica*, 75(2), 553–574.

——— (2009). "Opening the Black Box of Intrahousehold Decision Making: Theory and Nonparametric Empirical Tests of General Collective Consumption Models," *Journal of Political Economy*, 117(6), 1074–1104.

Cherepanov, V., T. Feddersen, and A. Sandroni (2013). "Rationalization," *Theoretical Economics*, 8(3), 775–800.

Chernoff, H. (1954). "Rational Selection of Decision Functions," *Econometrica*, 22(4), 422–443.

Chiappori, P.-A. (1988). "Rational Household Labor Supply," *Econometrica*, 56(1), 63–90.

Chiappori, P.-A., O. Donni, and I. Komunjer (2012). "Learning from a Piece of Pie," *The Review of Economic Studies*, 79(1), 162–195.

Chiappori, P.-A., and J.-C. Rochet (1987). "Revealed Preferences and Differentiable Demand," *Econometrica*, 55(3), 687–691.

Chipman, J. S. (1960). "Stochastic Choice and Subjective Probability," in *Decisions, Values and Groups*, edited by D. Willner, pp. 70–95. Symposium Publications Division, New York: Pergamon Press.

Choi, S., R. Fisman, D. Gale, and S. Kariv (2007). "Consistency and Heterogeneity of Individual Behavior under Uncertainty," *American Economic Review*, 97(5), 1921–1938.

Choi, S., S. Kariv, W. Müller, and D. Silverman (2014). "Who Is (More) Rational?" *American Economic Review*, 104(6), 1518–50.

Chung-Piaw, T., and R. Vohra (2003). "Afriat's Theorem and Negative Cycles," Mimeo, Northwestern University.

Colonius, H. (1984). *Stochastische Theorien individuellen Wahlverhaltens*. Berlin *et al.*: Springer.

Cooper, W. W., L. M. Seiford, and K. Tone (2007). *Data Envelopment Analysis: A Comprehensive Text with Models, Applications, References and DEA-Solver Software*, 2nd ed. Berlin *et al.*: Springer.

Coxeter, H. (1969). *Introduction to Geometry*, 2nd ed. New York: John Wiley & Sons, Inc.

Craig, W. (1956). "Replacement of Auxiliary Expressions," *Philosophical Review*, 65(1), 38–55.

Craig, W., and R. L. Vaught (1958). "Finite Axiomatizability Using Additional Predicates," *The Journal of Symbolic Logic*, 23(3), 289–308.

Crawford, I., and B. De Rock (2014). "Empirical Revealed Preference," *Annual Review of Economics*, 6, 503–524.

Davenport, J. H., and J. Heintz (1988). "Real Quantifier Elimination is Doubly Exponential," *Journal of Symbolic Computation*, 5(1), 29–35.

de Clippel, G., and K. Eliaz (2012). "Reason-Based Choice: A Bargaining Rationale for the Attraction and Compromise Effects," *Theoretical Economics*, 7(1), 125–162.

de Clippel, G., and K. Rozen (2012). "Bounded Rationality and Limited Datasets," working paper.

Dean, M., and D. Martin (2013). "Measuring Rationality with the Minimum Cost of Revealed Preference Violations?" Working paper, Brown University.

Deaton, A. S. (1974). "The Analysis of Consumer Demand in the United Kingdom, 1900-1970," *Econometrica*, 42(2), 341–367.

Deb, R. (1976). "On Constructing Generalized Voting Paradoxes," *The Review of Economic Studies*, 43(2), 347–351.

Deb, R., and M. M. Pai (2014). "The Geometry of Revealed Preference," *Journal of Mathematical Economics*, 50, 203–207.

Debreu, G. (1951). "The Coefficient of Resource Utilization," *Econometrica*, 19(3), 273–292.

Debreu, G. (1954). "Representation of a Preference Ordering by a Numerical Function," in *Decision Processes*, edited by R. Thrall, C. Coombs, and R. Davis, pp. 159–165. New York: John Wiley & Sons.

——— (1960a). "On An Identity in Arithmetic," *Proceedings of the American Mathematical Society*, 11(2), 220–221.

——— (1960b). "Review of RD Luce, Individual Choice Behavior: A Theoretical Analysis," *American Economic Review*, 50(1), 186–188.

——— (1974). "Excess Demand Functions," *Journal of Mathematical Economics*, 1(1), 15–21.

Degan, A., and A. Merlo (2009). "Do Voters Vote Ideologically?" *Journal of Economic Theory*, 144, 1868–1894.

Diamond, P. A. (1967). "Cardinal Welfare, Individualistic Ethics, and Interpersonal Comparison of Utility: Comment," *The Journal of Political Economy*, 75(5), 765.

Diewert, W. E. (1973). "Afriat and Revealed Preference Theory," *The Review of Economic Studies*, 40(3), 419–425.

——— (2012). "Afriat's Theorem and some Extensions to Choice under Uncertainty*," *The Economic Journal*, 122(560), 305–331.

Diewert, W. E., and C. Parkan (1983). "Linear Programming Tests of Regularity Conditions for Production Functions," in *Quantitative Studies on Production and Prices*, edited by W. Eichhorn, R. Henn, K. Neumann, and R. W. Shephard. Berlin *et al.*: Springer Verlag.

Dobell, A. R. (1965). "A Comment on A. Y. C. Koo's 'An Empirical Test of Revealed Preference Theory,' " *Econometrica*, 33(2), 451–455.

Dowrick, S., and J. Quiggin (1994). "International Comparisons of Living Standards and Tastes: A Revealed-Preference Analysis," *The American Economic Review*, 84(1), 332–341.

Dushnik, B., and E. W. Miller (1941). "Partially Ordered Sets," *American Journal of Mathematics*, 63(3), 600–610.

Dvoretzky, A., A. Wald, and J. Wolfowitz (1951). "Elimination of Randomization in Certain Statistical Decision Procedures and Zero-Sum Two-Person Games," *The Annals of Mathematical Statistics*, 22(1), 1–21.

Dziewulski, P., and J. Quah (2014). "Testing for Production with Complementarities," Mimeo, University of Oxford.

Echenique, F. (2008). "What Matchings Can Be Stable? The Testable Implications of Matching Theory," *Mathematics of Operations Research*, 33(3), 757–768.

——— (2013). "Testing for Separability is Hard," Mimeo, California Institute of Technology.

Echenique, F., T. Imai, and K. Saito (2013). "Testable Implications of Models of Intertemporal Choice: Exponential Discounting and Its Generalizations," SS working paper 1388, California Institiute of Technology.

Echenique, F., S. Lee, and M. Shum (2011). "The Money Pump as a Measure of Revealed Preference Violations," *Journal of Political Economy*, 119(6), 1201–1223.

Echenique, F., S. Lee, M. Shum, and M. B. Yenmez (2013). "The Revealed Preference Theory of Stable and Extremal Stable Matchings," *Econometrica*, 81(1), 153–171.

Echenique, F., and K. Saito (2013). "Savage in the Market," *Econometrica*, 83(4), 1467–9.

Ehlers, L., and Y. Sprumont (2008). "Weakened WARP and Top-Cycle Choice Rules," *Journal of Mathematical Economics*, 44(1), 87–94.

Eliaz, K., and E. A. Ok (2006). "Indifference or Indecisiveness? Choice-Theoretic Foundations of Incomplete Preferences," *Games and Economic Behavior*, 56(1), 61–86.

Ellsberg, D. (1961). "Risk, Ambiguity, and the Savage Axioms," *The Quarterly Journal of Economics*, 75(4), 643–669.

Epstein, L. G. (2000). "Are Probabilities Used in Markets?" *Journal of Economic Theory*, 91(1), 86–90.

Epstein, L. G., and A. J. Yatchew (1985). "Non-Parametric Hypothesis Testing Procedures and Applications to Demand Analysis," *Journal of Econometrics*, 30(1), 149–169.

Falmagne, J. (1978). "A Representation Theorem for Finite Random Scale Systems," *Journal of Mathematical Psychology*, 18(1), 52–72.

Famulari, M. (1995). "A Household-Based, Nonparametric Test of Demand Theory," *The Review of Economics and Statistics*, 77(2), 372–382.

——— (2006). "Household Labor Supply and Taxes: A Nonparametric, Revealed Preference Approach," Mimeo, UC San Diego.

Färe, R., S. Grosskopf, and H. Lee (1990). "A Nonparametric Approach to Expenditure-Constrained Profit Maximization," *American Journal of Agricultural Economics*, 72(3), 574–581.

Färe, R., S. Grosskopf, and C. K. Lovell (1987). "Nonparametric Disposability Tests," *Journal of Economics*, 47(1), 77–85.

Farkas, J. (1902). "Theorie der einfachen Ungleichungen," *Journal für die Reine und Angewandte Mathematik*, 124(124), 1–24.

Farrell, M. (1957). "The Measurement of Productive Efficiency," *Journal of the Royal Statistical Society. Series A (General)*, 120(3), 253–290.

Fawson, C., and C. R. Shumway (1988). "A Nonparametric Investigation of Agricultural Production Behavior for US Subregions," *American Journal of Agricultural Economics*, 70(2), 311–317.

Featherstone, A. M., G. A. Moghnieh, and B. K. Goodwin (1995). "Farm-Level Nonparametric Analysis of Cost-Minimization and Profit-Maximization Behavior," *Agricultural Economics*, 13(2), 109–117.

Ferguson, T. S. (1967). *Mathematical Statistics: A Decision Theoretic Approach*, Vol. 7. New York: Academic Press.

Fiorini, S. (2004). "A Short Proof of a Theorem of Falmagne," *Journal of Mathematical Psychology*, 48(1), 80–82.

Fishburn, P. C. (1969). "Preferences, Summation, and Social Welfare Functions," *Management Science*, 16(3), 179–186.

——— (1973a). "Summation Social Choice Functions," *Econometrica*, 41(6), 1183–1196.

——— (1973b). *The Theory of Social Choice*. Princeton University Press.

——— (1974). "Separation Theorems and Expected Utilities," *Journal of Economic Theory*, 11, 16–34.

——— (1976). "Representable Choice Functions," *Econometrica*, 44(5), 1033–1043.

Fitzpatrick, S. (1988). "Representing Monotone Operators by Convex Functions," in *Workshop/Miniconference on Functional Analysis and Optimization (Canberra 1988), Proceedings of the Centre for Mathematical Analysis, Australian National University*, Vol. 20, pp. 59–65.

Forges, F., and E. Minelli (2009). "Afriat's Theorem for General Budget Sets," *Journal of Economic Theory*, 144(1), 135–145.

Fostel, A., H. Scarf, and M. Todd (2004). "Two New Proofs of Afriat's Theorem," *Economic Theory*, 24(1), 211–219.

Galambos, A. (2010). "Revealed Preference in Game Theory," working paper.

Gale, D. (1960a). "A Note on Revealed Preference," *Economica*, 27(108), 348–354.

——— (1960b). *The Theory of Linear Economic Models*. University of Chicago press.

Geanakoplos, J. (1984). "Utility Functions for Debreu's 'Excess Demands,' " *Journal of Mathematical Economics*, 13(1), 1–9.

Ghouila-Houri, A. (1962). "Caractérisation des Graphes Non Orientés dont on Peut Orienter les Arêtes de Manière à Obtenir le Graphe d'une Relation d'Ordre," *CR Acad. Sci. Paris*, 254, 1370–1371.

Gilboa, I., and D. Schmeidler (1989). "Maxmin Expected Utility with Non-Unique Prior," *Journal of Mathematical Economics*, 18(2), 141–153.

Gilmore, P., and A. Hoffman (1964). "A Characterization of Comparability Graphs and of Interval Graphs," *The Canadian Journal of Mathematics*, 16, 539–548.

Gomberg, A. (2011). "Vote Revelation: Empirical Content of Scoring Rules," in *Political Economy of Institutions, Democracy and Voting*, edited by N. Schofield, and G. Caballero, pp. 411–417. Berlin *et al.*: Springer-Verlag.

——— (2014). "Revealed Votes," Manuscript.

Green, E., and K. Osband (1991). "A Revealed Preference Theory for Expected Utility," *The Review of Economic Studies*, 58(4), 677–695.

Green, J., and D. Hojman (2007). "Choice, Rationality, and Welfare Measurement," working paper.

Green, R. C., and S. Srivastava (1986). "Expected Utility Maximization and Demand Behavior," *Journal of Economic Theory*, 38(2), 313–323.

Gul, F., P. Natenzon, and W. Pesendorfer (2014). "Random Choice as Behavioral Optimization," *Econometrica*, 82(5), 1873–1912.

Gul, F., and W. Pesendorfer (2006). "Random Expected Utility," *Econometrica*, 74(1), 121–146.

Hanoch, G., and M. Rothschild (1972). "Testing the Assumptions of Production Theory: A Nonparametric Approach," *Journal of Political Economy*, 80(2), 256–275.

Hansson, B. (1968). "Choice Structures and Preference Relations," *Synthese*, 18(4), 443–458.

Harbaugh, W., K. Krause, and T. Berry (2001). "GARP for Kids: On the Development of Rational Choice Behavior," *American Economic Review*, 91(5), 1539–1545.

Hausman, J. A., and D. A. Wise (1978). "A Conditional Probit Model for Qualitative Choice: Discrete Decisions Recognizing Interdependence and Heterogeneous Preferences," *Econometrica*, 46(2), 403–426.

Heufer, J. (2007). "Revealed Preference and the Number of Commodities," working paper.

Hey, J., and N. Pace (2014). "The Explanatory and Predictive Power of Non Two-Stage-Probability Theories of Decision Making Under Ambiguity," *Journal of Risk and Uncertainty*, 49(1), 1–29.

Hicks, J. R. (1956). *A Revision of Demand Theory*. Oxford University Press.

Hoderlein, S. (2011). "How Many Consumers are Rational?" *Journal of Econometrics*, 164(2), 294–309.

Hoderlein, S., and J. Stoye (2014). "Revealed Preferences in a Heterogeneous Population," *Review of Economics and Statistics*, 96(2), 197–213.

Hong, C. S. (1983). "A Generalization of the Quasilinear Mean with Applications to the Measurement of Income Inequality and Decision Theory Resolving the Allais Paradox," *Econometrica*, 51(4), 1065–1092.

Houthakker, H. S. (1950). "Revealed Preference and the Utility Function," *Economica*, 17(66), 159–174.

——— (1957). "Mr. Newman on Revealed Preference," *Oxford Economic Papers*, 9(2), 234.

Houtman, M., and J. Maks (1985). "Determining All Maximal Data Subsets Consistent with Revealed Preference," *Kwantitatieve Methoden*, 19, 89–104.

Huber, J., J. W. Payne, and C. Puto (1982). "Adding Asymmetrically Dominated Alternatives: Violations of Regularity and the Similarity Hypothesis," *Journal of Consumer Research*, 9(1), 90–98.

Hurwicz, L., and M. K. Richter (1979). "Ville Axioms and Consumer Theory," *Econometrica*, 47(3), 603–619.

John, R. (1997). "A Simple Cycle Preserving Extension of a Demand Function," *Journal of Economic Theory*, 72(2), 442–445.

——— (2001). "The Concave Nontransitive Consumer," *Journal of Global Optimization*, 20(3–4), 297–308.

Kalai, G. (2004). "Social Indeterminacy," *Econometrica*, 72(5), 1565–1581.

Kalandrakis, T. (2010). "Rationalizable Voting," *Theoretical Economics*, 5, 93–125.

Kamiya, D. (1963). "A Note on the Strong Axiom of Revealed Preference," *Economica*, 30(117), 83–84.

Kehoe, T., and A. Mas-Colell (1984). "An Observation on Gross Substitutability and the Weak Axiom of Revealed Preference," *Economics Letters*, 15(3), 241–243.

Kehoe, T. J. (1992). "Gross Substitutability and the Weak Axiom of Revealed Preference," *Journal of Mathematical Economics*, 21(1), 37–50.

Kihlstrom, R., A. Mas-Colell, and H. Sonnenschein (1976). "The Demand Theory of the Weak Axiom of Revealed Preference," *Econometrica: Journal of the Econometric Society*, 44(5), 971–978.

Kim, T. (1987). "Intransitive Indifference and Revealed Preference," *Econometrica*, 55(1), 163–167.

——— (1991). "The Subjective Expected Utility Hypothesis and Revealed Preference," *Economic Theory*, 1(1), 251–263.

——— (1996). "Revealed Preference Theory on the Choice of Lotteries," *Journal of Mathematical Economics*, 26(4), 463–477.

Kim, T., and M. K. Richter (1986). "Nontransitive-Nontotal Consumer Theory," *Journal of Economic Theory*, 38(2), 324–363.

Kitamura, Y., and J. Stoye (2013). "Nonparametric Analysis of Random Utility Models," Mimeo, Yale University.

Knoblauch, V. (1992). "A Tight Upper Bound on the Money Metric Utility Function," *The American Economic Review*, 82(3), 660–663.

——— (1993). "Recovering Homothetic Preferences," *Economics Letters*, 43(1), 41–45.

——— (2005). "Characterizing Paretian Preferences," *Social Choice and Welfare*, 25(1), 179–186.

——— (2010). "Recognizing One-Dimensional Euclidean Preference Profiles," *Journal of Mathematical Economics*, 46(1), 1–5.

Koo, A. Y. C. (1963). "An Empirical Test of Revealed Preference Theory," *Econometrica*, 31(4), 646–664.

Krauss, E. (1985). "A Representation of Arbitrary Maximal Monotone Operators via Subgradients of Skew-Symmetric Saddle Functions," *Nonlinear Analysis: Theory, Methods & Applications*, 9(12), 1381–1399.

Krivine, J.-L. (1964). "Anneaux Préordonnés," *Journal d'Analyse Mathématique*, 12(1), 307–326.

Kubler, F., L. Selden, and X. Wei (2014). "Asset Demand Based Tests of Expected Utility Maximization," *American Economic Review*, 104(11), 3459–3480.

Kuhn, H., and A. Tucker (1956). *Linear Inequalities and Related Systems.(AM-38)*, Vol. 38. Princeton University Press.

Kumbhakar, S. C., and C. K. Lovell (2003). *Stochastic Frontier Analysis*. Cambridge University Press.

Landsburg, S. E. (1981). "Taste Change in the United Kingdom, 1900–1955," *Journal of Political Economy*, 89(1), 92–104.

Ledyard, J. O. (1986). "The Scope of the Hypothesis of Bayesian Equilibrium," *Journal of Economic Theory*, 39(1), 59–82.

Lee, S. (2011). "The Testable Implications of Zero-Sum Games," *Journal of Mathematical Economics*, 48(1), 39–46.

Little, I. M. (1949). "A Reformulation of the Theory of Consumer's Behaviour," *Oxford Economic Papers*, 1(1), 90–99.

Lo, K. C. (2000). "Rationalizability and the Savage Axioms," *Economic Theory*, 15(3), 727–733.

Luce, R. D. (1959). *Individual Choice Behavior: A Theoretical Analysis*. New York: John Wiley and Sons.

Luce, R. D., and P. Suppes (1965). "Preference, Utility, and Subjective Probability," in *Handbook of Mathematical Psychology*, edited by R. D. Luce, R. R. Bush, and E. Galanter, Vol. 3, pp. 249–410. New York: John Wiley and Sons.

Machina, M. J. (1985). "Stochastic Choice Functions Generated from Deterministic Preferences over Lotteries," *The Economic Journal*, 95(379), 575–594.

——— (1989). "Dynamic Consistency and Non-Expected Utility Models of Choice Under Uncertainty," *Journal of Economic Literature*, 27(4), 1622–1668.

Machina, M. J., and D. Schmeidler (1992). "A More Robust Definition of Subjective Probability," *Econometrica*, 60(4), 745–780.

Mantel, R. (1974). "On the Characterization of Aggregate Excess Demand," *Journal of Economic Theory*, 7(3), 348–353.

——— (1976). "Homothetic Preferences and Community Excess Demand Functions," *Journal of Economic Theory*, 12(2), 197–201.

——— (1977). "Implications of Microeconomic Theory for Community Excess Demand Functions," *Frontiers of Quantitative Economics*, 3, 111–126.

Manzini, P., and M. Mariotti (2007). "Sequentially Rationalizable Choice," *American Economic Review*, 97(5), 1824–1839.

Mariotti, M. (2008). "What Kind of Preference Maximization Does the Weak Axiom of Revealed Preference Characterize?," *Economic Theory*, 35(2), 403–406.

Marker, D. (2002). *Model Theory: An Introduction*. New York *et al.*: Springer.

Marshall, M. (2008). *Positive Polynomials and Sums of Squares*. Providence, RI: American Mathematical Society.

Mas-Colell, A. (1977). "On the Equilibrium Price Set of an Exchange Economy," *Journal of Mathematical Economics*, 4(2), 117–126.

——— (1978). "On Revealed Preference Analysis," *Review of Economic Studies*, 45(1), 121–131.

——— (1982). "Revealed Preference after Samuelson," in *Samuelson and Neoclassical Economics*, edited by G. R. Feiwel, pp. 72–82. New York *et al.*: Springer.

Mas-Colell, A., M. Whinston, and J. Green (1995). *Microeconomic Theory*, Vol. 1. New York: Oxford University Press.

Masatlioglu, Y., D. Nakajima, and E. Y. Ozbay (2012). "Revealed Attention," *American Economic Review*, 102(5), 2183–2205.

Masatlioglu, Y., and E. A. Ok (2014). "A Canonical Model of Choice with Initial Endowments," *The Review of Economic Studies*, 81(2), 851–883.

Matzkin, R. L. (1991). "Axioms of Revealed Preference for Nonlinear Choice Sets," *Econometrica*, 59(6), 1779–1786.

Matzkin, R. L., and M. K. Richter (1991). "Testing Strictly Concave Rationality," *Journal of Economic Theory*, 53(2), 287–303.

McFadden, D. (1974). "Conditional Logit Analysis of Qualitative Choice Behavior," in *Frontiers in Econometrics*, edited by P. Zarembka, p. 105. New York: Academic Press.

McFadden, D., A. Mas-Colell, R. Mantel, and M. K. Richter (1974). "A Characterization of Community Excess Demand Functions," *Journal of Economic Theory*, 9(4), 361–374.

McFadden, D., and M. Richter (1971). "On the Extension of a Set Function on a Set of Events to a Probability on the Generated Boolean σ-Algebra," UC Berkeley, working paper.

——— (1990). "Stochastic Rationality and Revealed Stochastic Preference," in *Preferences, Uncertainty, and Optimality, Essays in Honor of Leo Hurwicz*, edited by J. S. Chipman, D. McFadden, and M. K. Richter, pp. 161–186. Boulder, CO: Westview Press Inc.

McGarvey, D. C. (1953). "A Theorem on the Construction of Voting Paradoxes," *Econometrica*, 21(4), 608–610.

Mosteller, F., and P. Nogee (1951). "An Experimental Measurement of Utility," *Journal of Political Economy*, 59(5), 371–404.

Motzkin, T. S. (1936). "Beiträge zur Theorie der linearen Ungleichungen," Dissertation.

Newman, P. (1955). "The Foundations of Revealed Preference Theory," *Oxford Economic Papers*, 7, 151–169.

——— (1960). "Complete Ordering and Revealed Preference," *The Review of Economic Studies*, 27(2), 65–77.

Ok, E. A., P. Ortoleva, and G. Riella (2014). "Revealed (P)reference Theory," *American Economic Review*, forthcoming.

Papadimitriou, C. H., and M. Yannakakis (2010). "An Impossibility Theorem for Price-Adjustment Mechanisms," *Proceedings of the National Academy of Sciences*, 107(5), 1854–1859.

Papandreou, A. G. (1953). "An Experimental Test of an Axiom in the Theory of Choice," *Econometrica*, 21, 477.

Pareto, V. (1906). *Manuale di Economia Politica*. Societa Editrice.

Park, I.-U. (1998). "A Revealed-Preference Implication of Weighted Utility Decisions under Uncertainty," *Economic Theory*, 11, 413–426.

Parrilo, P. A. (2003). "Semidefinite Programming Relaxations for Semialgebraic Problems," *Mathematical Programming*, 96(2), 293–320.

——— (2004). "Sum of Squares Programs and Polynomial Inequalities," in *SIAG/OPT Views-and-News: A Forum for the SIAM Activity Group on Optimization*, Vol. 15, pp. 7–15.

Peleg, B., and S. Tijs (1996). "The Consistency Principle for Games in Strategic Form," *International Journal of Game Theory*, 25(1), 13–34.

Peters, H. J., and P. Wakker (1994). "WARP Does not Imply SARP for More than Two Commodities," *Journal of Economic Theory*, 62(1), 152–160.

——— (1996). "Cycle-Preserving Extension of Demand Functions to New Commodities," *Journal of Mathematical Economics*, 25(3), 281–290.

Pfanzagl, J., V. Baumann, and H. Huber (1971). *Theory of Measurement*. Heidelberg, Germany: Physica-Verlag.

Plott, C. R. (1974). "On Game Solutions and Revealed Preference Theory," working paper.

Poincaré, H. (1895). "Complément a l'Analysis Situs," *Rendiconti del Circolo Matematico di Palermo*, 13, 285–343.

Polisson, M., and J. Quah (2013). "Revealed Preference in a Discrete Consumption Space," *American Economic Journal: Microeconomics*, 5(1), 28–34.

Polisson, M., L. Renou, and J. Quah (2013). "Revealed Preference Tests under Risk and Uncertainty," working paper 13/24, University of Leicester.

Popper, K. R. (1959). *The Logic of Scientific Discovery*. London: Hutchinson.

Quah, J. K.-H. (2013). "A Revealed Preference Test for Weakly Separable Preferences," working paper, University of Oxford.

Quah, J. K.-H., H. Nishimura, and E. A. Ok (2013). "A Unified Approach to Revealed Preference Theory: The Case of Rational Choice," Mimeo, University of Oxford.

Rader, T. (1963). "The Existence of a Utility Function to Represent Preferences," *The Review of Economic Studies*, 30(3), 229–232.

Ray, I., and L. Zhou (2001). "Game Theory via Revealed Preferences," *Games and Economic Behavior*, 37(2), 415–424.

Ray, S. C., and D. Bhadra (1993). "Nonparametric Tests of Cost Minimizing Behavior: A Study of Indian Farms," *American Journal of Agricultural Economics*, 75(4), 990–999.

Rehbeck, J. (2014). "Every Choice Correspondence is Backwards-Induction Rationalizable," *Games and Economic Behavior*, 88, 207–210.

Reny, P. (2014). "A Characterization of Rationalizable Consumer Behavior," *Econometrica*, forthcoming.

Richter, M. K. (1966). "Revealed Preference Theory," *Econometrica*, 34(3), 635–645.

——— (1971). "Rational Choice," in *Preferences, Utility and Demand*, edited by J. S. Chipman, L. Hurwicz, M. K. Richter, and H. F. Sonnenschein, pp. 29–58. Orlando, FL: Harcourt Brace Jovanivic Inc.

——— (1975). "Rational Choice and Polynomial Measurement Models," *Journal of Mathematical Psychology*, 12(1), 99–113.

Richter, M. K. (1979). "Duality and Rationality," *Journal of Economic Theory*, 20(2), 131–181.

Richter, M. K., and L. Shapiro (1978). "Revelations of a Gambler," *Journal of Mathematical Economics*, 5(3), 229–244.

Richter, M. K., and K.-C. Wong (2004). "Concave Utility on Finite Sets," *Journal of Economic Theory*, 115(2), 341–357.

Rochet, J. (1987). "A Necessary and Sufficient Condition for Rationalizability in a Quasi-Linear Context," *Journal of Mathematical Economics*, 16, 191–200.

Rockafellar, R. T. (1966). "Characterization of the Subdifferentials of Convex Functions," *Pacific Journal of Mathematics*, 17(3), 497–510.

——— (1997). *Convex Analysis*. Princeton University Press.

Rose, H. (1958). "Consistency of Preference: The Two-Commodity Case," *The Review of Economic Studies*, 25(2), 124–125.

Rota, G.-C. (1964). "On the Foundations of Combinatorial Theory I. Theory of Möbius Functions," *Probability Theory and Related Fields*, 2(4), 340–368.

Rubin, D. B. (1973). "Matching to Remove Bias in Observational Studies," *Biometrics*, 29(1), 159–183.

Rudin, W. (1976). *Principles of Mathematical Analysis*. New York: McGraw-Hill.

Rynasiewicz, R. A. (1983). "Falsifiability and the Semantic Eliminability of Theoretical Languages," *The British Journal for the Philosophy of Science*, 34(3), 225–241.

Samuelson, P. A. (1938). "A Note on the Pure Theory of Consumer's Behaviour," *Economica*, 5(17), 61–71.

——— (1948). "Consumption Theory in Terms of Revealed Preference," *Economica*, 15(60), 243–253.

——— (1950). "The Problem of Integrability in Utility Theory," *Economica*, 17(68), 355–385.

——— (1963). "Problems of Methodology—Discussion," *American Economic Review*, 53, 232–236.

——— (1964). "Theory and Realism: A Reply," *American Economic Review*, 54, 736–739.

——— (1965). "Professor Samuelson on Theory and Realism: Reply," *American Economic Review*, 55, 1162–1172.

Savage, L. J. (1954). *The Foundations of Statistics*. New York: John Wiley and Sons.

Schipper, B. C. (2009). "How Mindless is Standard Economics Really?" Working papers, University of California, Department of Economics.

Schrijver, A. (1998). *Theory of Linear and Integer Programming*. New York: John Wiley & Sons.

Scott, D. (1964). "Measurement Structures and Linear Inequalities," *Journal of Mathematical Psychology*, 1(2), 233–247.

Seidenberg, A. (1954). "A New Decision Method for Elementary Algebra," *The Annals of Mathematics*, 60(2), 365–374.

Selten, R. (1991). "Properties of a Measure of Predictive Success," *Mathematical Social Sciences*, 21(2), 153–167.

Sen, A. (1969). "Quasi-Transitivity, Rational Choice and Collective Decisions," *The Review of Economic Studies*, 36(3), 381–393.

——— (1971). "Choice Functions and Revealed Preference," *The Review of Economic Studies*, 38(3), 307–317.

Shafer, W. (1977). "Revealed Preference Cycles and the Slutsky Matrix," *Journal of Economic Theory*, 16(2), 293–309.

Shafer, W., and H. Sonnenschein (1982). "Market Demand and Excess Demand Functions," in *Handbook of Mathematical Economics*, edited by K. J. Arrow, W. Hildenbrand, M. D. Intriligator, and H. Sonnenschein, Vol. 2, pp. 671–693. Amsterdam: North-Holland.

Shen, W.-M., and H. A. Simon (1993). "Fitness Requirements for Scientific Theories Containing Recursive Theoretical Terms," *The British Journal for the Philosophy of Science*, 44(4), 641–652.

Shirai, K. (2010). "On the Existence of a Submodular Utility Function," Mimeo, Waseda University.

Shmaya, E., and L. Yariv (2012). "Experiments on Decisions Under Uncertainty: A Theoretical Framework," working paper.

Simon, H. A. (1955). "A Behavioral Model of Rational Choice," *The Quarterly Journal of Economics*, 69(1), 99.

——— (1979). "Fit, Finite, and Universal Axiomatization of Theories," *Philosophy of Science*, 46(2), 295–301.

——— (1983). "Fitness Requirements for Scientific Theories," *The British Journal for the Philosophy of Science*, 34(4), 355–365.

——— (1985). "Quantification of Theoretical Terms and the Falsifiability of Theories," *The British Journal for the Philosophy of Science*, 36(3), 291–298.

Simon, H. A., and G. J. Groen (1973). "Ramsey Eliminability and the Testability of Scientific Theories," *The British Journal for the Philosophy of Science*, 24(4), 367–380.

Sippel, R. (1997). "An Experiment on the Pure Theory of Consumer's Behaviour," *The Economic Journal*, 107(444), 1431–1444.

Slater, M. L. (1951). "A Note on Motzkin's Transposition Theorem," *Econometrica*, 19(2), 185–187.

Smeulders, B., L. Cherchye, B. De Rock, and F. C. R. Spieksma (2013). "The Money Pump as a Measure of Revealed Preference Violations: A Comment," *Journal of Political Economy*, 121(6), 1248–1258.

Sneed, J. (1971). *The Logical Structure of Mathematical Physics*. Dordrecht: D. Reidel.

Snyder, S. (1999). "Testable Restrictions of Pareto Optimal Public Good Provision," *Journal of Public Economics*, 71(1), 97–119.

Sondermann, D. (1982). "Revealed Preference: An Elementary Treatment," *Econometrica*, 50(3), 777–779.

Sonnenschein, H. (1972). "Market Excess Demand Functions," *Econometrica*, 40(3), 549–563.

Sprumont, Y. (2000). "On the Testable Implications of Collective Choice Theories," *Journal of Economic Theory*, 93, 205–232.

——— (2001). "Paretian Quasi-Orders: The Regular Two-Agent Case," *Journal of Economic Theory*, 101(2), 437–456.

Stegmüller, W., W. Balzer, and W. Spohn (1982). *Philosophy of Economics: Proceedings, Munich, July 1981*. Berlin *et al.*: Springer-Verlag.

Stengle, G. (1974). "A Nullstellensatz and a Positivstellensatz in Semialgebraic Geometry," *Mathematische Annalen*, 207(2), 87–97.

Stigum, B. P. (1973). "Revealed Preference—A Proof of Houthakker's Theorem," *Econometrica*, 41(3), 411–423.

Stoer, J., and C. Witzgall (1970). *Convexity and Optimization in Finite Dimensions*. Berlin *et al.*: Springer-Verlag.

Sturmfels, B. (2002). *Solving Systems of Polynomial Equations*. Providence, RI: American Mathematical Society.

Suzumura, K. (1976a). "Rational Choice and Revealed Preference," *The Review of Economic Studies*, 43(1), 149–158.

——— (1976b). "Remarks on the Theory of Collective Choice," *Economica*, 43(172), 381–390.

——— (1977). "Houthakker's Axiom in the Theory of Rational Choice," *Journal of Economic Theory*, 14(2), 284–290.

Swofford, J. L., and G. A. Whitney (1986). "Flexible Functional Forms and the Utility Approach to the Demand for Money: A Nonparametric Analysis: Note," *Journal of Money, Credit and Banking*, 18(3), 383–389.

——— (1987). "Nonparametric Tests of Utility Maximization and Weak Separability for Consumption, Leisure and Money," *The Review of Economics and Statistics*, 69(3), 458–464.

Szpilrajn, E. (1930). "Sur l'Extension de l'Ordre Partiel," *Fundamenta Mathematicae*, 16, 386–389.

Tarski, A. (1951). "A Decision Method for Elementary Algebra and Geometry (2nd ed., revised)," Berkeley and Los Angeles: Rand Corporation monograph.

——— (1954). "Contributions to the Theory of Models I," *Indagationes Mathematicae*, 16, 572–581.

Tauer, L. W. (1995). "Do New York Dairy Farmers Maximize Profits or Minimize Costs?" *American Journal of Agricultural Economics*, 77(2), 421–429.

Tversky, A. (1967). "A General Theory of Polynomial Conjoint Measurement," *Journal of Mathematical Psychology*, 4, 1–20.

Tyson, C. (2008). "Cognitive Constraints, Contraction Consistency, and the Satisficing Criterion," *Journal of Economic Theory*, 138(1), 51–70.

Uzawa, H. (1956). "Note on Preference and Axioms of Choice," *Annals of the Institute of Statistical Mathematics*, 8(1), 35–40.

——— (1960a). "Preference and Rational Choice in the Theory of Consumption," in *Mathematical Methods in the Social Sciences, 1959: Proceedings of the First Stanford Symposium*, edited by K. J. Arrow, S. Karlin, and P. Suppes, pp. 129–150. Palo Alto, CA: Stanford University Press.

——— (1960b). "Walras' Tâtonnement in the Theory of Exchange," *The Review of Economic Studies*, 27(3), 182–194.

——— (1971). "Preference and Rational Choice in the Theory of Consumption," in *Preferences, Utility, and Demand: A Minnesota Symposium*, edited by J. S. Chipman, L. Hurwicz, M. K. Richter, and H. F. Sonnenschein, pp. 7–28. Orlando, FL: Harcourt Brace Jovanovich, Inc.

Van Benthem, J. (1976). "A Problem Concerning Expansions and its Connections with Modal Logic," working paper.

Varian, H. R. (1982). "The Nonparametric Approach to Demand Analysis," *Econometrica*, 50(4), 945–974.

——— (1983a). "Non-Parametric Tests of Consumer Behaviour," *Review of Economic Studies*, 50(1), 99–110.

——— (1983b). "Nonparametric Tests of Models of Investor Behavior," *Journal of Financial and Quantitative Analysis*, 18(3), 269–278.

——— (1984). "The Nonparametric Approach to Production Analysis," *Econometrica*, 52(3), 579–598.

——— (1985). "Non-Parametric Analysis of Optimizing Behavior with Measurement Error," *Journal of Econometrics*, 30, 445–458.

——— (1988a). "Revealed Preference with a Subset of Goods," *Journal of Economic Theory*, 46(1), 179–185.

——— (1988b). "Estimating Risk Aversion from Arrow-Debreu Portfolio Choice," *Econometrica*, 43(4), 973–979.

——— (1990). "Goodness-of-Fit in Optimizing Models," *Journal of Econometrics*, 46(1–2), 125–140.

——— (1991). "Goodness-of-Fit for Revealed Preference Tests," working paper, Department of Economics, University of Michigan.

——— (2006). "Revealed Preference," in *Samuelsonian Economics and the Twenty-First Century*, edited by M. Szenberg and L. Ramrattan, pp. 99–115. Oxford University Press.

Veblen, O., and J. Alexander (1912–1913). "Manifolds of *n* Dimensions," *Annals of Mathematics*, 14(1/2), 163–178.

Ville, J. (1946). "Sur les Conditions d'Existence d'une Ophélimité Totale et d'un Indice du Niveau des Prix," *Annales de L'Université de Lyon*, 9, 32–39.

Ville, J., and P. Newman (1951–1952). "The Existence Conditions of a Total Utility Function," *Review of Economic Studies*, 19(2), 123–128.

Von Neumann, J. (1953). "A Certain Zero-Sum Two-Person Game Equivalent to the Optimal Assignment Problem," *Contributions to the Theory of Games*, 2, 5–12.

Wald, A. (1947a). "An Essentially Complete Class of Admissible Decision Functions," *The Annals of Mathematical Statistics*, 18(4), 549–555.

——— (1947b). "Foundations of a General Theory of Sequential Decision Functions," *Econometrica*, 15(4), 279–313.

——— (1950). *Statistical Decision Functions*. New York: John Wiley and Sons.

Wilson, R. (1970). "The Finer Structure of Revealed Preference," *Journal of Economic Theory*, 2(4), 348–353.

Xiong, S. (2013). "Every Choice Correspondence is Backwards-Induction Rationalizable," working paper.

Xu, Y., and L. Zhou (2007). "Rationalizability of Choice Functions by Game Trees," *Journal of Economic Theory*, 134(1), 548–556.

Yannakakis, M. (1982). "The Complexity of the Partial Order Dimension Problem," *SIAM Journal on Algebraic and Discrete Methods*, 3, 351.

Yanovskaya, E. (1980). "Revealed Preference in Noncooperative Games" (in Russian), *Mathematical Methods of Social Science*, 13, 73–81.

Yatchew, A. (1985). "A Note on Non-Parametric Tests of Consumer Behaviour," *Economics Letters*, 18(1), 45–48.

Yellott, J. I. (1977). "The Relationship between Luce's Choice Axiom, Thurstone's Theory of Comparative Judgment, and the Double Exponential Distribution," *Journal of Mathematical Psychology*, 15(2), 109–144.

Index

Other titles in the series (*continued fron page iii*)

A. Colin Cameron and Pravin K. Trivedi, *Regression analysis of count data*, 9780521632010, 9780521635677

Steinar Strom, Editor, *Econometrics and economic theory in the 20th century: The Ragnar Frisch Centennial Symposium*, 9780521633239, 9780521633659

Eric Ghysels, Norman R. Swanson, and Mark Watson, Editors, *Essays in econometrics: Collected papers of Clive W. J. Granger (Volume I)*, 9780521772976, 9780521774963

Eric Ghysels, Norman R. Swanson, and Mark Watson, Editors, *Essays in econometrics: Collected papers of Clive W. J. Granger (Volume II)*, 9780521792073, 9780521796491

Cheng Hsiao, *Analysis of panel data, second edition*, 9780521818551, 9780521522717

Mathias Dewatripont, Lars Peter Hansen, and Stephen J. Turnovsky, Editors, *Advances in economics and econometrics – Eighth World Congress (Volume I)*, 9780521818728, 9780521524117

Mathias Dewatripont, Lars Peter Hansen, and Stephen J. Turnovsky, Editors, *Advances in economics and econometrics – Eighth World Congress (Volume II)*, 9780521818735, 9780521524124

Mathias Dewatripont, Lars Peter Hansen, and Stephen J. Turnovsky, Editors, *Advances in economics and econometrics – Eighth World Congress (Volume III)*, 9780521818742, 9780521524131

Roger Koenker, *Quantile regression*, 9780521845731, 9780521608275

Charles Blackorby, Walter Bossert, and David Donaldson, *Population issues in social choice theory, welfare economics, and ethics*, 9780521825511, 9780521532587

John E. Roemer, *Democracy, education, and equality*, 9780521846653, 9780521609135

Richard Blundell, Whitney K. Newey, and Thorsten Persson, *Advances in economics and econometrics – Ninth World Congress (Volume I)*, 9780521871525, 9780521692083

Richard Blundell, Whitney K. Newey, and Thorsten Persson, *Advances in economics and econometrics – Ninth World Congress (Volume II)*, 9780521871532, 9780521692090

Richard Blundell, Whitney K. Newey, and Thorsten Persson, *Advances in economics and econometrics – Ninth World Congress (Volume III)*, 9780521871549, 9780521692106

Fernando Vega-Redondo, *Complex social networks*, 9780521857406, 9780521674096

Itzhak Gilboa, *Theory of decision under uncertainty*, 9780521517324, 9780521741231

Krislert Samphantharak and Robert M. Townsend, *Households as corporate firms: An analysis of household finance using integrated household surveys and corporate financial accounting*, 9780521195829, 9780521124164

Rakesh Vohra, *Mechanism design: A linear programming approach*, 9781107004368, 9780521179461

Daron Acemoglu, Manuel Arellano, Eddie Dekel, *Advances in economics and econometrics – Tenth World Congress (Volume I)*, 9781107016040, 9781107638105

Daron Acemoglu, Manuel Arellano, Eddie Dekel, *Advances in economics and econometrics – Tenth World Congress (Volume II)*, 9781107016057, 9781107674165

Daron Acemoglu, Manuel Arellano, Eddie Dekel, *Advances in economics and econometrics – Tenth World Congress (Volume III)*, 9781107016064, 9781107627314

Andrew Harvey, *Dynamic models for volatility and heavy tails: With applications to financial and economic time series*, 9781107034723, 9781107630024

Cheng Hsiao, *An analysis of panel data* (second edition), 9781107038691, 9781107657632

Jean-François Mertens, Sylvain Sorin, Shmuel Zamir, *Repeated games*, 9781107030206, 9781107662636